APPLIED

DEVELOPMENTAL PSYCHOLOGY

Volume 1

CONTRIBUTORS

DANIEL R. ANDERSON

S. FARNHAM-DIGGORY

NORMAN GARMEZY

DANIEL P. KEATING

CATHERINE LORD

FREDERICK J. MORRISON

BILLIE NELSON

WILLIAM D. ROHWER, JR.

ROBIN SMITH

AUKE TELLEGEN

APPLIED

DEVELOPMENTAL PSYCHOLOGY

Edited by

FREDERICK J. MORRISON

DEPARTMENT OF FAMILY STUDIES
FACULTY OF HOME ECONOMICS
THE UNIVERSITY OF ALBERTA
EDMONTON, ALBERTA, CANADA

CATHERINE LORD

DEPARTMENT OF PSYCHOLOGY
GLENROSE HOSPITAL
AND DEPARTMENT OF PEDIATRICS
THE UNIVERSITY OF ALBERTA
SCHOOL OF MEDICINE
EDMONTON, ALBERTA, CANADA

DANIEL P. KEATING

DEPARTMENT OF PSYCHOLOGY
UNIVERSITY OF MARYLAND
BALTIMORE COUNTY
CATONSVILLE, MARYLAND

VOLUME 1

1984

ACADEMIC PRESS, INC.
(Harcourt Brace Jovanovich, Publishers)

Orlando   San Diego   San Francisco   New York   London
Toronto   Montreal   Sydney   Tokyo   São Paulo

ACADEMIC PRESS, INC.
Orlando, Florida 32887

United Kingdom Edition published by
ACADEMIC PRESS, INC. (LONDON) LTD.
24/28 Oval Road, London NW1 7DX

ISBN 0-12-041201-2
ISSN 0735-164-X

This publication is not a periodical and is not
subject to copying under CONTU guidelines.

PRINTED IN THE UNITED STATES OF AMERICA

84 85 86 87   9 8 7 6 5 4 3 2 1

CONTENTS

An Invitation to a Developmental Psychology of Studying

William D. Rohwer, Jr.

Young Children's TV Viewing: The Problem of Cognitive Continuity

Daniel R. Anderson and Robin Smith

The Development of Peer Relations in Children with Autism

Catherine Lord

Studies of Stress-Resistant Children: Methods, Variables, and Preliminary Findings

Norman Garmezy and Auke Tellegen

CONTRIBUTORS

Numbers in parentheses indicate the pages on which the authors' contributions begin.

DANIEL R. ANDERSON (115), Department of Psychology, University of Massachusetts, Amherst, Massachusetts 01003

S. FARNHAM-DIGGORY (21), Department of Educational Studies, University of Delaware, Newark, Delaware 19711

NORMAN GARMEZY (231), Department of Psychology, University of Minnesota, Minneapolis, Minnesota 55455

DANIEL P. KEATING (1), Department of Psychology, University of Maryland Baltimore County, Catonsville, Maryland 21228

CATHERINE LORD[1] (1, 165), Department of Psychology, Glenrose Hospital and Department of Pediatrics, The University of Alberta School of Medicine, Edmonton, Alberta T5G 0B7, Canada

FREDERICK J. MORRISON (1), Department of Family Studies, Faculty of Home Economics, The University of Alberta, Edmonton, Alberta T6G 2M8, Canada

[1] Mailing address: Department of Psychology, Glenrose Hospital, 10230 111th Avenue, Edmonton, Alberta T5G 0B7, Canada.

BILLIE NELSON (21), Department of Educational Studies, University of Delaware, Newark, Delaware 19711

WILLIAM D. ROHWER, JR. (75), Department of Education, University of California Berkeley, Berkeley, California 94720

ROBIN SMITH[2] (115), Department of Psychology, University of Massachusetts, Amherst, Massachusetts 01003

AUKE TELLEGEN (231), Department of Psychology, University of Minnesota, Minneapolis, Minnesota 55455

[2]Present address: Institute of Child Development, University of Minnesota, Minneapolis, Minnesota 55455.

PREFACE

The present volume and series represent an attempt to put forth a vision of the nature of developmental science somewhat at variance with current attitudes and practices. For several decades now the study of human development has been dominated by a relatively uniform set of standards and practices about what constitutes "good" scientific research: in brief, relatively exclusive emphasis on laboratory-based experimentation, coupled with a preference for studying simple issues amenable to experimental methodology. The hope was that careful examination of elementary processes in controlled laboratory environments would, in the fullness of time, yield cumulatively greater understanding of the complex nature of human development. A direct attack on complex real-world issues was deemed impossible prior to full consideration of the simpler processes composing them.

Nevertheless, in the recent past, diverse sets of events have contributed to a growing uneasiness about the "business-as-usual" science being practiced. Primary concern has been expressed by scientists themselves. A growing body of literature and commentary points to two conclusions, with rather dramatic implications for the current science of development. First, it has become clear that developmental changes in supposedly basic psychological processes observed in the laboratory may result in large part from growth in knowledge and skills gained from specific experiences in the natural environment. Second, the realization has surfaced that developmental changes observed in one environment, context, or even culture may not readily generalize to another. The most critical implication of these two conclusions is that, for a fuller understanding of human development and the forces that shape it, developmental scientists must refocus their attention on the everyday world of the child, for it is this world that holds the key to what really develops.

Additional forces in the larger social and cultural milieu have served to catalyze the process of questioning the current state of developmental science. While Western societies at least have traditionally not required "social relevance" or "accountability" in their basic sciences, and with good reason, there comes a time in the evolution of a science when natural questions do surface about what a particular science has contributed to understanding or aiding the society that supports it. Such has been the fate of developmental (indeed most social) science recently. In part, the card has been called by the serious social problems and harsh economic circumstances of the past two decades. To deal with increased crime and violence, to comprehend the academic regressions in our schools, and to ascertain the implications of social perturbations such as drug use and teenage pregnancy, or of major shifts in life style such as increased divorce, working women, and day-care, our society naturally has turned to its professional scientists for help. Yet too often they have discovered these scientists focused on relatively esoteric pursuits, not because these pursuits are necessary precursors to understanding complex real-world problems, but because they are more consonant with current academic standards of acceptable scientific practice.

Beyond the exigencies of current social problems, there is a recurring cycle in relations between society and science, one-half of which gives basic science free rein, the other half of which requests some accounting of its societal contribution.

The cumulative impact of changes in these many domains has been to highlight developmental psychology's "applied" dimensions, in two senses. First is the examination of the science's major contribution to dealing with society's problems, which has forced professional scientists to reexamine the importance of the questions they have been asking. The second, and ultimately more powerful, applied aspect of developmental psychology involves the realization that a complete understanding of the nature and causes of psychological growth must include a thoroughgoing analysis of the real-world environments that impinge on the life of the child and that shape or otherwise serve as the basis for the child's developing knowledge, feelings, and skills.

From the foregoing, it should be clear that we feel strongly that the perspective of an applied developmental psychology, in the two senses just described, can serve a vital function for growth and change in our science. Happily, a growing number of other scientists share our vision and have realized some of the necessary changes in their own research. This series will provide an ongoing forum for the presentation and exchange of ideas from an applied perspective. In this volume and the next we have chosen to celebrate the diversity and variety that presently characterize work in the area. Where appropriate, subsequent volumes will adopt a more thematic format.

In choosing the contributions to be included, we hope to highlight and illustrate some important features of applied developmental psychology that can contribute significantly to our science. As you read the following articles, you will note at least four salient characteristics. First is a direct, frontal assault on complex questions. In contrast to the more atomistic assumptions inherent in previous work, there is growing realization that complex psychological phenomena need to be examined at their own level of complexity. In other words, understanding of simple component processes does not automatically produce cumulative understanding of the complex phenomena they compose. In some cases isolating components may lead in the wrong direction. Second, consideration of these complex phenomena necessitates a multidisciplinary approach. For example, complete understanding of reading acquisition requires the combined insights of cognitive psychologists, psycholinguists, clinical psychologists, reading specialists, educators, and neuropsychologists. Such widened vision, we feel, promotes professional interchange and ultimately leads to more complete understanding of psychological growth. Third, there can be seen a healthy balance of basic and applied work. Where appropriate, important insights from basic research are brought to bear on complex applied problems. In addition, valuable suggestions from an applied domain serve to enrich and revitalize a basic research issue. The positive feedback of such a cycle facilitates growth in both domains. Finally, there is a central focus on real-world issues or the everyday lives of children. Sustaining such a focus not only provides a check on the importance of the questions being researched, it also serves to direct attention to sources of developmental change currently considered crucial to psychological growth.

The contributions of the present volume provide excellent examples of the characteristics just described. We know you will share our excitement in exploring these new frontiers.

Finally, we would like to thank those individuals who have helped us so immensely in bringing this project to fruition. We are indebted to the staff of Academic Press for their thorough, competent, and rapid editorial work. Finally we are most thankful to the authors of each article, our colleagues who provided scholarly substance to our initial idea in ways that surprised even us.

FREDERICK J. MORRISON
CATHERINE LORD
DANIEL P. KEATING

APPLIED DEVELOPMENTAL PSYCHOLOGY

Frederick J. Morrison,* Catherine Lord,†
and Daniel P. Keating‡

*DEPARTMENT OF FAMILY STUDIES
FACULTY OF HOME ECONOMICS
THE UNIVERSITY OF ALBERTA
EDMONTON, ALBERTA, CANADA

†DEPARTMENT OF PSYCHOLOGY, GLENROSE HOSPITAL
AND DEPARTMENT OF PEDIATRICS
THE UNIVERSITY OF ALBERTA SCHOOL OF MEDICINE
EDMONTON, ALBERTA, CANADA
AND
‡DEPARTMENT OF PSYCHOLOGY
UNIVERSITY OF MARYLAND BALTIMORE COUNTY
CATONSVILLE, MARYLAND

*Applied Developmental
Psychology, Volume 1*

For some eras of child study, there has been an enthusiastic anticipation that all problems are reducible by the science of the moment; intellectual technology can succeed (and imitate) the 19th century's commercial and industrial technology in the progressive and ultimate betterment of humankind. The optimism of the founders of child study and their immediate successors is dimmer today—"The sky's the limit" may be replaced by "You win a few, you lose a few"—and serious questions have been posed even for the basic assumptions underlying the scientific analysis of human behavior (Barrett, 1978). Child psychology may soon have to face anew the question of whether or not a scientific account of human development can be given without bringing in its wake the false claims of scientism and the arrogance of an ethic based on current findings. (Kessen, 1979, p. 818)

If cross-cultural psychology has mounted a challenge to developmental psychology in recent years it is because it has forced recognition of the fact that no context of observation, despite the care taken in its construction, is culturally neutral. Settings for behavior are socially organized, and they are embedded in larger systems of social organization which influence them. Membership in the society that organizes the observational setting provides participants with "special knowledge."

Whether the setting is a laboratory or a forest, participants in any setting of observation use cultural knowledge to make sense of the task and to organize their behavior in it. (Cole, 1979, p. 829)

Relative to behavioristic psychology, cognitive science is a fledgling, at the present time, in the application of its findings and techniques to practical human endeavors even though the development of new cognitive theories was, to some extent, motivated by applied problems. Thus, while the older behavioristic theories were developed in the laboratory and then extrapolated to practical uses, modern cognitive theory was shaped by the practical problems of skilled and complex human performance. As a result of this, a lesson has perhaps been learned: not only might laboratory work and theory be useful for application, but application can also be a significant generator and test of psychological theory. This lesson certainly has been well learned in other sciences. (Glaser, 1981, p. 114)

Today, in child development circles, there is frequent, even compulsive, reference to the value of interdisciplinary research, although the reasons are rarely mentioned. To the researcher, half drowned in the minutia of his own problem puddle, this emphasis on the whole child as a unifier for a science may seem a hollow appeal to some forgotten piety. Regrettably enough, it often is. But to those who struggled with the infinite variety of human problems presented in the child guidance clinics of the four decades before World War II, the piety is alive and genuine, for the need was—and is—ineradicable. (Sears, 1975, pp. 18–19)

My first plea is to educate for breadth of perspective. This means a knowledge of the fundamentals of one's discipline as a whole and a reasonable familiarity with those of a cognate discipline or disciplines as well. I am proposing a flexible integration of the historical strengths of liberal education with the strengths of the professional school, a matter not so much of substance as of style. For the behavioral sciences, breadth of experience means embedding our sciences in the real world more firmly than we have been wont to embed them in the past. Scholarship is not debased by being directed toward the concerns of ordinary life, for at its best it offers a deeper and, hopefully, more coherent vision of the human condition. To tie scholarship to the real world means to base our theories on practice. (Bevan, 1980, p. 5)

Now, a half century later, child development is a reflection of the tremulous partnership that always seems to exist when pure and applied science, and the services of scientists, are directed toward fulfilling social rather than purely intellectual needs. Today's novitiates in the "science" of child development must not complain when they feel the heat of social demands put upon them. The field grew out of relevance. Its content and its multidisciplinary structure are a product of the demands for social usefulness. Furthermore, there is some risk that it will fractionate into its component disciplines—and disappear as an entity in the world of science—if that relevance is not maintained. (Sears, 1975, p. 4)

Many prominent developmental scientists are troubled about the state of their discipline. The scientific study of human development, beginning almost a century ago with the pioneering efforts of G. Stanley Hall and others such as William Preyer, James Mark Baldwin, and Alfred Binet, has undergone significant transformations since its inception (Cairns & Ornstein, 1979; White, 1979). From its beginnings as a multidisciplinary, multifaceted endeavor representing diverse methodologies and theoretical persuasions, developmental psychology emerged during the middle decades of the twentieth century as a more streamlined discipline, embodying greater uniformity in working assumptions and working habits. There are reasons to believe that we are witnessing the beginnings of another major reorganization of perspectives on human development, involving a reassessment of priorities and a realignment of emphases (Kessel, 1980). Specifically there are signs that, for predominantly scientific but also for economic and social reasons, the mainstream discipline of developmental psychology is returning to a more multifaceted approach to the study of human development (White, 1980).

In the present article, we sketch the historical background leading to the present changing perspective. In so doing we highlight major characteristic assumptions underlying scientific activity of the past 30 years. We document recent empirical findings that pose challenges to the prevailing views and that point toward a more integrated perspective, combining basic and applied elements. We outline the nature of this emerging perspective on developmental issues. Finally we conclude with suggestions for a new research strategy for understanding human development.

I. The Study of Development: A Historical Sketch

A. Laying the Foundation: An "Empathic Ethos"

Historical analysts have documented that the science of child development did not evolve quite like other traditional scientific disciplines (Sears, 1975; White, 1979). Other life sciences, essentially self-contained within universities, developed more or less according to a classic model of scientific evolution, founded on theory construction, data accumulation, and refinement of instrumentation. In contrast, the scientific study of children and their development evolved from a variety of social and professional roots, encompassing legal, educational, medical, and religious issues as well as more academic concerns. The origins of the discipline lay in a broad range of social changes that occurred during the late eighteenth and nineteenth century, the cumulative effect of which was to foster an "empathic ethos" toward children and their welfare, as well as to point up the desirability of obtaining knowledge about children and how they grow up (Sears, 1975).

Starting with Pinel's pronouncement in 1792 that madness should be viewed as the result of illness rather than the operation of evil spirits, an atmosphere of social and professional concern for the unfortunate members of society, including troubled children, began to emerge. An early example of this concern came in 1825 with the establishment of a House of Refuge for delinquent children in New York City. Such children, formerly viewed as morally corrupt and in need of salvation, came to be considered as disadvantaged and in need of care and instruction. The value of formal instruction became gradually recognized, and compulsory education as well as tax support for schools were introduced during the early nineteenth century. In subsequent years, progressive establishment and growth of orphanages, institutions for handicapped children, foster care services, and juvenile courts added further testimony to the broad climate of concern which swept society during the nineteenth century.

The question of how to best care for children and promote their well-being and growth was naturally linked to and dependent upon knowledge of how children grew and developed normally. Hence medical, educational, and social statistics were gradually compiled, charting children's physical growth, tooth development, and school attendance. Beyond the informative value of the statistics themselves, such activity contributed greatly to the vision of science as an important instrument in social change. As such, a spirit of inquiry was born and nurtured as an essential ingredient in enhancing the lives of children and ultimately in changing society.

This brief sketch of the early period (for more details see Cairns & Ornstein, 1979; Sears, 1975; Siegel & White, 1983) highlights the elements of the soil in which the fledgling science of child study would take root. The focus on children was *multidisciplinary*: it included medical, educational, social, and academic professionals; the multidisciplinary focus fostered both *basic and applied perspectives* as necessary and complementary features of child study; and the focus of inquiry and concern was directed to relatively *complex* issues—juvenile delinquency, proper nutrition, how to teach what to whom. Finally, the questions and concerns of professionals originated in *real-world* problems or issues in the lives of children.

B. The Science of Child Study Emerges

"Child study was not a simple outgrowth of either scientific progress or social change. It was something that happened at a meeting-place of science and society" (Siegel & White, 1983, p. 57).

As the foregoing section illustrates, the forces behind the growth of a formal field of child study represented a mixture of social concern and professional curiosity about the nature and development of children. These same forces can be discerned as child study became a more formalized discipline, groping toward scientific status.

1. "POLYGLOT EMPIRICISM AND COSMIC THEORIZING"

The early scientific studies of the pioneers of child study—G. Stanley Hall, James Mark Baldwin, William T. Preyer, and Alfred Binet—were characterized by White (1979) as representing a "sprawling polyglot empiricism" lightly joined by "some cosmic theorizing." On the research side, early writings on children ranged far and wide in topic as well as in methodology, often coupled with practical advice to teachers, practitioners, and parents. In 1896, Barnes (quoted in Siegel & White, 1983) cataloged nine different methods of child study being utilized at that time. They ranged from undirected observation in everyday home and school life, to personal journals or letters of children, through autobiographies and fictional literary treatments of childhood, to the more rigorous and sophisticated methods involving direct studies of children, systematic observation (such as Preyer's baby biographies), and statistical studies. Topics ranged from children's knowledge of basic facts and concepts (in Hall's "The Contents of Children's Minds"), to Binet's studies of children's memory for words and sentences, to charting the developmental course of children's laughing, smiling, and motor behavior (in Preyer's "The Mind of the Child"), to clinical pieces in Hall's journal *Pedagogical Seminary* on "delinquents, stammerers, masturbators, deaf-mutes, psychopaths, slow readers, prodigies, the feeble-minded, children with digital malformations, blind children,

children of the insane, children who withdraw from school" (White, 1979, p. 812). Although topic and methodology, choice of question, and level of analysis varied widely, one senses from the historical record a common interest among these investigators and clinicians in what Sears (1975) has called the "whole child." The centrality of the growth and welfare of children to these professionals kept the focus on relatively complex, real-world issues. Since complete understanding of these issues usually exceeded the grasp of any one profession, the need for multidisciplinary input and interaction was sustained. On the negative side, this sprawling enterprise was also characterized by a relative lack of methodological rigor and sophistication, which tainted the image of child study as a scientific discipline. In addition, an inherent tendency toward "cosmic theorizing" further eroded the progress of the science. Child study as a discipline inherited from the early social and religious activists a level of theorizing about human nature and development that was heavily laden with philosophical and even theological assumptions. Human nature was seen by philosophical developmentalists such as Vico and Hegel (see White, 1979) as representing on an individual plane certain universal truths about the growth and evolution of society and of history. When wedded to Darwin's scientifically respectable theory of evolution, child development came to be seen as recapitulating the phylogenetic history of mankind. At one level the ethical overtones of such theorizing led to the notion that moral salvation or human happiness lay in understanding and promoting optimal growth and development in the individual child.

The atmosphere of such theorizing infused itself into the otherwise scientific writings of the period. As a consequence, research articles tended to draw relatively broad conclusions or to contain direct practical advice on the basis of limited empirical data. Clearly, though having made great strides, much work needed to be done to make the fledgling child study movement into a more solid, respectable empirical science. Nevertheless one cannot conclude without remarking, as did Cairns and Ornstein (1979), that in this early period "we find astute discussions of concepts that are currently hailed as providing 'new directions' for research in the 1970s and 1980s"—the emphasis on memory organization and on molar assessment from Binet, as well as discussions of basic versus applied perspectives and the proper methodology for developmental research.

2. FROM CHILD STUDY TO CHILD DEVELOPMENT

The first four decades of the twentieth century witnessed significant progress on major aspects of the science of development. The substantive activity and hence the identity of the discipline were solidified and greatly advanced by a series of events over this period. The most celebrated event involved establishment of the Child Welfare Research Station at the University of Iowa, spearheaded by Mrs. Correy Bussey Hillis, who felt that increased knowledge about children's health and development could prevent many childhood and family problems. In addition, private and public funds were utilized to set up other child development research centers around North America, including university-based centers at California, Columbia, Minnesota, Toronto, and Yale, and the Fels Research Institute in Ohio, as well as others (see Sears, 1975).

In addition to the solidification of professional identity, a series of events resulted in an increased measure of scientific respectability, albeit not without its controversial elements. It was during this period that behaviorism began to flourish in North American academic circles. John B. Watson, the acknowledged founder of behaviorism, considered development to be a fundamental cornerstone of the behaviorist perspective. Reliance on principles such as conditioning, reinforcement, and association highlighted the centrality of modification and change in understanding human behavior. In addition, the mental testing movement provided an aura of scientific respectability through development of the Stanford–Binet by Lewis Terman and its concomitant statistical refinements, as that movement expanded into a universal tool of personnel and academic selection (Cairns & Ornstein, 1979). Whether the theoretical base of such developments can be substantiated remains controversial (Gould, 1981; Keating, 1983), but clearly the testing movement played a major role in the perception of the field as methodologically rigorous and hence scientific.

Other related methodological advances served to distance the new science of child development from the earlier child study movement. Development and refinement of longitudinal methods of investigation paved the way for large-scale studies of development at Berkeley, Fels, and Stanford. Moreover, systematic improvements in use of observational methods in studies of young children and infants were instituted at Minnesota and elsewhere.

Finally, significant theoretical advances were made during these opening four decades. The efforts of Lewin, Freud, Werner, Piaget, and social learning theorists such as Dollard, Miller, Mohwer, Sears, and Whiting, though equally grand in scale, represented an adherence to canons of scientific theory construction which far surpassed the cosmic theorizing of their child study predecessors.

3. From Child Development to Developmental Psychology: The Process of "Streamlining"

The years up to the second world war saw vigorous growth for the field of child development. As in the earlier period, the enterprise had a distinct multidisciplinary character, employed diverse methodologies, and focused on both basic and applied issues. However, beginning soon after the war and continuing through the 1970s, child development began to take on a new look.

Advances in theory and methodology began gradually to impart respectability to the study of children in the eyes of the parent discipline, psychology. Developmental researchers began to appear on faculties in psychology departments, and graduate training programs in "developmental psychology" were begun in the mid-1960s at several universities, including Harvard and Brown.

While the mutual effects of this gradual and cautious liaison on the two disciplines are still in debate (White, 1980), several outcomes for the study of development were immediately apparent. Consonant with the previous generation's concern with methodological soundness, theory and research on development migrated toward the even more analytic thinking and methodology practiced in experimental psychology. Child development, as characterized by White, (1980), became "streamlined," shedding some of its bulkier and messier features for the sleeker, cleaner look of experimental psychology. Increasing use of the term *developmental psychology* (and even *experimental child psychology*) in place of *child development* signaled an evolving identity shift as the discipline entered the modern ranks of "real" science. More importantly, laboratory-based experimentation came to dominate the study of developmental issues.

Super (1982) recently documented this trend in looking at the changing nature of publications in the journal *Child Development* from 1930 to 1979. Prior to about 1960, articles were predominantly by single authors from development-centered research institutes. The research utilized a variety of methodologies including naturalistic observation, tests, interviews, and use of archival records. After 1960, the typical article was coauthored by several different people, each housed in psychology departments of different universities, with the strong predominance of laboratory experimentation.

What were the results of the "streamlining" process for developmental research and for the discipline of child development as a whole? At the time, the identity change was viewed as a perfectly natural, indeed very exciting, development by its participants, heralding the possibility of theoretical and professional integration of developmental with adult researchers, especially in cognition. The larger outcome was the gradual adoption of a set of assumptions and practices toward the study of development, which Sears (1975) has termed "experimentalism." In addition there were implications for the interdisciplinary identity of child development and for the philosophy and practices of graduate training.

   a. The Rise of Experimentalism. Experimentalism came to signify an attitude that laboratory experimentation was the sine qua non of good research. Laboratory-based research had multiple distinct advantages over other methods—greater control over variables, more precise measurement, and ultimately more accurate statements of cause–effect relations. For its rigor and precision, laboratory research came to be viewed as "better" than other methods, independent of the importance of the question being addressed (Sears, 1975).

A separate aspect of experimentalism included a constellation of beliefs that laboratory research produced findings about development that were, in some sense, more *universal* as well as more *basic* than results obtained from other methods. The first belief was that conclusions about development drawn from laboratory methodology were less prone to confounding and contamination by outside factors operating at the time of testing. As such the results were seen to be more universal, i.e., they told us facts about developmental processes that had greater generality and hence power. Second was the related belief that conclusions drawn from laboratory findings were more basic or elementary, in the sense that they formed the solid groundwork of developmental findings, upon which the effects of more global, complex factors such as social class or meaningfulness would be overlaid. In general, laboratory-based research was assumed to yield fundamental differences between different age groups, which were relatively independent of outside factors such as experience and which formed the foundation for analyzing more complex, real-world developmental phenomena.

Finally was the choice of research question itself. Typically the universalist assumption in laboratory research encouraged investigators to focus on general processes (such as attention, memory, attachment, or dependency) which presumably applied to all behavior at all times. Sears (1975) has called this type of work "process" research, and contrasts it with "substantive" research intended to apply to specific developmental situations, e.g., memory for prose materials, reading disability, toilet training, or child abuse. Laboratory-based methods tended to promote process research and have, until recently, downplayed the role of situational factors or special knowledge in explaining developmental phenomena. The natural bias toward process research both was motivated by and reinforced the universalist tenet just described. Having chosen to focus on general process research, the investigator most often elected to investigate simple processes, whose nature and development could be examined in isolation from other contaminating factors. As with laboratory experimentation itself, the choice and isolation of elementary cognitive or social variables became equated with sound scientific practice, and investigation of more complex issues regarded as messy and time consuming fell out of favor (see also Farnham-Diggory & Nelson, this volume).

b. Disciplinary Isolation. At a professional level, the domination of experimentalism produced a degree of insularity (and perhaps snobbishness) on the part of developmental scientists toward other disciplines relevant to child development—anthropology, pediatrics, sociology and social work, psychiatry, and even clinical psychology. For those who did attempt some interdisciplinary excursions (e.g., with anthropology or clinical practice) the early activity most often involved exporting laboratory-based techniques to a different culture or subject population (Cole, 1979).

Other subtle but powerful factors caused the new scientists of development to increasingly turn inward for identification and standards of conduct (Super, 1982). The sheer complexity and detail of experimental research, even on simple psychological processes, demanded all the time and energy a scientist could give. Hence the majority of effort was devoted to increasingly sophisticated analysis of specific processes, coupled with highly refined methodological fine tuning. For a researcher studying newborn eye movements using sophisticated corneal reflection techniques, it was hard enough to understand the work of the person in the next lab, using time-sequential analyses of social interaction in triads of 8 year olds, let alone to converse with someone working in a hospital or day-care.

Finally, disciplinary isolation was reinforced through changing practices governing the editorial process, a central mechanism for reflecting and controlling standards of professional conduct. Super (1982) pointed out that in the opening decade of its operation, *Child Development* included on its editorial board psychologists and other social scientists, with no single group predominating. By the early 1960s, the board consisted almost exclusively of psychologists. As a natural correlate, greater homogeneity was seen in the kinds of research questions addressed and methods utilized—essentially simple process questions amenable to laboratory experimentation.

c. Graduate Training. The education and training of prospective developmental scientists reflected the changing professional values rather directly (Bevan, 1980; Super, 1982). Developmental graduate students were drawn increasingly from undergraduate psychology programs and were strongly encouraged to maintain their knowledge and contacts with the main discipline. Heavier emphasis was placed on courses and experience in design and methodology, in advanced statistics, and on topics dealing with "basic" processes (perception and cognition, learning and memory, motivation and emotion). The resulting graduates were relatively narrow specialists, whose strengths lay in technique and methodology (Bevan, 1980).

A relative deemphasis was placed on practical experience in everyday settings, partly because there was not time but also due to a fundamental belief that learning about science was more crucial for apprentice developmentalists than learning about the daily lives of children. With the exception of a practicum during the first year (essentially a succession of short tours of, e.g., day-cares or schools for the deaf) many graduate students in developmental psychology obtained a Ph.D. without ongoing experience with their objects of study!

This type of graduate training coupled with the underlying experimentalist orientation produced a markedly different science of development from that seen in early periods. The current science has flourished for almost three decades, yet there are signs of change on the near horizon. Recent research, ironically most from the laboratory itself, is leading some developmental psychologists to question the generality and accuracy of recent conclusions about human development, conclusions drawn largely from research conducted in laboratory settings with heavy emphasis on the experimental method.

II. Some Emerging Doubts

To be sure, advances in understanding development for which experimental child psychology was directly responsible are significant and undeniable. Our understanding of the nature of infant perceptual and cognitive growth has been greatly enhanced by the technical and methodological advances of experimental studies initiated in that field (Cohen, De Loache, & Strauss, 1979). The systematic hypothesis testing applied to Piagetian theory has greatly clarified the contribution and limitations of that theory (Brainerd, 1978; Gelman, 1969; Trabasso, 1977). The same can be said for research examining the ethological theory of attachment applied to humans (Herbert, Sluckin, & Sluckin, 1982; Chess & Thomas, 1982). Finally, important advances in our understanding of the nature and growth of cognitive skills have come directly from the laboratory (Kail & Hagen, 1977; Siegler, 1978).

Despite its undisputed importance, the laboratory has recently spawned diverse research findings that cast doubt on the validity of an exclusively laboratory-based science. Two broad classes of findings have emerged. The first group focuses on the role of domain-specific skills and knowledge in explaining developmental differences found in selected cognitive tasks. The second set refers to some direct tests of the generalizability of laboratory research findings to other contexts or situations.

A. Laboratory Studies of Cognition and Development

1. DOMAIN-SPECIFIC SKILLS

One set of results provides evidence that skills developed in real-world domains, such as formal school environments, or in the course of learning other real-world tasks, such as reading, may explain a major portion of the variance observed in laboratory tests of supposedly basic information-processing and memory skills. For example, in an early series of studies, Marshall Haith and his colleagues (Haith, 1971) examined age differences in early information processing. Using a standard partial report procedure, they found that the earliest stages of processing (the first 300 msec assessing amount of information initially available and trace duration) were developmentally invariant. However, major age differences emerged in the post-300-msec interval, in which prevailing theory postulated that subjects were actively coding and transferring information to more permanent storage. From the pattern of position errors, they tentatively concluded that older children and adults were employing a systematic serial scanning strategy, derived, they hypothesized, from experience with reading materials. Later, Schwantes (1979) showed that the increased availability of information for older subjects in the later intervals was directly a result of rapid left-to-right scanning in older children. More crucially, perhaps, Schwantes went on to show that the differences observed across age could also be demonstrated across levels of reading skill; high-ability readers scanned left-to-right more systematically than low-ability readers. While the cause–effect status of these findings is still unclear, they raised the possibility that some of the age differences observed in laboratory assessments of information-processing skills were due to age-linked strategies acquired in the course of learning to read.

Additional findings have come from laboratory work on the development of memory skills—in particular on rehearsal and organization. In a series of studies Ornstein and Naus (1978) demonstrated that a fundamental determinant of age differences in immediate memory span is the degree of organized rehearsal by different age subjects. Corroborating cross-cultural work by Cole and associates and recently by Rogoff has indicated that similar differences in memory capacity can be observed between school and unschooled children or adults. In fact Rogoff (1981) recently demonstrated that, independent of potentially biasing family background variables, number of years of school experience significantly predicted performance on a series of memory tests. Further, Rogoff and Waddell (1982) and Mandler (1979) have recently shown that cross-cultural differences in memory performance may be limited to laboratory-type situations involving formal presentation of strings of unrelated items. With contextual organization of spatial material, a technique more commonly used by nonwestern people, cross-cultural differences in memory performance disappeared (see also Mandler, Scribner, Cole, & De Forest, 1980). Finally, Bauer (1979) has demonstrated that identical differences to those observed by Ornstein in children of different ages can be seen in comparisons of children differing in reading ability. The point of these and similar studies is that one central determinant of increases in basic memory capacity with age involves use of processing skills that are themselves acquired in specialized contexts such as school or as a by-product of developing reading skills and habits.

From such results, one is compelled to ask whether these laboratory assessments of elementary cognitive processes are yielding *basic* findings at all, or whether they constitute a dim Platonic shadow of more substantive changes occurring in real-world contexts. Further, the findings raise the issue of how *universal* these differences are, since they appear or disappear as a function of the equivalence of task contexts or task demands across age, culture, or reading skill.

2. THE SPECIFICITY OF KNOWLEDGE DOMAINS

Other evidence concerns some now well-known but still dramatic demonstrations of the specificity of human knowledge and the crucial role of domain-specific knowledge in explaining developmental and indeed cross-cultural differences in cognitive processing skills. For example, D'Andrade (1982) recently examined college-age students' ability to solve abstract versus concrete syllogistic reasoning problems. He found that undergraduate students had great difficulty with abstract forms of the syllogism (of the "if *a* then *b*" variety) as well as with concrete but arbitrary relations among the elements (e.g., if there is an *a* on the front of the card, there is a *3* on the back). However, with familiar materials (e.g., if it rained, the roof is wet) the students had very little trouble figuring out the various parts of the syllogism. The study illustrates that, contrary to certain univeralist assumptions, the use and success of selected cognitive skills appears to be strongly tied to specific realms of experience and familiarity. Evidence corroborating this conclusion has been obtained by Anderson and his colleagues (Reynolds, Taylor, Steffensen, Shirey, & Anderson, 1982; Steffensen, Joag-Dey, & Anderson, 1979) and by Engle and Bukstel (1978). In one study Steffensen *et al.* (1979) compared memory and comprehension scores of Americans versus eastern Indians for stories of weddings taking place in the two cultures. They found that reading speed, memory for factual details, overall comprehension, and accuracy of inferences were intimately linked to understanding of culture-specific events in the two wedding stories. In this context, Cole and Means (1981) provide an extended discussion with numerous examples of the pitfalls of making "process" inferences that fail to take into account underlying knowledge differences between different cultural groups.

Finally, the research of Chi (1978) and others has revealed that children with specific knowledge (e.g., of dinosaurs) or specific skills (e.g., in chess) demonstrated superior memory skills in those special domains compared to unskilled or less knowledgeable adults. In contrast, outside these domains, more traditional (for the laboratory at least) age differences in memory were observed.

B. Comparisons of Developmental Phenomena across Contexts

The second group of findings comes from studies comparing selected developmental phenomena across contexts. In one sense the work of Cole, Rogoff, and Chi just described also fits this category in showing that context is a crucial determinant of whether or not a developmental phenomenon will be observed.

However, a separate group of studies strikes at the heart of a different issue—the notion of a developmental stage or milestone. Most psychologists are familiar with Piaget's construct of egocentrism, its ubiquity, and its importance in explaining the cognitive limitations of the preoperational child. Several pieces of research in recent years have questioned the generality of the egocentrism of the preschool child and with it the experimental methods used to assess it. For example, Glucksberg and Krauss (1966) found that in laboratory communication tasks, young children appeared to be unable to take into account the information needs of the listener. But Shatz and Gelman (Shatz, 1978; Shatz & Gelman, 1973) have demonstrated that children of the same age, in more naturalistic settings, routinely adapt their messages to the needs of those with whom they are interacting. Similar conclusions were reached by Clarke-Stewart (1978) in her examination of infants reactions to strangers. Contrary to the appearance of "stranger anxiety" as a central and developmentally crucial milestone, Clarke-Stewart and others earlier (Rheingold and Eckerman, 1971, 1973) found that the extent and nature of an infant's negative reaction to a stranger was dependent on a host of variables including stranger characteristics, background, and ongoing behavior.

Finally, the importance of context has recently been examined more directly by Belsky and others (Belsky, 1979; Graves & Glick, 1978). Observing the degree to which mothers attended to, responded to, stimulated and praised, or prohibited and ignored their infants, Belsky failed to find behavioral stability (in mean performance) or consistency (across individuals) in maternal behavior in a free-play laboratory context versus a home environment. These studies and others point up quite directly that what is or is not defined as a developmental phenomenon may be crucially dependent on the manner of assessment.

C. Overview of Recent Trends

As the foregoing discussion illustrates, there is persuasive evidence that major changes may be needed in the focus and conduct of scientific inquiry in human development. Some changes can be accomplished simply by asking different questions (e.g., about the growth of knowledge and how it affects processing). However, if fuller understanding of the centrality of knowledge and context on development is to be gained, we must move beyond the confines of the laboratory setting and the experimental method. In one sense, recent events have completed a kind of cycle in the history of child study. The early workers in the field, from different professions and perspectives, promoted the scientific study of children as necessary for advancing their well-being. They advocated and developed diverse methodologies and generally focused on relatively complex, practical issues. Subsequent advances in more recent times involved greater refinement of methodology, closer attention to experimental rigor, and simplification of the questions and processes under investigation. Consequently there was movement away from complex substantive problem areas and less need for interdisciplinary communication. Yet the trend of recent findings appears to be pulling scientific inquiry precisely back to a focus on complex issues requiring diverse methodologies and an interdisciplinary perspective.

III. Restoring the Balance: An Emerging "Applied" Perspective

To the extent that the last 30 years produced a certain imbalance in our perspective and conduct, built-in restorative forces have alerted us to important issues and perspectives that were overlooked. In particular, the current twin emphases on growth of real-world knowledge and on the centrality of context in developmental study have sensitized scientists to the importance of local, everyday tasks and settings to the knowledge and skills individuals acquire and display. As such, there has been emerging (or reemerging) a kind of "applied" perspective on human development, which it is felt can provide valuable insights into the nature and sources of developmental change. While the outlines of this nascent perspective are barely visible currently, there are discernible changes in the activities and attitudes of some working scientists in the field that foreshadow major scientific and professional redirection. In an attempt to better understand the nature and purpose of this viewpoint, we need to address some important questions regarding the status of the "applied" perspective.

A. Is a Basic–Applied Distinction Valid or Useful?

The pattern of recent research findings, we have argued, necessitates some heightened appreciation for specialized knowledge and everyday contexts in developmental investigations. But why the need to reify this concern into a loftier-sounding "perspective" and to contrast it with a basic perspective? Isn't it all just the same science, with the same standards and conduct?

Other things being equal, a strong distinction between basic and applied research is probably not necessary. Nevertheless, some psychologists (including ourselves) are persuaded that, *at this point in the history of the field,* the distinction is both valid and useful. The fundamental aspects of an applied perspective—the focus on substantive and meaningful questions, analysis of complex issues, and promotion of interdisciplinary approaches—can add greatly to our understanding of human development. Further, they are not at present integral features of the current scientific ethos.

Admittedly, the great danger lies in viewing an applied perspective as a contrast to a supposedly different "basic" perspective. In simply resurrecting the distinction, one runs the risk of muddying the conceptual waters and fostering misconceptions about what scientists do, thereby creating differences and disagreements where none need exist.

While concerns about the potential problems of a strong distinction between basic and applied perspectives are legitimate, we feel that at the present time, the study of development and the profession of developmental psychology will benefit by an explicit emphasis on a perspective that is distinct yet complementary to more traditional scientific views. When the distinction is no longer necessary or useful, it should be abandoned. Thus we view the distinction as a historical, not a logical, issue. But at this historical juncture, we argue that the distinction is important and fruitful.

B. Is Applied Developmental Psychology a Separate Discipline?

In discussing an applied perspective (indeed, in creating the present series), one can give the appearance of creating a separate field and hence splintering unnecessarily an otherwise unitary domain of inquiry. To be explicit, there is no intention of creating a new field—in fact just the opposite is the case. The ultimate goal of those with an applied perspective is to return the study of development to a more balanced and integrated state, in which the important task is to understand human development, utilizing the most appropriate tools and methods for the question being investigated.

C. What Is Applied Developmental Psychology?

Applied developmental psychology, *at present,* represents a unique perspective on the study of human development, with implications for the major questions being addressed, for the disciplines and methodologies involved, and also for the training of future professionals and developmental and related fields.

With regard to the questions addressed, an applied perspective takes several different forms. At one end of the spectrum lies the basic researcher who is developing a sensitivity to the role of context in social or cognitive development. In the middle resides the investigator who has chosen a real-world task such as reading, mathematics, or day-care as the major focus of inquiry. On the other end is the scientist examining development in atypical children or the clinical researcher evaluating the nature and efficacy of assessment and intervention techniques. While varying in focus and conduct, applied scientists share a common perspective, which emphasizes the substantive and complex phenomena or problems encountered by individuals in their everyday lives. Such an orientation, it is felt, can greatly enhance and enrich our understanding of human nature and development.

A major result of sustaining the focus on substantive problems is realization of the inadequacy of any one discipline to fully explain important developmental phenomena. For example, complete understanding of reading disability, reading acquisition, and even aspects school-age cognitive development will ultimately require coordinating the insights of experimental and comparative psychologists, educators, linguists, pediatricians, neurologists, social workers, and parents. An applied perspective helps to expand the vision of individual disciplines by providing additional, sometimes challenging, information or ideas, while maintaining the focus on a concrete important question.

Finally, taking everyday tasks as a central focus implies that practicing as well as apprentice developmental scientists need to be intimately familiar with their objects of inquiry, children, as well as with the tasks children face as they grow and the environments that surround them. Hence there will need to be relatively greater emphasis in the future on in-depth practicum experiences for developmental graduate students as well as on course content focused on more substantive questions.

On the issue of training, it is important to make a statement to applied professionals from disciplines related to developmental psychology. Great strides have been made in recent decades in our understanding of human development and in the rigor and sophistication of our methodology. Basic research in developmental psychology has a great deal to offer the applied professional in medicine, education, and elsewhere. As developmental scientists are gaining greater appreciation for the perspective of the applied professional, further progress in our field requires reciprocal acceptance of the legitimate accomplishments made by basic developmental science. Hence medical students, nursing students, clinical trainees, and educational students would benefit from greater exposure to a developmental perspective. Beyond the domain of training, practicing applied professionals should become more aware of the progress made in understanding and in studying human development.

IV. Toward a New Research Strategy for Developmental Science

From the pattern of recent empirical findings and the trend of events in the field as a whole, some psychologists are persuaded that a reexamination of the relative exclusivity and centrality of laboratory-based experimentation and training is needed (Cole, 1979; Keating, 1983). Two kinds of changes will be needed. First, in the conduct of laboratory experiments themselves, more attention will need to be focused on what might be termed "real-world tasks and knowledge domains." As a consequence, stimulus materials, apparatus, and methods of procedure will need to more closely approximate those found in the real-world environment. Despite the obvious fragmentation and deemphasis of universal elements of development which such a strategy entails in the short run, this road in the long run should arrive at the more comprehensive understanding of development we seek.

The second change entails a more radical shift in research strategy to take into account the domain specificity of knowledge and skills and the centrality of context in shaping developmental phenomena. Both Cole (1979) and Keating (1983) have proferred some tentative proposals on developing a new research strategy. Briefly, the crucial features of a new approach appear to involve at least three elements. First, some important developmental phenomenon is chosen for inquiry. Though perhaps not necessary, both Cole and Keating seem to prefer to ground the research question in some clearly identifiable and important real-world task or context. Second, examination of important developmental changes in that domain is undertaken, using task-analytic and laboratory techniques, including assessment of whether the developmental changes can be induced. Finally comes examination of the degree of specificity or transfer of the developmental change to new tasks or contexts. Such assessment would require the equivalent of a series of converging operations, some involving finely grained laboratory tasks, others approximating real-world situations. Clearly the hope is that the pattern of findings would allow clearer specification of what really changes developmentally, how those changes occur, and how specific or general they are.

Acknowledgments

Preparation of this article was supported by grants from the Clifford E. Lee Foundation and the National Science and Engineering Research Council (to Frederick J. Morrison), and the Alberta Mental Health Advisory Council (to Catherine Lord). Portions of this paper were presented by the first author at the annual meeting of the Psychonomic Society, Minneapolis, November 1982.

References

Bauer, R. H. Memory acquisition and category clustering in learning-disabled children. *Journal of Experimental Child Psychology,* 1979, **21,** 365-383.

Belsky, J. The effects of context on mother-infant interaction: A complex issue. *Quarterly Newsletter of the Laboratory of Comparative Human Cognition,* 1979, **1,** 29-31.

Bevan, W. Graduate education for the earthquake generation. *S.R.C.D. Newsletter,* Fall 1980, pp. 4-5.

Brainerd, C. J. *Piaget's theory of intelligence.* New York: Prentice-Hall, 1978.

Cairns, R. B., & Ornstein, P. A. Developmental psychology. In E. Hearst (Ed.), *The first century of experimental psychology.* Hillsdale, New Jersey: Erlbaum, 1979.

Chess, S., & Thomas, A. D. Infant bonding: Mystique and reality. *American Journal of Orthopsychiatry,* April 1982, **52.**

Chi, M. T. H. Knowledge structures and memory development. In R. S. Siegler (Ed.), *Children's thinking: What develops?* Hillsdale, New Jersey: Erlbaum, 1978. Pp. 73-96.

Clarke-Stewart, A. Recasting the lone stranger. In J. Glick & A. Clarke-Stewart (Eds.), *The development of social understanding.* New York: Gardner, 1978.

Cohen, L. B., De Loache, J. S., & Strauss, M. S. Infant visual perception. In J. D. Osofsky (Ed.), *Handbook of infant development.* New York: Wiley, 1979, Pp. 393-438.

Cole, M. Cross-cultural psychology's challenges to our ideas of children and development. *American Psychologist,* October 1979, 827-833.

Cole, M., & Means, B. *Comparative studies of how people think.* Cambridge, Massachusetts: Harvard Univ. Press, 1981.

D'Andrade, R. G. *People reason a lot, but rarely use logic.* Paper presented at conference "The ecology of cognition," Tanglewood Park, North Carolina, April 1982.

Engle, R. W., & Bukstel, L. Memory processes among bridge players of differing expertise. *American Journal of Psychology,* 1978, **91,** 673-689.

Gelman, R. Conservation acquisition: A problem of learning to attend to relevant attributes. *Journal of Experimental Child Psychology,* 1969, **7,** 167-187.

Glaser, R. Instructional psychology: Past, present, and future. *Pedagogishe Studien,* 1981, **58,** 111-122.

Glucksberg, S., & Krauss, R. M. Referential communication in nursery school children: Method and some preliminary findings. *Journal of Experimental Child Psychology,* 1966, **3,** 333-342.

Gould, S. J. *The mismeasure of man.* New York: Norton, 1981.

Graves, A., & Glick, J. The effect of context on mother-infant interaction: A progress report. *Quarterly Newsletter of the Laboratory of Comparative Human Cognition,* 1978, **2,** 41-46.

Haith, M. M. Developmental changes in visual information-processing and short-term visual memory. *Human Development,* 1971, **14,** 249-261.

Herbert, M., Sluckin, W., & Sluckin, A. Mother-to-infant bonding. *Journal of Child Psychology and Psychiatry,* 1982, **23,** 205-221.

Kail, R. V., & Hagen, J. W. *Perspectives on the development of memory and cognition.* Hillsdale, New Jersey: Erlbaum, 1977.

Keating, D. P. The emperor's new clothes: The "new look in intelligence research." In R. J. Sternberg (Ed.), *Advances in the psychology of human intelligence* (Vol. 2). Hillsdale, New Jersey: Erlbaum, 1983.

Kessel, F. S. Developmental psychology's applied and interdisciplinary dimensions: The issue of training. *S.R.C.D. Newsletter,* Fall 1980, 4-9.

Kessen, W. The American child and other cultural inventions. *American Psychologist,* October 1979, 815-820.

Mandler, J. M. Categorical and schematic organization in memory. In C. R. Puff (Ed.), *Memory organization and structure.* New York: Academic Press, 1979.

Mandler, M. J., Scribner, S., Cole, M., & DeForest, M. Cross-cultural invariance in story recall. *Child Development,* 1980, **51,** 19–26.

Ornstein, P. A., & Naus, M. J. Rehearsal processes in children's memory. In P. A. Ornstein (Ed.), *Memory development in children.* Hillsdale, New Jersey: Erlbaum, 1978. Pp. 69–100.

Reynolds, R. E., Taylor, M. A., Steffensen, M. S., Shirey, L. L., & Anderson, R. C. Cultural schemata and reading comprehension. *Reading Research Quarterly,* 1982, **3,** 353–366.

Rheingold, H. L., & Eckerman, C. O. *Fear of the stranger: A critical examination.* Paper presented at the biennial meeting of the Society for Research in Child Development, Minneapolis, April 1971.

Rheingold, H. L., & Eckerman, C. O. Fear of the stranger: A critical examination. In H. W. Reese (Ed.), *Advances in child development and behavior.* New York: Academic Press, 1973. Pp. 185–222.

Rogoff, B. Schooling's influence on memory test performance. *Child Development,* 1981, **52,** 260–267.

Rogoff, B., & Waddell, K. J. Memory for information organized in a scene by children from two cultures. *Child Development,* 1982, **53,** 1124–1128.

Schwantes, F. M. Cognitive scanning processes in children. *Child Development,* 1979, **50,** 1136–1143.

Sears, R. R. Your ancients revisited: A history of child development. In E. M. Hetherington (Ed.), *Review of child development research* (Vol. 5). Chicago, Illinois: Univ. of Chicago Press, 1975. Pp. 1–74.

Shatz, M. The relationship between cognitive processes and the development of communication skills. In B. Keasey (Ed.), *Nebraska Symposium on Motivation* (Vol. 26). Lincoln, Nebraska: Univ. of Nebraska Press, 1978.

Shatz, M., & Gelman, R. The development of communication skills: Modification of listener. *Monographs of the Society for Research in Child Development,* 1973, **38** (5, Serial No. 152).

Siegel, A. W., & White, S. H. The child study movement: Early growth and development of the symbolized child. In H. W. Reese (Ed.), *Advances in child development and behavior.* New York: Academic Press, 1983.

Siegler, R. S. *Children's thinking: What develops?* Hillsdale, New Jersey: Erlbaum, 1978.

Steffensen, M. S., Joag-Dev, C., & Anderson, R. C. A cross-cultural perspective on reading comprehension. *Reading Research Quarterly,* 1979, **1,** 10–29.

Super, C. M. Secular trends in child development and the institutionalization of professional disciplines. *S.R.C.D. Newsletter,* Spring 1982, 10–11.

Trabasso, T. The role of memory as a system in making transitive inferences. In R. V. Kail & J. W. Hagen (Eds.), *Perspectives on the development of memory and cognition.* Hillsdale, New Jersey: Erlbaum, 1977. Pp. 333–336.

White, S. W. Children in perspective: Introduction. *American Psychologist,* October, 1979, **34,** 812–814.

White, S. W. Graduate training in a developing field. *S.R.C.D. Newsletter,* Fall 1980, 6–7.

COGNITIVE ANALYSES OF BASIC SCHOOL TASKS

S. Farnham-Diggory and Billie Nelson

DEPARTMENT OF EDUCATIONAL STUDIES
UNIVERSITY OF DELAWARE
NEWARK, DELAWARE

I. Introduction

Applied questions have always been among the most interesting problems, but psychology has not always been willing to devise adequate methods of studying them. It has been easier to study special laboratory tasks,

Applied Developmental
Psychology, Volume 1

some of which, like nonsense syllables, have a hundred years of tradition behind them. The hope was that knowledge derived from this rather strange world of the laboratory could be generalized to the real world, although no one was quite sure how or when.

In fact, such generalizations have seldom occurred. Consider the 10 year old in the laboratory struggling to learn a list of nonsense syllables. The child will never perform as well as a college sophomore, and indeed that has been the prevailing view in the developmental literature: children are not as good at anything as adults are. For a long while, no one seemed to notice that outside on the playground, children were making up games and codes far more intricate than nonsense syllables, and were mastering them with alacrity. There was no way the serial position effect could explain that.

But from time to time, experimental psychologists wandered out of the laboratory to gaze upon the world around them, and to worry about discrepancies between what they knew how to do, and what needed to be done. The need to make precise predictions about the limits of human skill, especially in man–machine environments, gave rise to a field called *human performance,* and to its important chronometric technology for measuring decision times, attention switches, mental rehearsal rates, and other high-speed cognitive processes (Posner & Rogers, 1978; Sperling, 1960; Sternberg, 1969). The advent of computers made possible a new type of theorizing: the representation of psychological theory as a computer program (Anderson, 1976; Hunt & Poltrock, 1974; Newell & Simon, 1972; Schank & Abelson, 1977). Psychology was at last freed of S–R oversimplifications, and was on its way toward the construction and evaluation of theories adequate to a science at least as complex as theoretical physics and molecular biology—for, after all, it is the mind's capacity to invent those theories that is under investigation. The juxtaposition of methods from the field of human performance and theoretical strategies from the field of artificial intelligence has resulted in a new science, information-processing psychology, that is adequate to the study of complex, real-world problems (Chase, 1978).

This article presents some of the ways that we have tried to apply these new methods of information-processing psychology to the old tasks of reading and spelling. We have tried to study these tasks in some of their real-world forms, or as close to them as we can get while still obtaining precise measurements. Precision is necessary because switches in attention, decisions, and other mental processes occur at high speed, even in children. This fact has been known for a long time. A happy bonus of information-processing psychology is that it has put us back in touch with some of our distinguished forebears, such as William James and Frederic Bartlett. We therefore begin with a brief survey of the early history of reading and spelling psychology.

II. Curriculum Psychology When the Century Began

At the turn of the century, as psychology struggled to become a science, it polarized around mentalistic philosophy on the one hand, and empiricism on the other. The two poles appeared in educational psychology as well (Monroe, 1952). In an article called "The Development of Educational Psychology" published in 1924, Daniel Leary identified two "trends of thought." One was represented (he said) by William James, John Dewey, and Edward Thorndike and reflected a spirit of scientific inquiry and an inductive, pragmatic approach to educational problems. The other, represented by William Harris and G. Stanley Hall, was "more mystical, more moral in the popular sense of that term, more deductive than inductive, not particularly keen about concrete observation, prone to argue about technicalities, and inclined to worry about words" (Leary, 1924, p. 94). Leary's choice of exemplars is interesting, since we often think of James and Dewey as philosophical in outlook, and of Hall as our first developmental empiricist. Yet, look closely at the quality of Jamesian thought in the following excerpt from *Talks to Teachers,* delivered first in 1892 and published in 1899:

Assume the case of a young child's training in good manners. The child has a native tendency to snatch with his hands at anything that attracts his curiosity; also to draw back his hands when slapped, to cry under the latter conditions, to smile when gently spoken to, and to imitate one's gestures.

Suppose now you appear before the child with a new toy intended as a present for him. No sooner does he see the toy than he seeks to snatch it. You slap the hand; it is withdrawn, and the child cries. You then hold up the toy, smiling and saying, "Beg for it nicely,—so!" The child stops crying, imitates you, receives the toy, crows with pleasure; and that little cycle of training is complete. You have substituted the new reaction of "begging" for the native reaction of snatching, when that kind of impression comes.

Now, if the child had no memory, the process would not be educative. No matter how often you came in with a toy, the same series of reactions would fatally occur, each called forth by its own impressions: see, snatch; slap, cry; hear, ask; receive, smile. But, with memory there, the child, at the very instant of snatching, recalls the rest of the earlier experience, thinks of the slap and the frustration, recollects the begging and the reward, inhibits the snatching impulse, substitutes the "nice" reaction for it, and gets the toy immediately, by eliminating all the intermediary steps. . . .

One can easily represent the whole process by a brain-diagram. . . . Figure 1 [Part (a)] shows the paths of the four successive reflexes executed by the lower or instinctive centers. The dotted lines that lead from them to the higher centres, and connect the latter together, represent the processes of memory and association which the reactions impress upon the higher centres as they take place.

In [Part (b)], we have the final result. The impression *see* awakens the chain of memories, and the only reactions that take place are the *beg* and *smile*. The thought of the *slap,* connected with the activity of Centre 2, inhibits the *snatch* and makes it abortive, so it is represented only by a dotted line of discharge not reaching the terminus. Ditto

a

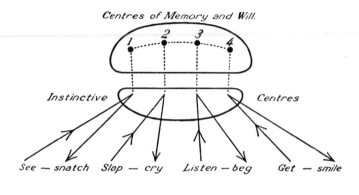

b

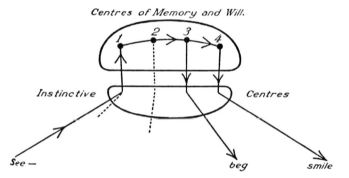

Fig. 1. William James' diagrams showing how education changes the flow of brain energy from sensorimotor to higher centers. (From James, 1958, p. 44.)

of the *cry* reaction. These are, as it were, short-circuited by the current sweeping through the higher centres from *see* to *smile*. *Beg* and *smile,* thus substituted for the original reaction *snatch,* become at last the immediate responses when the child sees a snatchable object in someone's hands.

    The first thing, then, for the teacher to understand is the native reactive tendencies—the impulses and instincts of childhood—so as to be able to substitute one for another, and turn them on to artificial objects. (James, 1958 edition, pp. 43–45)

That is the style of modern empiricism, although of course it was not so identified at the time. Early psychology, influenced by the brand of empiricism exemplified by Pavlov, Watson, and other radical behaviorists, abandoned both cognition and education in its quest for the vestments of hard science. It has taken us almost a hundred years to recover, to develop rigorous strategies for examining what James was talking about, and to conventionalize his flow charts.

The return to the study of cognition has also meant a return to the study of school tasks. Psychology was originally interested in school tasks—*common branches* they were called on the elementary level, and *higher branches* on the secondary. The early literature is replete with careful reasoning and intelligent speculation about cognitive processes involved in reading, writing, arithmetic, and many other school-based activities. It is a serious exercise in humility, as well as genuinely instructive, to review the work of our forerunners.

A. Psychology of the Common Branches

In early textbooks of educational psychology, the common branches included writing, drawing, reading, music, spelling, grammar, history, geography, mathematics, natural science, civics, hygiene, and ocasionally foreign languages (Cameron, 1927; Charters, 1913; Freeman, 1916; LaRue, 1924). Each was thought to develop particular faculties of the mind. For example, handwriting represented learning of a basic sensorimotor character.

> When the child takes pencil and paper and makes his first attempt to write, he is beginning a long course of training in the particular form of learning which we call "sensori-motor." His first attempt is to make a mark which shall look like the marks which are set before him as a copy, and the progress which he makes as he practices consists in getting better and better control over his movements so as to be able to produce letters and words which look more and more like the copy. Writing does not require in any large degree the exercise of memory, of imagination, or of reasoning. (Freeman, 1916, p. 1)

Writing was thus distinguished from spelling, in which learning particular letter sequences was emphasized. Spelling exemplified the *fixing of associations or bonds,* as Thorndike called them. Reading, drawing, and music were all thought to represent *perceptual learning,* defined as the organization of sensory impressions. Natural science developed the ability to *generalize from experience.* History and geography were forms of *imaginative learning,* and mathematics trained *capacities for abstraction.* This was not a formal faculty psychology, but was merely a convenient way of organizing psychological topics.

1. SPELLING

The study of spelling was sometimes introduced as an arbitrary matter which must be done correctly for social reasons. "The school is compelled to take the situation as it is," Freeman wrote, although "until recent times

even educated people expressed their meaning through writing in a satisfactory way without spelling with any high degree of uniformity" (Freeman, 1916, p. 116). Charters (1913), however, viewed spelling as having a
more essential function.

> The real reason for learning to spell correctly is that we may be understood.
> In writing words we place the letters in a certain order so that people will know exactly
> what we mean.
> An automobile dealer received the following letter from a correspondent:
> "Dear Sire: Because you send me A Paid Envellope I SEnd you an answer I Have
> no Recolection of Applying to you to Purchase an Automobile I am 82 years Old and
> very nervous Could Not possibly use one and would not accept one if you would Give
> it to me Would Not undertake to Operate One No how Have No no money only a Little
> Pension money I draw as a Wounded Soldier was badly wounded on the Yazoo river in
> 1863 could not Operate Car no-how Rid in one only with great ereluctance Please excuse
> me from wanting such a charge to worry out my life Farewell "
> Here we are inclined to think the writer an object of ridicule; and we have difficulty,
> moreover, in knowing exactly what he means. . . . Every time a word is misspelled, the
> writer has to trust to the mercy of the one who reads it. He has no right to expect to be
> understood. (Charters, 1913, pp. 2–3)

Such was the humorless disgrace that awaited children who shirked their
spelling practice. Charters (1913) referred somberly to the pedagogical goal
of instilling a *spelling conscience*.

By 1915, a number of experiments had been done on the best way to
teach spelling. There were three domains of research preoccupation: *modality, attention,* and *automaticity.*

> The first interesting thing about learning to spell is the fact that there are different
> types of imagery used by people who spell . . . visual, auditory, and motor imagery, the
> last of which originates in the muscles that control the fingers and the vocal cords.
> The presence of auditory images is seen in the case of those who say, "The spelling
> of that word does not *sound* right." They can hear the sounds "in their heads" just as
> many people can hear tunes in their heads. The visual image is seen in the case of those
> who say, "That spelling does not *look* right." They compare the spelling with a memory
> picture stored in their minds. The motor imagery is seen in the case of people who cannot
> be sure of a spelling until they have spelled it over to themselves and have recognized
> the "feel" in their throats, or have written it out rapidly and allowed the hand to have
> full play in the writing.
> Some are visualists, some audiles, and others motiles; but most people combine all
> three types, with the visual as the strongest. That is, the majority of people, in deciding
> whether a word is right or wrong, spell it aloud or . . . write it out and look at it, but
> usually resort to visual images first. (Charters, 1913, pp. 16–17)

An experiment reported by Cameron (1927) was conducted on 3000 German children in grades 3–8. The children practiced one of seven spelling
methods listed in Table I. From their error percentages on later tests, it was

Table I

Percentage of Spelling Errors Made by German Schoolchildren in Seven Training Conditions[a]

Training condition	Percentage of errors
Hearing—pupils not making any speech movements	3.04
Hearing—pupils repeating silently	2.69
Hearing—pupils repeating aloud	2.25
Seeing—pupils not making any speech movements	1.22
Seeing—pupils repeating silently	1.02
Seeing—pupils repeating aloud	.95
Copying—pupils repeating silently	.54

[a] From Cameron (1927, p. 318).

concluded that (1) the visual drill method was superior to the auditory, (2) both methods were improved by the addition of kinesthetic factors, (3) copying was the best method, since it involved both visual and kinesthetic processes, (4) copying was also the best way of controlling attention, and (5) copying incorporated the further advantage that "the studying of the word takes the form in which it is eventually reproduced" (p. 329).

Cameron also pointed out that good spellers have cultivated "an attitude toward words that leads to careful observation of their details" (p. 319). Teachers were urged to instill this attitude.

Repetition made without giving attention is of little value. This principle is some-times . . . designated by the term *focalization*. When there is focalization of attention, the child has his mind called sharply to the thing he is doing. In the case of spelling, this means that when he is learning to spell a word, he is thinking primarily of its spelling, and not of its meaning, or of the form of the letters as he writes them, or of some other fact connected with it. . . . Spelling drill, in which the words are studied particularly for the sake of knowing how to spell them, calls the child's attention to this one fact or aspect of the word, and therefore brings about the condition of focalization. (Freeman, 1916, p. 127)

The development of automaticity was explicitly emphasized.

The ability to write a word without having to think about the spelling is spoken of as the ability to spell *automatically*. To set up automatic spelling habits is the aim of all attempts to teach the subject. . . . Unless the spelling of a word is made automatic, all the labor is lost. That is to say, in the spelling of *superficial* as *s-u-p-e-r-f-i-c-i-a-l,* the letters must follow with rapidity or certainty, and without thought. It will not do to spell *sup* and then stumble over *er,* or spell *superf* and stumble over *icial.* This is very important. If the child cannot do this at one sitting, he should try it at a second sitting or a third sitting. In order to make the sequence of letters very stable, the words have to be spelled at many different times. Reviews are essential, and speed is to be striven for at the expense of everything but accuracy. (Charters, 1913, pp. 18–22)

Some idea of the amount of practice involved is given in the following quotation from one of the most influential research reports of the time, that of *Spelling Efficiency* by J. E. W. Wallin (1911).

Ten words focalized during the week recur as subordinate words during the next two weeks. They are also made the subject of a special review once a week. At the end of every eighth week oral and written interschool contests between the same grades in all the schools of the [Cleveland] system are conducted, based upon the eighty words focalized and reviewed during this period. Similar annual contests are also held, and the following year the words are again reviewed as subordinates. Each focalized word is reviewed, therefore, four times (or five, including the initial assignment) in two years. Recourse is had to the interschool contests in order to secure attentive repetitions and to vitalize the process. Motivation is thus secured by appealing to the child's instincts of emulation, rivalry and pride in the prestige of his class and school.

This method of thoroughgoing initial focalization and attentive repetition should have yielded a high degree of automatic mastery of the spelling of a considerable number of words. As a matter of fact, spelling efficiency engendered by this spelling technique in the Cleveland schools is quite remarkable. (Wallin, 1911, pp. 18–19)

2. READING

The process of reading was defined broadly and meaningfully in the early part of the century as *the reproduction of experience from symbols* (LaRue, 1924, p. 277). The writer first organizes his experience "according to the rules of language. He may throw it into the form of exposition. . . . On the other hand, he may throw it into the form of a narrative" but in any case, "the reader has to build up in his experience the same experience that the writer had when he wrote" (Charters, 1913, pp. 105–106). For children to do this, Charters believed, their reading materials must reflect their own experiences. Concepts of "readiness" and child-centered content were therefore central to the early psychology of reading.

When you find, in the reading period, the pupils curling the pages of the primer, rolling pencils, and pulling playthings out of their pockets, in spite of all the efforts of the teacher, the chances are that there is something the matter with the story. It is said in the apple market that "the mouth merely eats the apple; the eye buys it." The child merely reads the book; the teacher or superintendent buys it. When McGuffey was writing his good old readers, about the middle of the last century, he called in the children of the neighborhood and tried out his literature on them. It would be well if we could still have committees of children to help in making selections. (LaRue, 1924, p. 293)

But if interest flagged, the shame of illiteracy was quickly trotted forth.

If one cannot read, there is the sting of disgrace. A young man of about twenty-seven found himself called upon to read aloud before the Lodge to which he belonged, a part of its proceedings, and was forced to confess himself unable to do so. He felt the humiliation so keenly that he at once hunted out someone to teach him to read. He became later a prominent superintendent of schools. (LaRue, 1924, p. 293)

It was generally recognized that spelling was related to reading, but that the processes involved were sufficiently different to warrant separate courses of instruction.

On the sensory side, spelling is related to reading since it deals with the same materials. The object of perception in spelling, however, is quite different from the object of perception in reading. While reading is more efficient the larger the unit of perception becomes, in the case of spelling the unit of perception must be the letter. Undoubtedly in the case of practised spellers the writing of words may be in response to large units, such as words and especially syllables; but in the case of the child each letter is written individually, and in any case each letter must be thought of in a sense that does not hold good for the act of reading.

It is for this reason that the best method of teaching reading may not be, and probably is not, the best method of producing good spellers. Indeed, the two processes are naturally opposed, since spelling requires analysis of words into their component elements, while reading is the more effective the longer the unit apprehended within the limits required for getting the thought without mistakes. (Cameron, 1927, pp. 316–317)

Controversy over "whole word" vs "phonetic" reading pedagogy is longstanding (Fries, 1963). But at the turn of the century, when the psychology of reading was becoming conscious of itself as such, textbooks of educational psychology had adopted a fairly uniform stance. Children were initially taught a pool of sight words, and were then taught phonetic or alphabetic principles contained in them. There were three learning stages: first, becoming aware of the general fact that something written stands for something spoken. "The experience of seeing other persons read, the realization of the meaning of street signs, of store signs, etc., will give this early type of recognition" (Freeman, 1916, p. 71). The second stage was learning to connect particular written forms with particular words. This was, in the opinion of the early psychologists, similar to any other form of object recognition.

Your beginner may know that the longest word teacher writes on the board is "bumblebee," that the one with the two round eyes in the middle is "book," and so on— and that may be practically all he does know about them. A word, for a beginner, is more of an *object*, like a toy, about so long and so wide and with prongs sticking out here and there. They often recognize words with equal ease whether the card that holds it is right side up or upside down, just as they know the dog when he is lying on his back, and as you can recognize a Ford car even when it is upset. One child, on being asked to find "shoes," said that "dress" looked so much like "shoes" she was afraid she would make a mistake. These two words are of the same length, both curly at the end, and each has one letter that sticks up at the beginning. (LaRue, 1924, p. 285)

An important point was the child had not yet developed an *analytical* approach to reading.

> A written word is perceived as a shape or form in which the individual letters are merged into a characteristic pattern just as in the case of our perception of any ordinary object. As we go along the street and a horse passes us, it is unnecessary in order to recognize it as a horse to examine individually its head, ears, and tail. It is recognized immediately as a form or shape with certain characteristic features. The recognition of words takes place in a similar manner. (Cameron, 1927, p. 299)

The third stage of learning to read therefore focused on what would later be called the *distinguishing features* of familiar patterns. Ideally, this instruction began after the children knew 200 or 300 sight words, and had discovered that they needed to learn new words for themselves. This was called the *phonics* method. "Some people have worked out primary reading by . . . using phones or letter-sounds instead of letter-names. They are said to use, then, a *phonic* method instead of an *alphabetic* method" (Charters, 1913, p. 121).

Analytical thinking was clearly recognized as a different type of cognitive activity having its own time course.

> This process of phonetic analysis is necessarily slower than that in which recognition takes place by vision alone, just because it *is* a process of analysis rather than immediate apprehension of relatively large units. If analysis is resorted to, there must be synthesis of the elements into the total word sound before recognition takes place. Evidently the eye must be slowed up to the extent that analysis becomes necessary. Hence phonetic analysis should be regarded as a supplementary aid to visual recognition, rather than the fundamental basis for reading instruction. It must not be thought . . . that the mature reader goes to the extreme of resolving words into the sounds of the individual letters when he is making use of the method of phonetic analysis. (Cameron, 1927, pp. 309–310)

Cameron went on to point out that the mature reader dealt with syllables rather than with individual letters. LaRue discussed at some length the reader's need to master *inclusive units*—first, "groups of letters that remain together in many different words, as *ap* in *cap, nap, rap,* and *tap,*" (p. 287), and later, words and phrases. LaRue advised introducing "but one difficulty at a time" and diagrammed the general process as shown in Fig. 2. Analytical instruction thus explicitly encouraged the formation of what we now call *chunks.*

$$\begin{array}{ccc}
\textit{Sight Words} & \textit{Phonic Parts} & \textit{New Words} \\
\left.\begin{array}{l} \text{rat} \\ \text{can} \end{array}\right\} > \longrightarrow & \left\{\begin{array}{l} \text{r\ at} \\ \text{c\ an} \end{array}\right\} > \longrightarrow & \left\{\begin{array}{l} \text{ran, } \textit{studied as } \text{r--an} \\ \text{cat, \quad `` \quad `` \quad c--at} \end{array}\right.
\end{array}$$

Fig. 2. "The general process of mastering new words so as to introduce but one difficulty at a time." (From LaRue, 1924, p. 288.)

Studies in the learning of telegraphy, and typewriting, and everything else of the sort, show that there is first a *letter* stage; and then, as the bonds go on working better and more cooperatively, [a *letter-group* stage]; a *word* stage; a *phrase* stage; and in the case of the very skillful, a *still-larger-unit* stage. In fact, the size of the unit that can be handled as a unit is the royal mark of skill. (LaRue, 1924, p. 290)

The size of the unit was inferred from eye movements in the case of silent reading, and from the eye–voice span in the case of oral reading. By 1920, a method had been developed for recording on film a spot of light reflected from the cornea during reading. Figure 3a shows an example of eye movements obtained from a slow fourth-grade reader. Figure 3b shows the eye movements of a skilled adult reader. The numbers at the top of the vertical lines are the fixation orders; the numbers at the bottom, durations in fiftieths of a second.

The development of smooth and economical eye movements was thought to signify the development of smooth and economical cognitive processing. The assumption then, as now, was that drill was necessary to automate unit recognition and to free attention for dealing with comprehension demands.

The processes of recognition . . . are in the case of the slower readers so difficult that they . . . make demands on the attention which would otherwise be directed to the meanings conveyed by the words (p. 306).

The ability to get the [meaning] is in large measure made possible by making certain elements of the process automatic and mechanical. The skill of the teacher will be taxed chiefly in providing a maximum of drill without at the same time making the activity such a formal exercise that the drill becomes the end, instead of the means, of increased ability to acquire meanings. (Cameron, 1927, pp. 298–300)

With reference to the psychology of reading comprehension, it is important to understand that silent reading was only just coming into fashion. Until the early part of this century, people considered oral reading to be the only kind of reading there was. Silent reading had to be explicitly advocated. Here are some of the reasons why LaRue rather reluctantly did so.

In most reading situations, we are . . . compelled to proceed silently for our neighbor's sake. . . . If we have been well schooled in oral reading, we learn to "reproduce the

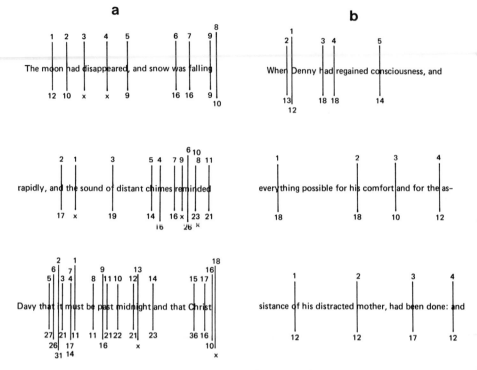

Fig. 3. Eye fixations of (a) a slow fourth grader, and (b) a skilled adult reader. Each vertical line indicates a fixation. The order of fixations are the numbers above the line; the duration of each (in fiftieths of a second) are the lower numbers. (From Cameron, 1927, pp. 34–35.)

experience," or as much of it as we want, without the aid of the voice, just as a pupil who has had practice in thinking-talking-writing will at length write his thought silently without the middle step of talking, at the same time testing out by inner speech how his sentences will feel and sound when his reader lifts them from the paper. If we are willing to sacrifice what the voice contributes, we can also gain in speed, for if we uncouple our talking machinery and let the inner speech run on alone, it keeps on going when we are breathing in as well as when we are breathing out, and even faster than when the lips are moving. We often wish to "skim through" our reading matter; for much that is printed is to be "tasted" only—it is not all real literature by any means. And even if it were, we may want to glean from it some one theme and not to grasp it as a whole. Such gleaning and skimming is likely to be a rapid, flitting kind of process, with words slurred, half pronounced, or omitted, and so it can best be carried on silently. (LaRue, 1924, pp. 279–280)

Nevertheless, a substantial portion of reading instruction was directed toward the development of expressive oral reading skills, including posture, intonation, and gaze management. "Read it to yourself first, then look at me and say it." LaRue's teachers were advised to instruct, "with expression." Young readers were thus forced to look and plan ahead—LaRue said to *prevision*.

> One important reason for so much muddling and blundering by our pupils is that they either do not see what is coming next, or they are not ready for it when it piles up before them. In reading, as the pupil speaks one phrase he must, with his eye, be scooping up the next one. As he speaks or writes one word or sentence, his thoughts must be prospecting ahead, preparing the next. The very spirit of speed in typewriting lies in letting the mind run over, in a quick, anticipatory way, what is to be written next. Life itself, if we live well, is largely a matter of looking ahead. But a word of warning here: do not expect prevision nor speed from a beginner. "Introduce but one difficulty at a time." Now, speed itself is a difficulty. In the beginning, go slow, work for *accuracy*, and let speed, for the most part, take care of itself. Prevision comes only with practice: The old road reminds us which turn is coming next. (LaRue, 1924, p. 81)

There was dispute even then over whether reading aloud forced the development of comprehension strategies or worked against them, producing word callers who failed to understand what they were saying. LaRue took the former position, as evidenced by his sequencing of the skills summarized below:

> To you, as teacher, the aim will be "reading for meaning." As aids to this ultimate object, the chief exercises to be conducted are (1) the drill on sight words and phrases; (2) the study of phonics; (3) the application of phonics to the mastery of new words; (4) reading [aloud] for expression; and (5) the mastering of large inclusive units. (LaRue, 1924, p. 298)

Thorndike was also interested in reading comprehension, and wrote in 1917 on "Reading as Reasoning: A Study of Mistakes in Paragraph Reading."

> It seems to be a common opinion that reading . . . is a rather simple compounding of habits. Each word or phrase is supposed, if known to the reader, to call up its sound and meaning. . . . [But] reading is a very elaborate procedure, involving a weighing of each of many elements in a sentence, their organization in the proper relations one to another, the selection of certain of their connotations and the rejection of others, and the cooperation of many forces to determine final response. (Thorndike, 1917, p. 323)

Thorndike was especially interested in what he called the *under-potency* or *over-potency* of particular words. In his experiment, children first read the following paragraph:

> In Franklin, attendance upon school is required of every child between the ages of seven and fourteen on every day when school is in session unless the child is so ill as to be unable to go to school, or some person in his house is ill with a contagious disease, or the roads are impassable.

Children then answered questions about the paragraph, and Thorndike analyzed the significance of their errors.

> The second question was: "On what day would a ten-year-old girl not be expected to attend school?" We find under-potency of *not* resulting in answers like "When school is in session" or "Five days a week." We find under-potency of *day* resulting in responses like "She is allowed to go to school when 6 years."
> We find over-potency of *day* shown by "Monday," "Wednesday," and "Friday;" of *ten-year-old girl* in "The ten-year-old girl will be in [grade] 5A."
> *Ten-year-old* is over-potent in an interesting way, namely, in the very large number of responses of "On her birthday." (Thorndike, 1917, p. 328)

Thorndike was perhaps wishing he could develop a quantitative formula for predicting comprehension.

> To make a long story short, inspection of the mistakes shows that the potency of any word or word group in a question may be far above or far below its proper amount in relation to the rest of the question. The same holds for any word or word group in the paragraph. Understanding a paragraph implies keeping these respective weights in proper proportion from the start or varying their proportions until they together evoke a response which satisfies the purpose of the reading.
> Understanding a paragraph is like solving a problem in mathematics. It consists in selecting the right elements of the situation and putting them together in the right relations, and also with the right amount of weight or influence or force for each. The mind is assailed as it were by every word in the paragraph. It must select, repress, soften, emphasize, correlate and organize, all under the influence of the right mental set or purpose or demand. (Thorndike, 1917, p. 329)

Thorndike noted that the children could recognize the absurdity of their errors if confronted with them directly. What the children failed to do, he said, was "of their own accord test their responses by thinking out their subtler or more remote implications" (p. 330). He therefore recommended explicit training in comprehension strategies, noting that "it is in their outside reading of stories and in their study of geography, history, and the like, that many school children really learn to read" (p. 332).

We cannot help wonder how Thorndike and others who have been quoted in this historical overview might have made use of the information-processing concepts and paradigms of today. As in Pirandello's play *Six Characters in Search of an Author,* many propositions put forth by early theorists seem in search of modern empirical language. We have now, we think, more elegant paradigms, more accurate terms, and more sensitive technologies for dealing with the same issues. But perhaps, as Piagetians would point out, that comment reveals only the egocentrism of our own stage of formal operations.

B. Then What Happened?

In a word, *tests*. With the advent of the testing movement, the psychology of school tasks was submerged and almost extinguished. This historical sequence is illustrated in Fig. 4, which graphs the percentage of school task vs testing articles that appeared in the *Journal of Educational Psychology* from 1910 (the year of its inception) through 1981.

The graph is based on a content analysis of every volume from 1910 through 1920, and every tenth volume thereafter, plus the volume for 1981. Twelve mutually exclusive categories were identified:

1. *School tasks*—articles concerned with the pedagogy or structure of the content areas, including reading, literature, poetry, grammar, handwriting, composition, spelling, arithmetic, geometry, hygiene, science (chemistry, botany, etc.), psychology, drawing, music, agriculture, etc. The percentage of these articles, fluctuating over the 70-year period, is graphed in Fig. 4 as the black bars.

The next categories were testing articles, and are combined in the Fig. 4 open bars.

2. *Individual differences*—articles concerned with intelligence, motor

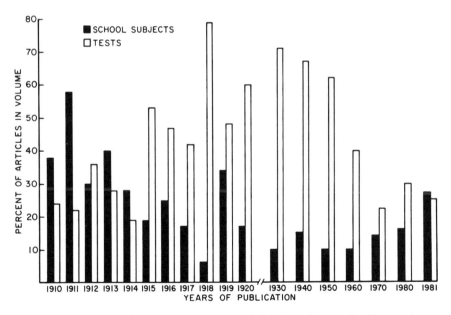

Fig. 4. Proportions of articles per volume sampled dealing with school subjects and tests in *Journal of Educational Psychology,* 1910–1981.

skills, sensory skills, etc. arising from the Binet, Galton, and Cattell traditions.

3. *School achievement*—articles concerned with standardized achievement testing in content areas. This category also included evaluation of teachers and programs.

4. *Statistics and research design*—articles concerned with the mathematics of test development.

In addition, eight categories were identified that are not graphed in Fig. 4.

5. *Exceptional children*—articles concerned with deaf, blind, retarded, gifted, and special education generally. These accounted for ~3% per volume sampled.

6. *Language and speech development*—articles concerned with onset of language and with school remediation (1%).

7. *Physical development*—articles concerned with growth and sensory capacities (1%).

8. *Theory*—articles concerned with the application of psychological theory to education (1%).

9. *Management*—articles concerned with administration, teacher training, and demonstration programs (4%).

10. *Laboratory: learning*—experiments that used artificial stimuli (e.g., nonsense syllables) rather than pedagogical materials (9%).

11. *Laboratory: cognitive processes*—experiments also using artificial stimuli, but concerned with cognition rather than with traditional learning paradigms. These did not appear in this journal until 1970, but now account for ~8% of its publications.

12. *Motivation*—articles concerned with interest, preference, reinforcement, personality, social interactions, etc. These appeared infrequently until 1950. Since then, they have accounted for 22% of articles in the volumes sampled.

As Fig. 4 clearly illustrates, educational psychology, strictly defined as the papers accepted for publication in the sole official journal of that title, preoccupied itself with standardized tests from about 1915 onward, at the expense of all other categories. Particularly devastating was the abandonment of the rich and productive theorizing represented by early curriculum research. However, as psychology has generally broadened itself in recent years, so educational psychology has begun to include, again, a concern with curriculum. As Fig. 4 reveals, in 1981, for the first time since 1914, articles concerned with school tasks outranked articles concerned with tests and measurements. Elsewhere, books and periodicals are burgeoning with evidence of increasing interest in school tasks on the part of research psychologists (Anderson, Spiro, & Montague, 1977; Farnham-Diggory, 1972, 1977; Frith, 1980; Green, 1980; Klahr, 1976; LaBerge & Samuels, 1977; Lesgold, Pellegrino, Fokkema, & Glaser, 1978; Reber & Scarborough, 1977; Resnick & Ford, 1981; Simon & Simon, 1978; Snow, Federico, & Montague, 1980; Tuma & Reif, 1980; and see also the new journal *Cognition & Instruction*). There has been a resounding turn in the tide.

III. Curriculum Psychology As the Century Ends

By the beginning of the 1980s, the testing movement was undergoing massive political and theoretical reappraisals (Chase, 1977; Feuerstein, 1979; Glaser & Bond, 1981). Coming under fire was the basic notion that the products of a test (answers to test questions) could be evaluated independently of the processes of producing them. The child answering a test question was acknowledged to be assembling and activating complex programs of mental operations. It was no longer acceptable for researchers to ignore those operations in favor of simple, easy-to-count "right" or "wrong" answers. If wrong, why wrong? What particular stages of answering particular questions was the child unable to accomplish? The statistics of the mental testing movement were being recognized as potentially illusory; a table of correlations might be a gloss for ignorance of the complex mental processes that produced them. The job now was to face up to the problem of specifying exactly what was going on.

What do children do inside their heads when they spell? What do they do inside their heads when they read? Not until those questions are answered will it be possible to design appropriate methods of assessing skill. Research is moving "back to the basics" of school tasks themselves. As forthcoming examples from our own laboratory will illustrate, information-processing psychology now offers methods for tracing high-speed mental processes involved in school tasks. We can, for example, detect particular letter combinations that spellers assemble as units, or the amount of time it takes a third grader to process a conditional clause. This type of research exemplifies three main paradigmatic principles. (1) A model, crude or elaborate, is specified. In our case, the models are far from being full simulations, and we therefore refer to them as *protomodels*. They are Jamesian in spirit (pp. 23–25, above) but follow modern information-processing formats. (2) Parameters of the model are being sought: How fast does memory work? How many letters can be accessed at once? There is no attempt as yet to formulate and test hypotheses. Not enough is known about the phenomena themselves. (3) Subject behaviors are described with painstaking precision. Sequences of cognitive operations are not random. There is always a pattern but it may not be discoverable unless data can be examined in slow motion and in fine detail.

We illustrate this modern approach to curriculum psychology by excerpts from two projects of our own. The first is a brief sample of a long-term project on spelling. The second is a more detailed examination of pilot data from a new project on reading.

A. Spelling

Over the past 4 years we have been engaged in studying the process of producing written words. We have videotaped normal and learning-disabled children, and normal adults, as they wrote words. We have examined not merely spelling products, correctly or incorrectly spelled words, but also the millisecond-by-millisecond processes of producing them. We call this type of research *microethology,* since it borrows from the biologists a concern with naturally unfolding behaviors, and from the human performance researchers, a concern with the split-second time course of human cognition.

As noted by our pedagogical forebears at the turn of the century (pp. 25–28, above), the modality of the spelling process is of special importance. There are visual, aural, and kinesthetic representational components. We have tried to assess the relative contribution of visual and aural components while holding kinesthetic contributions constant. We have focused also on the development of writing automaticity, particularly on the question of how many letters are produced as cohesive sets.

1. METHODS

There are many kinds of spelling tasks: spelling out loud, writing words down on paper, writing words on a blackboard, studying a list of words and then writing them, writing words in the context of sentences, typing, playing anagrams, etc. We asked our subjects to write on a vertical surface as they would on a blackboard, only in this case they were writing on a transparent Plexiglas panel. We videotaped subjects *through* the panel, recording the movements of writing hands. The analyses reported here were obtained from close-ups of the hands.

Subjects sat in an adjustable chair about 18 in. from the panel. A "space helmet" attached to a rigid bar held their heads still. An opaque visor came down from the helmet. By raising and lowering this visor, we controlled the subject's visual input. In particular, we did not let the subjects see what they were writing, because, for these studies, we wanted their output to be uncontaminated by visual feedback. Subjects rehearsed this "blind writing," and had no difficulty with it. They wrote with a felt pen, and were instructed to print.

There were two conditions. In the aural condition, subjects were primed by an aural matching task, and were then instructed to concentrate, while printing, on the sounds of the words that were being dictated to them. We called this *sound spelling*. In the other condition, subjects were primed by a visual matching task, and were then shown words printed on tagboard. These subjects were instructed to concentrate on their visual images of the words as they printed them. We called this *sight spelling*. All subjects, in counterbalanced order, were assigned to both conditions. Words (blocked by condition) were displayed one at a time, and the subjects were given as much time as they needed to write each one. The Plexiglas was wiped clean after each trial.

Numbers, incrementing in 16.6-msec intervals, were superimposed on the videotapes during recording. This made it possible to measure *letter-writing time* and *preletter latencies* with high reliability. Letter-writing time was measured from the time the pen began moving on the Plexiglas until the movement stopped. Preletter latencies were measured from the time the pen stopped until it touched down and began the next letter.

All data reported here are for correctly spelled words only.

2. SUBJECTS AND STIMULI

Only normal children and adults are discussed here. There were 12 7-year-old and 12 11-year-old children, and 20 adults. Both sexes were equally represented in each group. All subjects were of normal intelligence and reading ability.

The words spelled by the children were CHILDREN, PICTURE, WINDOW, STUPID, BROKEN, COMPUTE, SIGNAL, HISTORY, SOLUTION, and MEDICINE. The words spelled by the adults were VERBALIZE, BOMBARD, MEDICATION, SIGNATURE, COMPUTATION, STUPIDITY, MUSCULAR, COMPOSITION, MALIGNANT, and GRADUATION.

3. PROTOMODEL OF THIS SPELLING TASK

Roughly, the task could be decomposed into the following sequence of cognitive procedures:

Segmentation Protomodel

Step 1 Register the word
Step 2 Parse word into segments
Step 3 Get (next) segment
Step 4 Write its letters
Step 5 Test: Finished yet?
        If not, return to Step 3
        If so, stop

Note this particular protomodel does not include a test of whether or not written letters, or sets of them, "look right," ordinarily a normal and important aspect of spelling. That test is absent because it was prevented by the visor.

When a task is broken down in this way, its steps can be examined theoretically and empirically. What could be said about Step 1? If sight and hearing are normal, and if the stimulus is presented clearly, frequencies will be coded by neurons and maintained for a brief period in a sensory buffer—primary projection areas in the occipital (seeing) or temporal (hearing) cortex. However, from that point onward, there is no compelling neurological reason why sight spelling should differ from sound spelling. Theoretically, the same brain subroutines could be triggered by either eyes or ears. Nevertheless, our data show that presentation modality continues to influence the entire sequence of cognitive procedures. That is, subjects who saw words conducted Steps 2, 3, and 4 differently from subjects who heard them.

4. PARSING A WORD INTO SEGMENTS

When you spell a word, you usually write a few letters in a burst, pause, write a few more letters in a burst, pause again, and continue in that manner until the word is finished. Those little bursts are what we call *segments*. The segmentation model specifies that when a word is registered, it is marked off mentally into segments. Each segment is then taken up in turn. If that were not the case, how would you know when you had reached the end of the word? You could not have initially marked the last letter of the word, because you would not have retrieved it yet. Instead, you must have "set a flag" on some portion of the pattern that was initially registered—a portion of the intonation pattern in the case of sound spelling, or a portion of the spatial array in the case of sight spelling.

A major objective of our research has been to identify *segment boundaries*. How long does a preletter latency have to be, to qualify as a *presegment latency*? Somewhat longer than the latencies within a segment, but how much longer? Similar questions have been asked about typing (Sternberg, Monsell, Knoll, & Wright, 1978), and the placement of chess pieces (Chase & Simon, 1973). Following those theoretical leads, we eventually discovered a surprisingly simple way to identify segment boundaries: if a latency increase amounted to 50% or more of the previous change, this increase was considered to mark a segment boundary. The full story of our search, and details of the statistical evidence supporting it, are in Farnham-Diggory, Nelson, and Rohrlich, *Microethology of Spelling Behavior* (in preparation). The point is that a presegment latency must be defined in terms of its location within a word. Latencies generally speed up as spelling proceeds. A presegment latency near the end of a word may be shorter than one occurring earlier. Hence, it is necessary to have a locally relative measure.

Given this measure, we can ask about the nature of segments. Table II shows the number of segments produced by the three age groups during sight and sound spelling, as well as the number of letters in each segment. You can see that all three groups parsed their words into more segments during sight spelling. That may be because spatial arrays are easier to subdivide than sound patterns are. As the N columns show, more words are correctly spelled following visual presentation, a fact that seems intuitively obvious, but is by no means easy to account for theoretically (Farnham-Diggory & Simon, 1975; Henderson & Chard, 1980).

As Table II shows, the number of segments per word increases with age. Remember, however, that adults were spelling longer words than children were. One interesting possibility is that the number of letters per segment may remain constant, regardless of word length. Segments are composed of about three letters each. In the event of long words, the number of segments would have to increase.

After discovering this apparent three-letter constancy, we found a strongly confirmatory article by Broadbent (1975), who presented several kinds of evidence suggesting that in adults, long-term memory data are output in clusters of three or four items. Development of control processes for such an output strategy may underlie the increase in *analytical attitude* described by the early spelling researchers (e.g., Cameron, 1927, as quoted above). We have other bits of evidence to support this. Consider the 7- and 11-year-old children, who spelled the same words. We might expect the older group to produce more of these words as single segments. In fact, the younger children were more likely to produce single-segment words, if they could spell the words at all. They could spell *window,* for example. There were 10 productions of that word as a single segment, compared to 4 such productions in the older group. However, when the older group spelled words

Table II

Number of Segments per Word and Letters per Segment for Correctly Spelled Words [a]

	Sound spelling			Sight spelling		
	Segments per word	Letters per segment	(N)	Segments per word	Letters per segment	(N)
7 year olds	1.93	3.47	(43)	2.24	3.03	(68)
11 year olds	2.12	3.23	(112)	2.29	3.00	(117)
Adults	3.07	3.00	(188)	3.13	2.34	(195)

[a] Data are pooled. The numbers in parentheses are the number of correctly spelled words in each group.

that were more difficult for them than *window* was, a whole-word strategy appeared in their group as well: in seven cases, *signal* was produced as a single segment, and in seven cases *history* was.

Our working hypothesis has therefore come to be that two protomodels should be specified. The first has been listed above, the segmentation model. A second one would be the following:

Look-Up Protomodel

Step 1   Register word
Step 2   Access its list of letters
Step 3   Write the (next) letter
Step 4   Test: Have I finished the list yet?
          If not, return to Step 3
          If so, stop

Both beginning and experienced spellers can activate the look-up procedures. Beginners, however, may need to rely on a look-up model almost entirely until their segmentation skills and capacities develop. That is probably why immature (poor) spellers sometimes substitute incorrect whole words (e.g., *house* instead of *home*) for words they are supposed to be spelling. However, once segmentation skills have begun to develop, the segmentation model and its three-letter/segment parameter may take over.

5. Presegment Latencies

Figure 5 shows the mean presegment latencies during sight and sound spelling in the three age groups. In all three groups, the latencies are shorter during sight spelling. The effect is especially strong in 7 year olds, who require more than 1100 msec, on the average, to get segments during sound spelling, as compared to 900 msec during sight spelling. This effect is consistent with a large literature showing that aural processing inefficiency is associated with developmental immaturity (Vellutino, 1979). By the age of 11, however, presegment latency differences between sound and sight spelling have dropped to about 30 msec, essentially the adult level.

What is occurring during those little pauses? In part, presumably, the assembly of a program to produce a forthcoming segment. If so, then the size of the pause should predict the size of the segment. To obtain a measure of segment size, we added together all the latencies and letter-writing times within a segment, producing a *total segment time*. That total time could then be correlated with the length of the boundary latency that preceded it. The results are summarized in Table III.

Although one 7-year-old child produced a significant correlation in the sound-spelling condition, it was generally true among 7 year olds that no

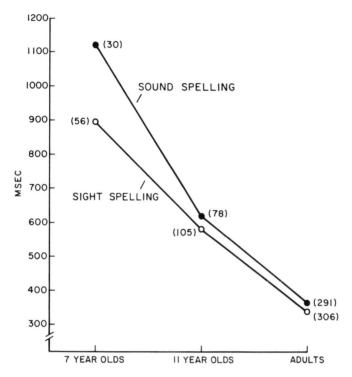

Fig. 5. Presegment latencies (ordinate) by age and mode of representation. Numbers in parentheses are the number of data points.

Table III

Correlational Data on Proportion of Group Displaying Significant Individual Rank-Order Correlations of Presegment Latencies with Total Segment Production Times, Average Size of Correlations, and Average Significance Levels

	Sound spelling			Sight spelling		
	Proportion of group (%)	Mean rho	Mean significance level	Proportion of group (%)	Mean rho	Mean significance level
7 year olds	8	.943	.002	—	—	—
11 year olds	25	.413	.03	33	.701	.005
Adults	85	.637	.01	80	.557	.01

stable correlations appeared. Among the 11 year olds, the proportion of significant correlations was between 25 and 35%, and among the adults, that proportion grew to 85%. As the table shows, the correlations, when they appeared, were highly significant.

The increasing number of significant correlations suggests, again, that the ability to implement a segmentation strategy increases with age. We further believe that the appearance of a significant correlation in an individual case may serve as an index of strategy development. However, that remains to be tested longitudinally.

6. LETTER-WRITING TIMES

The letters graphed in Fig. 6 were written in the context of correctly spelled words. We extracted them from those contexts in order to compute average writing times. Three consonants and three vowels with *N*s of at least 20 per data point are shown.

There is a tendency for letters to be written more slowly during sight spelling than during sound spelling. That was true for over half the letters written by the children, and for 98% of those written by adults. It is likely

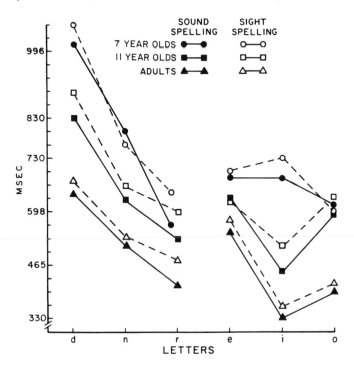

Fig. 6. Mean printing time (ordinate) for six letters printed in word contexts during sound and sight spelling by children and adults.

that the additional milliseconds go into a feedback test—"Did the letter I wrote look like the one I saw?"—even though the subjects were writing blind.

With the exception of the letter *i,* adults and children spend the same relative amounts of time on particular letters. *D*s are written more slowly than *r*s, etc. Among the younger children, dotting the *i* was of special concern. Even blindly, the children were careful (and remarkably accurate) in their placement of the dot. With age, this procedure was given less attention. Only among the younger children did we ever see the entertaining variation of placing the dot first, and drawing the vertical stroke under it— a clear sign that dotting was a salient subroutine.

Letters are generally written more quickly with age, which may be a straightforward function of practice. Letter writing has many more opportunities to become automated with age.

7. SUMMARY AND THEORETICAL IMPLICATIONS

This sample of our work on spelling has illustrated the paradigmatic points discussed earlier: specification of process models, search for parameters, and detailed analysis of behavior. Our results indicate that representational modality, visual or aural, influences the way a word is parsed into segments, speed of retrieving segments, and speed of writing. The results further show that there are both quantitative and qualitative changes with age. Speed of writing, speed of accessing segments, and number of segments increase with age. Qualitatively, 7-year-old children appear to have special difficulty retrieving segments during sound spelling. Also, the size of a presegment pause does not predict the total size of the segment in their case. In the 11-year-old group, significant correlations are beginning to appear, and presumably index increasing skill in coordinating steps of the spelling process.

There has been only one detailed spelling model, that of Dorothea Simon (1976), but several other protomodels have been discussed (Farnham-Diggory & Simon, 1975; Morton, 1980; Seymour & Porpodas, 1980). Our work to date indicates that microethological data will eventually yield the parametric information needed for more complete model specification, but much additional research remains to be done.

For example, we need information about aspects of visual and aural stimuli that govern the marking of segments. Letter frequencies, orthographic regularities, etc., as well as dimensions of the physical signal, are critical. Meaning or meaning roots are important. Optimal exposure durations must be determined. Automatization of letter writing frees up some processing capacity, but exactly how much?

A number of questions concern the nature of the data stores that spellers draw upon. Presegment latencies are relatively short during visual spelling.

Is this because subjects are accessing or assembling information that is temporarily available in a working memory? Or is it because they are accessing long-term visual letter stores that are easier to deal with generally than long-term aural stores are? Often, different letters can represent the same sound. Choosing the correct letter(s) should be faster following visual presentation of a word, since an entire memory list of possible representations would not have to be searched.

Another question concerns the two protomodels listed above, segmentation and look-up. How is the decision made between them? Is there a fast preliminary scan of word knowledge, "Do I have a complete letter list for that word?" Once the more advanced segmentation model has been constructed, will it become dominant? Must some degree of automaticity be achieved for hard new words, before the segmentation model "fires"?

8. IMPLICATIONS FOR INSTRUCTION

Our data explicate some of the reasons why methods involving visualization (e.g., copying) have long been preferred instructionally. Sight spelling encourages the development of the analytical attitude: more segments are produced, segmentation is easier, and letters are written more attentively. Visual presentation of words provides segmentation cues that expedite children's spelling procedures. Aural presentation creates difficulties for them. The relatively slow presegmentation latencies of 7 year olds signify the presence of special effort. Before imposing that effort, teachers should automate other procedures so that spare capacity will be available. Weeks of copying practice, then, should precede spelling from dictation. This would serve not only to automate letter writing, but also to build up knowledge of orthographic frequencies, so that decisions about phoneme–grapheme equivalencies could be made reliably and efficiently. Research should be done on the possibility that providing beginners with segmentation cues (i.e., spaces between letter groups) would help them. But it is by no means clear that we know what the optimal letter groups should be (Venezky, 1967).

In general, this analysis of spelling shows how information-processing methodology can be applied to real-world tasks, and how the application advances us beyond intuitive beliefs of an earlier historical period. We do in fact know more about spelling cognition than we used to. Theories of instruction can now be predicated upon a more rigorous data base.

B. Reading

The work to be reported next is part of a school-based research and development program, the overall aim of which is to increase the coordination of laboratory research with classroom practice. Through the cooperation of a local elementary school, we have installed a PLATO laboratory convenient to the classrooms of children in the primary grades (kindergarten through grade 3). The basic unit consists of an IST-1 terminal with microprocessor capability, and an EIS Instavox Rapid-Access Audio Unit with earphones, for auditory stimuli. Through telephone lines, the unit has access to the PLATO system of the University of Delaware (one of 13 in the country), with its extensive libraries, programming facilities and routines, and data manipulation resources.

The microprocessor runs psychological experiments that require precision timing and displays. All data are continuously recorded on-line, and are processed on the larger system.

The availability of the laboratory makes it possible for us to run computer-controlled analyses of classroom tasks, and thus help close the gap between research and practice. In the case of reading, we have begun a taxonomy of elementary reading tasks, and designed several ways of tapping reading cognition that occurs in classrooms: reading span, phoneme–grapheme matching, and several measures of on-line comprehension.

As in the above work on spelling, we are illustrating three design principles: the construction of task models (protomodels, in our case), the search for parameters, and fine-grained analysis of behavior. Our general objective is to show how this type of research points the way toward new and better forms of instruction, while at the same time adding to our basic knowledge.

C. Reading in Classrooms versus Laboratories

There are hundreds of different types of school tasks that have some bearing on learning to read. Most primary teachers use a basal reading program that includes readers, workbooks, tests, and supplementary (remedial or enrichment) materials, but modify them in various ways. There is seldom a theoretically guided sequence of reading activities. The choice of activity is determined partly by the child's interests and level of skill, partly by administrative convenience, and partly by a curriculum guide of some sort, not necessarily the one provided by the basal publisher.

Typically, the first formal lesson of the day will be a lesson that bears on the small-group reading activity to follow. For example, a teacher may explain the difference between the sounds of *ow* in *bowl* and *cow,* because that distinction will appear in the forthcoming story. In the course of that task, the children pronounce words that the teacher points to, recall rules ("When two vowels come together ____"), and locate matching words and letters in their readers. That would be a class-wide lesson that includes a number of different tasks.

Reading groups (e.g., "Bluebirds") of five or six children then assemble consecutively in a "reading corner," while the remainder of the class engages in "seat work," for example, copying *long e* words (*bead, beet, sheep, leaf,* etc.) from the blackboard, and illustrating them. The small-group reading lesson typically begins with top-down pointers from the teacher ("This is a story about friends. Do you have a friend?"), and includes a number of subtasks such as pointing to words with the eraser of a pencil (see Fig. 7), observing rules for taking turns, and responding to questions inserted by the teacher to guide comprehension ("What other story is this like?"). Each child reads aloud, usually one sentence or paragraph. Sometimes roles are cast, and the children read the story as if it were a play with a narrator.

Fig. 7. A reading subtask: pointing to words with the eraser of a pencil.

Color all words rhyming with
took [blue].
Color all other words [yellow]

fog	book	mop	hook	sock
top	cook	pot	book	mop
roof	hook	look	hook	rock
moon	dock	lock	cook	pop
boot	cool	log	look	mob

Fig. 8. Typical independent reading activity in primary grades.

Following the reading, the teacher introduces a workbook page (e.g., Fig. 8) that provides supplementary practice, and/or a more complex activity located in a "learning station." Gradually over the months, the children build up procedural knowledge for doing a large variety of activities independently. The list in Table IV is typical of what can be observed in a primary-grade classroom during almost any morning.

Meanwhile, back in the laboratory, researchers have generally divided themselves into two camps: those who study decoding, and those who study comprenension (LaBerge & Samuels, 1977). A wide variety of laboratory tasks could be cataloged accordingly. A typical decoding study will use pseudowords that control frequencies, orthographic rules, etc., and will show that good readers pronounce pseudowords faster than poor readers do (Hogaboam & Perfetti, 1978). A typical comprehension study will contrast information embedded in a story with information listed in sentences, and will show that children miss a good deal in stories (Johnson & Smith, 1981). Much laboratory research falls into the category of existence demonstrations—poor readers cannot read, comprehending paragraphs is different from comprehending sentences, etc. Much reading research continues to utilize traditional laboratory tasks. The theoretical and empirical complexity of real classroom reading tasks, when noticed at all by researchers, is truly daunting, as Table IV shows. Bringing coherence into reading research and practice will be a formidable problem. We have tried to take a few small steps in that direction by means of the research program to be described next.

Table IV

Reading Activities in a Primary Grade Classroom

Worksheets

Materials	Instructions
1. Picture of a whip ___ip Picture of a ship ___ip	Fill in missing letters
2. *did not could not*	Write contractions
3. Sentence: *The girl didn't go.*	Underline contractions
4. Read short story	Draw picture to go with story

5. The flower . . .
 	
A lady . . .
	Pick correct ending from list:
	  is big and red
	  a small flower
	  looked out the window

6. I (laughed, liked) at Bob. The (lady, like) will make cookies.	Pick correct word
7. *jacks, bake, gave, acorn, days, fun*	Put words in alphabetical order
8. *platexp, mshaves*	Find embedded words
9. Picture of a shirt followed by list: *th, sh, ch, wh*	Circle starting sound
10. List: *bugle, cure, huge, cube, fuse,* *mule, tube*	Circle the long *u* words
11. Ted will fl__t his boat on the lake. Can you t__ your shoes?	Fill in blanks with letters from this list: *es, oa, ai, ie*
12. you for Thank me helping	Arrange words into sentence
13. Read short selection about giraffes, then read following sentences: *A giraffe is* *taller than an elephant.* (etc.)	Write *yes* after sentence that is true, *no* after sentence that is not true
14. Crossword puzzle; pictures are clues	Write words in crossword boxes
15. *sick, look, small, ill, little, see*	Find words that mean the same thing
16. Sentences about story in reading book, followed by list of characters: He was too big to run after rabbits.__ He ran after rabbits.__	Write name of the character the sentence refers to
17. Read short selections, then a list of sentences	Circle the sentence that restates the main idea
18. Pictures of bat, lion, coat, turkey, etc.	Say name of picture, then write be- ginning letter
19. *a, an*	Put articles into sentences
20. Story written in mixed up sentences	Put sentences in right order, so story makes sense

Activity stations

1. "Vowel Graph"—Look at pictures, say word, listen for vowel sound, place counter in egg carton marked with vowel sounds, count the number of markers for each sound, draw graph showing number of times *a, e, i, o, u* was heard in the words
2. "Lobster Pot"—Pick a fish, look at picture on fish, decide if picture has long or short *o* sound, place fish in long or short *o* lobster pot
3. "Mailbox Match"—Pick a word, decide what has to be done to add *ing*, put word in "mail-box" that has the correct rule and example
4. "Syllables"—Pick word, clap while saying word to find out how many syllables it has, find number card, place it on word card

1. PROTOMODEL OF THE READING TASK

We have been working within the framework of the following proto-model of reading:

Reading Protomodel

Step 1   Construct a schema of the reading task
Step 2   Pick up (next) set of letters
Step 3   Test: Do I recognize this word?
         If not, go to Step 4
         If so, go to Step 5
Step 4   Analyze word
         —sound it out
         —identify root
         —seek analog
           etc.
Step 5   Get its meaning
Step 6   Test: Is its meaning consistent with
           previous meanings?
         If not, go to Step 7
         If so, go to Step 8
Step 7   Correct interpretation
         —check word meaning (Step 5)
         —check analysis (Step 4)
         —check schema (Step 1)
           etc.
Step 8   Test: Is passage finished yet?
         If not, return to Step 2
         If so, stop

While that is far from a complete listing, it does provide a hub to which a variety of reading tasks can be temporarily anchored—at least long enough to speculate about some of their interrelationships. Step 1 puts us in touch with the schema literature (Bower, 1978; Schank & Abelson, 1977), including the literature on story grammars (Mandler, Scribner, Cole, & DeForest, 1980). Steps 2, 3, and 4 comprise the decoding phase, and include letter perception, letter groupings (Samuels, LaBerge, & Bremer, 1978), lexical decisions, and a variety of word analysis techniques. The listing in Step 4 means that some analytical strategy is likely to be applied if Step 3 fails. (Most of the school tasks in Table IV represent attempts to give children practice in analytical techniques, a point that is discussed shortly.) Steps 5, 6, and 7 comprise the comprehension phase, and imply that we are currently in agreement with the type of model suggested by Just and Carpenter (1980). This model specifies that information is integrated as the reader moves from word to word, in contrast to models that postulate that a "batch" of words is picked up, held in a buffer, and, when "enough" words have accumulated, integrated all at once. Step 8 simply keeps the reading process going until it is finished.

2. READING SPAN

As the protomodel implies, concurrent reading processes may exceed the limit of immediate apprehension, especially in children. That means some steps must proceed automatically while others receive conscious attention. An underlying assumption is that there exists some fixed limit with reference to which reading resources must be allocated (Case, 1978). Traditionally, this limit has been estimated by digit-span, digits-backwards, and other tests bearing little resemblance to reading (Chi, 1977; Farnham-Diggory & Gregg, 1975). In Curtis's (1980) study, for example, letters were presented one at a time and were reported backwards. But Dempster (1978) has shown that capacity estimates vary greatly with the nature of the material used to assess them. Included in any such estimate are unspecified mental operations, some of which may become automated at a later stage in an individual's development, some of which may become unitized with practice (LaBerge, 1976), and so forth. Since we cannot yet distill these components from the overall capacity estimate, it is essential to make sure the estimate includes only those (unspecified) components that are probably involved in the task of interest. That is especially critical where the hope is to construct quantitative models.

Now consider the following typical school task. First, the child reads the sentences:

The little sheep went into the water.
Shep [a dog] saw the sheep in the water.
He went in to get the sheep.

Then the child is asked by the teacher, "Where did the sheep go? How do you think the little sheep felt? What did Shep do next?" This material is from the Teacher's Edition of *Pets and People* (Evertts, Hunt, Weiss, & Smith, 1973), and represents an everyday component of the small-group reading lesson described earlier. Children in such groups soon come to learn they must read for the purpose of answering questions of two types: (1) questions requiring the recall of particular facts, and (2) questions requiring inferences. We are concerned here only with questions of the first type, which should transform the basic reading protomodel as follows:

Reading-for-Facts Protomodel

Step 1   Schema: Plan to "flag-and-hold"
             proper names, key verbs, key adjectives, color
             terms, etc.
Step 2   Pick up (next) set of letters
Step 3   Test: Do I recognize word?
             If not, go to Step 4
             If so, go to Step 5
Step 4   Analyze word
Step 5   Get its meaning
Step 6   Test: Is word in "flagged" category?
             If not, go to Step 8
             If so, go to Step 7
Step 7   Store and rehearse
Step 8   Test: Passage finished yet?
             If not, return to Step 2
             If so, stop

Note that the protomodel does not mean the passage will be understood, only that key words in it will be remembered long enough for questions about them to be answered.

In traditional span tests, the protomodel would be

Traditional Span Protomodel

Step 1   Register (hear or see) a string of digits
Step 2   Test: Finished yet?
             If not, return to Step 1
             If so, report

The components are not clearly relevant to the reading-for-facts protomodel. But recently, Daneman and Carpenter (1980) developed a span task that requires subjects to remember the last word in a series of unrelated sentences. A protomodel of that task would be

Reading Span Protomodel

Step 1   Plan to "flag-and-hold" final words
Step 2   Pick up (next) set of letters
Step 3   Test: Do I recognize word?
             .
             .
             etc.

The rest is isomorphic to the reading-for-facts protomodel. The task produces an estimate of the capacity available to an individual who is actively engaged in processing linguistic information. An even more accurate version of the test might be to ask children to remember proper nouns, verbs, color terms, etc., but such stimuli are difficult to deal with in developmental paradigms. Asking children to remember the last word in a sentence is a workable alternative.

Accordingly, we followed Daneman's (1981) specifications, and constructed stimuli composed of unrelated sentences three to six words in length. The words were taken from the children's own reading books. Typical sentences were *My dog is big* and *Here is a blue horn.*

There were three sets of two sentences, three sets of three sentences, three sets of four sentences, and three sets of five sentences. Subjects had to be correct on two out of three sets, to be accorded a span of the set length. For example, subjects who were correct on at least two of the three four-sentence sets, were scored as having a span length of 4. If subjects got only one set correct, they were given a credit of .5. Thus a subject who got two of the four-sentence sets right, and one of the five-sentence sets right, would be accorded a span size of 4.5. Subjects had to fail all three sets before testing was terminated.

Both listening and reading versions of the test were presented in counterbalanced order to all subjects. In the listening version, stimuli were presented over earphones. For the reading version, stimuli were presented (consecutively) on the PLATO screen and subjects read them aloud.

For pilot work, approximately three girls and three boys were tested at each of three grade levels. The results are in Table V.

Note first the combined (mean) column, where it is shown that first graders have an average span of 2.25, second graders, one of 2.58, and third graders, 2.90. Such a combined span was used by Daneman (1981) to predict certain facets of children's reading behavior, for example, gaze duration on words that were inconsistent with context. For children with relatively large spans (usually fourth and fifth graders) gaze was longer even if a disambiguating word were three to five words removed from an ambiguous word (e.g., *There were tears in her brown dress* as compared to *There were tears in her brown eyes*). For small-span readers, second and third graders like those in our sample, gaze was longer only if the distances were one or two words, excluding articles and auxiliaries. That clearly shows the span measure to be a logical one.

Daneman did not report listening and reading spans separately, but it is important to do so in the case that, as in our sample, listening span exceeds reading span and increases at a faster rate than reading span does (Table V, columns 1 and 2). This difference could be an important parameter. If

Table V
Span Length of Children from First, Second, and Third Grades

Grade	Sex	Span type		Combined (mean)
		Listening	Reading	
First	Girls	1.0	Could not read	—
		2.5	2.0	2.25
	Boys	2.5	2.0	2.25
		3.0	Could not read	—
		2.0	Could not read	—
		1.5	Could not read	—
	Mean	2.1	2.0	2.25
Second	Girls	2.5	2.0	2.25
		3.0	1.0	2.00
		4.0	2.0	3.00
	Boys	2.0	2.5	2.25
		3.0	3.0	3.00
		3.5	2.5	3.00
	Mean	3.0	2.2	2.58
Third	Girls	3.5	2.5	3.00
		4.0	2.0	3.00
	Boys	3.5	3.0	3.26
		2.0	2.0	2.0
		4.5	2.0	3.25
	Mean	3.5	2.3	2.90

comprehension operations are constant from listening to reading, then differences between listening and reading spans could represent the additional costs of decoding operations (Sticht, 1979). Since so few of the first graders could read, this is not a meaningful index in their case. But among the second and third graders, a large portion of their available capacity appeared to be drained off by decoding.

In preparation for further research on this issue, we have been developing independent measures of decoding ability, one of which is reported next.

3. A DECODING MEASURE

As the reading protomodel indicates, decoding processes of skilled readers are guided by top-down comprehension directives, i.e., the schema in Step 1 and the correction procedures in Step 7, but controversy has raged for a hundred years over whether or not such directives should be incorporated into beginning reading instruction. For example, in the so-called language experience methods, children generate sentences about meaningful events, e.g., *Mary is wearing a red dress,* where Mary is a smiling classmate who is indeed wearing a red dress. Such sentences, written on the blackboard, then form the basis of a decoding lesson (Stauffer, 1969). Alternatively, a curriculum may drill words that embody salient decoding patterns (*mat, rat, pat*) even though they are not high frequency words in a 6 year old's life, nor embedded in sentences (Fries, 1963). Most reading curriculums today tread an uneasy path between those two extremes, as the above *Shep* and *sheep* selection indicates. Hence, most primary children are being provided with contextual aids to decoding.

A strategy that children may construct, then, would be the following. (Since this fits into Step 4 of the reading protomodel, its steps are numbered accordingly.)

Word Analysis Protomodel

Step 4.1   Generate word (expected) from context
Step 4.2   See first letter of written word
Step 4.3   Test: Does the word I'm expecting
          begin with this letter?
      If so, go to Step 5 (get its meaning)
      If not . . . (try another analytical routine)

It is likely that the "word expected from context" is in an aural format (Kleiman, 1975). The following task should therefore capture the above sequence: a word is delivered through earphones; a letter is presented on the screen; if the word has begun with that letter, press YES, otherwise, NO.

Variants of this task are indigenous to primary classrooms as well as to decoding tests. A teacher says, "I'm going to say a word, and you point to the letter it begins with." There is also the ubiquitous version where a picture is presented, the child (or teacher) says the name of the picture, and then points to (or writes) the letter the name begins with. In our version of this class of tasks, the protomodel would be the following:

Word–Letter Protomodel

Step 1   Hear word
Step 2   Peel off first sound
Step 3   Get its letter and hold
Step 4   See letter on screen
Step 5   Test: Does that letter match
          the letter in memory?
      If so, press YES
      If not, press NO

If there is a relatively long pause between Steps 1 and 4, then subjects should have completed the first three stages of processing, and be ready to respond quickly to the appearance of the letter. If there has not been a sufficiently long pause, then subjects would have some additional processing to do even though a letter is waiting on the screen. In that case, response times should be slower.

Stimulus words were chosen from readers the children were using, and were presented in 16-trial blocks that interspersed two delay intervals, 300 msec and 800 msec. The probes were the first letters (all consonants) from the same 16 words. On half the trials they matched the words, and on half they did not. Sampling was random without replacement from word and consonant pools, subject to the above constraints.

Letters were centered on the terminal screen within a 6 × 8 mm matrix. When the child pressed the space bar, a small fixation cross appeared in the center of the screen. After a 1.5-second pause, the stimulus word was presented through the earphones. After the variable delay, the letter probe replaced the fixation cross, and the child pressed the YES or NO key in response. The letter remained on until the response. The child's hand was held comfortably but firmly in place by a Velcro bracelet anchored to a spot in front of the keyboard. After the response, the child saw either a smiling face or a frowning one as feedback for a correct or an incorrect response. Accuracies were recorded, as well as response times from letter onset to key press. Complete trial-by-trial specifications and results were preserved on line.

Two boys and two girls each from first, second, and third grades were our pilot subjects. They received a minimum of 10 practice trials, followed by 32 experimental trials. Error rate was 6%, and only correct responses are reported here.

As Table VI shows, in all cases the responses following the 800-msec delay were faster than those following the 300-msec delay. Even 6 year olds displayed the spontaneous strategy of utilizing the additional 500 msec to get ready for the letter. That is of considerable interest, since the strategy is never explicitly taught in classrooms.

Also of interest is the absence of evidence that this strategy becomes more efficient with age. Figure 9 graphs the means of the three groups, and shows that, although third graders are faster overall, they are not making better use of their extra 500 msec than first and second graders are, relative to respective speed levels. What we might like to see, instead, is a function showing that, with age and practice, children become progressively better at expediting Steps 1–3 of the word–letter protomodel, given an extra 500 msec in which to do so.

The fact that no such progression appeared is consistent with the fact that reading span also showed no marked increase in this sample (Table V).

Table VI

*Response Times[a] on Word–Letter Task by Children
from First, Second and Third Grades*

		Delay from word onset to letter onset	
Grade	Sex	300 msec	800 msec
First	Girls	2813	2071
		1722	1670
	Boys	1573	1238
		2253	1673
Second	Girls	2360	1595
		2041	1903
	Boys	1875	1504
		2108	1740
Third	Girls	1228	975
		1555	1361
	Boys	1853	1516
		2523	2308

[a] In milliseconds.

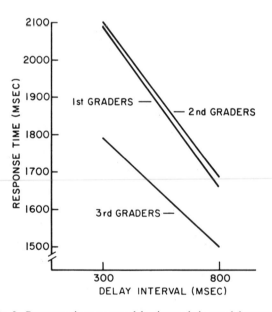

Fig. 9. Response times to two delay intervals in word–letter task.

However, it must be remembered that subjects in Table V and VI were randomly sampled from the same classrooms, but are not the same children.

4. COMPREHENSION MEASURES

As in the work on reading span and decoding, our pilot work in the area of comprehension has been primarily methodological. A popular measure of comprehension is the *cloze* procedure, in which a blank is left somewhere in a sentence, and the subject must provide, choose (from a list), or verify a filler.

Fischler and Bloom (1980) reviewed this literature and provided completion norms for 329 sentence contexts (Bloom & Fischler, 1980). The general finding is that response times are facilitated when a word fits a sentence context, and are inhibited when it does not. Schwantes, Boesl, and Ritz (1980) conducted a developmental study, and showed that third graders, compared to sixth graders and adults, are especially sensitive to this manipulation. Children, being relatively inexperienced readers, apparently depend on context more heavily than adults do.

To test the utility of the cloze procedure, we adapted Frederiksen's method (1980) for presenting materials on a computer screen. All but the final word of a sentence was first presented on one line. As soon as the line was read, the child pressed the space bar and the final word appeared below. The child now indicated if the word "made sense" or not by pressing a YES or NO key. Timing began with the onset of the final word, and was terminated by the key press. We also timed the rate at which the child read the preceding sentence.

Sentences suitable for use with children were chosen from the Bloom and Fischler (1980) corpus. Strongly contextualized stems included *The children went outside to . . .* [*play* vs *grow*]. Weakly contexualized stems included *After school he went to the . . .* [*circus* vs *shoe*]. The correct answers to the words in brackets would have been *yes* vs *no* in that order.

Twenty-one first, second, and third graders participated in this pilot work. There were 10 girls and 11 boys divided into strong and weak context groups. Each child read 10 sentences clozed by suitable words, and 10 sentences clozed by unsuitable ones. Both speed and accuracy were emphasized during practice sessions. Accuracy was high, and only data from correct responses are reported here.

Since children varied in reading speed, we later separated their reaction-time data on that basis rather than on the basis of grade. Most of the slower readers were, of course, first and second graders, and most of the faster readers were third graders, but some exchanges occurred. The slower readers had an average of 1.16 words per second; the faster readers, an average rate of 1.85 (not a strikingly large difference). There were, then, about five fast readers and five slow readers in each of the context groups.

The results are graphed in Fig. 10. Clearly there is only one meaningful effect; slower readers, as Schwantes *et al.* (1980) might have predicted, made the most use of strong contextual clues. When a word was highly predictable, slow readers predicted it—and were measurably "taken aback" when another word appeared.

But, the absence of quantifiable effect among faster readers indicated to us that this particular method was not going to be sufficiently sensitive and therefore we have been developing alternative comprehension measures.

Reading rate is an attractive dependent variable for our purposes. It can be easily recorded, and, assuming children become interested in what they are reading, should be a stable indicator of skill, persistence, and various semantic and syntactic manipulations (Kintsch, 1974). To prepare the study reported next, we took our lead from Cirilo and Foss (1980), who examined the influence of prose structure on both reading rate and recall. General predictions in research of this type are straightforward; if a person is men-

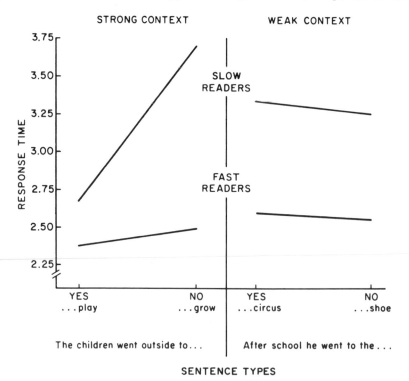

Fig. 10. Cloze response times (in seconds) of fast and slow readers to strong and weak sentence contexts.

tally constructing a concept that organizes forthcoming concepts, then (1) reading time should be longer, and (2) recall should be better.

To examine this, we assembled expository paragraphs typical of those that third-grade children are expected to comprehend in the context of social studies. These were presented in sets of three, as illustrated below. (Line numbers were not presented, but are listed here for easy reference.)

(Line 1) Boats are made of every size.
(Line 2) Large boats can cross the ocean.
(Line 3) If a boat is too small,
(Line 4) it may sink under the waves.
(Line 5) Rowboats are often used on rivers.
(Line 6) Toy boats are safe in the tub.

(Line 1) People traveled in wagons long ago.
(Line 2) A wagon trip was not easy.
(Line 3) The seats were made of wood.
(Line 4) Roads were bad and the wheels hard.
(Line 5) A ride on a wagon was bumpy.
(Line 6) Sometimes a trip took many days.

(Line 1) A jeep is a small car.
(Line 2) Jeeps are useful in the Army.
(Line 3) If soldiers find very poor roads,
(Line 4) they know their jeep can still go.
(Line 5) Sometimes jeeps drive through woods.
(Line 6) Jeeps can even go through streams.

We presented these paragraphs one line at a time on a PLATO screen. Each line was shown in the same location, but the previous line was erased before the second one appeared. Each line remained in view until the child summoned the next line by a press of the space bar. This time was recorded, and the number of words read per second was later calculated.

While this is not a totally natural mode of reading, it is the only mode that permits accurate calculation of reading rates on a line-by-line basis. If the entire paragraph is in view, we have no way of knowing how many words remain within the field of vision, or when the child is checking back instead of attending to a new line. (Someday, when simple eye-movement apparatus is available, field and check-back information will be a valuable addition to monitoring routines.)

Nine third-grade children, four females and five males, served as our pilot subjects. Each child saw three different sets of three paragraphs each, thematically related. The above comprised the "Vehicle" set. Also included were "Spices" (paragraphs about pepper, sugar, and mustard) and "Animals" (paragraphs about birds, bears, and dogs). Each paragraph was six lines long, and each line contained six or seven words. The order of paragraphs within each set was randomized, as was the order of themes.

No attempt was made to prepare this material according to linguistic formulas. Instead, we utilized materials routinely assigned by teachers. These particular paragraphs were not familiar to our subjects, but they were similar to paragraphs that were. For classwork, the children usually answered a single multiple-choice question about the "main idea" of each paragraph. To increase our data base, we asked the children, instead, to recall everything they could about each set of three paragraphs. Instructions and practice sets emphasized the fact that there would be *three* different "stories," and that subjects should try to remember as much as possible about all *three*.

The free-recall literature tells us that two recall protomodels should be specified.

Itemized Recall

Step 1   Recall (next) "flagged" item
Step 2   Test: Am I at the end of the list yet?
         If not, return to Step 1
         If so, stop

Categorized Recall

Step 1   Recall (next) topic
Step 2   Recall all "flagged" items under that topic
Step 3   Test: Are topics finished?
         If not, return to Step 1
         If so, stop

The following protocol was obtained from Subject 15 who had just read the stories in the order *wagon, boat,* and *jeep.*

> Jeeps are used in the Army.
> People used to ride in wagons.
> People often use rowboats and canoes
>   on lakes or whatever.
> If you take a small boat then it may
>   sink under the waves.
> Let's see.
> Jeeps can go over hard roads and
>   jeeps are small cars.
> That's all I remember.

The following protocol was obtained from Subject 9, who read the paragraphs in the order *boat, jeep,* and *wagon.*

> I read about some boats and their
> being all different sizes.
> And big boats can cross the ocean.
> Little boats would get sunk under the waves.
> And usually rowboats are supposed to be
> for rivers.
> And toy boats are good for in the tub.
> And I read about how jeeps work.
> And they can go through mud.
> And they can go through steams.
> And they can even go through some woods.
> And I read about wagon rides.
> And they said the seats were made of wood.
> And it was very bumpy.
> And very uncomfortable.

The free-recall literature would lead us to expect children who categorize information to recall more than children who do not. While that was true of the above two subjects, it could not be tested for the remaining subjects, since all but two of them were categorizers.

Our interest was in the more subtle measure of the relation of reading time to recall. Our hope was that the children would indicate, by slowing down, their construction of new mental structures when paragraph topics changed. The children knew there would be three paragraphs in each set. New paragraphs were not indented, but were signaled by a change in the head noun (from *jeep* to *boat,* for example). When a new topic was encountered, a child should think, in effect, "Here comes the next story," and set up a new higher order address node. That should have slowed the child's reading rate for that first sentence relative to the second one.

A "slowdown" was identified in simple ordinal terms. Subject 9, for example, read *Boats are made of every size* at the rate of 1.91 words per second, and *Large boats can cross the ocean* at the rate of 1.99 words per second. That was counted as a first-sentence slowdown. Subject 15 read *A jeep is a small car* at 2.10 words per second, and *Jeeps are useful in the Army* at 1.91 words per second. That was not counted as a first-sentence slowdown. While a measure that takes account of the degree of slowdown will eventually be useful, a simple ordinal comparison was sufficient for pilot work, as will be shown.

To compute amount recalled, a content analysis was performed on the paragraphs. Initially, we hoped to apply a method of propositional analysis (e.g., Kintsch, 1974) but such methods turned out to be unnecessarily abstract. A simple count of concepts was sufficient for our purposes. For example, the concepts to be scored in Line 1 of the first paragraph above were *boats* and *every size;* in Line 2, *large boats* and *cross ocean;* in Line 3, *boat* and *small;* in Line 4, *sink* and *under waves;* in Line 5, *rowboats* and *used on rivers;* and in Line 6 *toy boats* and *safe in tub.*

The amounts recalled from Lines 1 and 2 were calculated separately from the amounts recalled from Lines 3, 4, 5, and 6. Subject 9, above, was scored as follows.

Line 1—boats, different sizes	2
Line 2—big boats, cross ocean	2
Total from Lines 1 and 2	4
Line 3—little, boats	2
Line 4—sunk, under waves	2
Line 5—rowboats, for rivers	2
Line 6—toy boats, good in tub	2
Total from Lines 3–6	8

These data were then listed separately for occasions when a child had displayed a first-sentence slowdown, and for occasions when that same child had not.

Table VII shows the amount recalled from the first two lines and from the remaining four lines, when a slowdown appeared for the first sentence relative to the second one. For all subjects except one, the amount recalled from the first two sentences was greater following a first-sentence slowdown. Although more variability appears, the amount recalled from the remaining four sentences continued to be greater, on the average, where there had been a first-sentence slowdown. Thus, this preliminary set of data supports the possibility that children were setting up topic nodes in their semantic networks, taking a measurable amount of extra time to do so, and recalling concepts better as a result.

However, local factors will also influence both reading speed and recall. For example, two of the sentences from the above material contain conditional clauses: *If a boat is too small, it may sink under the waves;* and *If soldiers find very poor roads, they know their jeep can still go.* The presence of a conditional term like *if* should trigger new mental activity; a node should be set up for subsuming incoming information. The conditional phrase should therefore be read more slowly.

Table VII

Mean Number of Items Recalled As a Function of Relative Speed
in Reading the First and Second Sentences of Nine Paragraphs

Lines scored	Subject number	First-sentence slowdown?			
		Yes	(N)	No	(N)
1 + 2	09	3.33	(6)	2.00	(3)
	10	2.50	(4)	1.40	(5)
	11	1.57	(7)	1.00	(2)
	12	2.20	(5)	2.00	(4)
	13	2.40	(5)	1.25	(4)
	14	3.00	(5)	2.50	(4)
	15	3.00	(6)	2.67	(3)
	16	3.40	(5)	3.00	(4)
	17	1.00	(6)	3.33	(3)
	Mean	2.48	(5.4)	2.12	(3.6)
3 + 4 + 5 + 6	09	6.17	(same as above)	4.00	(same as above)
	10	2.00		3.20	
	11	2.43		2.50	
	12	1.20		2.00	
	13	5.20		2.00	
	14	1.60		4.50	
	15	2.00		3.33	
	16	5.00		3.75	
	17	3.00		1.00	
	Mean	3.18		2.92	

Table VIII shows that in 14 of the 18 cases, the conditional information was read more slowly than was the incoming new information. Since so few children departed from this pattern, it was not possible to measure differences in their recall.

5. SUMMARY AND THEORETICAL IMPLICATIONS

Beginning with a protomodel of the reading process as a whole, we examined the following aspects of it in children from the first three grades: (1) capacity for allocating attention among stages of the reading process; our findings were that this capacity is smaller, on the average, than the capacity for allocating attention during listening, and develops more slowly; (2) use of a high-speed decoding subroutine for phoneme–grapheme matching; our findings were that 6 year olds were as facile in the use of their strategy as 8 year olds were; (3) use of contextual clues by slow and fast readers; our findings were that slow readers were more sensitive to contextual clues than fast readers were; (4) construction of comprehension anchor

Table VIII

Reading Rate[a] for Conditional and Dependent Clauses in Two Paragraphs

	Subject number								
Clause	09	10	11	12	13	14	15	16	17
Paragraph I									
If a boat is too small it	1.62	1.71	.99	1.62	2.03	1.39	1.98	2.48	1.18
may sink under the waves	2.40	2.05	1.56	3.81	1.88	2.10	1.23	2.45	1.45
Paragraph II									
If soldiers find very poor	1.54	1.94	1.26	1.70	1.58	1.55	1.48	1.50	1.28
roads they know their	2.83	1.67	1.34	2.73	1.87	1.93	1.88	1.77	1.83
jeep can still go.									

[a] In words per second.

points (topic sentences and conditionals); our findings were that line-by-line reading time reflects the constructive processes, and predicts recall.

There are a large number of reading protomodels, some of which are quite detailed (Davis, 1971; Farnham-Diggory, 1978). One often cited by information-processing psychologists is Rumelhart's (1977), which captures the intuition that different aspects of the reading process (perceiving letters, expecting particular words, etc.) proceed in concert and make use of one another's outputs. Thus, letter-recognition mechanisms work on incoming sensory stimuli, and syntactic mechanisms work on their outputs (letters) as soon as any letters become available, etc. This type of model is consistent with what we know of development. Children clearly have mechanisms which function quite well in some areas, but which must become coordinated in new ways within the framework of the strange new task called *reading*. One problem with much of the research literature is a failure to distinguish between tasks for which a mechanism functions efficiently, and tasks for which it does not. For example, any normal child has a normal working memory, i.e., a capacity to process normal amounts of everyday information. The working memory problem in reading arises from the specific requirements of reading, and can only be analyzed within the framework of some theory about what they are (Farnham-Diggory & Gregg, 1975).

Our preliminary data indicate that we must use extreme care in designing tasks for estimating span, decoding efficiencies, and comprehension operations. If 6 year olds spontaneously make use of a split second to initiate a mental strategy that no one is teaching them, then we are surely amiss to claim they are "not able to decode." What we must do, instead, is identify exactly which stages of which decoding tasks the children are not able to perform. Similarly, if reading rate slows when children detect a conditional phrase, then we are surely amiss to claim that "3rd graders cannot comprehend" (Markman, 1979). The research task is to identify factors that are deflecting children's mental operations from the directions in which we expect them to go.

We have known for a long time (e.g., Farnham-Diggory, 1967; not to mention Thorndike, 1917; and Wickersham, 1865, pp. 220–224) that children often fail to make the comprehension test in Step 6—"Is the meaning of this word consistent with previous meanings?" Contiguity plays a role, especially in children who have short reading spans (Daneman, 1981). While that is an important clue, does it signify the dissolution of memory trace in the presence of continuing visual stimulation? Or the absence of an adequate "flagging" strategy? We are hopeful that our on-line reading methodology will permit us to find out, for example, if children can be instructed to "set flags" (perhaps almost literally, given PLATO's graphic and touch capabilities) on words that are keys to comprehension, no matter how far in advance they occur. Most pressingly, we need to collect data on the same children longitudinally, so that individual differences in growth rates can be determined.

6. IMPLICATIONS FOR INSTRUCTION

Consider again the tasks listed in Table IV. Most of us would feel that children busily at work on such tasks are learning something useful compared to children who are sitting around idly. But are they learning to read? National reading achievement test results are discouraging. Children apparently are not learning to read very well (Munday, 1979). Even worse, neither are their teachers. On national college reading tests, education majors display the lowest reading scores of any group other than agricultural and clerical-office majors (Weaver, 1979, p. 30). Since teachers are products of the same instructional techniques they are passing on to their own pupils, the downward reading spiral that is currently afflicting our nation may not be capable of correcting itself without infusion from the research and development sector.

There are several ways in which such infusion can immediately proceed. First of all, through protomodeling techniques, tasks that are in fact germane to the overall process of reading can be distinguished from tasks that are not. An alphabetizing task, for example, while useful in its own right, is not going to advance a skill that has the achievement of meaning as a fundamental objective. Even the early stages of a science—and we are still in the very early stages of reading science—can produce useful taxonomies, and the suggestion here is that a theoretically grounded taxonomy of classroom reading tasks could be of immediate value to teachers (Gregg & Farnham-Diggory, 1979).

Secondly, reading instruction, like all instruction, should build on the capabilities that children already have. One example is immediately apparent: children have more resources available for understanding what they hear than for understanding what they are just learning to read. To help them read, therefore, we should make their own full resources available to them. One obvious way to do that is to read along with them, out loud. This tactic is well known to many parents, and it should not be surprising that they often turn out to be the parents of the best readers in the class.

A final type of infusion can be provided by computers. It is programmatically simple to present reading material on video screens, to keep track of a child's reading rate, to provide the child with feedback on both reading speed and comprehension, to keep lists of sight words a child must study, to provide practice on new orthographic rules, and to deliver—through earphones—words, sounds, comprehension directives, or any instructions required by individual children. Further, it is possible to monitor the child's high-speed mental activities in ways that a teacher cannot—and it is precisely these high-speed activities that must be monitored for effective instruction to occur. But it is essential for all such computer-based activities to proceed within the context of natural reading, or as close to it as we can get. Many computer-based programs on the PLATO system now, and on other systems, are merely extensions of classroom tasks that have little theoretical connection to natural reading, and that, like those classroom tasks, may not foster the development of reading skills. Given the safeguard of a natural reading format, computer-based systems can provide the extensive practice and detailed monitoring that children need, and thereby free teachers for interpersonal and inspirational activities that teachers do best (Atkinson, 1974).

IV. Conclusion

As we look toward the next century, new technologies offer hope of high-powered educational futures (Abelson, 1982). In 1946, one of the first computers (ENIAC) took up 1500 ft^2 of space, consisted of 18,000 large vacuum tubes, cost millions of dollars, and required dozens of technicians to keep it running for only a few minutes at a time. In the late 1980s, IBM predicts, a far more powerful computer will be contained in a 6-in. box and run on a 9-V battery (Johnson, 1981). Communication networks—telephone, cable television, radio, etc.—are already in place, but transmission media are changing from air and wire to fiber optics (transmission of light beams) and lasers. A communications device, equipped with its own computerized decision-making system, will soon be able to make contact with any other communications device on the planet instantly. We will soon have the technological ability to deliver instruction, designed and transmitted by experts, whenever they are found, to any individual, anywhere in the world (Johnson, 1981; E.C. Posner, 1979).

Education's most pressing research and development need is twofold: (1) systems management, and (2) instructional design. Management talent will probably emerge from industries that already nurture relevant expertise, Bell Telephone, CBS, and the like. But it will be up to cognitive and developmental scientists to provide instructional strategies that can be adapted to individuals of all ages, interests, and backgrounds.

Computers have introduced powerful new representational systems for both theory and experimental design. Curriculum psychology now has a machine that can construct an on-line theory of how an individual student is learning, instruct the student accordingly, and collect data at the same time. Allen Collins (1977) has illustrated this elegantly for the field of geography (see also Stevens & Collins, 1980).

It is important to note the difference between this general approach, and the approach currently described as *componential analysis*. In the latter, as in factor analysis, the assumption is made that a few underlying sources of variance can be identified, and can account for a wide range of surface variability (Carroll, 1980, 1981; R. Sternberg, 1977, 1980). Such work begins with the administration of fleets of tests. While such tests used to be haphazardly selected, the trend in recent years is toward theoretically governed selections (Curtis, 1980; Frederiksen, 1980; Hunt, 1978; Pelligrino & Glaser, 1980). But problems often remain. A test is after all just another task. Unless we have an explicit model of the test task, as well as an explicit model of the criterion task, we are likely to miss some fundamental incompatibilities.

At this stage of our return to the study of school tasks, it is probably advisable to postpone a search for abstract learning factors, and concentrate on the close analysis of one task at a time. Identifying and measuring what Sternberg (1980) calls *performance components* is enough of a job for now.

Basically, we can look toward the day when children practicing reading, writing, and arithmetic will be monitored by video and computational devices programmed to respond sensitively to the children's high-speed mental operations as revealed by their motor and ocular patterns—assuming that we will be scientifically capable of telling those devices what to do. New information-processing methods—microethology, chronometric analysis, and protomodeling—are beginning to provide the engineering specifications we need. Eventually, the logic and precision of psychological measurement will equal the logic and precision of powerful new systems for delivering instruction and monitoring learning. Meanwhile, it is good to know that curriculum research is pursuing again the theoretical notions that interested William James a hundred years ago.

Acknowledgments

The work reported here has been supported in part by Grant BNS 77–18106 from the National Science Foundation, and in part by a Unidel Grant for Interdisciplinary Studies to the College of Education, University of Delaware. We are grateful to Karen Schilling, Sr. Theresa, and the children of Immaculate Heart of Mary School for help with the spelling studies; to Mike Frank for PLATO programming; to Judy Sandler for public relations assistance; and to Edward Smith, Principal, and the teachers and children of Downes School, who so cheerfully cooperated in this project.

References

Abelson, P. H. The revolution in computers and electronics. *Science,* 1982, **215,** 751–753.

Anderson, J. R. *Language, memory and thought.* Hillsdale, New Jersey, Erlbaum, 1976.

Anderson, R. E., Spiro, R. J., & Montague, W. E. (Eds.), *Schooling and the acquisition of knowledge.* Hillsdale, New Jersey: Erlbaum, 1977.

Atkinson, R. C. Teaching children to read using a computer. *American Psychologist,* 1974, **29,** 169–178.

Bloom, P. A., & Fischler, I. Completion norms for 329 sentence contexts. *Memory & Cognition,* 1980, **8,** 631–642.

Bower, G. H. Experiments on story comprehension and recall. *Discourse Processes,* 1978, **1,** 211–231.

Broadbent, D. E. The magic number seven after 15 years. In A. Kennedy & A. Wilkes (Eds.) *Studies in long term memory.* New York: Wiley, 1975.

Cameron, E. H. *Educational psychology.* New York: Century, 1927.

Carroll, J. B. Remarks on Sternberg's "Factor theories of intelligence are all right almost." *Educational Researcher*, September 1980.

Carroll, J. B. Ability and task difficulty in cognitive psychology. *Educational Researcher,* January 1981.

Case, R. Intellectual development from birth to adulthood: A neo-Piagetian interpretation. In R. W. Siegler (Ed.), *Children's thinking; What develops?* Hillsdale, New Jersey: Erlbaum, 1978.

Charters, W. W. *Teaching the common branches.* Boston, Massachusetts: Houghton-Mifflin, 1913.

Chase, A. *The legacy of Malthus.* New York: Knopf, 1977.

Chase, W. G. Elementary information processes. In W. K. Estes (Ed.), *Handbook of learning and cognitive processes. Vol. 5: Human information processing.* Hillsdale, New Jersey: Erlbaum, 1978.

Chase, W. G., & Simon, H. A. Perception in chess. *Cognitive Psychology,* 1973, **4,** 55–81.

Chi, M. T. H. Age differences in memory span. *Journal of Experimental Child Psychology,* 1977, **23,** 266–281.

Cirilo, R. K., & Foss, D. J. Text structure and reading time for sentences. *Journal of Verbal Learning and Verbal Behavior,* 1980, **19,** 96–109.

Collins, A. Processes in acquiring knowledge. In R. C. Anderson, R. J. Spiro, & W. E. Montague (Eds.), *Schooling and the acquisition of knowledge.* Hillsdale, New Jersey: Erlbaum, 1977.

Curtis, M. E. Development of components of reading skill. *Journal of Educational Psychology,* 1980, **72,** 656, 669.

Daneman, M. *The integration processes of reading: Individual and developmental differences.* Unpublished doctoral dissertation, Carnegie-Mellon University, 1981.

Daneman, M. & Carpenter, P. A. Individual differences in working memory and reading. *Journal of Verbal Learning and Verbal Behavior,* 1980, **19,** 450–466.

Davis, F. B. (Ed.), *The literature of research on reading with emphasis on models.* New Brunswick, New Jersey: Rutgers State Univ. Press, 1971.

Dempster, F. N. Memory span and short-term memory capacity: A developmental study *Journal of Experimental Child Psychology,* 1978, **26,** 419–431.

Evertts, E. L., Hunt, L. C., Weiss, B. J., & Smith, N. *Pets and people* (Teachers' ed.). New York: Holt, 1973.

Farnham-Diggory, S. Symbol and synthesis in experimental "reading." *Child Development,* 1967, **38,** 221–231.

Farnham-Diggory, S. *Cognitive processes in education.* New York: Harper, 1972.

Farnham-Diggory, S. The cognitive point of view. In D. J. Treffinger, J. K. Davis, & R. E. Ripple (Eds.), *Handbook on teaching educational psychology.* New York: Academic Press, 1977.

Farnham-Diggory, S. How to study reading: Some information processing ways. In F. B. Murray & J. J. Pikulski (Eds.), *The acquisition of reading.* Baltimore, Maryland: Univ. Park Press, 1978.

Farnham-Diggory, S., & Gregg, L. W. Short term memory function in young readers. *Journal of Experimental Child Psychology.* 1975, **19,** 279–298.

Farnham-Diggory, S., & Simon, H. A. Retention of visually presented information in children's spelling. *Memory & Cognition,* 1975, **3,** 599–608.

Feuerstein, R. *The dynamic assessment of retarded performers.* Baltimore, Maryland: Univ. Park Press, 1979.

Fischler, I., & Bloom, P. A. Rapid processing of the meaning of sentences. *Memory & Cognition,* 1980, **8,** 216–225.

Frederiksen, J. R. Component skills in reading: Measurement of individual differences through chronometric analysis. In R. E. Snow, P. Federico, & W. E. Montague (Eds.), *Aptitude, learning and instruction* (Vol. 1). Hillsdale, New Jersey: Erlbaum, 1980.

Freeman, F. N. *The psychology of the common branches.* Boston, Massachusetts: Houghton-Mifflin, 1916.

Fries, C. C. *Linguistics and reading.* New York: Holt, 1963.

Frith, U. (Ed.). *Cognitive processes in spelling.* New York: Academic Press, 1980.

Glaser, R., & Bond, L. (Eds.). Testing: Concepts, policy, practice, and research. *American Psychologist,* 1981, **36,** 997–1189.

Green, J. G. Some examples of cognitive task analysis with instructional implications. In R. E. Snow, P. Frederico, & W. E. Montague (Eds.), *Aptitude, learning, and instruction* (Vol. 2). Hillsdale, New Jersey: Erlbaum, 1980.

Gregg, L. W., & Farnham-Diggory, S. How to study reading: An information processing analysis. In L. B. Resnick & P. A. Weaver (Eds.), *Theory and practice of early reading* (Vol. 3). Hillsdale, New Jersey: Erlbaum, 1979.

Henderson, L., & Chard, J. The reader's implicit knowledge of orthographic structure. In U. Frith (Ed.), *Cognitive processes in spelling*. New York: Academic Press, 1980.

Hogaboam, T. W., & Perfetti, C. A. Reading skill and the role of verbal experience in decoding. *Journal of Educational Psychology,* 1978, **70**, 717–729.

Hunt, E. B. Mechanics of verbal ability. *Psychological Review,* 1978, **85**, 109–130.

Hunt, E. B., & Poltrock, S. E. The mechanics of thought. In B. Kantowitz (Ed.), *Human information processing: Tutorials in performance and cognition*. Hillsdale, New Jersey: Erlbaum, 1974.

James, W. *Talks to teachers: On psychology; and to students on some of life's ideals*. New York: Norton, 1958. (Originally published in 1899.)

Johnson, H., & Smith, L. D. Children's inferential abilities in the context of reading to understand. *Child Development,* 1981, **52**, 1216–1223.

Johnson, J. W. Education and the new technology: A force of history. *Educational Technology*, October 1981.

Just, M. A., & Carpenter, P. A. A theory of reading: From eye fixations to comprehension. *Psychological Review,* 1980, **87**, 329–353.

Kintsch, W. *The representation of meaning in memory*. Hillsdale, New Jersey: Erlbaum, 1974.

Klahr, D. (Ed.), *Cognition and instruction*. Hillsdale, New Jersey: Erlbaum, 1976.

Kleiman, G. M. Speech recoding in reading. *Journal of Verbal Learning and Verbal Behavior,* 1975, **14**, 323–339.

LaBerge, D. Perceptual learning and attention. In W. K. Estes (Ed.), *Handbook of learning and cognitive processes. Vol. 4: Attention and memory*. Hillsdale, New Jersey: Erlbaum, 1976.

LaBerge, D., & Samuels, S. J. (Eds.). *Basic processes in reading: Perception and comprehension*. Hillsdale, New Jersey: Erlbaum, 1977.

LaRue, D. W. *The child's mind and the common branches*. New York: Macmillan, 1924.

Leary, D. B. Development of educational psychology. In L. Kandel (Ed.), *Twenty-five years of American education*. New York: Macmillan, 1924.

Lesgold, A. M., Pellegrino, J. W., Fokkema, S. D., & Glaser, R. (Eds.). *Cognitive psychology and instruction*. New York: Plenum, 1978.

Mandler, J. M., Scribner, S., Cole, M., & DeForest, M. Cross-cultural invariance in story recall. *Child Development,* 1980, **51**, 19–26.

Markman, E. M. Realizing that you don't understand: Elementary school children's awareness of inconsistencies. *Child Development,* 1979, **50**, 643–655.

Monroe, W. S. *Teaching-learning theory and teacher education 1890 to 1950*. Urbana, Illinois: Univ. of Illinois Press, 1952.

Morton, J. The Logogen model and orthographic structure. In U. Frith (Ed.), *Cognitive processes in spelling*. New York: Academic Press, 1980.

Munday, L. A. Changing test scores especially since 1970. *Phi Delta Kappan,* 1979, **61**, 496–499.

Newell, A., & Simon, H. A. *Human problem solving*. New York: Prentice-Hall, 1972.

Pelligrino, J. W., & Glaser, R. Components of inductive reasoning. In R. E. Snow, P. Federico, & W. E. Montague (Eds.). *Aptitude, learning and instruction* (Vol. 1). Hillsdale, New Jersey: Erlbaum, 1980.

Posner, E. C. Information and communication in the third millenium. *IEEE Communications Magazine*, January 1979.

Posner, M. I., & Rogers, M. G. K. Chronometric analysis of abstraction and recognition. In W. K. Estes (Ed.), *Handbook of learning and cognitive processes. Vol. 5: Human information processing.* Hillsdale, New Jersey: Erlbaum, 1978.

Reber, A. S., & Scarborough, D. L. (Eds.). *Toward a psychology of reading.* Hillsdale, New Jersey: Erlbaum, 1977.

Resnick, L. B., & Ford, W. W. *The psychology of mathematics for instruction.* Hillsdale, New Jersey: Erlbaum, 1981.

Rumelhart, D. E. Toward an interactive model of reading. In S. Dornic & P.M.A. Rabbitt (Eds.), *Attention and performance* (Vol. 6). Hillsdale, New Jersey: Erlbaum, 1977.

Samuels, S. J., LaBerge, D., & Bremer, C. Units for word recognition: Evidence for developmental changes. *Journal of Verbal Learning and Verbal Behavior,* 1978, **17,** 715–720.

Schank, R. C., & Abelson, R. P. *Scripts, plans, goals, and understanding.* Hillsdale, New Jersey: Erlbaum, 1977.

Schwantes, F. M., Boesl, S. L., & Ritz, E. G. Children's use of context in word recognition. A psycholinguistic guessing game. *Child Development,* 1980, **51,** 730–736.

Seymour, P. H. K., & Porpodas, C. D. Lexical and non-lexical processing of spelling in dyslexia. In U. Frith (Ed.), *Cognitive processes in spelling.* New York: Academic Press, 1980.

Simon, D. P. Spelling—A task analysis. *Instructional Science,* 1976, **5,** 277–302.

Simon, D. P., & Simon, H. A. Individual differences in solving physics problems. In R. S. Siegler (Ed.), *Children's thinking: What develops?* Hillsdale, New Jersey: Erlbaum, 1978.

Snow, R. E., Federico, P. A., & Montague, W. E. *Aptitude learning and instruction* (Vols. 1 and 2). Hillsdale, New Jersey: Erlbaum, 1980.

Sperling, G. The information available in brief visual perceptions. *Psychological Monographs,* 1960, **74** (11).

Stauffer, R. G. *Teaching reading as a thinking process.* New York: Harper, 1969.

Sternberg, R. J. *Intelligence, information processing, and analogical reasoning: The componential analysis of human abilities.* Hillsdale, New Jersey: Erlbaum, 1977.

Sternberg, R. J. Factor theories of intelligence are all right almost. *Educational Researcher,* September 1980.

Sternberg, S. Memory-scanning: Mental processes revealed by reaction time experiments. *American Scientist,* 1969, **57,** 421–457.

Sternberg, S., Monsell, S., Knoll, R. L., & Wright, C. E. The latency and duration of rapid movement sequences: Comparisons of speech and typewriting. In G. E. Stelmach (Ed.), *Information processing in motor control and learning.* New York: Academic Press, 1978.

Stevens, A. L., & Collins, A. Multiple conceptual models of a complex system. In R. E. Snow, P. A. Frederico, & W. E. Montague (Eds.), *Aptitude, learning and instruction* (Vol. 2). Hillsdale, New Jersey: Erlbaum, 1980.

Sticht, T. G. Applications of the audread model to reading evaluation and instruction. In L. B. Resnick & P. A. Weaver (Eds.), *Theory and practice of early reading* (Vol. 1). Hillsdale, New Jersey: Erlbaum, 1979.

Thorndike, E. L. Reading as reasoning: A study of mistake in paragraph reading. *Journal of Educational Psychology,* 1917, **8,** 323–332.

Tuma, D. T., & Reif, F. (Eds.). *Problem solving and educational issues in teaching and research.* New York: Wiley, 1980.

Vellutino, F. R. *Dyslexia.* Cambridge, Massachusetts: MIT Press, 1979.
Venezky, R. L. English orthography: Its graphical structure and its relation to sound. *Reading Research Quarterly,* 1967, **2,** 75–106.
Wallin, J. E. W. *Spelling efficiency.* New York: Warwick & York, 1911.
Weaver, W. T. In search of quality: The need for talent in teaching. *Phi Delta Kappan,* 1979, **61,** 29–46.
Wickersham, J. P. *Methods of instruction.* Philadelphia, Pennsylvania: Lippincott, 1865.

AN INVITATION TO A DEVELOPMENTAL PSYCHOLOGY OF STUDYING

William D. Rohwer, Jr.

DEPARTMENT OF EDUCATION
UNIVERSITY OF CALIFORNIA, BERKELEY
BERKELEY, CALIFORNIA

Applied Developmental
Psychology, Volume 1

I. Rationale for a Focus on Studying

Broadly conceived, studying is the principal means of self-education throughout life. It consists of all those activities, both covert and overt, that individuals independently engage in to acquire knowledge or skill. A young girl studies the behavior of her hamster; an adolescent reads manuals to study the intricacies of computer programming or of "Dungeons and Dragons"; an adult studies the processes of making and enjoying wine; a retired person studies the sources of stock market fluctuations.

Even conceived more narrowly, as preparation essential to meet explicit performance criteria, reliance on studying is pervasive. Musicians, actors, lawyers, and football coaches, for example, all report spending numerous hours in private study. A reliance on studying is also evident in the context of formal education. By assigning homework, teachers explicitly acknowledge the necessity that students engage in independent study to meet prescribed achievement standards. Students discover, or to their disadvantage fail to discover, this necessity themselves. Thus, brief consideration suggests that studying, because of its pervasiveness and potential instrumental importance, is a proper subject of systematic psychological research.

Further consideration suggests, moreover, that such research, especially when focused on an educational context, should incorporate a central developmental component. As many parents could testify, the role of studying markedly expands across the years of schooling. Teachers in the primary grades, K–3, rarely expect their students to engage in unsupervised study, not even in the form of structured homework. As grade level increases, however, the necessity of studying increases as well. Teachers in upper elementary grades begin to assign structured homework and occasional reports to be prepared outside of class. In the secondary school years, such study assignments grow in both frequency and scope, as the amount of structure provided shrinks. In the typical college course, instructors explicitly acknowledge their expectation that students will devote at least twice as much time to independent study as to class attendance, while leaving the character and procedures of this studying entirely unspecified. Thus, the demands placed on students for independent study activity change dramatically over the school years. In the absence of systematic research, however, the question remains whether the development of student capabilities for such activity keeps pace with these growing demands. It is this question, then, that issues the invitation to a developmental psychology of studying.

This article represents a tentative response to that invitation. The initial step is to consider the past and current status of studying in an attempt to determine why it has not yet emerged as a visible and coherent focus of psychological inquiry. Next, a case is made that recent trends, both societal and psychological, portend the formation of such a focus. Then, using a preliminary framework, a selective review is made of available research on studying phenomena with the aim of distinguishing among more and less promising approaches. Finally, the results of this review are used to refine the framework and to suggest an agenda of future research priorities.

II. Status of Studying

The apparent prominence of studying, as a means of both self-education and academic success, contrasts with its low visibility as a field of psychological research. This contrast might be comprehensible if research of relevance had simply not been attempted, but psychologists have already created some of the components essential to this field. They have formulated theories containing conceptions relevant to the analysis of studying. They have adapted empirical methods useful in investigating selected aspects of studying. They have even charted age differences in a number of psychological capabilities that appear germane to studying. Yet, these achievements have not proved sufficient; the connections among them are desultory, and the promise of a developmental psychology of studying remains to be fulfilled.

The low visibility of this field might also be comprehensible if psychologists were generally averse to the formation of such specialties. This explanation, however, runs counter to the facts. In addition to the more generic field of educational psychology, previously established specialties include psychologies of teaching, reading, and mathematics. An even more relevant parallel, the specialty of instructional psychology, gained formal status in 1969 with the publication of a review bearing this title in the *Annual Review of Psychology* (Gagné & Rohwer, 1969). Notably, at the time of this review, few of the cited studies had direct bearing on instruction. Despite this inauspicious beginning, however, the field of instructional psychology has since flourished. Its growth in extent, coherence, and visibility is documented in a succession of *Annual Reviews* (Glaser & Resnick, 1972;

Wittrock & Lumsdaine, 1977; Resnick, 1981) and is marked by the recent inception of the publication, *Advances in Instructional Psychology* (Glaser, 1978). Modest beginnings are evidently no bar to the development of a field.

Thus, the low status of studying as a research specialty cannot be traced to its inherent unimportance, or to an absence of relevant research, or to a lack of precedent in psychology. What, then, are the obstacles responsible for its comparative invisibility? A way of answering this question was offered a little more than a decade ago by Robert McClintock (1971) in his documentation of a marked historical shift in the educational role of studying. Prior to the eighteenth century, study was the principal means of education; now it is merely ancillary to teaching and instruction. "No longer the source," McClintock (p. 180) observes, "study itself has become a consequence of instruction." He attributes this shift to a variety of sources. For demographic, political, and economic reasons, education became a mission of the state, which then demanded accountability of its educational agents, that is, teachers. Prodded by the state and armed with empiricist assumptions about the environmental sources of learning, teachers imposed instruction on students, relegating study to a distinctly subsidiary role. Learning became entirely vested in teaching. Perhaps, then, the lowly state of studying as a subject of attention in psychology has resulted from the same societal and philosophical factors that led to its subservient place in the world of education.

Consistent with this interpretation, for approximately half the present century psychology was dominated by the theoretical assumption that learning stems principally from the controlling effects of external conditions. By the early 1960s, for example, operant conditioning had found educational expression in the form of programmed instruction. By providing total external control of discriminative stimuli and response contingencies, this system promised to produce effective learning in all students, making the activities of independent study entirely superfluous. Thus, it appears that psychological assumptions as well as societal conditions coincided to divert attention from the potential importance of studying.

III. Recent Societal and Psychological Trends

During the last 30 years, however, events in both the society at large and within psychology constitute trends that may culminate in an elevation in the status of studying. The relevant trend in the larger society is made up of events that have repeatedly evoked public dissatisfaction with the effectiveness of schooling. In psychology the trend consists of a shift in explanatory principles from a reliance on external factors to an emphasis on internal cognitive factors. Brief examination of each of these trends suggests that they may converge in a focus of attention on independent learning activities.

A. Dissatisfaction with Education

In the United States over the last three decades, the particular objects of public discontent with education have varied with fluctuations in the surrounding context of political, social policy, and economic concerns. In the 1950s, for example, Sputnik evoked widespread denouncement of curricula in science and mathematics. In the 1960s and 1970s, those who demanded an end to discrepancies among ethnic groups in rights, opportunities, and attainments traced these disparities to a pervasive educational inequality. At present, unemployment coupled with unmet manpower needs, in technological industries and in the volunteer army, for example, have spurred charges of general inadequacy in basic skills education. These charges of underpreparation have been buttressed by evidence of low average levels of literacy among high school graduates and by declining average scores on standardized tests of aptitude and achievement.

Despite the heterogeneity of these problems the remedies that have been prescribed up to now are strikingly similar; all involve the augmentation of instruction. In response to the dissatisfaction of the 1950s, new curricula in science and mathematics were developed and then installed in elementary schools. Later, Head Start and its supplement, Follow Through, added more teachers and increased instructional time to the schooling regimen. Even now, the remedies proposed to meet current problems include increases in the numbers of English and mathematics courses required for high school graduation and college entrance. In keeping with McClintock's (1971) analysis, then, the character of these responses reveals a continuing commitment to the assumption that instruction is the determining force in education. If instruction proves inadequate, a larger dose is prescribed (cf. Rohwer, 1980a).

Yet, for all the apparent continuity of this commitment, it may soon weaken. This prospect arises partly from the fact that the instructional initiatives of the past 30 years have produced only modest gains. Levels of mathematics achievement and literacy rates remain unacceptably low; the educational attainments of different ethnic and social class groups continue to be discrepant. Outcomes such as these work steadily to diminish public faith in the curative power of direct instruction. Current economic conditions may exert additional force in turning attention toward less expensive alternatives to instructional remedies, for education must now compete for shrinking real-dollar amounts of public funds. Thus, confidence in and willingness to pay for instructional solutions may eventually wane.

B. Shift in Psychological Theory

Changes in psychological conceptions of human learning and development are also congenial to a reformulation of the role of studying in education. In the 1950s, behaviorism was a dominant influence in psychology. But now, only a quarter century later, behaviorism has been dethroned by the "cognitive revolution." The resulting cognitive psychology makes educational phenomena one of its central foci (Greeno, 1980); indeed, cognitive approaches currently dominate the field of instructional psychology (Resnick, 1981). Moreover, according to these conceptions, effective learning does not stem chiefly from external control. While often stimulated and nourished by the cultural context (Vygotsky, 1978), internal structures and processes are conceived as having an autonomous impulse of their own. In current conceptions, then, instruction is no longer seen as the absolute master of learning, but as its handmaiden.

Two major forces have contributed to this shift in psychological assumptions. One was the advent of information-processing models of human performance. Models introduced early in the period (e.g., Miller, Galanter, & Pribram, 1960; Newell & Simon, 1972), as well as the more elaborate ones developed later (e.g., Bower, 1975; Gagné, 1977), mirrored the components and processes of high-speed computers. They also posited mental contents, such as networks and hierarchies, of far greater complexity than the simple or even the mediated connections of the prior S-R models.

The second major force was supplied by Piagetian theory. Like virtually all contemporary views, Piagetian theory stipulates that learning results from interactions of the human being with the physical and social environment. The theory is distinctive, however, in its insistence that such interactions are instigated by the learner's own mental or sensorimotor activity. When, to the contrary, the source of instigation is entirely external, effective learning simply does not occur. In keeping with these propositions, Piaget and Inhelder (1973, p. 396) have criticized certain educational practices: "the absurdity of a number of school practices is precisely that they divorce the memory of spontaneous activities from the intelligence and its operational schemata." Although this viewpoint would not exclude instruction as a means of education, it would nevertheless accord studying a more central role, for the hallmark of study is the spontaneous activity of the learner.

Currently then, influential psychological conceptions, as well as emerging societal conditions, provide a congenial context for the creation of a psychology of studying. Moreover, at least one of these conceptions, Piagetian theory, affords a developmental perspective on phenomena arising from increases with age in the prominence of study demands. The stage is thus set for the creation of a developmental psychology of studying, and the time is ripe to assess the current research base for this enterprise.

IV. A Provisional Framework

Brief reflection about the dimensions of a developmental psychology of studying quickly reveals a potential for complexity that threatens to be overwhelming. In part, this complexity stems from the sheer number of factors that may be at work in determining studying phenomena. Further enhancing the potential for complexity is the variety of these factors. Finally, complexity inheres in the dual roles that must be accorded to study activities. When viewed as the outcomes of other factors, these activities serve as dependent variables; in contrast, when viewed as determinants of academic achievement, they serve as independent variables. Because of these several sources of complexity, a provisional framework is needed even to begin an orderly examination of research on studying.

The major components of such a framework are displayed in Fig. 1. Central among these components is that of study activities. As indicated in Table I, studying can be subdivided into three broad categories: overt and covert cognitive procedures, affective procedures, and procedures of resource management and use. The entries in this table do not exhaust all possibilities. Instead, they represent those procedures that have appeared prominently in traditional conceptions of studying (e.g., time allocation), in educational research (e.g., notetaking), and in contemporary research on cognition (e.g., elaboration).

Four of the remaining components shown in Fig. 1 can be thought of as forming a 2 × 2 matrix like that in Table II. The columns of the matrix contrast components that are immediate to studying and achievement with components that are in the background. The rows distinguish between factors that characterize students and those that characterize the context of studying and achievement. Although the potential number of constituents of each cell is very large indeed, only a few examples are listed in the table for illustrative purposes.

Also displayed in Fig. 1 is a hypothetical structure of the relationships among the major components in the framework. Three aspects of this structure deserve emphasis. First, study activities and the immediate components of student and context characteristics are each presumed to exert a direct and independent influence on achievement level. Second, study activities

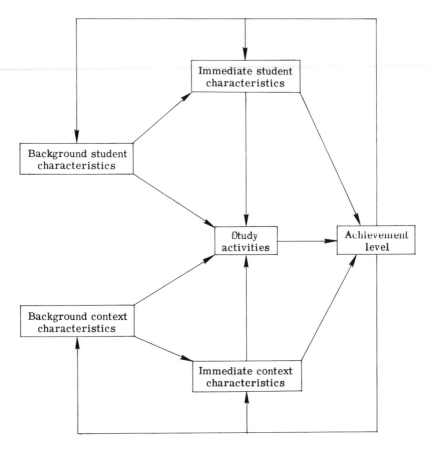

Fig. 1. Hypothetical structure of relationships among student characteristics, context characteristics, study activities, and achievement level.

themselves are expected to vary as a function of student and context characteristics. Thus, in terms of an analysis of variance metaphor, study activities are expected to have not only main effects on achievement but, in combination with student and context factors, interaction effects as well. For example, successful achievement might result from quite divergent study activities, depending on the developmental processing capabilities of students and the character of the performance demanded. The evaluation of this interaction hypothesis, then, is one of the principal goals of the present review. Finally, note in Fig. 1 the feedback loops from Achievement Level to Student and Context Characteristics. As these loops indicate, the outcomes of studying can, over time, affect the capabilities and motivation of students as well as their access to educational opportunities.

Table I

Examples of Study Activities

Cognitive procedures	
Overt	Covert
Notetaking	Selection
Outlining	Rehearsal
Tabulating	Elaboration
Working problems	Organization
Writing answers	Mental review

Affective procedures
Anxiety reduction
Scheduling
Goal setting
Self-reinforcement
Self-talk

Resource management and use
Time and effort allocation
Consulting ancillary texts
Consulting teachers
Arranging study conditions
Consulting prior tests

Table II

*Examples of Background and Immediate Student
and Context Factors*

	Background	Immediate
Student	Age	Processing capabilities
	Study knowledge	Selection knowledge
	Ability	Task experience
	Locus of control	Test anxiety
	Achievement motives	Subject-matter interest
Context	Home attributes	Criterion type
	Parent attributes	Criterion information
	Peer attributes	Subject matter
	Major field	Study time
	School attributes	Study materials

Published research of relevance to the proposed framework is extraordinarily heterogeneous. In some lines of investigation study activities are aggregated into multivariate composites; in others, they are analyzed more specifically. Even within the latter category, there are wide variations in the particular study activities examined. The available research also varies methodologically, from large-scale self-report surveys to small-scale, focused experiments. Yet, many of these variations are correlated. It is rare, for example, to find investigations designed to assess the effects of immediate context characteristics on composites of study activities. This state of affairs has dictated the organization of the present review. Examined first is evidence about the magnitude of relationships between composite study activities and cumulative levels of achievement, ignoring the roles of immediate and background characteristics. Next, an appraisal is made of such general studying–achievement relationships as a function of background characteristics. The last set of investigations to be examined includes those pertaining to specific study activities and their interrelationships with student characteristics, context characteristics, and achievement.

V. Composite Study Activities

A. Relationships with Achievement

For a very practical reason, relationships between composite study activities and achievement have been assessed chiefly by means of self-report surveys. The reason behind this methodological choice is the need for large samples; numerous observations are required in order to detect relationships when activities are aggregated across quite heterogeneous student and context characteristics. Even self-report surveys are arduous, for they depend on the development, standardization, and psychometric evaluation of reporting instruments. Nevertheless, several such instruments are now available. Among these, the one that has been used most often is the Survey of Study Habits and Attitudes (SSHA).

1. SURVEY OF STUDY HABITS AND ATTITUDES

The SSHA, initially designed for administration to high school seniors and college freshmen (Brown & Holtzman, 1953), has undergone a lengthy process of development and revision. Two versions are now available, one version for college students, Form C, and one for students in grades 7–12, Form H (Brown & Holtzman, 1967). The two versions are similar in providing scores on four subscales, Delay Avoidance, Work Methods, Teacher Approval, and Education Acceptance. Forms C and H are also similar in that items on the Delay Avoidance and Work Methods subscales ask for information about traditional aspects of study activities rather than underlying cognitive and affective procedures, while the Teacher Approval and Education Acceptance scales appear to elicit attitudinal information.

The validity of the SSHA has been assessed with respect to two kinds of criteria. The first of these criteria is the actual study behavior of students, as reflected in ratings made by their peers. The one such investigation discovered involved a comparatively small sample ($n = 32$) of university students (Goldfried & D'Zurilla, 1973). While only suggestive, therefore, the results were nevertheless encouraging: the average correlation between the total SSHA scores of students and peer ratings of their academic effectiveness was .45.

Of more direct relevance to the present topic, the validity of the SSHA has also been assessed with respect to the criterion of grade point average (GPA). This kind of assessment, then, furnishes information about the relationship between composite study activities and general levels of academic achievement. Across a number of samples of college students, according to Brown and Holtzman (1967), correlations of scores on SSHA Form C with GPA at the end of the term of administration have averaged approximately .36, ranging between .16 and .48. In a sample of more than 10,000 students in grades 7–12, the average correlation between subscale scores on Form H and GPA ranged between .35 and .48, and the average correlation for total score was .49. In the latter investigation, even when scores on the Scholastic Aptitude Test (SAT) were held constant, the partial correlation of SSHA total score with GPA was .43. As the magnitude of these correlations is as high as those of direct correlations between the SAT and GPA, they appear consistent with the notion that study effectiveness is a general and stable source of student differences in academic achievement.

This initial appearance, however, is belied by additional evidence and psychometric analysis. For example, in a validation study of a British adaptation of the SSHA, the Student Attitude Inventory, the highest of the observed correlations with academic performance was only .35 (Entwistle, Nisbet, Entwistle, & Colwell, 1971). Furthermore, the interpretation of even such modest relationships is clouded by certain psychometric properties of the SSHA. In particular, the integrity of the four subscales is in doubt in two respects. First, according to Bray, Maxwell, and Schmeck (1980), the reliabilities of the subscales are only marginal, as indexed by coefficient alpha, a measure of internal consistency. Second, the Brown–Holtzman assignment of items to subscales provides a poor fit to the results of an empirical factor analysis. Indeeed almost 20% of the items failed to load appreciably on any of the four factors. This lack of fit is also suggested by the results of another analysis reported by Khan and Roberts (1975).

Unlike the subscale scores, the total score yielded by the SSHA survives psychometric evaluation in the sense that it is adequately reliable (Bray *et al.*, 1980). Yet, the items that make up this inventory are strikingly heterogeneous, apparently tapping attitudes toward self and schooling as well as work methods. Thus, relationships between total SSHA scores and academic achievement shed little analytic light on the relationship between such achievement and the effectiveness of particular study activities.

2. INVENTORY OF LEARNING PROCESSES

Of more recent vintage than the SSHA, the Inventory of Learning Processes (ILP) (Schmeck, Ribich, & Ramanaiah, 1977) has also been validated in a way that provides information about relationships between omnibus study activities and achievement. The ILP consists of 62 true–false items that constitute four scales: Synthesis–Analysis, Study Methods, Fact Retention, and Elaborative Processing. The Study Methods scale resembles the Work Methods scale of the SSHA in tapping traditional study activities (e.g., "I have regular weekly review periods."). In contrast to the SSHA, items that define the other scales were formulated to reflect cognitive procedures that have emerged in recent information-processing research (e.g., "When I study something, I devise a system for recalling it later."). Also unlike the SSHA, the ILP is homogeneous in its focus on study activities, excluding items concerning attitudes toward self, education, and learning.

Psychometrically, the ILP appears to have certain advantages over the SSHA. The scales were initially defined by factor-analytic methods rather than by a priori item assignment, and each is sufficiently reliable, as indexed by test–retest correlations, to warrant confidence, at least for group assessment (Schmeck *et al.*, 1977). Extensive effort has also been expended in assessing the construct validity of the ILP scales (Schmeck & Ribich, 1978).

Despite its several laudable features, however, the ILP has yielded little evidence to support the hypothesis that individual differences in composite study activities account for substantial variation in general levels of academic achievement. The relevant data were obtained by computing correlations between scores on each of the ILP scales and the cumulative GPAs of 70 university undergraduates. Except for the Study Methods scale, all of these correlations differed significantly from zero. Nevertheless, in absolute magnitude, the highest of the correlations, .23 for Synthesis–Analysis, was quite modest. Even when the scales were combined by means of multiple correlations, the ILP accounted for only 16% of the variance in GPA.

Viewed as a source of general achievement differences, then, variations in composite study activities have little evident power. Yet, it remains possible that the importance of such variations is obscured in investigations such as the preceding ones by underlying interactions with student and context characteristics. If so, composite study activity as well as achievement should in fact vary as a function of such characteristics. The appraisal of this supposition entails an examination of variations in study activities and achievement as a function of relevant background characteristics.

B. Student Background Characteristics

Among investigations of composite study activity as a function of student background characteristics, several factors have received attention. These factors include age, educational attainment, various personality characteristics, attitudes, and values.

1. AGE

A major presumption of the present perspective, as previously indicated, is that both the character and the effectiveness of study activities should vary substantially with age. This presumption derives from both developmental principles and from the results of empirical research conducted to verify those principles. Indeed, laboratory research on the development of cognitive procedures for learning and memory has increased dramatically in the last 20 years. It is both surprising and disappointing, therefore, to find that age differences in composite study activities have been ignored almost entirely in the field of educational research. In the category of self-report survey investigations, for example, it appears that only two such efforts have even included age as a classification variable. Furthermore, the possibility of age differences in study activities was of no more than secondary interest in either investigation.

One of these surveys was that of Holtzman and Brown (1968). In evaluating Form H of the SSHA, as described previously, these investigators administered the instrument to large samples of students in grades 7–12. While statistically significant differences in SSHA mean scores were associated with grade level, they were curiously unsystematic. Similarly, the slight decrease with grade level in correlations between SSHA and GPA, attributed by the investigators to the attrition of poorer students at higher grade levels, is of no substantive importance.

The results of a second survey investigation, also conducted with the SSHA, are comparably uninformative about age differences (Weigel & Weigel, 1967). A sample of 225 college students was stratified with respect to sex and class (freshman, sophomore, upperclassmen). Among females, mean SSHA scores increased significantly with class level, whereas for males, the mean for freshmen fell approximately midway between that for sophomores and upperclassmen. This sex difference and the trends within sexes are largely uninterpretable, however, since the representativeness of the within-cell samples was not determined and their sizes were quite small ($\bar{n} = 19$).

The paucity of the information available about systematic relationships between age and omnibus study activities may be a significant impediment to the formation of a developmental psychology of studying. If so, an obvious recommendation is that investigations should be designed to obtain this missing information. Still, the kind of information needed may be different from that obtained through typical composite approaches, a possibility discussed in subsequent sections.

2. KNOWLEDGE OF STUDY PROCEDURES

Another student background characteristic of presumptive relevance to studying and achievement is that of knowledge about generally effective study procedures. Unfortunately, however, here too there is a paucity of relevant research evidence. One of the three investigations located for the present review was that of Weigel and Weigel (1967), cited in the immediately preceding section. The male ($n = 20$) and female ($n = 16$) college freshmen in the sample responded to the SSHA under two instructional sets. In one instructional set, students were asked to describe their own study habits and attitudes, while in the other they were asked for descriptions of those characteristics for an ideal student. Responses under the latter instructions, then, can be regarded as an index of knowledgeability about effective study activities. The results were puzzling. The correlations of real and ideal SSHA scores with GPA were .43 and .86 for males, whereas for females they were .39 and .10, respectively. Additionally, the extent of agreement between real and ideal scores added negligibly to these relationships with GPA.

A second investigation of general knowledge of study procedures also involved the SSHA (Robyak & Downey, 1979). This instrument served as the index of actual study activities in a sample of 65 university students who had enrolled in a campus study skills course. These participants were also administered a section of the Study Skills Test (Raygor, 1970) intended to measure knowledge of effective study techniques. On the basis of the relationship between their cumulative GPAs and their American College Testing Program (ACT) scores, the students were divided into underachievers and nonunderachievers, a distinction between students whose actual grades did and did not fall below projections derived from the college aptitude test. A discriminant analysis revealed that SSHA scores were unrelated to this distinction, but that nonunderachievers were characterized by both greater study skill knowledge and a higher tendency toward introversion than underachievers.

The implications of both of these studies are doubtful. Not only do the results defy interpretation, but the samples are disturbingly small and probably unrepresentative. Furthermore, the index of study activity in each investigation was the SSHA which, as previously noted, is of doubtful content and psychometric characteristics.

The sample size ($n = 230$) was more adequate in a third investigation of the relationship between general study knowledge and achievement level (Kirkland & Hollandsworth, 1979). Knowledge of study procedures among university students enrolled in introductory summer-term psychology and sociology courses was indexed by scores on the Effective Study Test (Brown, 1975). This self-report inventory consists of scales intended to measure knowledge about organizing study activities, examination preparation, reading, and writing. The correlation between total score on this test and cumulative GPA was .37. Study knowledge was also related to another background characteristic, indexed by total ACT score, which itself correlated substantially with GPA ($r = .55$). While these relationships are of potential importance, for present purposes their value is limited by the fact that the actual study activities of the participants were not assessed, either directly or indirectly. Accordingly the relationship between study knowledge and study activities cannot be estimated.

3. PERSONALITY CHARACTERISTICS, ATTITUDES, AND VALUES

Investigations of relationships among student background factors, studying, and achievement have not been limited to the cognitive domain but have included affective characteristics as well. Among these investigations, some have focused on single traits, such as anxiety and locus of control. Others have encompassed a multiplicity of affective characteristics, including personality variables, attitudes, and values.

a. Anxiety. Kirkland and Hollandsworth (1979), in the investigation described in the preceding section, obtained several measures of anxiety on their sample of college students. Of these, the debilitating anxiety index from the Achievement Anxiety Test (Alpert & Haber, 1960) and the Test Anxiety Scale (Sarason, 1972) exhibited significant negative correlations (approximating $-.30$) with both GPA and scores on the study knowledge test. As mentioned previously, however, this investigation included no index of actual study behavior.

Such indexes were included in another investigation of anxiety and achievement (Culler & Holahan, 1980). In an extreme-groups design, scores on the Test Anxiety Scale were used to select from among university freshmen enrolled in an introductory psychology course those in the upper ($n = 65$) and lower ($n = 31$) quartiles. These high- and low-anxiety students also responded to the Study Habit scale of the SSHA and provided estimates of their total weekly study time. As compared with the low-anxiety group, the high-anxiety students reported investing more time in studying, but they obtained significantly lower scores on the SSHA. Furthermore, they also earned significantly lower GPAs at the end of the semester than their low-anxiety counterparts. It is tempting to conclude that these outcomes confirm the present hypothesis that study activities mediate between the background characteristic of anxiety and achievement level. This temptation, however, must be resisted for two reasons: the relevant correlations were not appropriately partitioned by, for example, path-analytic techniques, and the use of an extreme-groups design, in all likelihood, resulted in inflated estimates of the relationships that were computed.

b. Locus of Control. Unfortunately, uncertainty also plagues the results of two investigations of relationships between locus of control and study activities. In one of these (Ramanaiah, Ribich, & Schmeck, 1975), 253 college students in an introductory psychology course were administered the SSHA and an Internal–External Locus of Control Scale (I–E Scale, Rotter, 1966). The results showed that the greater the tendency toward internal locus of control, the higher the scores on three of the SSHA scales, Work Methods, Teacher Approval, and Educational Acceptance ($\bar{r} = .29$). Due, however, to the intercorrelations among the SSHA scales and the lack of an achievement index, it is impossible to estimate the remaining relationships among locus of control, study activities, and academic performance.

An achievement index was included in a more recent investigation involving the characteristic of locus of control (Keller, Goldman, & Sutterer, 1978). The sample consisted of 138 college students enrolled in an introductory psychology course conducted by means of the Personalized System of Instruction (PSI). Performance scores in this course served as the achievement criterion, and all students were administered the I–E Scale and the SSHA. Correlational analysis revealed no significant relationship between locus of control and achievement. Furthermore, the results of regression analyses indicated that a single scale of the SSHA, the Teacher Acceptance index of attitudes, accounted for the entire relationship of the SSHA with the I–E scale. Similarly the relationship between the SSHA and achievement was entirely accounted for by the Delay Avoidance Scale. Thus, unlike anxiety, locus of control has neither a direct relationship with achievement, nor one that is mediated by study activities (although this conclusion may be specific to PSI courses).

c. Multiple Affective Characteristics. Nowhere is the potential complexity of studying phenomena more evident than in investigations involving multiple affective characteristics. This potential is revealed in even so ostensibly a straightforward approach as that of administering a single personality inventory along with an inventory of study activities. Rutkowski and Domino (1975), for example, administered the California Psychological Inventory (CPI) and the SSHA to a sample of 201 freshmen university students. Scores on the 18 scales of the CPI and on the four scales of the SSHA were entered into a principal component factor analysis. Apart from a factor defined largely by the SSHA, its individual scales exhibited relationships with distinctly different collections of CPI scales. The two attitude scales, for example, loaded on a factor together with those CPI scales' regarded as measures of general adjustment. In contrast, the Work Methods scale loaded with the CPI scales regarded as measures of social poise and confidence. Beyond noting the differentiation of these relationships, little can be gained from attempting to interpret these outcomes, partly due to the limitations of the SSHA and partly because no index of achievement was included in the investigation.

Such an index was used by Entwistle and Brennan (1971) in an assessment of relationships between study activity and an even larger collection of background characteristics. More than 800 British university and college students were given the Student Attitude Inventory (British adaptation of the SSHA), the Eysenck Extraversion and Neuroticism scales, the Allport–Vernon and Lindzey value scales, and they responded to five additional self-rating items (hours studied weekly, hard working, ambitious, sociable, and likeable). Also available for each student were scores on tests of verbal and quantitative ability, along with information about two characteristics of their contextual background, father's occupation and mother's education. Finally, the index of achievement level was academic performance at the college level.

These variables were entered into a cluster analysis designed to allot students to groups that differed in terms of score profile. Twelve such clusters were identified, and the distinctiveness of the score profiles supported the investigators' contention (p. 268) "that there are a variety of paths leading to either success or failure." The average achievement level in two of the clusters, for example, was virtually identical, falling at the mean for the entire sample, Yet students in the two clusters exhibited sharply contrasting scores on study activities, extraversion, neuroticism, theoretical values, and religious values. Thus, although this investigation must be regarded as descriptive, its results suggest that background characteristics may indeed interact with study activities in determining achievement.

A similar interpretation of survey self-report data has been given by Biggs (1978), author and developer of the Study Process Questionnaire (SPQ). The SPQ comprises 80 items that tap a wide variety of student characteristics in the domains of motivation, values, and study procedures. Factor analyses of responses to the SPQ over a series of administrations have led to the identification of 10 scales, including ones referred to as academic motivation, academic neuroticism, study skills, and test anxiety. While each of these scales has a moderate degree of internal consistency (Briggs, 1976; Watkins & Hattie, 1980), none survives a test for unidimensionality (Watkins & Hattie, 1980). Moreover, no one of the scales has exhibited more than a modest degree of relationship with general levels of academic achievement (Biggs, 1978).

Nevertheless, the results of second-order factor analyses suggest that relationships between study procedures, as indexed by the SPQ, and achievement may be obscured by interactions with background personality characteristics and values (Biggs, 1978; Watkins & Hattie, 1980). According to Biggs (1978), for example, each of three higher order factors is made up of three distinct groups of items: one related to study strategies, another to values, and a third to motivation. Thus, a rote-reproductive study emphasis combines with pragmatic values and high test anxiety; a study emphasis on comprehension and integration of new with old knowledge combines with value placed on self-growth and intrinsic motivation; an emphasis on structured, well-organized study combines with competitive values and high extrinsic motivation. Although the magnitudes of the relationships between these combinations and achievement level have yet to be determined empirically, the composites themselves imply that the effectiveness of a given study procedure should vary as a function of student background characteristics.

C. Background Context Characteristics

While research on student background characteristics thus far yields only a fragmentary picture, it nevertheless appears voluminous in comparison to research on background context characteristics. Almost no attention has yet been given to characteristics of students' homes, of their neighborhoods, of the educational institutions in which they are enrolled, or of their fellow students (for an exception, see Biggs, 1972). Indeed, only one context characteristic has been exposed to repeated empirical appraisal. This characteristic concerns the general subject matter to be studied, as indicated by the student's major field.

MAJOR FIELD

Brown and Dubois (1964) conducted one of the earliest investigations of variations in study effectiveness as a function of major field. The sample consisted of two groups of male college freshmen enrolled at one university, but in two distinct colleges: Engineering ($n = 125$), and Science and Humanities ($n = 76$). The students in both groups were drawn from the highest quartile of the incoming class, as defined by high school GPA and score on a math placement test. The resulting restriction of range, then, may have limited the magnitudes of the various relationships obtained.

Each student was administered a variety of instruments, including the SSHA, and also obtained for each was the cumulative GPA for the first two quarters of the academic year. Among the Sciences and Humanities students, Educational Acceptance, an index of attitudes, was the only scale of the SSHA that entered into a significant correlation with achievement (r = .22). For the Engineering students, in contrast, significant correlations with GPA emerged for all four scales, yielding a coefficient of .49 for the combination of the two Study Habit scales. Thus, even though no direct tests were made between the SSHA–GPA correlations of the two colleges, the apparent difference in their magnitudes is consistent with the interaction hypothesis. Nevertheless, the status of this interpretation must remain tentative due to the oft-repeated limitations of the SSHA.

A direct test for interaction has been made by Biggs (1976), using the SPQ. In an early study (Biggs, 1970), the SPQ was administered at the beginning of their freshman year to students enrolled in either the Faculty of Arts (n = 246) or the Faculty of Sciences (n = 68), at an Australian university. Significant correlations were found in the Arts group between end-of-year GPA and four of the SPQ scales, including ones regarded by the author as indexes of reproductive studying and transformational studying. In the Science group, however, no significant correlations were obtained, suggesting an underlying interaction, although this suggestion is weakened by the discrepancy in sample sizes. In a more recent study, direct tests were made of this implied interaction, using data furnished by university Arts and Sciences students in Canada (Biggs, 1976). While patterns of responses to the SPQ differed significantly across the two groups, none of the scale scores interacted significantly with the Arts–Sciences factor in terms of achievement level.

A similar outcome has been reported by Goldman and Warren (1973; also see Goldman & Hudson, 1973). These investigators developed a study strategies questionnaire consisting of items drawn from students' own descriptions of their study procedures. This questionnaire was administered to third- and fourth-year university students whose major fields were in either the Physical Sciences (n = 82), Biological Sciences (n = 188), Social Sciences (n = 168), or Humanities (n = 100). Within each of these groups, students were divided into two achievement levels (above and below a B average), based on self-reported cumulative GPA. A multivariate analysis of variance of questionnaire responses revealed a significant difference in reported study procedures (1) between achievement levels and (2) among major fields. Contrary to the hypothesis, however, no significant interaction emerged.

For two reasons, this latter outcome is potentially more damaging to the interaction hypothesis than other similar ones such as that reported by Biggs (1976). First, the questionnaire used by Goldman and Warren (1973) consists of items that predominantly tap study procedures, the focus of the interaction hypothesis, rather than being devoted heavily to personality and attitude characteristics. Second, the method of data analysis was, in an important respect, more appropriate for testing the hypothesis than any of those reviewed previously. Other investigators have subdivided their self-report inventories into a series of fixed scales that are scored uniformly regardless of the student's major field. Accordingly, differences across fields in patterns of responses at the item level, the level of specific study activities, might well have been obscured. The multivariate analysis applied by Goldman and Warren (1973), however, was designed to detect differences at this level and nevertheless failed to reveal any evidence of the predicted interaction. These results, then, must be given serious weight in evaluating the hypothesis.

Yet, they should not be regarded as conclusive. Little information has been reported about the psychometric characteristics of the Goldman and Warren questionnaire, in particular about the reliabilities of its items. Furthermore, yet to be established are the validities of its items with reference to the criterion of the study procedures actually followed by students. This validity limitation is not unique to the Goldman and Warren instrument; indeed it characterizes all the self-report inventories reviewed here. Finally, even though the Goldman and Warren analysis was specific with respect to reported study activities, their investigation was excessively general in two other respects: students were asked to report study activities without regard for possible variations across course types, and correspondingly, the achievement index was also insensitive to course differences.

For the purpose of establishing a developmental psychology of studying, then, the method of self-reports, as used so far, is limited in a number of ways. Central among these is the practice of treating study activities in a composite fashion. With the exception of Goldman and Warren (1973), self-report data have been summed into scale scores for amalgams of items rather than being analyzed so as to expose variations in specific study activities. Accordingly, these composite approaches have failed to provide descriptions of differences in the reported study activities of groups of students that vary with respect to any particular background characteristic such as anxiety or major field. Such approaches are thus foredoomed to be uninformative about relationships between variations in study activity and achievement.

A comparable lack of descriptive specificity also characterizes the achievement criteria that have been employed. Such criteria themselves are composites, typically consisting of GPA cumulated across courses, terms, and even years. Aggregation of this kind not only blurs descriptive precision, but also may obscure potential interactions of study activities with course characteristics in determining achievement. The consequences of this practice may be particularly serious if, as seems likely, quite divergent study activities prove to be effective in different kinds of courses.

Yet another limitation evident across the investigations reviewed in this section is their lack of density and coverage. Replication is almost nonexistent, except for Biggs' attempt (1970, 1976), and several potentially relevant background characteristics have been investigated only once or twice, if at all.

Finally, from a developmental perspective, especially frustrating is the lack of descriptive information about variations in specific study activities as a function of age. Until systematic information of this kind is obtained, progress toward a developmental psychology of studying will be impeded for lack of a proper descriptive base. Moreover, in the case of young students, the method of self-reports is severely limited in its potential for ever furnishing such information. Below the high school and college level, the younger the student the less likely that complete and accurate descriptions of study activities can be obtained from self reports.

VI. Specific Study Activities

In contrast to the emphasis of the preceding investigations on composite study activities is the emphasis in several other lines of research on specific study activities. Among the most pointed and systematic of these are laboratory investigations of learning and memory development. While these investigations are relevant to a psychology of studying and exemplify the kind of research needed in this field, they have not been framed by the context of academic achievement. Accordingly, they are only briefly summarized here. More extensive attention is given to research addressed directly to relationships between achievement and three specific study procedures: allocation of effort, selectivity, and recoding and recording.

A. Learning and Memory Development

List-learning tasks have provided the vehicle for much of the published research on learning and memory development. Moreover, this research has shown that the character of study activity accounts for a large share of the common variance in age and achievement. Tasks that require memory for the identity and sequence of list items, for example, have been shown to evoke rehearsal procedures that vary systematically with age across the years of early and middle childhood (Ornstein & Naus, 1978). Associated with this variation in study procedures is parallel variation in achievement, as indexed by memory performance. Such results, then, are consistent with the assumption reflected in the present framework, namely that the character of study activity mediates between the background characteristic of age and achievement.

Further evidence of this relationship is furnished by the results of another line of list-learning research. Performance on cued recall tasks, those requiring paired-associate learning, for example, varies dramatically as a function of age, especially across the period of adolescence. A variety of experimental manipulations have corroborated the hypothesis that this age–achievement relationship is largely due to the increasing use of elaboration, a study procedure for creating coherent relationships among initially disparate items (Rohwer, 1973; Rohwer, Raines, Eoff, & Wagner, 1977). Moreover, self-report methods have directly confirmed that this elaborative procedure mediates the age–achievement relationship (Pressley & Levin, 1977; Waters, 1982). Additionally, transfer of this procedure, when incorporated into the larger keyword study method, has been shown to be more probable for 18 year olds than for 12 year olds (Pressley & Dennis-Rounds, 1980). Thus, evidence for the mediating role of study activities is not confined to laboratory tasks, but extends to more school-like tasks as well.

Specific study procedures, including the preceding ones, would be expected to interact with student characteristics of more immediacy than age. Of relevance to this expectation is the burgeoning research on a problem area called metamemory (Flavell & Wellman, 1977). Metamemory refers to knowledge about memory, including knowledge about the effectiveness of specific study procedures. Research to date has established that the amount of such knowledge varies substantially with age, suggesting that it may exert a potent influence on relationships between study procedures and achievement. Thus far, however, research has failed to confirm this predicted interaction. Nevertheless, the reasons for this failure may stem more from conceptual and methodological limitations than from the substantive invalidity of the hypothesis, according to the thesis documented by Cavanaugh and Perlmutter (1982) in their recent critical review.

B. Effort Allocation

The allocation of effort to studying in preparation for a task should, by extrapolation from findings about total learning time (Carroll, 1963) and time on task (Bloom, 1976), relate directly to achievement. This presumptive relationship, however, has resisted simple corroboration (e.g., Hakstian, 1971). Some of the reasons for this difficulty are illuminated in the reports of two recent empirical investigations.

In one of these investigations, Covington and Omelich (1981) obtained self-ratings from 339 college students concerning their expenditure of effort in preparing for multiple-choice tests on one unit of an introductory college psychology course. All students took one test on the unit and among those who judged their performance on this test as a failure, some were permitted to take a second test as well. The students were also administered a scale designed to index their self-concepts of academic ability. The sample was cross-classified, then, with respect to self-concept of ability (high, low), and self-ratings of test performance (success, failure).

Although direct tests of effects associated with these classification factors were not made, the data reported suggest a complex interaction. On the first test, little variation in effort expended appears to be associated with either classification factor. After an initial failure, however, high-self-concept students appear to increase their study efforts substantially more than low-self-concept students. Thus, the results indicate that effort expenditure may vary as a function of both an immediate context characteristic, prior failure, and a student background characteristic, self-concept of academic ability.

A more direct measure of study effort expended was made by Owings, Petersen, Bransford, Morris, and Stein (1980). Sixteen fifth-grade students, classified as more or less successful on the basis of teacher judgments and standardized achievement test scores, were asked to read and study four one-paragraph stories in preparation for a sentence-completion test. Half of the stories were easy and half difficult with reference to the congruence of sentence subjects and predicates. Both the reading and the study intervals were self-paced, and the amount of time devoted to each activity was observed and recorded for each student.

The amount of time spent studying varied significantly as a function of the interaction of student background and story difficulty. More successful students devoted less study time to easy stories, but more to difficult stories than the less successful students. This interaction, however, was not mirrored in performance on the sentence completion test; the more successful students exhibited higher levels of achievement than the less successful across both kinds of stories, and achievement levels were higher for the easy than for the difficult stories across both kinds of students. Thus, a student background characteristic and an immediate context characteristic appear to exert direct effects on achievement. Moreover, these characteristics interact in determining a study activity, that is, effort allocation. Yet, these results provide no evidence for the central assertion in the present hypothesis, namely that study activities themselves interact with student and context characteristics in determining achievement.

C. Selectivity

Effort allocation is not an isolated study activity, for the allotment of more study effort to some resource materials than to others presupposes selectivity. In the various contexts of natural study activity, students confront amounts of information too large to be mastered in the time available. To achieve success, therefore, they must make astute decisions about the selection of information to be emphasized in studying. The preceding investigation by Owings et al. (1980) exemplifies two components of selectivity: that of making distinctions within materials to be studied, and that of using such distinctions to guide selective emphasis during study. In this case, the distinctions were between separate passages of resource material, whereas in a number of other investigations, the focus is on selection within single passages.

In examining selection phenomena, a number of investigators have adopted a qualitative methodology (Marton & Säljö, 1976; Pask, 1976; Svensson, 1977; Laurillard, 1979). Typically, college students are asked to read a passage of material, to recall the material, to describe their strategic approaches to the material, and to "teach back" or explain the content of the passage. Students' strategy descriptions are examined and classified, principally into either of two approaches. One approach involves a focus on specific details of passage content and sequence, whereas the other emphasizes main ideas, overall meaning, and a search for authors' intentions. This dichotomy has been variously labeled surface level vs deep level (Marton & Säljö, 1976), atomistic vs holistic (Svensson, 1977), and operation learning vs comprehension learning (Pask, 1976). Student explanations of passage content are similarly dichotomized in terms of whether they explicate the relationship between the facts presented and the conclusion reached in the passage.

When these two dichotomies are crossed to form a contingency table, they reveal a strong relationship between a holistic selective focus and the explication of fact–conclusion relationships (Svensson, 1977). This component of selectivity, then, appears to be a strong determinant of achievement. Still, the question remains whether the tendency to select holistic or atomistic aspects for study is context dependent. Svensson (1977) has hypothesized such a dependency, and Laurillard (1979) has reported confirming evidence. In the latter investigation, 30 college students provided descriptions of their study approaches to different task assignments within a single science course. Classification of these descriptions revealed that across tasks more than half the students varied their selection emphasis from deep level to surface level. According to Laurillard (1979), this variation depends on both the content to be learned and the student's aim in accomplishing a task.

This line of research, then, has produced evidence consistent with the present interaction hypothesis. Yet, the evidence is far from conclusive, for at least two reasons. The first reason is that results of the kinds obtained through this qualitative methodology have not yet been confirmed by experimental methods. Second, no one of the preceding investigations incorporated all of the elements in the hypothesized interaction. Svensson (1977), for example, did not directly examine intraindividual variation, and Laurillard (1979) did not relate such variation to outcome achievement levels.

A step toward filling these gaps has been taken by Biggs (1979), who asked 60 college students to study two- to three-page abstracts of two topically divergent psychological experiments. Selectivity was manipulated within subjects by instructions to study the two abstracts differently, that is, by concentrating on either the *purpose* of the experiment or on its *facts and details*. Student background characteristics were assessed by means of Biggs' inventory, the SPQ, providing scores for each student on the second-order scales of utilizing, internalizing, and achievement. After studying each abstract, the students were asked (1) to write an essay response to a question concerning the claims made, and (2) to answer factual questions about details of the experiment. Responses to the essay question were classified with respect to conceptual level, using a taxonomy similar to that developed by Martin and Säljö (1976). Unfortunately, these dependent variables were not augmented by any direct measures of selective emphasis during study.

Nevertheless, consistent with the present thesis, the results revealed complex interactions. As indexed by essay content, a study emphasis on purpose, compared with an emphasis on facts, produced higher level conceptual responses, but this effect differed across the two abstracts as a function of the student background characteristic of utilizing. A complementary interaction was also evident in factual recall. Thus, differences in selection decisions can affect achievement but, apparently, only in interaction with student background characteristics and with the immediate context characteristic of subject matter topic.

A similarly complex interaction was obtained by Brown and Smiley (1978, Experiment 3), in an investigation that stands out among those reviewed because it included direct measures of selectivity, namely, underlining and notetaking. The background characteristic of age was varied systematically by sampling from populations of elementary (fifth-grade), junior high (seventh- and eighth-grade), and high school students. All students were asked to study Japanese folktales and then to recall their gist. The constituent idea units of these relatively short texts (approximately 400 words) had been previously classified with respect to four levels of importance, providing a standard against which to compare students' selection decisions. An immediate context characteristic was manipulated by contrasting a long with a short study interval.

This context manipulation interacted with both age and importance level. Given additional study time, the older the students the greater the increase in their recall of the higher but not of the lower level units. This apparent variation in selective emphasis as a function of age and study time was corroborated by data on underlining and notetaking. These activities increased with age and, of more significance, the importance level of the units noted or underlined increased with both age and study time. Again, then, selectivity in studying affects achievement level by means of a complex in teraction involving an immediate context characteristic and a student background characteristic.

D. Recoding and Recording

While selectivity may be viewed as a study procedure in its own right, it also underlies a number of other study activities. In the investigation by Brown and Smiley (1978), for example, the conventional study activities of underlining and notetaking were presumed to depend on and, therefore, to reflect selection processes. These activities, along with other related ones such as summarizing, mapping, and networking, involve the recoding of information conveyed orally or in print in order to produce a selective written record. Each such activity, then, has both a public and a private aspect. The public aspect is the tangible product of recording activity, in the form of lecture notes for example. The private aspect, the recoding of information, involves processes such as reduction, integration, and elaboration. Psychologically, then, traditional recording activities stem from the underlying structures and processes that are of contemporary concern in cognitive psychology: the character of knowledge representation, knowledge integration, both within and between text segments, as well an encoding and retrieval processes. Thus, the private aspect of recording activities is quite complex and would be expected to interact with a number of student and background characteristics in determining achievement.

This potential for interactive relationships is well exemplified in the activity of notetaking. Numerous investigators, over a period of many years, have subjected notetaking to empirical examination. Yet, the effectiveness of this activity in promoting achievement still remains in doubt (Carrier & Titus, 1979). This ambiguity, according to the present hypothesis, is likely to continue in the absence of research designed to analyze the probable interactions involved in the notetaking–achievement relationship (cf. Anderson & Armbruster, 1982).

To appreciate this possibility, consider the variables that might plausibly affect notetaking. As already mentioned, for example, there is substantial variation with age in the capabilities of identifying the importance of available information, and of using such distinctions to guide decisions about selective emphasis. Age variation would also be expected, then, in the types of notes students take and use in studying. Another potentially important student variable concerns the way selected information is processed. By itself, astute selection cannot guarantee that information will be comprehensible and memorable, if it is processed only superficially (Craik & Lockhart, 1972). Furthermore, the impact of selection and processing skills may vary as a function of context characteristics. For example, effective selection and processing may depend on the availability of knowledge about what information will be relevant to the criterion task. Also of importance may be the character of the criterion task, whether it requires recall or recognition, for example. Finally, even though well-informed selection and capable processing may result in potentially effective notes, they may be of small assistance unless adequate opportunities for review are available.

The preceding conjectures about relationships among notetaking variables imply a particular interaction pattern. This pattern, however, has not yet been verified; no single investigation, or set of related investigations, has been designed to include all of the necessary variations. Yet, scattered across a variety of investigations is evidence suggestive of the potential importance of the variables and of their lower order interactions. Without duplicating the comprehensive review available elsewhere (Carrier & Titus, 1979; Anderson & Armbruster, 1982), the credibility of this assertion may be shown by describing a few illustrative investigations.

1. NOTE TYPE AND PEFORMANCE CRITERIA

Even in the absence of information about the particular performance criteria they must meet, students might be expected to vary in the types of written notes they take. A gross dimension of such variation is the amount of notetaking per unit of presented information. Applying this index to normal lecture notes of college students in an educational psychology course, Maqsud (1980) divided the students into groups of brief or detailed notetakers. Immediately after a subsequent lecture in the same course, the students were asked to engage in free recall of the information presented, without having access to the notes they had just taken. Although equated for vocabulary level, brief notetakers still outperformed detailed notetakers. Because the two kinds of notetakers were self-selected, however, the question remains whether the obtained effect should be ascribed to the comprehensiveness of notes per se.

One means of addressing this question is to manipulate the comprehensiveness of notes experimentally. Such manipulations have been made, although in somewhat unsatisfactory ways, in two investigations. In each investigation, students enrolled in a lecture course were assigned to one of three conditions: take *personal notes* on the lecture, receive *partial notes,* prepared by the lecturer, consisting of headings and key points in a format allowing space to record additional personal notes, or receive copies of the *full notes* of the lecturer without provisions for adding personal notes. With respect to the issue of comprehensiveness, this manipulation is less than satisfactory on two counts. First, the comparative comprehensiveness of the three sets of notes is unclear; the full notes would presumably be the most comprehensive, but the relative positions of personal and partial notes is indeterminate. Second, even the relatively clear comparison of full notes with the other two conditions is confounded with a presumptive difference in amount of student cognitive processing entailed. Nevertheless, for all this ambiguity with respect to the issue of comprehensiveness, the results of these investigations point up, once again, the likelihood that study-achievement relationships are interactive.

In one of the investigations (Collingwood & Hughes, 1978), the lecture content consisted of topics in electrical engineering, and the achievement test consisted entirely of multiple-choice items. The results indicated that the provision of full and parital notes produced higher achievement than personal notes. On the presumption that both kinds of provided notes were more comprehensive than personal notes, this outcome runs counter to Maqsud's (1980) conclusion that brief notes are superior to detailed ones. This apparent contradiction, however, may be resolvable by attributing the discrepancy to any of several differences between the two investigations. For example, one difference was in the subject matter content of the lectures. Another difference, of more pertinence to the topic of the present section, was the contrast between a free-recall (Maqsud, 1980) and a multiple-choice (Collingwood & Hughes, 1978) achievement criterion.

The possible importance of this criterion difference is illustrated by the results of a second investigation involving a personal–partial–full notes manipulation (Annis, 1981). This investigation, in which the lecture topic was developmental psychology, also included a criterion manipulation that contrasted performance on multiple-choice and short-answer essay items. This manipulation proved to be important, as the effect of notetaking condition varied with the type of criterion: multiple-choice achievement was highest for those receiving partial notes, whereas essay achievement was highest for those who took personal notes. Inasmuch as the full notes condition was the least effective as indexed by both criteria, the issue of comprehensiveness stands unresolved. Nevertheless, it appears that type of notetaking interacts with type of criterion, and perhaps with subject matter as well, in determining achievement.

2. REVIEW OPPORTUNITY

These already complex relationships grow even more complicated with an examination of the effects of yet another context variable, namely, that of review opportunities. Participants in the notetaking investigations reviewed in the preceding section all had opportunities to review their notes prior to completing a performance test. While such arrangements are congruent with conditions that usually obtain in natural settings, they leave open a theoretically important issue about notetaking effects. This issue is whether notetaking affects achievement because of the kind of processing it fosters at the time notes are taken or because it provides a record that can be reviewed later to improve retention.

A number of investigations have addressed this locus issue, but it nevertheless remains open due to discrepancies in the outcomes observed. The results of two recent invetigations are illustrative. Each involved the manipulation of notetaking from printed texts (rather than from lectures), in addition to the manipulation of review opportunities.

One of these investigations yielded results that were quite straightforward, placing the locus squarely at the time of notetaking (Bretzing & Kulhavy, 1979). High school students were asked to read an eight-page passage of social science content in preparation for a test. From the published description, each item on this short-answer test apparently required the integration of facts and main ideas presented in the passage. Some of the students were instructed only to read the passage, others to select and record verbatim the three lines from each page that best captured its main ideas, and still others to summarize or paraphrase these ideas in three lines of their own words. Half of the students in the notetaking groups were allowed to review their records prior to the criterion test, half were not. The results indicated that verbatim notes were of no more value than reading the passage, while paraphrase and summary notes significantly facilitated performance. More to the point, review opportunity exerted no appreciable effect on performance, nor did it interact with type of notetaking. Thus, the clear implication is that the benefits of notetaking accrue from and depend on the kind of processing it stimulates during initial encoding.

Contrasting sharply with this conclusion are the results of a second investigation (Santa, Abrams, & Santa, 1979). In addition to the manipulation of notetaking and review opportunity, this investigation also included two kinds of criterion tasks, multiple-choice and free recall, as well as two kinds of text, a history passage and a science article. College students, classified as either good or poor readers, were assigned to three notetaking conditions: no notes, restricted notes (notes of no more than two sentences per paragraph), or unrestricted notes. Only half the students in the restricted and unrestricted conditions were permitted to review their notes prior to a multiple-choice test which was followed immediately by a free-recall test on the passage.

The results revealed that neither the notetaking nor the review manipulation affected performance on the multiple-choice test. Nevertheless, these manipulations did exert effects on free recall, when performance was indexed in two separate ways: number of main ideas recalled, and number of details recalled. In recalling main ideas, students who took no notes performed as well as or better than students in any other condition. In fact, good readers constrained to take restricted notes, especially those prevented from reviewing their notes, recalled significantly fewer main ideas than those in the no-note condition.

These results differ substantially from those for recall of details. In virtually all cases of detail recall, notetaking of either kind was superior to not taking notes. Yet, even here, multiple interactions emerged. Among poor readers, for example, the effect of review opportunity varied with passage content. Among good readers, review opportunity made no discernible difference in number of details recalled by those who took restricted notes, whereas it was critical for those who took unrestricted notes.

Thus, unlike the results obtained by Bretzing and Kulhavy (1979), the outcomes of this study suggest a number of conditional relationships between notetaking and achievement. The value of taking notes at all appears to depend on the character of performance criteria; that is, notetaking improved recall of details but had little if any value for recognition or for recall of main ideas. Moreover, the locus of notetaking effects on detail recall varied with type of notes. Restricted notes appear to exert their effect at encoding, for review opportunity did not alter this effect; unrestricted notes, in contrast, were only effective given a review opportunity, suggesting that they function chiefly as a retrieval aid.

3. CRITERION KNOWLEDGE

Still another variable of presumptive relevance to the effectiveness of studying is the availability of information about the character of the criterion test. This variable can be construed as either an immediate context characteristic (availability) or an immediate student characteristic (knowledge of the criterion). In either case, the more information students have about the nature of the performance to be required, the more effective should be their notetaking and study activities. Although ostensibly a truism, this proposition has resisted empirical confirmation in both laboratory and more natural settings.

The typical aim of relevant laboratory investigations has been to verify the hypothesis that valid test expectations should produce optimal encoding of information during study (Lockhart, Craik, & Jacoby, 1976). Students are asked to study lists of words or pictures in preparation for a subsequent retention test. Their test expectations are manipulated either by informing them of the type of test to be given or by providing a succession of experiences with a single type of test. On the critical comparison task, half the students receive a test congruent with their expectations, while the other half receive an incongruent test.

The results of a series of experiments of this kind have been quite variable across test types and study materials. Positive effects of accurate expecations have been obtained for cued recall but not free recall (Jacoby, 1973), for free recall but not recognition (Connor, 1977), and for recognition but not free recall (Carey & Lockhart, 1973). In contrast to this variability, Tversky (1973) obtained positive expectation effects for both recognition and free recall, but only after informing students about effective ways of studying for the kind of test anticipated. Thus, outcomes that are otherwise discouragingly inconsistent may eventually be explicable in terms of variations in processing knowledge (cf. Anderson & Armbruster, 1982).

Inconsistency also marks the outcomes of investigations designed to examine the effects of criterion knowledge on performance in more school-like settings. In such settings, even entirely null outcomes have been reported. Hakstian (1971), for example, conducted two experiments in each of which college students were informed that they would receive either an essay test, an objective test, or a combined essay–objective test. In one of the experiments, this instructional manipulation occurred as an integral part of an undergraduate course, where study activities were assessed by means of self-reports and achievement by means of a combined essay–objective midterm examination. The other experiment was conducted in a single session, so that study activities, such as notetaking, could be assessed by direct observation. In neither experiment, however, did the manipulation of criterion information produce significant effects on either study activities or achievement.

A similar outcome was obtained by Carrier and Titus (1981), but only in one condition of their investigation. In this condition, high school students were informed either that they would receive an unspecified test, a multiple-choice test, or an essay test (which, in fact, was a free-recall test). They were then encouraged to take notes while listening to a lecture on the content to be examined. Consistent with the outcomes of the Hakstian (1971) experiments, the manipulation of criterion information produced no significant effects on achievement as indexed by either a multiple-choice or a free-recall test.

Students assigned to the other major condition of this investigation were given pretraining in notetaking techniques prior to the experiment proper. For these students, the anticipation of a multiple-choice test led to higher performance than anticipation of an essay test. Surprisingly, moreover, this difference emerged not only on the multiple-choice test, but on the free-recall test as well. While this outcome suggests that processing or notetaking knowledge may interact with criterion knowledge, the other expected interaction—with type of criterion—is not in evidence.

Rickards and Friedman (1978) introduced a further refinement in the methodology of assessing expectation effects. This refinement consisted of differentiating the criterion variables with respect to the importance levels of idea units from a text passage. College students were told to expect either a multiple-choice or an essay test covering a passage of text they were then asked to read. Within each expectation condition, two groups of students were allowed to take notes while reading, while another group was not. The notetaking groups were distinguished by whether or not they were allowed to review their notes prior to the completion and free-recall tests administered one week later.

This review opportunity facilitated performance significantly on both criterion tests. Even without review, notetaking was advantageous, but only on the completion test, not for free recall. Consistent with the results reported by Hakstian (1971), test expectation did not significantly affect either the total number of notes taken or overall achievement on the criterion test. Expectation differences did emerge, however, when performance was partitioned by importance level. For example, the average importance level of notes taken was higher for students who expected an essay test than for those who expected a multiple-choice test.

Presumably, the implied interaction of expectation and importance level should also have emerged in the achievement measures. Some such evidence was obtained in secondary analyses of performance on the completion test, but none at all was reported for the free-recall test. While apparently puzzling, this outcome may have stemmed from student ignorance about what information should be recorded in notes.

This interpretation is consistent with results reported by Brown, Smiley, and Lawton (1978). Samples of students, ranging from fifth grade to college age, listened to stories and were then asked to select those constituent idea units (up to approximately one-fourth of the total) that they would prefer to have available should they need to recall the story. Prior to a recall attempt, students at all ages showed a decided preference for the highest level idea units. Even after a recall attempt, this preference remained equally strong among all students of precollege age. Among college students, however, recall experience resulted in a shift of preference to idea units of middling importance levels. Thus, had Rickards and Friedman (1978) provided students with another notetaking task after they had experienced a recall test, expectation effects might have been more pronounced. Such a design would also have permitted an examination of individual differences in the interaction of notetaking, criterion knowledge, and achievement.

As Anderson and Armbruster (1982) have argued, information about the character of performance criteria can vary dramatically in specificity. At one end of the dimension, students can be provided with actual copies of the criterion items for use as they read, listen, and take notes; such inserted questions have a potent facilitative effect on achievement. At the other end of the dimension, the kind of criterion test to be expected may be described only in generalities. As the preceding review indicates, the availability of such general criterion information has little impact on notetaking–achievement relationships. Indeed, an analogous lack of specificity may well have muted many of the interactive effects examined in research on notetaking, whether they involved note type, criterion type, review opportunity, or criterion knowledge.

On the whole, this review of research on specific study activities is more encouraging than the preceding review of omnibus activities, but only to a limited degree. Encouraging are the findings of achievement effects attributable to variations in activities such as effort allocation, selection, and type of notetaking. Moreover, suggestive of the promise of the interaction hypothesis are results showing that these study activities themselves vary as a function of both immediate and background characteristics. Yet, such outcomes are hardly cause for unbridled optimism about the present state of a psychology of studying, for they are fragmentary and, at least superficially, inconsistent from one investigation to another. Similarly, research on developmental trends in relationships between specific study activities and achievement presents a mixed picture at best. Age differences are sometimes quite striking, as in the cases of processing and selection procedures, but the simple fact is that only a precious few developmental investigations have yet been made. Thus, a developmental psychology of studying must await future research.

VII. Agenda for Future Research

Despite its limitations, previous research on studying yields a number of suggestions about the contours and priorities that should characterize future research. The inchoate character of the field to date underlines the need for systematic classification schemes to guide the collection of descriptive information. This descriptive emphasis itself stems from the present paucity of information about basic attributes and variations in studying. The limitations of previous research also suggest that alternative methods might prove productive in collecting the descriptive information called for by the classification schemes. In addition to an emphasis on description, future research must also progress toward the construction of theories about particular studying tasks and about differences among students across task variations. Broadly speaking, then, research must proceed concurrently along explanatory as well as descriptive lines.

A. A Classification Scheme

In principle, of course, any number of alternative classification schemes could be constructed to guide descriptive research on studying. The framework presented in Fig. 1 is sufficiently general to encompass many of these options, but too general to guide a choice among them. To serve this selection function, specific advance hypotheses are needed, even though they may be only provisional ones.

Two such hypotheses are suggested by the present review. One of these hypotheses asserts that the effectiveness of particular study activities depends on specific attributes of both the students involved and of the courses for which they study. The second hypothesis concerns student differences in achievement across course attributes: effective students vary their study activities, tailoring them for specific differences in course demands. The hallmark of both hypotheses is specificity with respect to both student and context characteristics.

Of the multitude of such characteristics, which should be given initial priority? In keeping with the goal of making development a central dimension in a psychology of studying, the student characteristic of chronological age must be accorded high priority. The potential importance of this characteristic is also suggested by the results of previous research, especially those emanating from laboratory investigations and from investigations of selection processes (e.g., Brown & Smiley, 1978). Another student background factor of potential importance is that of type of achievement motivation (e.g., Biggs, 1978). Among more immediate student characteristics, the research reviewed suggests at least two that deserve initial attention. One of these characteristics is knowledge of and propensity to employ effective procedures for processing different kinds of information (Anderson & Armbruster, 1982; Rohwer, 1980b). A second immediate student characteristic is the capability of selecting information for study attention, depending on the criterion to be met (e.g., Brown et al., 1978). As for course characteristics, the present review indicates that early attention should be given to those of subject matter (e.g., Laurillard, 1979; Santa *et al.*, 1979), type of performance criterion (e.g., Annis, 1981), and availability of specific information about performance criteria (Anderson & Armbruster, 1982).

Even this small number of student and course variables, when factorially combined, sets a challenging agenda of descriptive research. This research, furthermore, would need to be programmatic rather than consisting of the kinds of isolated investigations that have typified the field of studying to date. Consider, for example, the number of groups involved in a single, relatively straightforward design for obtaining descriptive information about the study activities of students at, say, three levels of achievement. In addition to achievement level, the design might also include the factors of age and subject matter. The age samples could be drawn from three distinct grade levels, such as junior high school, high school, and college. Optimally, then, the subject matters selected would be divergent but representative of courses taught at all three grades, such as American history, mathematics, and English. This 27-cell design might also be replicated on two kinds of students, those bound for 4-year colleges and those bound for community colleges. Similarly large designs could also be elaborated from combinations of the other high-priority variables in the preceding list, and each would have the potential of furnishing more systematic information about study activities than is now available.

B. Methods of Descriptive Research

The methods used to collect this information would also depart from those employed in the past. Given a design like that in the example, initial steps might include interview and observational investigations of the actual study activities engaged in by small but representative samples of students in each cell. The information obtained could then be used to construct self-report inventories for the collection of data on larger samples. This self-report approach, however, would differ from most previous ones in that interest would center on variations in responses at the item level rather than at the factor-scale level (cf. Goldman & Warren, 1973). Another departure from previous practice would entail the examination, through direct observation, of item validities with respect to the criterion of actual study behavior.

The anticipated outcome of such series of programmatic investigations would be empirical generalizations about variations in the use and effectiveness of study procedures as a function of factors like age and subject matter. Given appropriate designs, ones in which achievement level and subject matter, for example, were treated as within-subjects factors, generalizations could also be obtained relevant to the hypothesis that effective students vary their study procedures depending on specific course demands. These generalizations would then need to be confirmed in experimental investigations involving the manipulation of study procedures.

C. *Explanatory Research*

Even experimental investigations of the kind just mentioned would, by themselves, be insufficient to create a viable psychology of studying. Substantially more analytic research would also be needed. The aim of these investigations would be to verify theories about the study procedures required for the successful accomplishment of particular academic performance tasks, for example, composing essay responses or selecting multiple-choice alternatives in order to draw comparisons among the attributes of major figures in history and in literature. Methodologically, this analytic research could be modeled after the approaches reviewed in the section on specific study activities (Section VI) and after other approaches described in detail by Anderson and Armbruster (1982). An additional provision, however, is critical; even analytical research to verify task performance theories should be replicated across different age groups and subject matters, preferably those about which descriptive information is available. Finally, while such research might center on studying as it occurs in the contexts of schooling, it should extend beyond these confines to encompass the wide variety of individual efforts toward self-education.

Although brief and incomplete, this sketch of a sample research agenda may give pause to recipients of the present invitation to a proposed branch of applied developmental psychology. To accept the invitation is to accept a challenge that is intimidating in its demands for inventiveness, endurance, and tenacity. Required in order to meet the challenge will be a protracted and concerted effort on the part of numerous investigators committed to the eventual creation of a visible and coherent developmental psychology of studying.

References

Alpert, R., & Haber, R. N. Anxiety in academic achievement situations. *Journal of Abnormal and Social Psychology,* 1960, **61,** 207–215.

Anderson, T. H., & Armbruster, B. B. Studying. In P. D. Pearson (Ed.), *Handbook of reading research.* New York: Longman, 1982.

Annis, L. F. Effects of preference for assigned lecture notes on student achievement. *Journal of Educational Research,* 1981, **74,** 179–182.

Biggs, J. B. Faculty patterns in study behaviour. *Australian Journal of Psychology,* 1970, **22,** 161–174.

Biggs, J. B. Study behaviour and matriculation performance in two school populations. *Australian Journal of Education,* 1972, **16**, 187–204.

Biggs, J. B. Dimensions of study behaviour: Another look at ATI. *British Journal of Educational Psychology,* 1976, **46**, 68–80.

Biggs, J. B. Individual and group differences in study processes. *British Journal of Educational Psychology,* 1978, **48**, 266–279.

Biggs, J. B. Individual differences in study processes and the quality of learning outcomes. *Higher Education,* 1979, **8**, 381–394.

Bloom, B. S. *Human characteristics and school learning.* New York: McGraw-Hill, 1976.

Bower, G. H. Cognitive psychology: An introduction. In W. K. Estes (Ed.), *Handbook of learning and cognitive processes* (Vol. 1). Hillsdale, New Jersey: Erlbaum, 1975.

Bray, J. H., Maxwell, S. E., & Schmeck, R. R. A psychometric investigation of the Survey of Study Habits and Attitudes. *Applied Psychological Measurement,* 1980, **4**, 195–201.

Bretzing, B. H., & Kulhavy, R. W. Notetaking and depth of processing. *Contemporary Educational Psychology,* 1979, **4**, 145–153.

Brown, A. L., & Smiley, S. S. Rating the importance of structural units of prose passages: A problem of metacognitive development. *Child Development,* 1977, **48**, 1–8.

Brown, A. L., & Smiley, S. S. The development of strategies for studying texts. *Child Development,* 1978, **49**, 1076–1088.

Brown, A. L., Smiley, S. S., & Lawton, S. Q. C. The effects of experience on the selection of suitable retrieval cues for studying texts. *Child Development,* 1978, **49**, 829–835.

Brown, F. G., & Dubois, T. E. Correlates of academic success for high-ability freshman men. *Personnel and Guidance Journal,* 1964, **42**, 603–607.

Brown, W. F. *Effective study test: Manual of directions.* San Marcos, Texas: Effective Study Materials, 1975.

Brown, W. F., & Holtzman, W. H. *Survey of study habits and attitudes.* New York: Psychological Corp., 1953.

Brown, W. F., & Holtzman, W. H. *Survey of study habits and attitudes forms C and H.* New York: Psychological Corp., 1967.

Carey, S. T., & Lockhart, R. S. Encoding differences in recognition and recall. *Memory & Cognition,* 1973, **1**, 297–300.

Carrier, C. A., & Titus, A. The effects of notetaking: A review of studies. *Contemporary Educational Psychology,* 1979, **4**, 299–314.

Carrier, C. A., & Titus, A. Effects of notetaking pretraining and test mode expectations on learning from lectures. *American Educational Research Journal,* 1981, **18**, 385–397.

Carroll, J. B. A model of school learning. *Teachers College Record,* 1963, **64**, 723–733.

Cavanaugh, J. C., & Perlmutter, M. Metamemory: A critical examination. *Child Development,* 1982, **53**, 11–28.

Collingwood, V., & Hughes, D. C. Effects of three types of university lecture notes on student achievement. *Journal of Educational Psychology,* 1978, **70**, 175–179.

Connor, J. M. Effects of organization and expectancy on recall and recognition. *Memory & Cognition,* 1977, **5**, 315–318.

Covington, M. V., & Omelich, C. L. As failures mount: Affective and cognitive consequences of ability demotion in the classroom. *Journal of Educational Psychology,* 1981, **73**, 796–808.

Craik, F. I. M., & Lockhart, R. S. Levels of processing: A framework for memory research. *Journal of Verbal Learning and Verbal Behavior,* 1972, **11**, 671–684.

Culler, R. E., & Holahan, C. J. Test anxiety and academic performance: The effects of study-related behaviors. *Journal of Educational Psychology,* 1980, **72**, 16–20.

Entwistle, N. J., & Brennan, T. The academic performance of students. II. Types of successful students. *British Journal of Educational Psychology,* 1971, **41**, 268–276.

Entwistle, N. J., Nisbet, J., Entwistle, D., & Cowell, M. D. The academic performance of students. I. Prediction from scales of motivation and study methods. *British Journal of Educational Psychology,* 1971, **41,** 258-267.

Flavell, J. H., & Wellman, H. M. Metamemory. In R. V. Kail, Jr. & J. W. Hagen (Eds.), *Perspectives on the development of memory and cognition.* Hillsdale, New Jersey: Erlbaum, 1977.

Gagné, R. M. *The conditions of learning.* New York: Holt, 1977.

Gagné, R. M., & Rohwer, W. D., Jr. Instructional psychology. *Annual Review of Psychology,* 1969, **20,** 381-414.

Glaser, R. (Ed.). *Advances in instructional psychology* (Vol. 1). Hillsdale, New Jersey: Erlbaum, 1978.

Glaser, R., & Resnick, L. B. Instructional psychology. *Annual Review of Psychology,* 1972, **23,** 207-276.

Goldfried, M. R., & D'Zurilla, M. R. Prediction of academic competence by means of the Survey of Study Habits and Attitudes. *Journal of Educational Psychology,* 1973, **64,** 116-122.

Goldman, R. D. Effects of a logical versus a mnemonic learning strategy on performance in two undergraduate psychology classes. *Journal of Educational Psychology,* 1972, **63,** 347-352.

Goldman, R. D., & Hudson, D. J. A multivariate analysis of academic abilities and strategies for successful and unsuccessful college students in different major fields. *Journal of Educational Psychology,* 1973, **75,** 364-370.

Goldman, R. D., & Warren, R. Discriminant analysis of study strategies connected with college grade success in different major fields. *Journal of Educational Measurement,* 1973, **10,** 39-47.

Greeno, J. G. Psychology of learning, 1960-1980. One participant's observations. *American Psychologist,* 1980, **35,** 713-728.

Hakstian, A. R. The effects of type of examination anticipated on test preparation and performance. *Journal of Educational Research,* 1971, **64,** 319-324.

Holtzman, W. H., & Brown, W. F. Evaluating the study habits and attitudes of high school students. *Journal of Educational Psychology,* 1968, **59,** 404-409.

Jacoby, L. L. Test appropriate strategies in retention of categorized lists. *Journal of Verbal Learning and Verbal Behavior,* 1973, **12,** 675-682.

Keller, J. M., Goldman, J. A., & Sutterer, J. R. Locus of control in relation to academic attitudes and performance in a personalized system of instruction course. *Journal of Educational Psychology,* 1978, **70,** 414-421.

Khan, S. B., & Roberts, D. M. Structure of academic attitudes and study habits. *Educational and Psychological Measurement,* 1975, **35,** 835-842.

Kirkland, K., & Hollandsworth, J. G., Jr. Test anxiety, study skills, and academic performance. *Journal of College Student Personnel,* 1979, **20,** 431-435.

Laurillard, D. The processes of student learning. *Higher Education,* 1979, **8,** 395-409.

Lockhart, R. S., Craik, F., & Jacoby, L. Depth of processing, recognition and recall. In J. Brown (Ed.), *Recall and recognition.* New York: Wiley, 1976.

Maqsud, M. Effects of personal lecture notes and teacher-notes on recall of university students. *British Journal of Educational Psychology,* 1980, **50,** 289-294.

Marton, F., & Säljö, R. On qualitative differences in learning: I. Outcomes and process. *British Journal of Educational Psychology,* 1976, **46,** 4-11.

McClintock, R. Toward a place for study in a world of instruction. *Teachers College Record,* 1971, **73,** 161-205.

Miller, G. A., Galanter, E., & Pribram, K. H. *Plans and the structure of behavior.* New York: Holt, 1960.

Newell, A., & Simon, H. A. *Human problem solving.* New York: Prentice-Hall, 1971.

Ornstein, P. A., & Naus, M. J. Rehearsal processess in children's memory. In P. A. Ornstein (Ed.), *Memory development in children.* Hillsdale, New Jersey: Erlbaum, 1978.

Owings, R. A., Petersen, G. A., Bransford, J. D., Morris, C. D., & Stein, B. S. Spontaneous monitoring and regulation of learning: A comparison of successful and less successful fifth graders. *Journal of Educational Psychology,* 1980, **72,** 250–256.

Pask, G. Styles and strategies of learning. *British Journal of Educational Psychology,* 1976, **46,** 128–148.

Piaget, J., & Inhelder, B. *Memory and intelligence.* New York: Basic Books, 1973.

Pressley, M., & Dennis-Rounds, J. Transfer of a mnemonic keyword strategy at two age levels. *Journal of Educational Psychology,* 1980, **72,** 575–582.

Pressley, M., & Levin, J. R. Developmental differences in subjects' associative-learning strategies and performance: Assessing a hypothesis. *Journal of Experimental Child Psychology,* 1977, **24,** 431–439.

Ramanaiah, N. V., Ribich, F. D., & Schmeck, R. R. Internal-external control of reinforcement as a determinant of study habits and academic attitudes. *Journal of Research in Personality,* 1975, **9,** 375–384.

Raygor, A. *Study skills test.* New York: McGraw-Hill, 1970.

Resnick, L. B. Instructional psychology. *Annual Review of Psychology,* 1981, **32,** 659–704.

Rickards, J. P., & Friedman, F. The encoding versus the external storage hypothesis in note taking. *Contemporary Educational Psychology,* 1978, **3,** 136–143.

Robyak, J. G., & Downey, R. G. A discriminant analysis of the study skills and personality types of underachieving and nonunderachieving study skills students. *Journal of College Student Personnel,* 1979, **20,** 306–309.

Rohwer, W. D., Jr. Elaboration and learning in childhood and adolescence. In H. W. Reese (Ed.), *Advances in child development and behavior* (Vol. 8). New York: Academic Press, 1973.

Rohwer, W. D., Jr. How the smart get smarter. *Educational Psychologist,* 1980, **15,** 35–43. (a)

Rohwer, W. D., Jr. An elaborative conception of learner differences. In R. E. Snow, P.-A. Federico, & W. E. Montague (Eds.), *Aptitude, learning, and instruction* (Vol. 2). Hillsdale, New Jersey: Erlbaum, 1980. (b)

Rohwer, W. D., Jr., Raines, J. M., Eoff, J., & Wagner, M. The development of elaborative propensity in adolescence. *Journal of Experimental Child Psychology,* 1977, **23,** 472–492.

Rotter, J. B. Generalized expectancies for internal versus external control of reinforcement, 1966, **80** (1, Whole No. 609).

Rutkowski, K., & Domino, G. Interrelationship of study skills and personality variables in college students. *Journal of Educational Psychology,* 1975, **67,** 784–789.

Santa, C. M., Abrams, L., & Santa, J. L. Effects of notetaking and studying on the retention of prose. *Journal of Reading Behavior,* 1979, **11,** 247–260.

Sarason, I. G. Experimental approaches to test anxiety: Attention and the uses of information. In C. D. Spielberger (Ed.), *Anxiety: Current trends in theory and research* (Vol. 2). New York: Academic Press, 1972.

Schmeck, R. R., & Ribich, F. D. Construct validation of the inventory of learning processes. *Applied Psychological Measurement,* 1978, **2,** 551–562.

Schmeck, R. R., Ribich, F., & Ramanaiah, N. Development of a self-report inventory for assessing individual differences in learning processes. *Applied Psychological Measurement,* 1977, **1,** 413–431.

Svensson, L. On Qualitative differences in learning: III. Study skill and learning. *British Journal of Educational Psychology,* 1977, **47,** 233–243.

Tversky, B. G. Encoding processes in recognition and recall. *Cognitive Psychology,* 1973, **5,** 275–287.

Vygotsky, L. S. *Mind in society.* Cambridge, Massachusetts: Harvard Univ. Press, 1978.

Waters, H. S. Memory development in adolescence: Relationships between metamemory, strategy use, and performance. *Journal of Experimental Child Psychology,* 1982, **33,** 183–195.

Watkins, D., & Hattie, J. An investigation of the internal structure of the Biggs Study Process Questionnaire. *Educational and Psychological Measurement,* 1980, **40,** 1125–1130.

Weigel, R. G., & Weigel, V. M. The relationship of knowledge and usage of study skill techniques to academic performance. *The Journal of Educational Research,* 1967, **61,** 78–80.

Wittrock, M. C., & Lumsdaine, A. A. Instructional psychology. *Annual Review of Psychology,* 1977, **28,** 417–459.

YOUNG CHILDREN'S TV VIEWING: THE PROBLEM

OF COGNITIVE CONTINUITY

Daniel R. Anderson and Robin Smith[1]

DEPARTMENT OF PSYCHOLOGY
UNIVERSITY OF MASSACHUSETTS
AMHERST, MASSACHUSETTS

[1]Present address: Institute of Child Development, University of Minnesota, Minneapolis, Minnesota.

*Applied Developmental
Psychology, Volume 1*

I. Television Viewing as a Cognitive Activity

A 4-year-old girl spends 25 hours a week in front of a television set. Sometimes she rarely looks at the screen; instead, she plays with toys or interacts with family and friends. On other occasions she pays careful attention, sitting quietly for many minutes at a time, resistant to distraction. Sometimes she gets up and leaves the room, while other times she asks her parents constant questions about the program. Her parents know that TV is having an impact since she talks about TV characters and situations and incorporates them into her play. Her parents notice that she watches some things and ignores others, and wonder what she understands of the many TV programs to which she is exposed.

Television viewing is a cognitive activity; it may be the single most common externally structured cognitive activity engaged in by American preschool children. Although TV viewing is often dismissed as merely passive reception of prepackaged stimulation, closer analysis reveals the television stimulus to be in many ways complex and dense. At the level of content, television presents an inexorable succession of people, situations, places, and words which are often unfamiliar to the preschool child. At the level of form, television presents a dynamic flow of image and symbol in two modalities. The child is thus presented with a problem of *cognitive continuity:* how to connect and make sense of this flow of information. The processing of other media and of many "real-life" activities in general may present problems analogous to that of television. Many situations present challenges of cognitive continuity requiring the strategic deployment of attention, resistance to distraction, temporal integration of multimodal information, and the comprehension of formal conventions. We and others have found that the child's approach to solving the problem of cognitive continuity in television viewing is active and unexpectedly sophisticated. This article examines this advance in our understanding of what happens when a child watches television.

II. Why Study Cognitive Processing of Television?

Compared to the amount of research that has been devoted to cognition and its development in general, there has been little work on the cognitive processing of television. The lack of research is due to a bias in academic psychology against "applied" research, to a lack of clearly formulated issues to be addressed by such research, and to a belief that general principles cannot be abstracted from much real-life activity because of its complexity. We believe that there are in fact a number of justifications for studying children's television viewing, including the abstraction of basic principles of cognition and its development.

A. Advancing the Study of Cognition and Its Development

We believe that systematic descriptive analysis of complex real-life cognitive behavior is essential to the advance of cognitive science. Such analysis complements more traditional process- and structure-oriented cognitive research, but it also holds potential advantages. In order to clarify the complementarity and advantages, it is necessary to characterize the two approaches.

Cognitive theory is often directly or indirectly based on a computer metaphor. A distinction which is made within this metaphor is process versus structure. A basic cognitive process is analogous to a machine instruction, whereas a cognitive structure is analogous to the data structure. Process-oriented cognitive research has typically examined individual cognitive processes in relative isolation from many other potentially interacting psychological processes. By carefully varying some aspects of the experimental situation while holding others constant, it is hoped that properties of the process may be revealed. Collectively, hundreds of experiments have been reported that examine basic processes such as iconic storage, attentional allocation, and memory scanning.

Research on cognitive structure is more difficult to characterize, but often it, too, examines some relatively stable and static aspect of knowledge in relative isolation from other structures and processes. Many studies on representation as image versus proposition or studies of prototypical concepts are examples of the study of cognitive structure.

Research examining process and structure in experimental isolation has led to major findings, concepts, and research techniques. But, as Neisser (1976) and Norman (1980) among others have pointed out, there are inherent limitations on the power and generality of such research. A major source of the limitations is the lack of generalizability to cognitive activity in almost any ongoing normal circumstance, which involves many interactions over time between knowledge structures and cognitive processes. Furthermore, many ordinary cognitive activities such as holding a conversation or watching TV involve the processing of dynamic, structured, multimodal stimulation. Research that examines process and structure in isolation cannot by itself account for the processing of such complex stimulation. Such an accounting requires direct analysis of the complex activities themselves.

Descriptive analysis of real-life cognitive behavior holds several potential advantages over process- and structure-oriented research. The data obtained from a descriptive analysis of real-life behavior are likely to have a greater useful longevity than the data obtained from experimental studies of process and structure. This follows insofar as many experimental studies of cognition employ tasks and behavioral situations that are meaningful only in relation to the hypothesized nature of some given process or structure. The problem is that since the research paradigm generated to study the process usually has no explicit relationship to a general theory of behavior, to other psychological processes, or to significant naturally occurring behaviors, the data produced in the research paradigm have little obvious importance except in relation to the original conceptions leading to the development of that research paradigm. Thus, many empirical investigations are deemed irrelevant to future research when new research paradigms are developed to study the same process, or when the tides of research interest shift and somewhat different conceptions of interesting cognitive processes become dominant. The data often have no descriptive value in and of themselves. When studying a "real" cognitive activity such as TV viewing, however, the problem is less likely to hold; since the activity is something people *do,* the data have descriptive value independent of the worth of the theoretical or process assumptions which generated the study.

When the behavioral system itself (as opposed to some presumed process or structural property) becomes the focus of analysis, descriptions of the system become highly useful and provide anchor points for subsequent theoretical development. Whereas disagreements may ensue about processes underlying observed phenomena, there is likely to be agreement about the descriptions of the phenomena themselves. The criterion for a successful theory thus becomes the ability to account for these observed phenomena, introducing the possibility of productive theoretical dialogue. The approach is more likely to be one of analysis, that is, dividing the observed behavioral system into component processes, structures, and relationships, rather than an approach of synthesis, that is, starting with presumed processes underlying the behavioral system, constructing a theory to account for the system, and then designing experiments that test the theory. One strength of a descriptive-analytic approach is that previously unsuspected processes and structures may emerge from the analyses (Mayr, 1982; see our discussion of attentional inertia in TV viewing, Section VI, this article). Such unsuspected findings may represent emergent properties present in a complex system but not apparent when hypothesized processes are studied in isolation.

The study of cognition and its development will, of course, advance through a variety of approaches. In our study of TV viewing as a complex cognitive activity, we make use of the ideas, techniques, and theories developed from process- and structure-oriented research. Our argument here, however, is that such research, while necessary, is unlikely to be sufficient in achieving the long-range goal of a data base and theory of cognition adequate to deal with a wide range of cognitive behavior and its development. Research on cognition in a variety of real-life activities such as reading, TV viewing, social interaction, and game playing will provide not only a valuable data base but also verification of the usefulness of theorized processes and structures as well as discoveries of new, emergent processes and structures.

B. Application to TV Production

An advantage to choosing a complex real-life behavioral system to study is that much of the obtained knowledge may be directly or indirectly applicable to practical concerns. In the case of television viewing, data and theoretical principles obtained from cognitive research have already proven useful in educational and commercial television production. Some TV production groups regularly engage in formative research directed at developing a specific TV program or series. The topics of interest often include attention and comprehension, and production groups frequently employ academic consultants to advise and conduct research (e.g., Lorch & Anderson, 1978). To the degree to which evaluations can be made, these efforts have contributed to the success of a number of educational TV programs (Crane, 1980; Lesser, 1974; Mates, 1980; Mielke, 1983; Palmer, 1974; Watkins, Huston-Stein, & Wright, 1980).

Formative research, however, is often of only limited general use. It is usually informal in nature, utilizing few subjects, and is oriented toward questions of little relevance outside the specific production. Unless the series has unusual longevity (as in the rare case of a program such as *Sesame Street*), formative research has little continuity and is rarely published. Other formative research done for advertising and some commerical children's programs is proprietary and unavailable to public scrutiny. Formative research is thus not a substitute for programmatic basic research if the goal is to develop principles that have general application.

C. Prevalence of TV Viewing

Apart from theoretical or practical considerations, the study of TV viewing is important because TV viewing is a predominant activity in the lives of Americans. While estimates of amount of TV viewing vary from study to study and are influenced by a large number of factors (Anderson, Alwitt, Lorch, & Levin, 1979; Comstock, Chaffee, Katzman, McCombs, & Roberts, 1978), it is clear that Americans, at least, spend substantial amounts of time in front of TV sets. The heaviest viewers are preschool children, who are often estimated to spend a third of their waking hours in front of TV. The study of television would seem to be justified simply because it is a large part of what people, especially young children, do.

D. Effects of TV Viewing

In parallel with the development of every mass medium in this century, the inception of television has brought waves of public concern over its effects on children (Reeves & Wartella, 1982). These concerns have ranged from physical effects (as in concern about possible radiation hazards) to effects on social behavior and cognitive skills. In response to these concerns, funding has been sporadically made available to determine the effects of TV viewing. In fact, most published behavioral research concerning television has been motivated and funded as a result of these public concerns. Such "effects" research has extended our understanding of the impact of television and has provided useful policy information. The work, however, often has not stemmed from conceptions of television and its effects as being of scientific interest, separate from current public concerns. Much of the research has been conducted by investigators with no prior interest in the issues, and has also been conducted in a crisis atmosphere conducive to unprogrammatic, hurried, simplistic research. In his review of research relating reading and schooling skills to TV viewing, for example, Hornik (1981) noted that every study was a singular effort by the investigators; there were no consistent programs of research. Since the work often tries to provide simple answers in terms of TV's "effects," there has been little interest in underlying processes, and the theory that has been employed has been taken whole cloth from research conducted outside the framework of television's effects.

Recently, however, several investigators have suggested that basic research into cognitive processing of television may reveal significant factors that mediate the effects of TV. Collins (1979, 1981, 1983), and Pingree and Hawkins (1982) have argued that the effects of TV content interact in complex ways with the viewer's background, cognitive skills, and goals such that a clear picture of TV effects cannot emerge without a detailed analysis of factors leading to the selection, interpretation, and retention of TV programming. Also, recent public concerns have been specifically cognitive in nature. Accusations that television shortens children's attention spans, induces "visual thought," reduces reading skills, and other similar accusations certainly suggest the importance of detailed analyses of the cognitive nature of TV viewing.

There are thus several justifications for the cognitive analysis of television viewing: as a means of advancing cognitive research and theory, for application to program production, because TV viewing is highly prevalent, and as a means to understanding TV's effects. Responding to some or all of these concerns, in the last decade a small group of investigators have begun programs of research on the cognitive nature of TV viewing. This "second generation" of television research (Kelly & Gardner, 1981a) has led to two recent volumes that emphasize cognitive processing of television (Bryant & Anderson, 1983; Kelly & Gardner, 1981b).

III. Television and the Problem of Cognitive Continuity

Television viewing presents the young child with a formidable array of on-line cognitive processing problems. These problems stem from the form and content of television programming, from the possibly unsupportive and distracting TV viewing environment, and from potential inadequacies of the young viewer's knowledge and information-processing abilities. Most discussions of these issues conclude that the young child is generally not capable of cognitively dealing with these problems and is overwhelmed by television. The argument in this article is that young children are far more able to cope with the information-processing demands of television than they have generally been given credit. Before presenting this argument and supportive research, however, we provide a brief task analysis of TV viewing and review the arguments for young children's cognitive limitations.

A. Content

Only about 50% of television programming seen by American preschool children is explicitly child oriented (e.g., Lyle & Hoffman, 1972). Virtually any given program presented on television may thus be viewed by at least some young children. As such, children can see an enormous variety of content ranging from cartoon fantasy characters operating in a fantasy environment, to dramatic presentation of a nineteenth-century midwestern farm family, to news films of diplomacy and war. It is thus apparent that much of the producer-intended content of television is incomprehensible to a young child. It should be recognized, however, that the content often bears several levels of analysis, and that the content from a producer's point of view and the same content from a young child's perspective may not be the same. For example, one of us observed a 5-year-old boy watching an automobile commercial which showed a young couple enjoying an elegant outdoor meal beside their new Mercedes. When asked what the commercial was about, the boy said "they want you to buy picnics." While such misunderstandings may reflect lack of comprehension from an adult perspective, they indicate that young children at least sometimes actively process content not intended for them and may assimilate that content according to their own limited fund of world knowledge. It is likely, nevertheless, that much television content is incomprehensible to the young child except, for example, at the uninteresting level of "grown-ups talking." To the young child, the amount, variety, complexity, and unfamiliarity of television content thus presents a significant problem of online comprehension.

B. Form

Regardless of the comprehensibility of the content, the form in which that content is presented also provides potential problems for cognitive processing. Television is an edited medium which can present visual and auditory information very rapidly. Information can be revealed by camera and lens through zooms, pans, and dollies, or by editing and special effects such as switches, cuts, inserts, dissolves, fades, compression, chromakey, and text. Audio techniques include voice-overs, sound effects, music, echo, compressed speech, and others. These techniques of manipulating sound and video have been called "formal features" (cf. Rice, Huston, & Wright, 1982).

Consider an analysis of a prime-time family TV program, *Little House on the Prairie,* commonly seen by young children. This program, which strikes the adult observer as being almost leisurely in its pacing, incorporates a remarkable number of formal features. In one randomly selected episode, we (Smith, Anderson, & Fischer, 1983) counted 311 cuts (about one per 9.1 seconds), 10 zooms, 56 pans, and 4 fades. There was thus a density of 8.1 of these formal features per minute. An action-adventure program popular with children (*Dukes of Hazzard*) provided an even greater density of such devices. Analysis of a randomly selected episode revealed 556 cuts (one every 5.0 seconds, on the average), 38 zooms, 6 freeze-frames, 118 pans, and 63 dolly or truck shots (movement of the camera as on a car in a chase scene). There were thus a total of 781 visual formal features in this rapidly paced program, or a density of about 16.7 formal features per minute.

Formal features may play several roles in young children's TV viewing: (1) maintenance of attention, (2) marking of significant content, and (3) transmission of meaning (cf. Huston & Wright, 1983). A formal feature could affect attention by eliciting an orienting reaction as a result of sudden stimulus change; it could mark significant content as a characteristic feature of the medium learned by the child; and it could convey concepts of time, space, action, and character psychology through the pragmatic logic of the sequence of events and settings. In film theory this last role of formal features is called "montage." Consider a sequence from a children's TV program previously discussed by Anderson *et al.* (1979). A jet airplane as seen from far below crosses the screen accompanied by characteristic engine noise. The scene abruptly changes to a shot up the aisle of the passenger section of an airliner showing rows of seats with passengers. The camera pans right and zooms to a close-up shot of a boy looking at a comic book. This entire sequence, which incorporates several formal features, is accomplished in about 6 seconds. Attention could, in principle, be elicited or maintained by the sound effect and visual changes; the cut to the interior shot may convey information about the location of subsequent action (the interior of an airliner which is currently in flight); and the pan and zoom to close-up can be interpreted as a conventional marker of a central character. In a space of a few seconds, formal features may thus play all three roles. Given the frequency and potential importance of formal features, it is clear that their use and interpretation must be central to the child's on-going cognitive processing of television. It is also clear that the many changes of scene, sound, and action must be integrated in some manner in order to comprehend the narrative. Television's form thus adds to the problem of cognitive continuity.

C. The TV Viewing Environment

Beyond content and form there is a growing appreciation that the *context* in which television is watched may have an influence on the child's processing of TV form and content. It is clear that TV is watched in widely varied situations at home and school. The context includes the availability of alternative activities other than looking at TV (e.g., by the availability of toys), distractions, social context (e.g., presence of coviewing peers or parents), situational demands (e.g., the prospect of being tested on the information, as in a school situation), as well as general attitudes of the family or larger cultural group toward TV. Each of these contextual factors has been suggested as a potential influence on the child's attention and comprehension. When watching television, the child often has more to deal with than television.

D. Cognitive Development and Television Viewing

The previous sections have presented the television stimulus as seriously challenging young children's meager stores of knowledge and understanding with unfamiliar content, and have described the rapid pace of formal features and the possibly distracting viewing environments experienced by children. These problems raise the question of how children in fact cognitively deal with television. Virtually all reports are that preschool children's comprehension of television is poor. For example, Friedlander, Wetstone, and Scott (1974) tested preschoolers on their comprehension of a 3-minute segment from *Captain Kangaroo* and found that over half of the children demonstrated comprehension of less than half of the information.

1. THE DEFICIT MODEL

Most discussions of young children's cognitive processing of television have been heavily influenced by Piagetian notions of development, particularly those dealing with preoperational thought. It is assumed that certain properties of preoperational cognitive structures make it difficult or impossible for young children to understand the meaning conveyed by a typical television show.

Three properties of preoperational thought that are commonly cited in the developmental literature on television viewing are egocentrism, centration, and difficulty in dealing with transformations from one state to another. The first, preoperational egocentrism, is described by Flavell (1963) as a very general characteristic, one manifestation of which is the inability to coordinate visual perspectives to represent the appearance of a display seen from various positions. Applying the concept to television, the Japanese psychologist Tada (1969) suggested that "to couple two shots of different camera angles is an intellectual task too difficult for a child of 4, who has not yet acquired the topological concept of space."

A second characteristic of the preoperational stage in Piagetian theory is centration. "Like the young sensorimotor infant in the field of direct action, the preoperational child is confined to the surface of the phenomena he tries to think about, assimilating only those superficial features which clamor loudest for his attention" (Flavell, 1963). The notion that the child moves from heavy reliance on perceptual aspects of television presentations to more reliance on conceptual aspects has been very influential in some theories of young children's attention to television (H. Lesser, 1977; Singer, 1980; Wartella & Ettema, 1974; Wright & Huston, 1981). This has led to suggestions that the young child's attention is "controlled" by the TV set. Anderson and Lorch (1983) have called these characterizations "reactive" theories of attention since they view the child as automatically reacting to superficial characteristics of the medium. It has also been suggested that children center on the visual component of the television stimulus, thereby preventing encoding of the auditory information and reducing comprehension of the meaning of the scene as a whole (Hayes & Birnbaum, 1980; Korac, 1981; Wackman & Wartella, 1977).

Finally, Piaget demonstrated the young child's difficulty in representing transformations that render two states logically coherent. In the "falling sticks" task (described by Flavell, 1963), children were asked to depict the successive states of a stick allowed to fall on its side from a vertical position. Apparently, preoperational children found it extremely difficult to reconstruct the intermediate positions (described by Flavell as "still-film") occupied by the stick during the transformation. Early research on film comprehension, influenced by Piagetian theory, reported that even 6-year-old children did not understand the relationship between film sequences and perceived them as a series of unrelated events (Flapan, 1965; Franck, 1955; Zazzo, 1956). Recent investigators, although not necessarily working from Piagetian theory, have also reported young children as having difficulty temporally integrating televised events. Leifer, Collins, Gross, Taylor, Andrews, and Blackmer (1971) found that 4-year-olds poorly ordered the three most central scenes from a 20-minute film. Noble (1975) also reported that young children were especially poor at sequencing events within a film and suggested that they perceive television narratives as separate and fragmentary incidents rather than as a story. In fact, Collins, Wellman, Keniston, and Westby (1978) reported that second-grade boys showed no evidence of being able to distinguish a normally presented detective show from the same story edited so that the major component scenes were presented in random sequence.

In summary, a deficit model of young children's cognitive processes has guided most of the early research and theory. Young children are described as "severely limited" in the ways they extract meaning from television (Wartella, 1981) due to the stimulus-bound, egocentric, and inflexible nature of their cognitive structures. This description of the young child suggests that the problem of cognitive continuity in TV viewing is not solved until late in childhood.

2. RECENT THEORETICAL TRENDS

While early research and theory supported the deficit model, other findings made it clear that young children can and do learn from television. They have favorite programs and can name their favorite characters from pictures of them (Lyle & Hoffman, 1972). Preschoolers can differentiate programs from commercials (Levin, Petros, & Petrella, 1982), make predictions about the outcomes of some depicted events (Rice, 1980; Sproull, 1973), incorporate program sequences into their play (Desmond, 1978), and learn specific content such as body parts, letters, and numbers from educational shows (Ball & Bogatz, 1972). In order to reconcile these findings with the evidence of preschoolers' cognitive deficiencies in television comprehension, we need to better understand how young children represent and process information from this medium.

Recent research and theoretical developments concerning cognition in the young child have identified new processes, structures, and strategies which may play a more central role in real-life everyday cognitive activity than the strictly logical structures described by Piaget. For example, Nelson and Gruendel (1981) describe the development of "generalized event representations" as basic building blocks of cognition. One of the new elements in their proposal is their attempt to understand how the child processes information from naturally occurring events, such as going to a birthday party or eating at McDonald's. They suggest that context-derived event representations of specific, meaningful activities are important organizing structures for the young child. Among other things, these representations enable prediction about what happens next, which reduces effort in processing real-life information in all its complexity. Other important new approaches to describing the nature of preschool thought include Fischer's skill theory (1980) and Siegler's (1982) rule-assessment approach in describing concept development.

In addition to new theoretical developments, there exists a growing awareness that preschool children's cognitive abilities deserve study in their own right (see Gelman, 1979). There is a new emphasis on uncovering the competencies of young children as precursors of more sophisticated thought. By altering task demands, examining activity in the context of naturalistic settings, and looking in domains of activity that are appropriate for preschoolers, it has been possible to reveal capacities that were previously unsuspected, and to trace development *within* the preschool years. For example, using short simple stories, Brown and Smiley (1977) demonstrated that young children spontaneously abstract the main ideas in oral and written text and favor the important units in recall. In her research on temporal ordering of events, Brown (1976) demonstrated that even preoperational children have some ability to exploit causal and logical links to infer the most probable order of events.

Research and theory on general cognitive development thus leave us with conflicting predictions of how young children deal with television. Classic developmental theory based on Piaget emphasizes the child's egocentrism, reactions to attention-demanding stimulation, and inability to understand the transformations that connect sequences of events. As applied to television the theory suggests that "young children see a series of separate and fragmentary incidents rather than a story" (Noble, 1975, p. 94). Writers influenced by this theory see little advance in the child's processing of television due to watching television, per se; rather, the older child solves the problem of cognitive continuity of TV viewing by entering a new *stage* of cognitive development. Children begin to perceive television as connected discourse by virtue of a general reorganization in their mental structures which renders them less reactive and egocentric, and more able to comprehend the transitions and transformations that connect scenes.

Newer trends in developmental research and theory have emphasized the importance of task-specific experience in developing cognitive skills appropriate to that task. Recent theory suggests that children abstract expectations about the canonical order of event sequences of ordinary living and apply these expectations in interpreting stories. If so, children may also be able to interpret sequences of scenes on television as long as these sequences conform with their experiences. Much of young children's experience, furthermore, is with television. Taken together, recent research trends are suggestive that young children may indeed be able to at least partially solve the problem of cognitive continuity. It is possible that research that shows poor comprehension by preschoolers either utilized insensitive testing techniques or utilized TV programming that simply exceeded their general knowledge of the world.

With particular reference to the conflict between the deficit model and more recent theoretical trends, recent research on attention and comprehension is reviewed in Section IV. Of central concern is the issue of cognitive continuity: How does the child process the dynamic multimodal flow of images, events, symbols, and formal features? Is attention and comprehension integrated and strategic, or is attention reactive and comprehension fragmentary?

IV. Paying Visual Attention to Television

In this article "attention" is considered equivalent to visual orientation toward the TV. This is not to say that the viewer fails to listen to the TV when not looking or that in principle the viewer does not have different "levels" of attention while looking. Rather, research on television viewing at this time has simply not developed measures to assess auditory attention or distinguish between levels of processing.

Visual orientation to the TV is typically measured in a continuous fashion in which an observer presses a button when the viewer looks at the TV and releases it when the viewer looks away. The judgment is easy to make and invariably yields high interobserver reliability. The observer's button is connected to a recording device which records the time from the beginning of the TV program of each look onset and offset. In this way looking at the TV can be related temporally to program content and formal features as well as to the behavior of other viewers (e.g., Levin & Anderson, 1976; Anderson, Lorch, Smith, Bradford, & Levin, 1981b).

A. Alternative Characterizations of Visual Attention to Television

1. VISUAL ATTENTION AS CONTINUOUS

Logically a young TV viewer could help solve the problem of cognitive continuity by looking at the TV screen continuously. Despite popular characterizations of the young child as constantly staring at the TV screen with rapt attention (e.g., Moody, 1980; Winn, 1978), quantitative analyses of preschool children's visual attention find that visual attention is intermittent (Alwitt, Anderson, Lorch, & Levin, 1980; Anderson & Levin, 1976; Anderson et al., 1981b; Becker & Wolfe, 1960; Sproull, 1973). Consider the distribution of look lengths illustrated in Fig. 1. The data are taken from 299 3- and 5-year-old children who each watched an hour of *Sesame Street* (Anderson et al., 1981b). The children looked at and away from the TV about 215 times per hour such that nearly 75% of the looks were under 6 seconds in length. In other studies (Alwitt et al., 1980; Anderson & Levin, 1976), frequencies of looks were about 150 per hour. If such laboratory observations are representative of TV viewing at home, then it is clear that the young viewer does not approach the problem of TV viewing by maintaining continuous attention.

Other characterizations consider young children's viewing as either reflexively reactive or cognitively active and strategic. The adequacy of either characterization must be judged in part against its ability to account for the details of the intermittency of visual attention to TV.

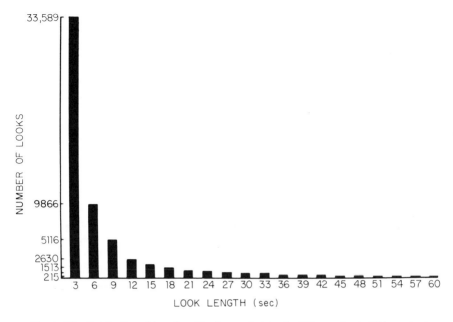

Fig. 1. The distribution of lengths of looks at television by 299 preschool children viewing *Sesame Street*.

2. Visual Attention as Reactive

If one has a cognitive deficit view of the young child, a reactive explanation of TV viewing is consistent. According to such a view, the child's visual attention is not strategically related to comprehension processes. Rather, a look at television is a reaction to stimulus change and novelty. If the pacing of formal features such as scene changes and sound effects is sufficiently rapid, then a series of orienting reflexes is elicited, and the child maintains visual attention to the TV (Singer, 1980). The intermittency of attention can be explained by variations in the frequency of these noncontent features; sometimes attention is lost when the pacing slows and attention habituates.

According to the reactive theory, the young child has not solved the problem of cognitive continuity in TV viewing (the theory is inexplicit about how it is solved). The child passively and episodically incorporates television content as a series of disconnected scenes, not recognizing the marker or content functions of formal features. In fact, the occurrence of these features, by eliciting the orienting reflex, is hypothesized by Singer (1980) as denying the child the opportunity for reflection necessary to the active reorganization and storage of information. The reactive theory has implicitly and explicitly guided most discussions of young children's TV viewing (cf. Anderson & Lorch, 1983), but until recently it has not been subject to empirical examination.

3. VISUAL ATTENTION AS ACTIVE

In contrast to the reactive theory, several investigators have proposed that young children's visual attention is active and strategic. Two versions of attentional strategies for TV viewing have been proposed. One version, suggested by Krull and Husson (1979), holds that children, when engaged in a simultaneous activity such as toy play, may "monitor" the content of the TV program by periodically glancing up at the screen. This strategy, which is not tied to events on the TV, implies that the longer it has been since the child last looked at the TV screen, the more probable it is that he or she would look back. The strategy can be rejected, however, because a plot of the probability of looking back at the TV as a function of time since the end of the last look reveals a decreasing rather than increasing function (Anderson et al., 1979).

A more complex active attentional strategy has been proposed by Anderson and his colleagues (Alwitt et al., 1980; Anderson, 1979; Anderson & Lorch, 1979, 1983; Anderson et al., 1981a,b; Lorch, Anderson & Levin, 1979). A similar theory has also been proposed by Huston and Wright (Huston & Wright, 1983; Rice et al., 1982; Wright & Huston, 1981). In our version of the theory, we have proposed that young children's visual attention to television is actively and strategically guided by their attempts to comprehend ongoing content. The children's initial TV viewing strategies are learned by about 2.5 years of age, due in part to their extensive experience with the medium. We suggest that children not only take into account many of the demands, distractions, and information provided by the viewing context, but they also learn the marker functions of formal features and other informative cues.

Briefly, the theory suggests that children initially learn to monitor the audio track of the TV program for cues that are predictive of comprehensible content. Cues that predict such content come to elicit attention, whereas cues that predict adult-oriented incomprehensible content come to inhibit attention. We also suggested that children use informative cues provided by other viewers to guide attention to comprehensible, entertaining parts of the TV program. Attention is maintained insofar as the content is comprehensible but not overly predictable. TV viewing is thus seen as a learned behavioral system involving an active transaction between the viewer, the TV, and informative aspects of the viewing environment. With experience, the child becomes a selective TV viewer able to distribute attention to informative parts of the TV program while often simultaneously engaging in toy play, social play, or other secondary activities. This theory strongly implies that the problem of cognitive continuity must be at least partially solved by the child in order for the content to be comprehensible and attention thus maintained. The child not only makes use of formal features as markers of comprehensible content, but also must have some knowledge of their use in conveying the meaning of that content.

Research bearing on the issue of reactive versus active visual attention to television focuses on at least three major issues: age trends, the relationship of visual attention to comprehension of TV, and attributes of TV which are related to attention. We argue that the results strongly support the hypothesis of visual attention as active.

B. The Development of Visual Attention to Television

There is a steady increase in the percentage of attention to the TV as a function of age during the preschool years. This increase has been observed in the laboratory and also in home observations. The trend is illustrated in Fig. 2, which plots data from several studies. The age trends shown are taken from Anderson and Levin (1976), Alwitt et al. (1980), and Anderson et al. (1981a,b) and were based on laboratory observations of 1–3 hours of children's programming. The Anderson, Nathan, Field, and Lorch (unpublished) data are based on time samples taken every 55 minutes from time-lapse videotapes, recorded in homes over 10-day periods, of 30 children ranging in age from 1 to 5 years from 18 families. The automated videotape equipment began recording the viewing area when the TV set was turned on and stopped recording when the TV set was turned off. These data were randomly selected from a larger sample of 106 families, each of which provided 10 days of time-lapse in-home recordings. Analyses from the full data set will be reported in later publications. The solid line representing these data is the best fitting linear function [$y = 9.2x + 24.8$, $r(28) = .58$, $p < .01$].

When the several studies that have reported age trends are considered together, the conclusion of a developmental trend of increased visual attention to television is compelling. A closer analysis of the age trend was provided by Anderson and Levin (1976), who reported a sharp increase in the frequency of looks at the television in the laboratory at age 2.5 years. This sharp increase was correlated with a similar sharp increase in the children's home viewing at 2.5 years of age as reported by the children's parents. Qualitatively, Anderson and Levin (1976) observed, "The younger children appeared to be far more interested in playing with toys and interacting with their mothers than watching television. Older children, on the

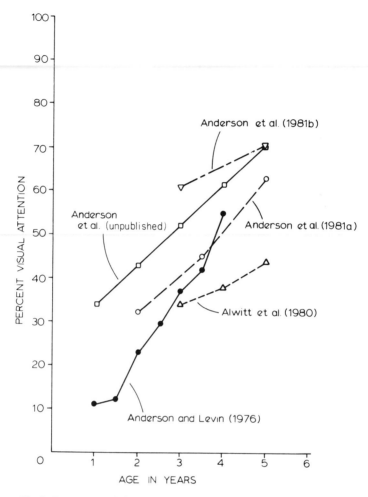

Fig. 2. Percentage of visual attention to television as a function of age.

other hand, appeared to more deliberately 'watch' television: they sat oriented toward the TV, often playing with toys, but glancing up at the screen frequently" (p. 810). Schramm, Lyle, and Parker (1961) and Carew (1980) also report that consistent TV viewing begins between 2 and 3 years of age. Schramm *et al.* (1961) reported 2.8 years as the average age of regular TV viewing as cited by parents. In a longitudinal study, Carew (1980) observed 23 children between the ages 12 to 33 months. She reported that looking at TV occupied less than 1% of a child's time at 12 months, 2% at 18 months, 3% at 24 months, and 8% at 30 months. Anderson and Lorch (1983) have suggested that this increase in viewing is not predicted by the reactive theory of TV viewing (Lesser, 1977; Singer, 1980), since the reactive attentional mechanisms posited by this theory as the basis for looking at TV are well established early in infancy (Appleton, Clifton, & Goldberg, 1975). If, on the other hand, visual attention to television reflects the child's active comprehension processes, such an increase is expected, given the considerable increase in cognitive and language skills observed during this period of development (Bruner, 1964; deVilliers & deVilliers, 1978; Piaget, 1952). As television becomes increasingly comprehensible to young children, they pay more attention.

C. The Relationship between Attention and Comprehension

A fundamental distinction between the active and reactive theories of TV viewing concerns the relationship between visual attention and comprehension. The active theory (Anderson & Lorch, 1983) holds that visual attention is in service of comprehension processes, which are in turn subject to the experience, plans, goals, and expectations of the viewer. When the theory is applied to the preschool viewer, to whom much of television is presumably difficult or impossible to comprehend, the relationship between attention and comprehension is central. The theory holds that very young viewers pay attention to content that is (to them) comprehensible. The primary causal relationship is thus from comprehension to attention. It is this principle that allows the active theory to account for the progressive increase in visual attention to television with age. According to the reactive theory, on the other hand, the TV set controls attention. Attention is elicited and maintained by a sensory bombardment of formal features which continuously provoke the orienting reaction. The causal chain of attention and comprehension is seen as straightforward; given that the TV elicits attention, the child passively absorbs content without reflection and reorganization. The relationship is from attention to comprehension. The two theories thus provide opposite assertions about the primary causal relationship between visual attention and comprehension. This relationship has been tested in a number of studies which will be briefly reviewed here. A more complete review of the tests of the two theories can be found in Anderson and Lorch (1983).

If, as asserted by the reactive theory, information acquisition by young children follows passively from visual attention, then presumably an increase in visual attention should be accompanied by an increase in information acquisition. Lorch et al. (1979) tested this prediction by presenting to 5-year-old children Sesame Street with or without toys in the viewing room. With toys, visual attention to the TV was moderate (44%), because the children played with the toys as well as looked at the TV. Visual attention without toys was nearly doubled (87%). Subsequent cued-recall measures revealed *no* advantage for the high-attention group. More detailed analyses, however, revealed a significant positive relationship between visual attention at the exact time the information necessary to answer a question was given by the TV program, and performance on that question.There was thus a seeming paradox in the results; experimentally doubling visual attention did not increase recall, but recall was greatest for those portions of the program that received greatest visual attention.

Lorch *et al.* (1979) suggested a resolution to the paradox, a resolution which provided the basis for an active theory of TV viewing: young children pay attention to content that is to them comprehensible. Furthermore, Lorch *et al.* (1979) proposed that "by age 5, children have developed a sophisticated strategy of TV viewing which allows them to effectively divide their visual attention between the television and other activities, such as toy play . . . the 5-year olds distributed their attention in a manner apparently optimally efficient given their level of understanding" (p. 726).

In two subsequent studies the relationship between comprehensibility of content and visual attention was explored further. Seeking an a priori measure of comprehensibility, Anderson *et al.* (1981a, Study 1) rated the dialogue of 15 *Sesame Street* programs as either having immediate or nonimmediate referents. Dialogue with an immediate referent concerned a topic that was visually or auditorily present. An example of immediate dialogue is an offscreen voice describing a puppet whose arms are too short to reach a nectarine (the puppet is simultaneously shown trying to reach the nectarine). An example of a nonimmediate dialogue is a discussion of a shopping trip which has occurred earlier.

It was assumed that immediate dialogue should be somewhat more comprehensible to young children than nonimmediate dialogue (cf. Brown, 1976; deVilliers & deVilliers, 1978). The prediction, therefore, was that young children should look at the TV more during immediate dialogue. Analysis of visual attention of 3 year olds and 5 year olds verified the prediction; both ages paid greater attention during immediate than nonimmediate dialogue.

In a further study, Anderson *et al.* (1981a, Study 2) experimentally reduced comprehensibility while holding the structures of formal features constant. They reduced comprehensibility (1) by randomly rearranging scenes within *Sesame Street* segments, (2) by reversing each utterance of the dialogue such that it was backwards but occupied the same video frames (thus preserving intonation, voice quality, and approximate lip synchronization), or (3) by using a professionally dubbed foreign language (Greek). With each of these techniques, there was no disturbance of any of the formal features such as movement, cuts, pans, zooms, and sound effects which are commonly cited as the reactive basis for young children's attention to TV. In comparison to normal versions of the same segments, Anderson *et al.* (1981a) reported that visual attention of 2, 3.5, and 5 year olds were reduced to the distorted segments. The reduction was especially great for the dialogue distortions, reflecting the greater disruption of comprehensibility created by these distortions, as independently rated by college students.

This series of studies demonstrates that the comprehensibility of TV content is a major determinant of a young child's visual attention to television. But how does the young child *know* when the content is comprehensible?

D. Cues to Comprehensibility

Lorch *et al.* (1979) provided a hypothesis of how young children guide their visual attention to comprehensible portions of a TV program. They suggested that "children monitor the sound track primarily at a superficial level of detecting the presence of auditory attributes which indicate informative content or which indicate changes in content. The children may, however, process the auditory information sufficiently to respond to certain signal words (e.g., 'cookie,' 'Big Bird'). These auditory attributes and signal words provide cues of informative and comprehensible program content to the children and thus elicit full attention. Insofar as the program content is informative and comprehensible, we suggest that visual attention is maintained until the content becomes either incomprehensible, redundant, or not otherwise visually and auditorily attractive (e.g., two adult men talking abstractly about a future event), at which time the children return to their alternative activity" (p. 726). According to this hypothesis, the children approach the problem of cognitive continuity by learning that certain auditory cues of the medium predict those portions of TV programs that are potentially understandable and to which, therefore, there is some point in paying attention. Use of such a strategy allows the child to make double use of TV viewing time by engaging in a secondary activity during periods in which the TV program is, from the child's point of view, uninformative.

Alwitt *et al.* (1980), Anderson and Levin (1976), and Calvert, Huston, Watkins, and Wright (1982) report research that may identify some of the auditory cues used to direct visual attention. By relating the occurrence of children's visual attention to the occurrence of various attributes of children's TV programs, they have consistently found, for example, depressed visual attention in the presence of adult male voices and enhanced attention in the presence of children's voices. Alwitt *et al.* (1980), furthermore, were able to show that these effects occurred primarily by eliciting or inhibiting visual attention given that the child was *not* looking at the TV at the time the attribute occurred. In their heterogeneous sample of children's programs, moreover, they demonstrated that enhanced attention to visual attributes such as puppets was due to the elicitation of attention by auditory attributes. In the case of puppets, for example, the auditory attribute was "peculiar voices" (defined as voices the child was unlikely to hear except as part of a mass medium experience). Alwitt *et al.* (1980) and Anderson and Lorch (1983) argued that the best explanation of these findings is that the children have learned that voice characteristics and other auditory cues have value in predicting comprehensible, informative, and entertaining content. Peculiar voices and children's voices, for example, virtually never occur on television except when the content is oriented toward children and thus is more likely to be comprehensible than adult-oriented content. Men's voices, on the other hand, are ubiquitous on television and are far more likely to be predictive of relatively abstract, adult-oriented content. If a child has learned these relationships over many hours of exposure to television, he or she can use them as cues to comprehensible content without having to pay continuous full attention.

Evidence that the cues are learned is provided by inspection of attribute effects as a function of age. Inspection of the age interactions of attributes (see Levin & Anderson, 1976) reveals that very few attributes have significant relationships to attention until about age 2.5 years, the age at which consistent TV viewing begins. If the attributes were functioning by eliciting primitive attentional mechanisms, they should be showing significant relationships to attention at earlier ages.

Using informative attributes as a basis for visual attention may aid children in comprehension. Calvert *et al.* (1982) report correlational data indicating that those children who attentionally differentiate attributes to the greatest extent also show the greatest comprehension.

Young children use more than television attributes to guide their attention to and from the TV; they also use as cues the behaviors of other viewers in the same room. We demonstrated this by presenting *Sesame Street* to 3- and 5-year-old children in groups of one, two, or three viewers (Anderson *et al.*, 1981b). The viewing context included a slide distractor which presented a new slide every 8 seconds. Observers continuously recorded the children's visual attention to the TV and the slide distractor. They also recorded active overt involvement with the TV program such as talking about the show, dancing to the music, and pointing at the screen. Since the data were synchronized to the beginning of the TV program, we were able to compare the times of onset and offset of attention and involvement both within and between viewing groups. We found that although the TV program had a general synchronizing effect on the children's behavior (e.g., they tended to look at and away from the TV at the same points in the program), the children were very much influenced by each others' behavior. When one child looked at or away from the TV or the slide distractor, or demonstrated overt involvement with the TV program, the other coviewers tended to do the same thing at the same time. This effect occurred above and beyond the common organizing influence of the TV program itself. In interpreting this finding, we suggested that the children use each others' viewing behavior to provide cues to the likely presence of comprehensible and entertaining content. Rather than the TV viewing dominating and eliminating social interaction, we proposed that "a reciprocal modulation occurs such that viewing the TV program is controlled in part by the ongoing social interaction and the social interaction is controlled in part by the ongoing TV program" (p. 452). In terms of the problem of cognitive continuity in TV viewing, rather than other children being distracting, the young TV viewer *uses* their viewing behavior to provide further direction to his or her own behavior.

E. A Summary and a Paradox

The research strongly supports the notion that young children learn to watch TV in an active and strategic manner and that their visual attention reflects active attempts at comprehension. There are a few bits of evidence that salient formal features can demand attention (Bryant, Zillman, & Brown, 1983; Krull, 1983), but the role they play appears to be small (Watt & Welch, 1983). If indeed young children's attention is active and strategically guided by comprehension processes, then the focus of inquiry necessarily shifts to comprehension. But here a further paradox is raised. The published literature seems to indicate that preschool children's comprehension of television is at best fragmentary and incomplete. At the basic level of understanding the continuity of settings, characters, and actions as conveyed by formal cinematic techniques, the young child's comprehension would appear to be inadequate.

The paradox is this: If young children's visual attention is effectively guided by comprehension strategies, then how can these strategies be so ineffective that no continuity of cognition obtains across scenes? In the program *Dukes of Hazzard* there is a change of scene or visual perspective every 5 seconds on the average, and yet, we recently found that 40% of 334 5 year olds in one of our studies watched *Dukes of Hazzard* in a 10-day period, as noted in family TV diaries. If the children truly do not comprehend the relationship between shots, their understanding of this popular program must be fragmented in the extreme, and watching it, inexplicable. A close examination of young children's comprehension of content as conveyed by editing and other cinematic techniques is thus a necessity.

V. Comprehension of Cinematic Montage

A. The Nature of Montage

Montage is defined as the "succession of images in a motion picture to illustrate the association of ideas" (Woolf, 1976). It is accomplished by film and tape editing and by other postproduction techniques which produce cuts, dissolves, fades, compressions, and a large number of other effects, as well as by techniques used during production such as camera switching, trucks, dollies, pans, and zooms. It is through these formal features (plus sound dubbing and editing) that the director accomplishes much of the sequencing, pace, and visual interest of a production. Film theorists, who often consider montage to be the essence of film and television, have long been interested in this "syntax," the "real and only code of the film" (Kjørup, 1977). Only recently, however, has there been interest in the psychological demands placed on the viewer by the use of different variables of montage (Salomon, 1979).

To illustrate the analogy of cinematic code to language syntax, consider an example taken from Whitaker (1970), which he calls "predispositional" montage. If a shot of a small cottage in the woods dissolves to a scene of a man sitting in his chair reading a book, viewers are likely to infer that the man is sitting inside the cottage. If, however, the shots are reversed, so that the man is seen reading and the camera dissolves to the cottage, viewers are more likely to infer that the man is reading about the cottage. The analogy to syntax is the fundamental change in meaning of the sequence when the order of the components is changed. It is important to realize that such techniques as dissolves, cuts, zooms, and pans do not necessarily convey meaning by themselves. Rather, the meaning is derived from the context in which the techniques are used.

Complementary to their functions of bridging scenes and advancing the flow of action, the formal features of montage have been shown to serve as "segmentation boundaries." Carroll and Bever (1976) reported that viewers use formal features to help parse film sequences. Cuts that coincided with true event boundaries furthered segmentation, but cuts that did not indicate an event change were not perceived as such. The point is that editing techniques are most often used in the service of advancing the plot and not as "events" by themselves [see Metz (1974) and Bellman and Jules-Rossette (1977) for a discussion of this issue]. It is our experience, in fact, that adults viewing heavily edited action sequences (as from *Dukes of Hazzard*) are usually unaware of the editing. This suggests that, perhaps due to many years of exposure to film and television, adults perceive film with such well-developed expectations that their temporal integration of scenes is automatic. This idea is reinforced by Baggett (1979) who demonstrated that adults' representations of a narrative are not necessarily dependent on the input medium. She demonstrated that the recall protocols based on structurally equivalent movie and text stories were very similar, even though the stories differed in details of content. It seems likely that, analogous to text, certain cues in audiovisual narratives such as the length, form, and content of shots assist the viewer in "parsing" the story. To the experienced adults, the information has the same meaning and structure regardless of whether it was in text or film form.

B. Is Comprehension of Montage Learned?

While considerable pedagogical effort is expended in teaching children to read, little or no effort is expended in teaching children to watch television. We have in this article, nevertheless, marshalled evidence and theory that children learn how to distribute their visual attention throughout a TV program, and that they use some formal features as attentional guides. Must they also learn to "read" the cinematic codes of television in order to comprehend the flow of depicted events?

The earliest evidence that such comprehension may not be automatic comes from anecdotal reports by anthropologists about "film illiteracy." For example, Forsdale and Forsdale (1966) cite an anecdote in which cinema-naive Africans, in viewing a film showing persons going off the edge of the screen, wanted to know how and why they had disappeared. They also give an example of an American filmmaker's discovery that an Iranian audience did not follow the connection between a close-up and a long-shot. In order to make it clear that a large isolated foot or eye belonged to the animal shown a moment before, the camera had to present the complete transition in motion. These anecdotes also illustrate the range of conceptions subsumed under the label of "film literacy." Among others, they include the ability to recognize depicted objects, to relate parts of objects to the whole, to distinguish between film and reality, and to deal with editing techniques (Forsdale and Forsdale, 1966).

Film theorists have claimed that increasing film literacy among Westerners has led to increased pacing of films each decade. Harrington (1973) reports that the average number of shots per hour has risen steadily since the 1940s and 1950s, and that the length of fades has shortened.

As a result of these examples, there is a common belief that film literacy is gradually acquired.[1] This is a particularly common assumption in the research and theoretical literature on children's comprehension of TV. In

---

[1]We are using the terms "montage" and "film literacy" in a more limited sense than they are typically used by film theorists. We are focusing on the comprehension of the event sequences portrayed by film and television, apart from the viewers' evaluations of artistic merit and aesthetic value of the program.

Section III, we reviewed research on preschool children's comprehension of TV that indicates their representations may often be fragmentary and incomplete. From such evidence it is often claimed that preschoolers are unable to cope with the editing techniques used on TV. For example, Baron (1980) claims that "eight appears to be the average age when understanding concepts related to TV technique appear. Such techniques as zoom and editing are not well understood by younger children." Citing evidence that only school-age children attempt to interrelate scenes from a TV program, Salomon (1979) claims that "for reasons of cognitive development, the preschooler evidently aims at extracting that kind of information from a TV program which does not require him mentally to transform or imitate novel coding elements. This means that the preschooler has a smaller chance of being affected by novel coding elements, as he ignores them altogether or transforms them mentally by applying skills that are already mastered but often inappropriate" (p. 171).

An alternative reason for the poor comprehension performance displayed by preschoolers in television research may be the use of testing procedures inappropriate for this age group. Particularly problematic is reliance on verbal recall, given the lack of expository skills in preschoolers (Brown, 1976). Many recent studies attempt to deal with this problem by using recognition items (Zuckerman, Ziegler, & Stevenson, 1978; Ward, Wackman, & Wartella, 1977), yes–no responses (Levin et al., 1983), or multiple-choice items (Calvert et al., 1982). Each of these techniques has advantages, particularly for comparison with the scores of older children and adults. But none is designed well enough to reveal the sequential and inferential quality of the young child's representation of TV content. These methods have also tended to give us negative information on the abilities of preschoolers; we know what they cannot do, not what they do. New methodologies which are informed by an understanding of the behavioral repertoire of the preschooler are needed to assess the competencies as well as deficiencies in their representation of TV content.

In addition to issues of task design, research on the effects of editing techniques on comprehension has been hampered in the past by the necessity of using already existing program material in which the use of editing techniques is confounded with familiarity of contextual variables such as setting and characters and with the complexity of the narrative structure of the program. Rice (1979) rated the use of formal features and linguistic features in six popular children's shows and found that the distribution of formal features was related to patterns of linguistic features within the show. For example, the shows with a moderate amount of verbal complexity also demonstrated a moderate use of formal features. Furthermore, TV program genres such as children's programs are characterized by particular constellations of formal features (Huston, Wright, Wartella, Rice, Watkins, Campbell, & Potts, 1981). Due to the nature of the medium, then, it has been impossible to directly assess the effects editing techniques have on comprehension independently of the familiarity of context and complexity of structure.

C. A New Procedure for Testing Young Children's Comprehension of Montage

We have developed a methodology that involves the preparation of original program material ideally suited for testing young children's recall. We shoot stop-animation films of Fisher–Price dolls enacting scenes in various sets such as a house, a school, or a street. The films are transferred to videotape, the tape is edited, and dialogue and sound effects are added. After showing the segments on a color monitor, we ask children to reconstruct the narrative "as if you were making the same TV show" with the actual set and dolls. Children express delight at the appearance of the same set after each viewing and seem to enjoy the task. The entire session is videotaped for later coding by two observers.

D. Study 1: An Experimental Manipulation of Montage

In our first experiment with this method (Smith, 1981), we used three sets to create three different scripts. Each script was filmed in three different editing conditions. In the first condition, the action unfolded in front of a stationary camera. No special techniques were used and no events in the script were edited out. In the second condition, the camera panned and zoomed in order to highlight and follow the action in the story. In the third condition, pans and zooms were combined with cuts, such that an event was eliminated by cutting from its previous to succeeding action or by cutting away to a different event. The design thus involved three stories each conveyed by three types of production technique.

Our analysis involved dividing the story into basic units of action and dialogue. Each story in our first study consisted of eight or nine of these units. After viewing the stories, children were given the chance to reconstruct the entire narrative without prompts first, and some did. After the first attempt, the experimenter systematically prompted the child to reproduce those units not reconstructed by reproducing for the child the unit previous to each unit the child missed. We tested 35 3 year olds and 36 5 year olds (ages are within 1 month of the child's birthday). Each child saw each of the three stories in one of the three editing conditions. Order of presentation was randomized.

We found no effect of the use of simple cinematic techniques on reconstruction performance as compared to the unedited, still camera conditions. The montage neither helped nor hindered the children's reconstruction of the event sequences at either age. This was our first evidence that preschoolers engage in active integration of information from edited sequences on television.

A major strength of this method is the opportunity it affords of observing the preschool child's sequential representation of the story. Figure 3 depicts the sequential reconstruction performance for one of the stories. Since an analysis of variance indicated no effect of editing, we combined the data across editing conditions. The graph is read from left to right. Arrows indicate transitions from one unit to another (the size of the arrows are proportional to the percentage of subjects who make the transition) and the size of the unit indicates the percentage of subjects reproducing the unit.

Analyses revealed an effect of age such that 5 year olds, as expected, reproduced more story units than 3 year olds. From Fig. 3, it is clear that children at both ages generally start reconstruction at the beginning of the story. There were very few order inversions, and of a total of 170 reconstruction attempts, there was not a single intrusion of elaboration. Deletion of units was common among 3 year olds, and in particular, the auditory units were more likely to be skipped than visual units. For children at both ages, there was a strong tendency to end their reconstruction at the major end state of the character (there was frequent skipping of the tag-ending phrases such as "Gee, this is fun"). Premature ending was more common among 3 year olds. A substantial proportion of 3 year olds gave the gist of the story, and the 5 year olds generally demonstrated connected, accurate reconstructions. Finally, we found no relationship between total score and the amount of the children's home TV viewing as estimated by their parents.

In summary, the results of our first study indicated that, relative to the unedited sequences, the use of editing techniques such as cuts, zooms, and pans did not disrupt the construction of the televised event sequence for preschoolers. The children demonstrated connected, accurate representations of the stories. There was no evidence that the varying perceptual characteristics of the three montage conditions had any effect on their ability to make sense of what they had seen. It must be kept in mind, however, that these stories were much shorter than those used in most studies of children's comprehension of television and that the editing manipulations were mild. In our second study with this method, we attempted to extend our research to somewhat longer sequences and to examine the effects of more challenging editing manipulations involving time, space, ellipsis (deleted actions), and character perspective.

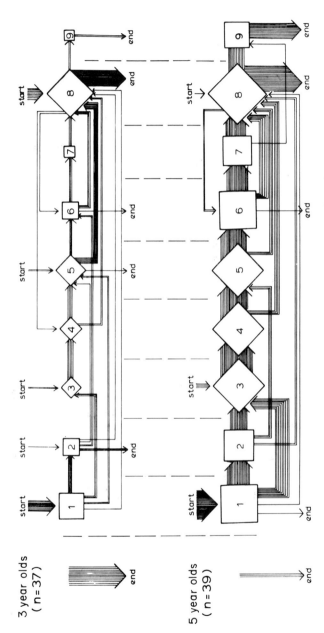

Fig. 3. The reproduction of units of a short television segment, "House," in sequence by children aged 3 and 5 years. Audio units are represented by squares, visual units by diamonds. The size of each is proportional to the number of children reproducing that unit. Each line in the arrows represents a subject's transition from reproducing one unit to another. The units are (1) "Mother may I go out and play with Susie?" (2) "Yes, you may." (3) Billy walks to the steps. (4) Billy walks down the steps. (5) Billy walks to the swings. (6) "Hi Susie, want to go on the other swing?" (7) "O.K." (8) Both get on the other swing. (9) "Gee, this is fun."

E. Study 2: Representation of Montage Conveying Concepts of Time, Space, Ellipsis, and Character Perspective

The goal of our second study (Smith *et al.*, 1983) was to discover the point at which young children's comprehension of event sequences conveyed through montage begins to break down. In the first study we demonstrated that their poor performance in comprehension research could not be attributed to the effects of camera techniques and editing, per se. Keeping in mind that these techniques did not convey meaning by themselves, we looked to the context in which they were embedded. For example, in order to comprehend a "predispositional montage" sequence, an inference is required of the viewer, and the type of inference varies with the order of the shots. In Whitaker's example cited earlier, the dissolve from the shot of the cottage to the man reading requires a spatiotemporal inference to understand that the man is inside the house. However, reversing the sequence from the shot of the man reading to the shot of the cottage requires an inference of psychological perspective—that is, the viewer must realize that the man is visualizing the content of the book. We reasoned that comprehension difficulty may vary in child viewers with the type of inference required by the montage.

We filmed 13 new stories, each incorporating camera techniques that conveyed either very simple or somewhat more complex changes in space, time, event sequence, or psychological perspective. We showed these films on a color video monitor to 38 4 year olds and 40 7 year olds and asked them to reconstruct the story.

We found that the 4 year olds performed far better than either developmental theory or the research literature would predict. In every segment, a substantial proportion of children indicated comprehension of the target inference, and in some segments, which seemed to us very difficult on an a priori basis, nearly all of the 4 year olds performed correctly. Of course, the 7 year olds performed at very high levels on almost all of the segments.

We categorized the segments into four groups based on the type of "target" inference required to get the gist of the story. In order to give a more detailed picture of how children performed on these segments, we describe below one segment from each category along with the reconstruction data.

1. SPACE

Almost all video action takes place in some kind of space shown directly, revealed by a succession of shots or movements of the camera, or simply implied by showing a part of the space. Within the cinematic space, objects and characters have locations relative to the space as a whole and also relative to each other. It is apparent, therefore, that spatial inferences from montage are a central aspect of film and TV comprehension.

Five segments were designed to test the children's ability to represent the cinematic space and place the depicted objects and characters correctly within that space. One such segment was entitled "Susie Takes a Nap." In this story, an establishment shot of two buildings (an "establishment shot" identifies the location of subsequent action) is followed by a zoom to Susie looking out one of the four windows. There is a cut to an interior shot of Susie, from behind, looking out the window. After a brief monologue, Susie gets into her bed.

The children were asked to reconstruct this sequence, placing Suise in the correct room and reenacting the story. We found that 83% of the 4 year olds and 93% of the 7 year olds placed the doll in the correct room without hesitation, thus showing their understanding of the space revealed by the exterior establishment shot, zoom, and cut to interior scene. The remaining children all placed the doll in the wrong room, indicating their failure to integrate these shots.

In general, across all segments in our study, we found that while the children only sometimes replicated the *exact* placement of characters and objects, they were generally quite good at placing them relative to each other, to the setting as a whole and to the camera.

2. Time

In three segments, we tested the children's ability to infer simultaneity of action or passage of time as revealed by camera cuts and fades. In "Tired Judy," we see an establishment shot of a hospital and a zoom to the second floor bedroom, where Judy is having a short conversation with her doctor. He leaves and she gets into her bed. The window above her bed is dark. The scene fades to black and slowly fades up again, revealing light coming through the window. Judy gets out of bed and walks over to a table, saying that she will wait for the nurse to bring her something to eat. After reenacting the story, the children are asked what meal (breakfast, lunch, or dinner) Judy will be eating and how it is that they know this. Fifty-six percent of the 4 year olds responded "breakfast," which is better than chance ($p < .05$), although few were able to provide a verbal explanation for why they responded correctly. Seventy-seven percent of the 7 year olds gave the correct answer and most gave an appropriate explanation. In this segment, then, at least some young children were able to understand the use of a formal feature to indicate the passage of time. In the other two segments, the majority of the 4 year olds correctly understood sequences of shots conveying simultaneity of action (i.e., two characters or two vehicles approaching each other.) They also demonstrated the likely outcomes of the simultaneous actions (the characters meeting or the vehicles colliding).

3. ELLIPSIS

Previous research has indicated that young children are unlikely to make plot-relevant inferences to connect two major sections of a story even when they remember the content of the component scenes. At the more local level of sequences of shots within such story units, inferences are constantly demanded by sequences of cuts, zooms, and pans to both reveal and imply action. We constructed three segments to test children's ability to make inferences about an event sequence when part of that sequence was deleted (called, in film theory, *ellipsis*).

One of these segments was entitled "Helping Doctor Bill." The story begins with Joe standing next to a stretcher and an ambulance and telling us that he needs to deliver the stretcher to Dr. Bill. The camera cuts to Dr. Bill standing outside of the hospital set and saying that he needs the stretcher. We then see a shot of Joe loading the stretcher into the ambulance. The last shot shows Dr. Bill standing next to the stretcher and then pushing it into the hospital. Deleted, of course, are explicit shots showing Joe getting into the ambulance, driving to the hospital, unloading the stretcher, and driving away. Figure 4 illustrates the children's performance. When reconstructing this story, 86% of the 4 year olds and 91% of the 7 year olds loaded the stretcher into the ambulance, put Joe in the driver's seat, drove the ambulance over to the hospital set, and unloaded it in front of Dr. Bill. They also drove the ambulance away at the end, since it was not in the last shot.

The vast majority of children correctly filled in the essential missing actions implied by the sequence of shots (and by the dialogue) in this story to obtain a coherent representation of the story. The results from the other segments in this category confirmed that young children readily make inferences required from sequences of shots which only imply an action or a series of actions.

4. CHARACTER PERSPECTIVE

A fairly common cinematic technique is to show what a particular character is seeing or thinking. For example, in the *Dukes of Hazzard* show that we analyzed, one shot portrayed a car mirror which was reflecting the image of the sheriff's patrol car as it was pursuing the boys. From the preceding shot, which shows one of the boys looking out the window as he is driving, we are to infer that we are looking through his eyes and seeing the sheriff in the car mirror. Given the egocentrism of young viewers hypothesized by Piagetian theory, we might expect that such an inference would be very difficult for the child viewer.

We produced a segment, "Things To Do," which portrayed a doll considering several alternative activities. The segment was filmed as if the al-

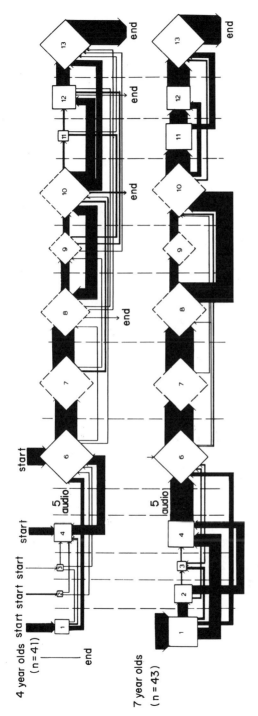

Fig. 4. "Helping Doctor Bill." The symbols represent visual and auditory units in the same manner as Fig. 3, except that the dashed diamonds represent inferred visual units. The units are (1) "I guess I'd better take this stretcher to Dr. Bill." (2) "Boy, I sure hope Joe brings that stretcher today." (3) "I guess it's time to go now." (4) "Let's see if I can get this into the back of the truck." (5) "Here we go." (6) Joe puts the stretcher into the back of the truck. (7) Joe gets into the truck. (8) Joe drives to Dr. Bill. (9) Joe gets out of the truck. (10) Joe takes the stretcher to Dr. Bill or Dr. Bill gets it from Joe. (11) "Boy, I sure am glad Joe brought that stretcher back. We sure do need it." (12) "I guess I'd better take it inside." (13) Dr. Bill pushes the stretcher into the hospital.

ternatives were seen through the doll's eyes. This was done by panning over a toy TV, an easel, an arts and crafts table, and a magazine rack. A voice-over simultaneously represented a child considering each of these activities, as they appeared on camera, as "things to do." The doll was never actually presented on screen. After viewing, the children were handed a doll and asked "What did Susie do in this show?" Fifty-eight percent of the 4 year olds and 98% of the 7 year olds correctly walked the doll past each of the items, in the correct order, *and* correctly repeated the voice-over. Even more impressive, the doll was always held so as to face the object the way the camera had portrayed the doll's perspective. The children correctly interpreted the segment as if they had seen it through the doll's eyes.

Similar results were obtained in a longer and considerably more complex segment. We conclude from this evidence that many young children are able to take the perspective of a TV character when the camera reveals that perspective.

There were many interesting subsidiary findings from this study, which we are currently exploring in a follow-up study. But our primary conclusion based on this research is that, contrary to speculation and the findings of research using less sensitive testing procedures, children as young as 4 years have a fundamental understanding of cinematic technique and that mastery of such comprehension is nearly complete by age 7.

F. Discussion of Montage Results

Based on the prior literature, we expected poor comprehension performance on these montage sequences which required inferences of space, time, implied action, and character perspective. Instead, in Study 1, we found that cinematic formal features neither enhanced nor diminished reconstruction performance. In Study 2, using a range of cinematic techniques requiring a variety of inferences, we found that 4 year olds were correct on an average of 58% of the key inferences and 7 year olds were correct on 84%. These figures should be considered in comparison to the children's figures for reconstructing any given simple action they had just seen that required no inferences—82 and 96%, respectively. If we take these latter figures as providing a baseline for performance on the task exclusive of cinematic techniques, then the children's performance is impressive; adjusting for these baseline limitations, the 4 year olds performed at 70% of their visual baseline reproductions and the 7 year olds at 88% of their baseline. For both ages, inferences concerning time were the most difficult (an average of 37 and 77% correct, respectively) whereas inferences concerning deleted actions were the easiest (78 and 98%, respectively). Inferences of space (59 and 88%, respectively) and of character perspective (59 and 65%, respectively) were intermediate in difficulty.

We must reconcile these findings of good comprehension of montage with the many reports of poor comprehension of film and television by young children. It is our guess that part of the difference lies in the tasks used to test the children's comprehension. Studies by Baron (1980), Flapan (1965), Friedlander et al. (1974), Noble (1975), and Salomon (1976), for example, used testing methods heavily dependent on the children's language abilities which are now generally believed to underestimate children's cognitive representations. The reproduction task appears to be particularly well suited to young children and is beginning to be used by other researchers (Jaglom & Gardner, 1981; Sturm & Jorg, 1981).

Another significant difference from other studies is in the stimulus material we used. Our segments are short (30–90 seconds) and minimally challenge or depart from the child's world knowledge. The segments, furthermore, are constructed so that inferences from montage are readily tested. The stimulus programs used in other studies, while more like broadcast television, are more complex with potentially large confounds between world knowledge required to interpret actions and the complexity of formal features used to convey those actions (cf. Rice, 1979). For example, Leifer et al. (1971) used a nonverbal picture sequencing task which is a potentially sensitive measure for preschoolers, but their stimulus program was a 20-minute "adaptation of a well-known fairy tale." The 4 year olds in their study performed very poorly at sequencing pictures of central incidents from the film, but the complexity of the film (confounding narrative complexity, formal features, comprehensibility of dialogue, for example) does not allow conclusions as to why performance was so poor.

If our findings and those of Leifer et al. (1971) are not in fact conflicting, then preschoolers' comprehension of montage at a local level of about a minute's duration can be quite good, but not over relatively lengthy TV programs of the variety ordinarily broadcast. Collins (1983) argues that the comprehension problems are not specifically due to excessive burdens on the young children's memory, but rather are due to their failure to integrate information across numerous scenes. Thus, an early scene indicating a character's innocence may not be integrated with later scenes indicating a character's duplicity.

This point can be expanded with respect to the issue of montage. It was previously stated that our analysis of *Dukes of Hazzard* revealed 781 visual formal features in a 47-minute production. Of these, 348 features were switches back and forth between characters talking to each other, simple reaction shots, shots following a continuous action, or other simple perspective shifts. Our subjects were very good at the simple spatial and action representations implied by these shots. Of the remaining, however, 24 involved character perspective, 163 represented simultaneous actions in two or more different locations, 76 involved implied actions, and 4 implied passage of time (the remainder are not easily classifiable). As an exercise, if we apply our percentages of correct inferences from Study 2 for these types of shots, we would predict that 4 year olds would not comprehend the meaning conveyed through 132 instances of formal features and 7 year olds would not understand 48. If so, 4 year olds would fail to comprehend about 2.7 cinematic transitions a minute, cumulatively more than enough to account for their poor comprehension of an entire program. This admittedly oversimplified calculation does not even take into account possible failures to understand dialogue and action due to lack of vocabulary and world knowledge. Our findings of good comprehension of montage at a very local level and other researchers' findings of poor comprehension of full-length programs are not, therefore, inconsistent.

G. How Is Comprehension of Montage Acquired?

Part of the problem of cognitive continuity in TV viewing is solved at an early age. Preschoolers clearly are capable of making a variety of local inferences demanded of them by montage. There is, nevertheless, substantial development of the ability to integrate information in longer and more complex cinematic narratives. In the findings of Collins et al. (1978), second-grade boys' comprehension of an adult TV detective show was not affected if the major scenes (one to several minutes in length) were randomly rearranged. Children a few years older show much greater temporal integration of televised programming and begin to approach adult levels of comprehension.

Some initial suggestions are here offered with regard to how very early temporal integration of television is accomplished. Through the first few years of life (up to about age 2.5 years), children do not watch television except very sporadically (as we have documented earlier). During this period, however, they develop knowledge about numerous routine event sequences from their daily experiences (Nelson & Gruendel, 1981).

Consider an event sequence as mundane as riding in an automobile, stopping at a house, getting out, walking up to the house, entering, and then being inside the house. Presumably most toddlers (in the United States, at least) have numerous experiences of this sort, both directly and perhaps vicariously (seeing other people arrive in autos, getting out, approaching the child's dwelling, and entering). Extending the experience, the child may be transported in a variety of vehicles, arriving at various possible buildings (stores, doctors' offices, etc.) and entering them. From these repeated experiences the child develops an expectation about the canonical order of events: a person is transported by a vehicle; the vehicle stops at a building; the person exits the vehicle; the person approaches the building; the person enters the building. Importantly, the representation of the event sequence is somewhat general; the event scheme can be instantiated with a large number of possible persons, vehicles, and buildings playing roles in the event sequence. The concept is very similar to Schank and Abelson's (1977) notion of "scripts," which are generalized event sequences with "slots" to be filled by particular instances (see also Collins, 1981).

Following the comprehensibility rule (the child attends to that which is understandable), the child begins to recognize numerous event sequences on television and by 2.5 years develops expectations about TV viewing itself as something to do (Anderson and Levin, 1976; Anderson and Lorch, 1983; Jaglom and Gardner, 1981). Early correct interpretation of montage occurs because the child has appropriate expectations of the depicted event sequence. Consider the following routine example: an automobile stops in front of a house; a passenger gets out and approaches the house; the scene changes to an interior shot of a door; the door opens, and the person earlier seen exiting the auto enters through the door. The challenge of relating the outdoor and indoor scenes is easily accomplished by the child because the highly familiar and generalized event scheme provides clear expectations concerning the temporal order of events and the outcome. In this way, the child masters basic montage and more and more of television becomes comprehensible. If, however, the child does not have an event scheme to apply to a particular transition, the transition may not be comprehended. Consider the earlier example of a shot of a man reading a book followed by a dissolve to a shot of a cottage. A young child who did not understand the experience of reading might well not be able to interpret the sequence.

The child's application of stereotyped expectations to understanding TV probably continues through the early school-age years, gradually becoming highly flexible and capable of dealing with a variety of exceptional situations. Collins and Wellman (cited by Collins, 1983) found that second graders were far less likely than fifth graders to report deviations from event stereotypes in their recall of an adult TV show. Collins has also found that younger school-age children's recall and evaluation is related to their personal familiarity with the context depicted by the TV program (Newcomb and Collins, 1979). Although Collins has not specifically studied montage, it should be clear in the present context that his findings have strong implications for its comprehension throughout later childhood.

We have suggested that children's acquisition of expectations concerning event sequences underlies their initial comprehension of montage. Through extensive experiences with film and television, we follow Salomon (1979) in suggesting that comprehension of montage becomes automatic and demands little mental effort. Older children and adults are thus able to devote more cognitive resources to the temporal integration of the narrative as a whole. The experienced viewer may no longer be required to decode the montage in terms of known event sequences, but instead be able to construct representations of new event sequences based in part on his or her knowledge of the cinematic conventions of montage.

There is, embedded in this argument, a contradiction. The comprehensibility principle was invoked to account for very young children's attention to television and the application of known event sequences in interpreting montage. But if a young child only pays attention to event sequences that are understood, how are new event sequences learned? A partial answer to this question may be provided by a phenomenon of television viewing called "attentional inertia."

VI. Attentional Inertia in Television Viewing

The longer a viewer continuously maintains visual attention to television, the longer he or she will continue to maintain attention (Anderson et al., 1979). This phenomenon, called attentional intertia, is illustrated in Fig. 5. There is a negatively accelerated, monotonic increase in the expected time a look will remain in progress, as a function of the time it has already been in progress. The attentional inertia function characterizes the data of adult as well as child viewers, and is apparent in individual as well as group data (Anderson et al., 1979; Anderson & Lorch, 1983).

Anderson and Lorch (1983) suggest that the phenomenon is not a strategic aspect of attention to television. Rather, we suggest attentional inertia may play a role analogous to attentional habituation, but to the opposite effect: "Since habituation is the attentional response to a repetitive, meaningless, static stimulus, then attentional inertia may be the attentional response to a somewhat unpredictable, meaningful, dynamic stimulus. Attentional inertia, we believe, provides the means by which attention is maintained to a source of information even across breaks in the continuity of that information. . . . Attentional inertia allows the child to keep processing a stimulus even when it is currently not understandable. Attentional inertia thus sometimes produces a dynamic tension with program comprehensibility: although in general the young child stops paying attention when the program becomes incomprehensible, attentional inertia serves to maintain attention further than it might otherwise go. As such, attentional inertia . . . may be part of the means by which [the child] . . . ventures into

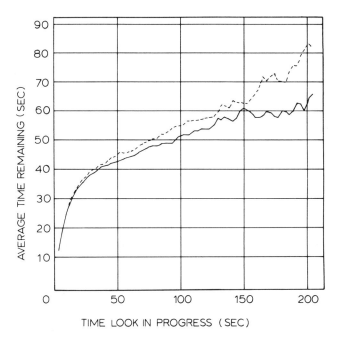

Fig. 5. The average time looks at the TV remain in progress as a function of time they have already been in progress. ------, 5 year olds; ———, 3 year olds.

unknown cognitive territory, occasionally leading to new cognitive discoveries.''

It is important to emphasize that attentional inertia appears to occur with respect to the *source* of the information and not directly with respect to the information itself. That is, inertia may be aroused in the young child by the processing of comprehensible information, but the arousal is not specific to the thematic content of that information. Support for this contention comes from an analysis reported by Anderson and Lorch (1983) in which they considered looks at the TV that were in progress at the time major content boundaries occurred. They reasoned that if attentional inertia is related to the source of the message and not the message itself, then there should be a positive relationship between the time a look has been in progress prior to a content boundary and the time that look remains in progress after the content boundary. If, on the other hand, attentional inertia reflects an increased involvement with the content, there should be no relationship between look length before and after content boundaries. The results of the analysis supported the former hypothesis; the longer a look was in progress prior to a content boundary, the longer it tended to remain in progress after a content boundary. Attentional inertia tends to "drive" looks across breaks in content.

The functional significance of attentional inertia remains to be fully explored, but a recent experiment (Anderson, Lorch, & Field, unpublished data) provides a clue. In this experiment in our laboratory, *Sesame Street* was shown to 3 and 5 year olds. At irregular intervals (ranging from 5 to 25 seconds) a slide was presented on a nearby screen accompanied by a loud "beep." The slide image (animals, posters, cartoon characters, flowers, etc.) remained for 4 seconds, then disappeared. Observers rated visual attention to the TV and whether or not the child turned and looked at the slide when it was presented (the slide would not go on if the child was already looking at the slide screen). Although at this time we have not finished analyzing the data, one result is clear. Slides were progressively less effective in distracting the child's attention from the TV set the longer the child had been continuously looking at the TV. The time course of this effect, furthermore, is quite similar to the time course for attentional inertia. Functionally, then, attentional inertia serves to render the child progressively less distractible from the source of information to which the child is attending.

Now consider the child's attention to event sequences. Ordinarily, we hypothesize, young children use informative cues to guide their attention to television when it promises to be comprehensible, maintaining attention until it becomes relatively incomprehensible. We hypothesize that comprehensibility, furthermore, is determined in part by the degree to which the depicted sequences of events conform to the child's stereotyped expectations based on experience. If a program has proved to be sufficiently comprehensible that the young child has paid extended attention, then attentional inertia builds up. We hypothesize that if the television then presents an unfamiliar event sequence, the child will continue to pay attention for some time, resistant to external distraction, actively processing the events, and attempting to comprehend their interrelationships. This, we suggest, is part of the mechanism by which new representations are acquired.

VII. Solving the Problem of Cognitive Continuity

A. *The Development of Cognitive Processing of Television*

We began this article by describing the TV viewing behavior of a 4 year old and suggested that such complex behavior can be understood by programmatic research analysis. We focused on a central problem of TV viewing, the problem of cognitive continuity, and reviewed research on attention and comprehension. In this section we present a schematic summary of that research in an accounting of the development of cognitive processing of television.

This accounting makes use of four major theoretical elements: event schemes, the comprehensibility rule, comprehensibility markers, and attentional inertia. The development of TV viewing occurs over at least three phases: the period of nonviewing, early partially integrated viewing, and fully developed TV viewing.

1. THE NONVIEWING PHASE

During the first 2 years of life the child pays little attention to television. We suggest this lack of attention reflects the operation of the comprehensibility rule; very young children attend to things that they can comprehend. Television is not yet comprehensible.

Under restricted circumstances an infant will pay attention to television and prefers an integrated audiovisual stimulus (sound consistent with depicted event) to a discrepant stimulus (Hollenbeck & Slaby, 1979). Although some attention to TV may be reactively elicited by salient formal features (Singer, 1980; Wright & Huston, 1981), we suggest that extended attention, when it occurs, indicates recognition of a familiar event sequence. But the rapid flow of events and language quickly replace the familiar with the unfamiliar, and the child loses interest. There is as yet no cognitive continuity in television viewing.

It is during these early years that the child develops the basic cognitive skills necessary for cognizant television viewing. Foremost among these are language comprehension and the formation of event schemes (Nelson & Gruendel, 1981).

2. PARTIALLY INTEGRATED EARLY TV VIEWING

At about 2.5 years of age children begin to pay consistent attention to television, showing clear preferences for children's programs as opposed to programs such as the news (Jaglom & Gardner, 1981). Visual attention to television steadily increases throughout the preschool years at least up until age 5, reflecting, we believe, the rapidly increasing comprehensibility of television to these young children. During these years, children develop an effective strategy of distributing their visual attention throughout a TV program so as to maximize the likelihood of paying attention during comprehensible portions of the TV program while avoiding incomprehensible portions. This strategy includes monitoring the audio track for attributes that mark comprehensible or otherwise important (to the child) content. An example of such a marker attribute is children's voices, which generally are predictive (across the broad range of television programming) of relatively comprehensible content meant for children. The effectiveness of the use of markers to guide attention is reflected in the finding by Calvert *et al.* (1983) that those children whose attention is most differentiated by markers also show the best comprehension. The young viewer also uses the viewing behavior of other children who are present to guide attention to and away from the TV.

By age 4 years the TV viewer is able to comprehend some montage requiring inferences of space, time, ellipsis, and character perspective, and thus has partially solved the problem of cognitive continuity. We hypothesize that the early comprehension of montage is strongly dependent on the degree to which the child can instantiate a well-formed event scheme as a basis for interpreting a sequence of scenes. Early comprehension of TV is strongly dependent on the child's experience and world knowledge, reflected in Collins' demonstrations that recall of TV programs by younger school-age children tends to reflect their socioeconomic backgrounds as well as their overapplication of common event schemes.

Although the TV viewing of young children is unexpectedly sophisticated and strategic, the problem of cognitive continuity is far from completely solved. Despite comprehending a good deal of montage, a preschooler or even a young school-age child probably fails to comprehend a significant number of cinematic transitions, and so comprehension is seriously fragmented. Beyond this problem, longer narrative structures may in general challenge the integrative capacities of young children regardless of the medium of input (e.g., Stein & Trabasso, 1983).

We suggested that part of the mechanisms that lead to new temporal integrations are due to attentional inertia in TV viewing. Attentional inertia, once aroused by consistent maintenance of attention (presumably due to comprehensible program material), may keep the child paying attention to new and unfamiliar content and also renders the child somewhat resistant to distraction. It is possible that this extended attention to unfamiliar or difficult program material provides a basis for new learning. In effect, attentional inertia serves to lengthen the young child's temporal attention span.

3. FULLY DEVELOPED TV VIEWING

Surprisingly, we know relatively little about the cognitive processes of TV viewing in the older child and adult. It is clear that mature TV viewers can plan their TV viewing and can adjust their cognitive processing of television in response to situational demands (Salomon, 1983). It is intuitively obvious that the comprehensibility rule accounts for little of the mature viewer's attention to television except in extreme and special cases (e.g., mistakenly tuning in to a foreign language TV program). Rather, it is likely that attention is differentiated on the basis of the narrative structure, the demands of secondary activities while TV viewing, and the goals, interests, and preferences of the viewer. The use of marker attributes to guide attention is probably differentiated far beyond their early use for prediction of comprehensible material. Attributes may be used to predict particular types of content based on interest value to the viewer, for example, an adult rapidly switching through the channels to find a news program.

Except for avant garde film techniques, comprehension of montage appears to be automatic, so much so that adults sometimes fail to realize that action sequences on television were conveyed by montage. Rather than using event sequences to interpret montage, it appears that highly overlearned cinematic conventions help the experienced film and TV viewer to parse and interpret the event sequence. If television viewing is cognitively challenging to the experienced adult, it is due to the nature of the content and not the medium.

B. Going beyond Television

In Section II we suggested that the study of real-life complex behavior is essential to the advance of knowledge about cognition and its development. The suggestion, we believe, is especially appropriate when the subjects are preschool children. Knowledge about cognitive development in the preschool years is extremely limited in scope. This is due, in part, to the predominance of theories of cognitive development that postulate one particular developmental mechanism or sequence to account for all growth in knowledge and skill. Perhaps the most obvious example is Piagetian theory, which views the development of logical operations as central to cognitive development. But, as Keating (1979), among others, has argued, levels of performance on many tasks typically used to "diagnose" logical structure are actually multiply determined. So, attempts to study a hypothesized developmental mechanism such as "logical structure" in isolation do not permit the discovery and assessment of the role of other, perhaps more important, sources of developmental variance.

The unidimensionality of major cognitive developmental theories also has had an impact on the choice of methods and tasks used to assess cognitive development, and on the interpretation of differences in performance on tasks claimed to be measuring the same thing. Briefly, the consequence is that "task effects" are not considered interesting or important sources of developmental variance. But "task effects" in performance during the preschool years are particularly prevalent (see Brown, 1976; Gelman, 1979). Such effects are, in part, responsible for the lack of positive information on the cognitive capacities of young children. We know a good deal about what preschoolers *cannot* do, but we know little about what they *can* and actually do. The problem is more than an unfair description of young children. Without valid positive information to contrast to negative information, findings of inability are difficult to interpret.

Examining cognitive development in preschoolers in the context of a central and meaningful activity in their lives offers a productive research strategy (see Perlmutter, 1980). Research on young children's cognitive processing of television has borne this out. The identification of phenomena such as the comprehensibility rule and informative attributes as comprehensibility markers would have been unlikely within a single structure- or process-oriented approach to research. Attentional inertia, in particular, would seem to qualify as an emergent process which could not have been discovered in the context of a detailed analysis of attention to a static stimulus at a given short interval of time. It would be surprising if these phenomena, furthermore, were limited only to television viewing. Part of the agenda for future research should be to explore the role of these determinants of attention in other common cognitive activities. Analysis of complex behavioral systems prevalent in day-to-day life, we believe, eventually will yield findings and insights of singular power, generality, and applicability.

Acknowledgments

This article was written while the first author held a Research Scientist Development Award from the National Institute of Mental Health. Much of the research discussed in this article has been supported by grants to D. R. Anderson from the National Science Foundation, the National Institute of Mental Health, the W. T. Grant Foundation, and research contracts from the Children's Television Workshop, which in turn received funds from the U.S. Office of Education. We would like to thank Catherine Fischer for her assistance in preparing this article and Alison Alexander, Diane Field, Leah Larkey, and Nancy Myers for their useful comments.

References

Alwitt, L. F., Anderson, D. R., Lorch, E. P., & Levin, S. R. Preschool children's visual attention to attributes of television. *Human Communication Research*, 1980, 7, 52–67.

Anderson, D. R. *Active and passive processes in children's television viewing*. Paper presented at American Psychological Association annual meeting, New York, 1979.

Anderson, D. R., Alwitt, L. F., Lorch, E. P., & Levin, S. R. Watching children watch television. In G. A. Hale & M. Lewis (Eds.), *Attention and cognitive development*. New York: Plenum, 1979.

Anderson, D. R., & Levin, S. R. Young children's attention to *Sesame Street*. *Child Development*, 1976, **47**, 806–811.

Anderson, D. R., & Lorch, E. P. *A theory of the active nature of young children's television viewing*. Paper presented at the biennial meeting of the Society for Research in Child Development. San Francisco, March, 1979.

Anderson, D. R., & Lorch, E. P. Looking at television: Action or reaction? In J. Bryant &

D. R. Anderson (Eds.), *Children's understanding of television: Research on attention and comprehension.* New York: Academic Press, 1983.

Anderson, D. R., Lorch, E. P., Field, D. E., & Sanders, J. The effects of TV program comprehensibility on preschool children's visual attention to television. *Child Development,* 1981, **52**, 151–157. (a)

Anderson, D. R., Lorch, E. P., Smith, R., Bradford, R., & Levin, S. R. Effects of peer presence on preschool children's television viewing behavior. *Developmental Psychology,* 1981, **17**, 446–453. (b)

Appleton, T., Clifton, R., & Goldberg, S. The development of behavioral competence in infancy. In F. D. Horowitz (Ed.), *Review of child development research.* Chicago, Illinois: Univ. of Chicago Press, 1975.

Baggett, P. Structurally equivalent stories in movie and text and the effect of the medium on recall. *Journal of Verbal Learning and Verbal Behavior,* 1979, **18**, 333–356.

Ball, S., & Bogatz, G. A. Summative research of *Sesame Street*: Implications for the study of preschool children. In A. Pick (Ed.), *Minnesota symposia on child psychology* (Vol. 6). Minneapolis, Minnesota: Univ. of Minnesota Press, 1972.

Baron, L. J. *What do children really see on television?* Paper presented at the annual meeting of the American Educational Research Association, Boston, 1980.

Becker, S. L., & Wolfe, G. J. Can adults predict children's interest in a television program? In W. Schramm (Ed.), *The impact of educational television.* Urbana, Illinois: Univ. of Illinois Press, 1960.

Bellman, B. L., & Jules-Rossette, B. *A paradigm for looking.* Norwood, New Jersey: Ablex, 1977.

Brown, A. L. The construction of temporal succession by preoperational children. In A. Pick (Ed.), *Minnesota symposia on child psychology* (Vol. 10). Minneapolis, Minnesota: Univ. of Minnesota Press, 1976.

Brown, A. L., & Smiley, S. S. Rating the importance of structural units of prose passages: A problem of metacognitive development. *Child Development,* 1977, **48**, 1–8.

Bruner, J. The course of cognitive growth. *American Psychologist,* 1964, **19**, 1–15.

Bryant, J., & Anderson, D. R. (Eds.). *Children's understanding of television: Research on attention and comprehension.* New York: Academic Press, 1983.

Bryant, J., Zillman, D., & Brown, D. Entertainment features in children's educational television: Effects on attention and information acquisition. In J. Bryant & D. R. Anderson (Eds.), *Children's understanding of television: Research on attention and comprehension.* New York: Academic Press, 1983.

Calvert, S. L., Huston, A. C., Watkins, B. A., & Wright, J. C. The relationship between selective attention to television forms and children's comprehension of content. *Child Development,* 1982, **53**, 601–610.

Carew, J. Experience and the development of intelligence in young children at home and in day care. *Monographs of the Society for Research in Child Development,* 1980, **45** (187), 1–89.

Carroll, J. M., & Bever, T. G. Segmentation in cinema perception. *Science,* 1976, **191**, 1053–1055.

Collins, W. A. Children's comprehension of television content. In E. Wartella (Ed.), *Children communicating: Media and the development of thought, speech, and understanding.* Beverly Hills, California: Sage, 1979.

Collins, W. A. Schemata for understanding television. In H. Kelly & H. Gardner (Eds.), *Viewing children through television.* San Francisco, California: Jossey-Bass, 1981.

Collins, W. A. Interpretation and inference in children's television viewing. In J. Bryant & D. R. Anderson (Eds.), *Children's understanding of television: Research on attention and comprehension.* New York: Academic Press, 1983.

Collins, W. A., Wellman, H., Keniston, A. H., & Westby, S. D. Age-related aspects of comprehension and inference from a televised dramatic narrative. *Child Development*, 1978, **49**, 389–399.

Comstock, G., Chaffee, S., Katzman, N., McCombs, M., & Roberts, D. *Television and human behavior*. New York: Columbia Univ. Press, 1978.

Crane, V. Content development for children's television programs. In E. L. Palmer & A. Dorr (Eds.), *Children and the faces of television: Teaching, violence, selling*. New York: Academic Press, 1980.

Desmond, R. J. Cognitive development and television comprehension. *Communication Research*, 1978, **5**, 202–220.

deVilliers, J. C., & deVilliers, P. A. *Language acquisition*. Cambridge, Massachusetts: Harvard Univ. Press, 1978.

Fischer, K. W. A theory of cognitive development: The control and construction of hierarchies of skills. *Psychological Review*, 1980, **87**, 477–531.

Flapan, D. P. *Children's understanding of social interaction*. Unpublished doctoral dissertation, Columbia University, 1965.

Flavell, J. H. *The developmental psychology of Jean Piaget*. Princeton, New Jersey: Van Nostrand-Reinhold, 1963.

Forsdale, J., & Forsdale, L. Film literacy. *Teacher's College Record*, 1966, **67**, 608–617.

Franck, G. J. *Über Geschehensgestaltungen in der Auffasung von Filmen durch Kinder*. Leipzig: Barth, 1955.

Friedlander, B. Z., Wetstone, H. S., & Scott, C. S. Suburban preschool children's comprehension of an age-appropriate informational television program. *Child Development*, 1974, **45**, 561–565.

Gelman, R. Preschool thought. *American Psychologist*, 1979, **34**, 900–905.

Harrington, J. *The rhetoric of film*. New York: Holt, 1973.

Hayes, D. S., & Birnbaum, D. W. Preschoolers' retention of televised events: Is a picture worth a thousand words? *Developmental Psychology*, 1980, **16**, 410–416.

Hollenbeck, A. R., & Slaby, R. G. Infant visual responses to television. *Child Development*, 1979, **50**, 41–45.

Hornik, R. Out-of-school television and schooling: Hypotheses and methods. *Review of Educational Research*, 1981, **51**, 193–214.

Huston, A., & Wright, J. C. Children's processing of television: The informative functions of formal features. In J. Bryant & D. R. Anderson (Eds.), *Children's understanding of television: Research on attention and comprehension*. New York: Academic Press, 1983.

Huston, A. C., Wright, J. C., Wartella, E., Rice, M., Watkins, B. A., Campbell, T., & Potts, R. Communicating more than content: Formal features of children's television programs. *Journal of Communication*, 1981, **31**, 32–48.

Jaglom, L. M., & Gardner, H. The preschool television viewer as anthropologist. In H. Kelly & H. Gardner (Eds.), *Viewing children through television*. San Francisco, California: Jossey-Bass, 1981.

Keating, D. P. Toward a multivariate life-span theory of intelligence. In D. Kuhn (Ed.), *Intellectual development beyond childhood*. San Francisco, California: Jossey-Bass, 1979.

Kelly, H., & Gardner, H. Tackling television on its own terms. In H. Kelly & H. Gardner (Eds.), *Viewing children through television*. San Francisco, California: Jossey-Bass, 1981. (a)

Kelly, H., & Gardner, H. (Eds.), *Viewing Children through television*. San Francisco, California: Jossey-Bass, 1981. (b)

Kjørup, S. Film as a meetingplace of multiple codes. In D. Perkins & B. Leondar (Eds.), *The arts and cognition*. Baltimore, Maryland: Johns Hopkins Press, 1977.

Korac, N. *Cognitive and semiotic factors in the development of audiovisual comprehension.* Unpublished manuscript, University of Minnesota, 1981.

Krull, R. Children learning to watch television. In J. Bryant & D. R. Anderson (Eds.), *Children's understanding of television: Research on attention and comprehension.* New York: Academic Press, 1983.

Krull, R., & Husson, W. Children's attention: The case of TV viewing. In E. Wartella (Ed.), *Children communicating: Media and development of thought, speech, understanding.* Beverly Hills, California: Sage, 1979.

Leifer, A. D., Collins, W. A., Gross, B. M., Taylor, P. H., Andrews, L., & Blackmer, E. R. Developmental aspects of variables relevant to observational learning. *Child Development,* 1971, **42**, 1509–1516.

Lesser, G. *Children and television: Lessons from Sesame Street.* New York: Random House, 1974.

Lesser, H. *Television and the preschool child.* New York: Academic Press, 1977.

Levin, S. R., & Anderson, D. R. The development of attention. *Journal of Communication,* 1976, **26**, 126–135.

Levin, S. R., Petros, T. V., & Petrella, F. W. Development of children's understanding of television advertising. *Child Development,* 1982, **53**, 933–937.

Lorch, E. P., & Anderson, D. R. *Paying attention to Sesame Street.* Technical Report to Children's Television Workshop, New York, 1978.

Lorch, E. P., Anderson, D. R., & Levin, S. R. The relationship of visual attention to children's comprehension of television. *Child Development,* 1979, **50**, 722–727.

Lyle, S., & Hoffman, H. R. Children's use of television and other media. In E. A. Rubinstein et al. (Eds.), *Television and social behavior* (Vol. 4). Washington, D.C.: U.S. Govt. Printing Office, 1972.

Mates, B. F. Current emphases and issues in planned programming for children. In E. L. Palmer & A. Dorr (Eds.), *Children and the faces of television: Teaching, violence, selling.* New York: Academic Press, 1980.

Mayr, E. *The growth of biological thought: Diversity, evolution, and inheritance.* Cambridge, Massachusetts: Harvard Univ. Press, 1982.

Metz, C. *Film language: The semiotics of the cinema.* New York and London: Oxford Univ. Press, 1974.

Mielke, K. W. Formative research on appeal and comprehension in *3–2–1 Contact.* In J. Bryant & D. R. Anderson (Eds.), *Children's understanding of television: Research on attention and comprehension.* New York: Academic Press, 1983.

Moody, K. *Growing up on television: The TV effect.* New York: Times Books, 1980.

Neisser, U. *Cognition and reality.* San Francisco, California: Freeman, 1976.

Nelson, K., & Gruendel, J. Generalized event representations: Basic building blocks of cognitive development. In M. E. Lamb & A. L. Brown (Eds.), *Advances in developmental psychology* (Vol. 1). Hillsdale, New Jersey: Erlbaum, 1981.

Newcomb, A. F., & Collins, W. A. Children's comprehension of family role portrayals in televised dramas: Effects of socio-economic status, ethnicity, and age. *Developmental Psychology,* 1979, **15**, 417–422.

Noble, G. *Children in front of the small screen.* London: Constable Press, 1975.

Norman, D. A. Twelve issues for cognitive science. *Cognitive Science,* 1980, **4**, 1–32.

Palmer, E. L. Formative research in the production of television for children. In D. Olson (Ed.), *Media and symbols: The forms of expression, communication and education.* Chicago, Illinois: Univ. of Chicago Press, 1974.

Perlmutter, M. (Ed.). *New directions for child development: Children's memory.* San Francisco, California: Jossey-Bass, 1980.

Piaget, J. *The origins of intelligence in children*. New York: International Universities Press, 1952.

Pingree, S., & Hawkins, R. P. What children do with television. In B. Dervin & M. Voight (Eds.), *Progress in communication sciences* (Vol. 3). Norwood, New Jersey: Ablex, 1982.

Reeves, B., & Wartella, E. *"For some children under some conditions": A history of research on children and media*. Paper presented at International Communication Association annual meeting, Boston, 1982.

Rice, M. *Television as a medium of verbal communication*. Paper presented at the annual meeting of the American Psychological Association, New York, 1979.

Rice, M. *What children talk about while they watch television*. Paper presented at the biennial meeting of the Southwestern Society for Research in Human Development, Lawrence, Kansas, March 1980.

Rice, M., Huston, A. C., & Wright, J. C. The forms and codes of television: Effects on children's attention, comprehension, and social behavior. In D. Pearl (Ed.), *Television and behavior: Ten years of scientific progress and implications for the 80's*. Washington, D.C.: U.S. Govt. Printing Office, 1982.

Salomon, G. Cognitive skill learning across cultures. *Journal of Communication*, 1976, **26**, 138–144.

Salomon, G. *Interaction of media, cognition, and learning*. San Francisco, California: Jossey-Bass, 1979.

Salomon, G. Television watching and mental effort: A social-psychological review. In J. Bryant & D. R. Anderson (Eds.), *Children's understanding of television: Research on attention and comprehension*. New York: Academic Press, 1983.

Salomon, G., & Sieber, J. Relevant subjective response uncertainty as a function of stimulus-task interaction. *American Educational Research Journal*, 1970, **7**, 337–349.

Schank, R., & Abelson, R. *Scripts, plans, goals, and understanding*. Hillsdale, New Jersey: Erlbaum, 1977.

Schramm, W., Lyle, J., & Parker, E. B. *Television in the lives of our children*. Stanford, California: Stanford Univ. Press, 1961.

Siegler, R., & Robinson, M. The development of numerical understandings. In H. W. Reese & L. P. Lipsitt (Eds.), *Advances in child development and behavior* (Vol. 16). New York: Academic Press, 1982.

Singer, J. L. The powers and limitations of television: A cognitive-affective analysis. In P. Tannenbaum (Ed.), *The entertainment functions of television*. Hillsdale, New Jersey: Erlbaum, 1980.

Smith, R. *Preschool children's comprehension of television*. Paper presented at biennial meeting of the Society for Research in Child Development, Boston, 1981.

Smith, R., Anderson, D. R., & Fischer, C. *Young children's comprehension of cinematic techniques*. Paper presented at Society for Research in Child Development biennial meeting, Detroit, 1983.

Sproull, N. Visual attention, modeling behaviors, and other verbal and nonverbal metacommunication of prekindergarten children viewing *Sesame Street*. *American Educational Research Journal*, 1973, **10**, 101–114.

Stein, N. L., & Trabasso, T. What's in a story: Critical issues in comprehension and instruction. In R. Glaser (Ed.), *Advances in the psychology of instruction*. Hillsdale, New Jersey: Erlbaum, 1983, in press.

Sturm, H., & Jorg, S. *Information processing by young children: Piaget's theory of intellectual development applied to radio and television*. Munich: Saur, 1981.

Tada, T. Image-cognition: A developmental approach. In *Studies of broadcasting*. Tokyo: Nippon Hoso Kyokai, 1969.

Wackman, D. B., & Wartella, E. A review of cognitive development theory and research and the implication for research on children's responses to television. *Communication Research*, 1977, **4**, 203–224.

Ward, S., Wackman, D. B., & Wartella, E. *How children learn to buy.* Beverly Hills, California: Sage, 1977.

Wartella, E. The child as viewer. In M. E. Ploghoft & J. A. Anderson (Eds.), *Education for the television age.* University of Utah, 1981.

Wartella, E., & Ettema, J. A cognitive developmental study of children's attention to television commercials. *Communication Research*, 1974, **1**, 69–88.

Watkins, B. A., Huston-Stein, A. C., & Wright, J. C. Effects of planned television programming. In E. L. Palmer & A. Dorr (Eds.), *Children and the faces of television: Teaching, violence, selling.* New York: Academic Press, 1980.

Watt, J., & Welch, A. J. The effects of static and dynamic complexity on children's attention and recall of televised instruction. In J. Bryant & D. R. Anderson (Eds.), *Children's understanding of television: Research on attention and comprehension.* New York: Academic Press, 1983.

Whitaker, R. *The language of film.* New York: Prentice-Hall, 1970.

Winn, M. *The plug-in drug.* New York: Bantam, 1978.

Woolf, H. B. (Ed.). *Webster's new collegiate dictionary.* Springfield, Massachusetts: Merriam, 1976.

Wright, J. C., & Huston, A. C. Children's understanding of the forms of television. In H. Kelly & H. Gardner (Eds.), *Viewing children through television.* San Francisco, California: Jossey Bass, 1981.

Zazzo, R. L'influence du cinema sur le developpement de la pensee de l'enfant. Paris: L'Ecole des Parents, 1956.

Zuckerman, P., Ziegler, M., & Stevenson, H. W. Children's viewing of television and recognition memory of commercials. *Child Development*, 1978, **49**, 96–104.

THE DEVELOPMENT OF PEER RELATIONS

IN CHILDREN WITH AUTISM

Catherine Lord

DEPARTMENT OF PSYCHOLOGY

GLENROSE HOSPITAL

AND

DEPARTMENT OF PEDIATRICS

UNIVERSITY OF ALBERTA SCHOOL OF MEDICINE

EDMONTON, ALBERTA, CANADA

*Applied Developmental
Psychology, Volume 1*

Copyright © 1984 by Academic Press, Inc.
All rights of reproduction in any form reserved.
ISBN 0-12-041201-2

I. Social Deficits and Autism

In his seminal paper on early infantile autism Leo Kanner stated, "the outstanding 'pathognomic' fundamental disorder [in autism] is the children's *inability to relate themselves* in an ordinary way to people and situations from the beginning of life" (Kanner, 1943, p. 33). Forty years later, Kanner's thoughtful description of the behavior of 11 children continues to represent the state of knowledge of the social development of autistic children. Although long recognized as a critical feature of the disorder, the social development of children with autism has received relatively little direct or systematic study (Howlin, 1978; Richer, 1978). Discussions by Wing and her associates (Wing, 1978; Wing & Gould, 1979) and by Rutter and colleagues (Rutter, 1978a, 1983; Rutter & Bartak, 1973) have highlighted the importance of social behavior, but until recently there have been relatively few empirical studies to support, refute, or expand Kanner's careful, but subjective, observations. Behavioral intervention studies such as those by Davison (1964) and Lovaas, Koegel, and colleagues (Koegel, Firestone, Cramme, & Dunlap, 1974; Lovaas, Koegel, Simmons, & Long, 1973) have provided information about the modifiability of specific behaviors such as eye contact and social approaches. Studies by Strain and colleagues (Ragland, Kerr, & Strain, 1978; Strain, Kerr, & Ragland, 1979) have shown increases in general positive social behavior as a function of the behavior of a playmate. Yet neither line of research has provided much information about specific social behaviors of autistic children in natural contexts. In part, the paucity of research may have stemmed from a lack of appropriate methods for studying behavior, as well as from a prevailing view that social impairments were derivative of more central deficits in learning strategies (Ferster, 1961), emotional status (Goldfarb, 1961), or cognition (Hermelin & O'Connor, 1970).

However, recently, social deficits have received renewed attention as a fundamental aspect of autism (Rutter, 1983; Wing, 1978). One impetus for this increasing emphasis on social deficits has been follow-up studies that have shown that the course of social development in individuals with autism can be separated to some degree from development in either language or cognition (Rutter, 1978b). By adolescence, some persons with autism possess quite sophisticated language skills, such as syntax, while social behaviors and functional communication continue to be severely delayed (Cantwell, Baker, & Rutter, 1978). Other autistic children may show marked improvements in social behaviors, while remaining mute and severely retarded in cognitive tasks (Rutter, 1978b). Though communication, cognitive abilities, and social skills are clearly intertwined, no single deficit (i.e., social, affective, cognitive, or language) has been shown to account for all the other deficits associated with autism. Thus, the description of social behavior associated with autism is a worthwhile goal in its own right, as well as for the information such observations provide for understanding other areas of development such as cognition and language.

The present article aims to provide a systematic, empirically based description of the social behavior of children with autism with their peers. An attempt is made to relate the behavior of autistic children to the social development or normally developing children. Much of this description is done in the context of observations made during three short-term treatment studies of the social behavior of autistic children with other children (Hopkins & Lord, 1981; Lord, Bream, & Hopkins, 1981). The underlying assumption is that observing social behavior over time can provide particularly useful information concerning social deficits. The purpose of the studies was not only to measure the effectiveness of treatment, but also to provide information, gleaned from hours of direct observation, on what autistic children do in social situations. One can then ask how these observations change or fit into our conceptualization of the social development and the social deficits associated with autism.

In the present article, Rutter's (1978c) definition of autism is employed. Thus, all children who are referred to as autistic (1) experienced the onset of symptoms before 30 months of age, (2) showed a profound and general failure to develop social relations, (3) exhibited language retardation with impaired comprehension and use of language, and (4) showed an insistence on sameness that involved ritualistic or compulsive phenomena. All of the children who participated in the treatment studies of autistic children reported here also met *DSM III* (American Psychiatric Association, 1979) criteria for autism including unusual responses to the environment and uneven patterns of development.

Recent epidemiological work by Lorna Wing (1978) has pointed to the need for a clearer definition of autism. Wing's studies of the relations among cognitive, language, social, and behavioral characteristics of severely retarded and/or autistic children led her to propose a new framework for categorizing pervasive developmental delays such as autism (Wing & Gould, 1979). This scheme was based heavily on observations of children's social behavior, particularly with peers. Wing proposed grouping together children who exhibited a triad of severe social impairments, consisting of significant delays in language comprehension, marked limitations in spontaneous, imaginative play, and severe deficits in social interaction, especially with other children. Deficits were categorized as *extreme aloofness, passivity*, and *active but odd* social behavior. On the basis of epidemiological studies, Wing identified about 50% of ambulatory, severely retarded children as possessing this triad of social deficits, in addition to general cognitive delays. Furthermore, a group of "autistic" children, some but not all of whom were also severely retarded, were identified as possessing the triad of impairments. Wing differentiated autistic children from children with the more general triad of deficits by defining an autistic subgroup as children who met criteria based on Kanner's original description: (1) extreme social aloofness, especially with peers, and (2) elaborate rituals. Both of these problems had to be present in the children in marked degrees from age 2½ to at least 7 years. This distinction between autism and other social deficits bears special consideration, because of the particular emphasis it places on the kind of social behavior a child exhibits (i.e., the distinction between aloofness and other categories of social deficit). While for the purposes of this article children are judged to be autistic on the basis of the broader Rutter criteria, Wing's three categories of social impairment are examined in detail below.

Both Wing (1976) and Rutter (1978b) have noted that, since interactions with adults often improve as autistic children grow older, the social impairments associated with autism are most clearly observed during interactions with peers, especially after age 5. Whereas relationships with adults may become more positive (Rutter, 1978b; Wing, 1976), serious social difficulties continue for most children with autism in interactions with peers and in many situations with adults. These difficulties are evident in the failure of most autistic children or adolescents to develop friendships and to be able to play or work cooperatively in a group.

What accounts for the discrepancy in how children with autism relate to adults as compared to other children? There are a number of possible explanations. If placed in a segregated classroom, a boy with autism may have little opportunity to interact with other children. His classmates who are also autistic may seldom attempt to initiate interactions with him, so that he may have few chances to respond to other children. His handicapped classmates may not consistently respond to his infrequent attempts to interact so that even if he does make a social overture, he has little or no reinforcement for doing so or incentive for trying again. This pattern of social behavior contrasts sharply with interactions between the same child with autism and familiar adults, such as parents and teachers. The adults would be expected to be much more responsive to the child's attempts to be social and would be more likely to take on the role of the initiator with him (Holmberg, 1980). Although many children with autism have normally developing siblings who also might be expected to be more interactive than other children, the amount of interaction between children in the same family appears to be extremely variable across families and often quite low (O'Neill & Lord, 1981).

With limited repertoires of appropriate behaviors with which to initiate interactions and to respond to others' overtures, the autistic child may be unlikely to find "behavioral matches" with other children, whose repertoires might be expected to be more limited than those of adults. Perhaps the social skills of autistic children improve sufficiently with maturation so that they can effectively cue adults to their intentions, and adults can respond appropriately. On the other hand, normally developing children may not understand what the autistic children intend or may not know how to modify their behavior to meet their needs. Other children may not typically provide the structure that adults do (Clark & Rutter, 1981). A mother of the children studied by DeMyer (1979) described the difference between her child's interactions with adults and children in terms of how hard the other person (i.e., child or adult) was willing to work to make her child feel comfortable. From the other child's perspective, interacting with an autistic child who provides little behavioral feedback may require too much effort and concentration for most nonhandicapped children. In a study of how normal 4 year olds talked to normal 2 year olds, Masur (1978) found that the older children showed more speech adjustment with 2 year olds who were socially responsive and who talked, even if not very clearly, than they did with 2 year olds who were silent.

Furthermore, children may interact with other children and with adults for quite different reasons. Nurturance, or making someone feel comfortable, is usually more, although not exclusively, an adult trait than something available from other children. Interactions with adults are more likely to contain affection seeking (which is rarely seen in peer interactions), emotional behavior such as smiling, clinging, or crying (Eckerman, 1979), requests for help (Barker & Wright, 1955), and requests for access to objects or activities (O'Neill & Lord, 1981). A high proportion of adult actions toward young children in everyday situations can be classified as either dominant or nurturant (Barker & Wright, 1955), two characteristics that are less typically found in child-to-child interactions. Obviously, these characteristics vary markedly with the situation and the age of the child (Hartup, 1980), but it is important to note that interactions with adults often provide different opportunities for children than do interactions with other children. An autistic child at a very simple developmental level may seek warmth and comfort from an adult that another child could not provide. On the other hand, an autistic child may interact with adults in order to satisfy needs that are not social; he or she may not need to interact with other children for the same purposes.

Interactions with other children often occur around play and imaginative use of objects (Eckerman, Whatley, & Kutz, 1975). These interactions are often quite repetitive (Hartup, 1975) and are usually relatively reciprocal, requiring roughly equal participation from both children. For autistic children who do not play imaginatively, the problems are immense.

More intense and frequent experience with adults (i.e., parents and teachers) than with other children may also account for some of these differences in autistic children. For example, in a recent study of spontaneous communicative speech produced by moderately to severely retarded autistic boys, those boys who had a normal sibling at home produced more spontaneous speech directed to peers at school and at home than did boys living in foster homes with only handicapped children (O'Neill & Lord, 1981). One implication of this discussion is that specific social skills taught by and with adults in behavioral paradigms may be helpful in strengthening adult-directed interactions, but they may be difficult to generalize to peers who behave in far less predictable fashions. In addition, the social skills needed by autistic children to interact with adults may be very different from the skills needed to participate in the object-oriented, egalitarian relationships typically seen between children (Hartup, 1976).

II. Social Development Measures in Nonhandicapped and Autistic Children

In beginning research on the social skills of children with autism, an initial question is the extent to which models of the social development of normally developing children are useful in understanding the problems and designing appropriate treatments for children with autism. Do comparisons of social behaviors of normally developing and autistic children have significant value? Autistic children have been described as missing social behavior such as eye contact and differential vocalizations typically used even by very young infants (Kubicek, 1980; Rutter, 1980). In addition, as they reach later school age and adolescence, many autistic children continue to experience difficulty with basic aspects of social interaction like appropriate proximity and the use of intonation for communication (Ricks & Wing, 1976), while mastering what appear at first glance to be more complex social behaviors such as making purchases at a store or introducing themselves to strangers. Thus, simple behavioral comparisons may not be very useful. Furthermore, comparisons based primarily on theory, such as Mahler's (1965) discussions of attachment, have often proved to be quite misleading (Rutter, 1983). For older autistic children and adolescents, social-educational goals must not only be reasonable for current levels of functioning, but also appropriate to the individual's chronological age and size (Donellan, 1980). At some point, playing "Peek-A-Boo" is no longer appropriate, even if the social aspects of the activity are needed. Especially in the older child, relationships among learning deficits, social skills, language, and cognition (Hermelin & O'Connor, 1970; Wing, 1976) appear to be sufficiently complex that the particular role of specifically social aspects of development may be nearly impossible to identify.

Greater knowledge about social behavior in autistic children has proceeded slowly until recently, partly due to the lack of basic understanding of social development in normal children, especially with peers. Although researchers have long been interested in describing the social behavior of normally developing children (Hartup, 1970), this task has been difficult for a number of reasons. Since social interaction inevitably involves at least two people whose behavior may change on a number of dimensions every second or two, quantification of "natural" situations is time consuming and inevitably open to multiple interpretations (Radke-Yarrow, 1975). On the other hand, one is never certain of the validity or relevance of experimental or quasi-experimental designs that deliberately vary one or two dimensions in artificial contexts (Belsky, 1979; Clarke-Stewart, 1978; see also discussion by Morrison, Lord, & Keating, this volume).

In addition, there is frequent disagreement on what is a fair measure of "good" social development. Though sociometrics, rate of interaction, success ratios of initiations, flexibility, and range of different social behaviors have all been used by various investigators to measure social skills (Wanlass & Prinz, 1982), empirical agreement on measures is often poor (Gresham, 1981). Moreover, theoretical agreement among investigators about the appropriate units of measurement is relatively poor as well (Gresham, 1981; Wanlass & Prinz, 1982).

However, there are a number of ways in which the study of social development in normally developing children could provide information for the researcher interested in the social abilities of children with autism. Specific units of measurement that have been found to be valid and reliable might be borrowed from the normal developmental literature and evaluated for their appropriateness to observations of children with autism (McHale, 1982; Sigman & Ungerer, 1981). In addition, developmental sequences of social behavior drawn from the study of normally developing children can provide the researcher studying atypical children with a framework to begin observation. While these sequences have seldom been as comprehensible and uniform as one might like (e.g., shifts from parallel play to cooperative play), knowledge that some behaviors typically precede others in a developmental sequence offers a starting point for observation and can provide initial goals for intervention (Flavell, 1981). For a child with an uneven pattern of development, where one enters the sequence (e.g., at his cognitive level, chronological age, or a level which best approximates his social skills) is a critical question.

For similar reasons, description of patterns of behavior within the interactions of normal children could prove useful to the study of social deficits. For example, the finding that the "technical quality" (i.e., understandability) of a preschool child's verbal initiation is a good predictor of whether he or she will receive a response from another child raises interesting questions about what may happen to the peer-directed communications of a language-delayed child (Mueller, 1972). If observations confirmed the relationship between quality of communication and likelihood of response for a particular child, an intervention could be planned based on the working hypothesis that improving the child's ability to communicate in a manner comprehensible to a large number of children (e.g., increasing his use of gesture or improving his articulation by encouraging the use of shorter, routine sentence frames) will improve his ability to initiate peer interactions. Techniques of intervention could also be devised using information about the contexts in which positive social behaviors are most likely to occur in normally developing children.

Whether this developmental approach is useful is an empirical question. Although the research described in this article does not really *test* this question, it provides an example of an attempt to use information and methods available from normal developmental research to accomplish the functional goal of improving the peer interactions of children with autism. Short-term observational studies of how autistic children interact with other children may begin to clarify the important factors related to successful interactions and to elucidate those factors subject to change. Since little systematic information is available, our research began by asking relatively straightforward questions: How do autistic children interact with nonautistic and autistic peers? How do these interactions change with familiarity? Finally, what general characteristics and specific behaviors of the playmates with whom the autistic children are expected to interact are most important for successful interaction?

Literature concerning social development was applied to the study of autism in three respects:

1. *Units of behavior* to be analyzed were drawn from basic research in child development. These units are discussed in Section III in relation to research concerning children with autism.

2. *Techniques of intervention* were devised using research reporting conditions in which positive social behaviors among normally developing children were most likely to occur.

3. Sequences of normal development were used to derive *goals for intervention*: (a) to identify patterns of behavior that one would expect to develop in conjunction with the children's other known abilities, and (b) to propose behaviors that were likely to precede and/or facilitate positive social interaction.

While units of analysis are discussed in relation to the general study of autism, goals and techniques of intervention are discussed primarily in relation to the three specific studies of interaction reported here.

III. Units of Analysis

One can measure social behavior by counting the frequency of certain social acts, here called *quantitative* units (i.e., asking how often something occurs), by making *qualitative*, often categorical, judgments about the content and meaning of the behaviors (i.e., asking what is happening), or finally, by observing relationships among specific qualitative behaviors pertaining to the interactions, here called *interactive* units (i.e., asking how behaviors relate to each other). Though many measures combine elements of these three types of units, these distinctions provide a useful starting point. Sociometric measures and methods requiring judgments on the part of subjects will not be discussed here because they are less relevant to the populations in question.

A. Quantitative Units

Autistic children have consistently been described as socially aloof and less interactive than other children, particularly at a young age (DeMyer, 1979; Wing, 1976). As a consequence, especially during the preschool years, one would anticipate fewer deliberate initiations of social interaction by autistic children than by other children (DeMyer, 1979; Hutt & Ounsted, 1966; Richer, 1978; Wing, 1976). Those initiations that did occur would most often be directed to a restricted group of people, usually adults, such as parents or teachers (Wing, 1976). When autistic children did interact with another person, one would expect less time spent in interaction, and shorter interactions sustained on a particular topic, than in comparable social exchanges between other children.

On the surface, many indications of the poor social functioning of autistic children are similar to descriptions of the social behaviors of infants and toddlers as compared to children of preschool and kindergarten age. For example, the positive relationship between age and interactive frequency among peers during the preschool years has been reported to be one of the most well-established findings in the study of social development (Tremblay, Strain, Hendrickson, & Shores, 1981). Since even infants have been shown to initiate interactions from a very early age (Becker, 1977; Rheingold & Eckerman, 1975), much of this overall increase in time spent during interaction can be attributed to increases in responsiveness to other children during the toddler and preschool years (Mueller & Brenner, 1977). Generally by preschool age, normally developing children have been found to be highly responsive to direct social initiations made by peers and adults. For example, the lowest ratio of responses to initiations found by Greenwood, Walker, Todd, and Hopps (1981) of preschool children to familiar peers was .84 responses for every initiation. Holmberg (1980) also reported steady increases in the number of positive responses made by children from 12 to 42 months old in familiar peers in day-care settings.

In addition, both Holmberg (1980) and Keane and Conger (1981) reported decreases in the number of topic changes during peer interaction with age. Thus, as part of normal development, children spend more time interacting with each other, respond to peers more consistently, and sustain interactions on particular topics or activities for longer periods. When and whether changes in initiations occur seems to be a more complex question. Studies of infants and familiar toddlers in dyads indicate high rates of initiation from very early on (Eckerman et al., 1975). However, studies of young children in larger groups with adults present have reported definite increases in peer-directed overtures from 12 to 42 months of age (Holmberg, 1980).

The autistic child's social behavior can be seen as part of a pervasive developmental delay in social skills. The ability to participate in and sustain peer interactions can be viewed as a set of skills that an autistic child acquires at a pace slower than other children (Sigman & Ungerer, 1981). Since social behavior is correlated with cognitive skills in normally developing children, and since many children with autism show delays in cognitive development, slower social development is not particularly surprising (Wing & Gould, 1979). Yet, a separate developmental model of social skills may prove useful for identifying and measuring areas of change. In fact, because of specific social deficits and generally uneven patterns of skills, social development may actually be less correlated with cognitive level for children with autism than for other children (Sigman & Ungerer, 1981). Based on the normal developmental literature, quantitative units of analysis useful to the study of children with autism could include the number of initiations and responses a child makes, the time he or she spends in interaction, and the length of time that individual social interactions are sustained.

In two well-known studies, behavioral methods were used to produce increases in quantitative measures in peer-directed social behavior in children with autism and related disorders. Romanczyk, Diament, Goren, Trunell, and Harris (1975) used passive shaping and food and verbal reinforcement to increase the amount of time four socially impaired children spent playing with each other. Time spent in social play increased significantly with the implementation of these procedures, but declined quickly when the intervention was terminated. By gradually fading adult prompts in a second study, the increases in social play were sustained more than in the first study, as long as reinforcements were continued. Though social play decreased greatly when reinforcements were discontinued, it remained substantially above baseline levels for all eight subjects in both studies for about three to five "extinction" sessions and then returned to near baseline levels. While a number of specific behaviors (e.g., vocalizations, touching) of the socially impaired children were observed, changes in these measures did not accompany changes in social or isolate play.

Strain and his colleagues (Strain et al., 1979) used a similar procedure with the modification that specially trained peers were used to provide prompts and reinforcements to autistic children. Dramatic increases in the number of positive motor-gestural and vocal-verbal behaviors were reported in conditions in which the nonhandicapped playmates either prompted and then reinforced play behaviors of the autistic children or repeatedly initiated play activities with the children with autism. Unfortunately, there was no generalization of increased positive social behaviors to sessions between two autistic children when the nonhandicapped playmates were not present. In a second baseline period, when the nonhandicapped peers stopped using the prompt/reinforcement or social initiation procedures, frequency of social interaction returned to virtually zero for the autistic children. Strain et al. (1979) concluded that prompt and reinforcement procedures would have had to be reduced systematically in a response-dependent fashion for maintenance of the changes in positive social behaviors to have occurred.

Analogies to developmental progressions are difficult to make on the basis of these behavioral interventions for several reasons. First, the contexts in which the children were observed, particularly the behaviors of the non-handicapped playmates, did not correspond to natural contexts observed in studies of the social interactions of the normally developing child. There are few situations in which a normal child would have an adult or child reinforcing their positive social behaviors on the average of every 30 seconds. Second, one could say that increases in interaction fit into a developmental model, since it is known that older children interact with each other more frequently than younger children, but it is not at all clear from either study, exactly *what* is developing. Because interactions were not differentiated by the roles taken by the handicapped and nonhandicapped children, distinctions between increases in initiations and increases in responsiveness cannot be made. To say that when any measure increases a developmental progression occurs becomes a bit meaningless.

On the other hand, differentiations made by Wing and Gould (1979) among categories of social deficits may provide a more fruitful basis for identifying the aspects of social behavior that differ in autistic children and nonhandicapped children and the aspects of social behavior that change with development. Working from Wing and Gould's (1979) description of their categories,[1] differentiating among them seems fairly straightforward on a quantitative basis, although terms are necessarily relative and defined by ranges rather than absolutes. For example, as shown in Table I, *aloof* children could be discriminated from *passive* children on the basis of their frequency of interaction and their responsiveness to other children's overtures. *Active but odd* children could be discriminated from *passive* or *aloof* children by the number of initiations they made and their ability to make some active contribution to sustaining an interaction. Thus, within the domain of social impairments, one could propose a developmental progression from *aloof* to *passive* in responsiveness and from *aloof* or *passive* to *active but odd* in rate of initiation. Again, this proposition is an empirical question, requiring data from longitudinal studies. However, one could ask, with regard to the studies both by Romanczyk *et al.* (1975) and Strain *et al.* (1979), whether the increases in interaction occurred because of changes in responsiveness of the autistic children (from *aloof* to *passive*) or changes in their initiations (from *aloof/passive* to *active but odd*) or both. The answer to this question might also provide some suggestions for improving ways of maintaining and generalizing gains in soical behavior.

[1]It should be noted that the measures and levels associated with Wing and Gould's categories were derived by this author, not Wing and Gould, and were based on their written description of the categories (Wing & Gould, 1979, pp. 14–15), not on the basis of the Handicap, Behavior, and Skills Schedule which they used to categorize individual children (Wing & Gould, 1979).

Table I

Autistic Children's Social Behavior with Peers

Quantitative measures	Social deficit categories		
	Aloof	Passive	Active but odd
Time spent in interaction	Very low	Low to high	Low to high
Ratio of autistic child's responses to number of initiations received	Very low	Low to high	Low to normal
Number of initiations made by child	Very low	Very low	Low to excessive
Length of sustained interaction	Very brief	Very brief	Brief

B. Qualitative Units

The social disorder of autistic children clearly goes beyond differences in frequency and length of interaction as compared to those of normal children, even if full maintenance and generalization of treatment effects were to be achieved (Howlin, 1978). Treatment studies have shown that simply increasing frequency of interaction does not make children with autism appear normal (Strain & Fox, 1981). Thus, qualitative analyses of patterns of behavior may be needed to gain a clearer description of the autistic child's social behavior (Howlin, 1978; Hutt & Hutt, 1970). Questions arise not only about whether children with autism are initiating or responding to others' overtures, but if so, how they are doing so. For example, some autistic children have been described as responding to other children's attempts to include them in social activities by actively avoiding or showing aggressive behavior to the other children (DeMyer, 1979; Strain & Cooke, 1976). Some children with autism have been described as friendly and positive, but naive about general rules of social contact, such as whom to hug or what constitutes a tactless remark (Wing, 1976). Wing's category of *active but odd* differentiates socially impaired "active" children from normally developing children on the basis of a qualitative judgment of an unusual manner in which "odd" socially impaired children behave.

Qualitative measures would include not only descriptions of socially directed actions but other behaviors expected to influence interaction. Whereas well-established patterns of social behaviors such as looking and directing actions have been observed in normally developing children under 6 months of age (Vandell, Wilson, & Buchanan, 1980), children with autism have been shown to spend less time looking at faces (Castell, 1970; Hutt & Ounsted, 1966) and more time looking at unusual parts of faces (Langdell, 1978) than other children. Lack of visual attentiveness becomes particularly significant in light of research showing that normally developing children are more responsive to another child's approach if they are already attending to that child and are more likely to approach a child who is attending to them (Mueller, 1972). A number of researchers working with normally developing children have also described being the "onlooker" as a first step in social play (Parten, 1932; Doyle, Connolly, & Rivest, 1980). Similarly, Wing and Gould's (1979) distinction between passivity and aloofness implies a difference in the readiness of the autistic children to interact if approached. This general phenomenon could be measured with such variables as the amount of time the autistic children spent visually attending to other children and how well they tolerated the proximity of another child.

Children with autism have been shown to tolerate more physical contact with an adult than other children of the same chronological age (Hutt & Ounsted, 1966), yet DeMyer (1979) reported that many parents of autistic children described their infants as becoming less social when they learned to walk or crawl. One interpretation of these seemingly discrepant results is that when "captured" by the physical contact of another person, autistic children, like younger children, will tolerate primary contact, but that autistic children may use their newfound mobility as infants more often to avoid contact and less often to seek contact than normally developing children.

One can ask whether play and the use of objects might serve the same function as mobility with older autistic children. Do autistic children use play only as a repetitive self-directed activity, or can it be seen as a step toward the development of social skills? An influential analysis of qualitative changes in play is Parten's (1932) description of normal developmental stages from unoccupied to onlooker, solitary to parallel, associative to cooperative interactions. More recent work has concluded that changes in play, as measured by Parten's categories, are not typically as stagelike as the author had described (Eckerman & Whatley, 1977; Mueller & Brenner, 1977; Rubin, 1977). However, Parten's categorization of play has proven useful to many researchers. Increases in the time children spend in parallel play with objects during the second year of life have been well documented (Mueller & Brenner, 1977). Increases in the amount of time children spend in group activities were observed when comparing 2–3 year olds with 4–5 year olds (Smith, 1978). Yet, solitary play and parallel play are no longer assumed to always be less complex or less mature than cooperative play, but are looked upon as activities that develop in their own right (Rubin, 1977). For example, Moore, Evertson, and Brophy (1974) described developmental shifts within solitary play from that of primarily watching other children, to expressive activities, to more constructive behaviors. Roper and Hinde (1978) found that the amount of time children spent in solitary play was not related to the time they spent in groups; more solitary play did not imply more or less group participation. Because the concept of parallel play involves two defining components, (1) proximity to another child without cooperative interaction and (2) appropriate play activity or use of objects, it has sometimes been treated as a higher form of social activity (because at least the children are close together) and sometimes as a form lower than solitary play (because if they really wanted to play together then one would expect cooperative play; otherwise solitary play would indicate more independence). One solution to this difficulty has been to avoid the categorization of play as a single entity and measure the separate components of proximity, interaction, and type of object use or game (Rubin, 1977).

A child learning to play is thus seen as acquiring two sets of skills: those involving use of objects (or in the case of dramatic play, skills such as imagination) and those involving interactions with playmates (Rubin, 1977). It may be possible for a child to be quite competent in one area and much less competent in the other. However, it also may be more common to see synergistic effects in which delays in one area are accompanied by delays in the other. Similarly, there are parellels between social and object-oriented aspects of play in normally developing children. Mueller and Brenner (1977) described changes in peer-directed social behavior that coincided with changes in the development of more complex use of toys. These changes involved shifts from socially directed behavior such as looking at other children or directing an action to them to coordinated social behaviors such as turn taking that were equivalent to more complicated play with objects.

In the infant, what may appear as more complex social behaviors such as turn taking may be initially dependent on the adult structuring the interaction, and thus may be highly context specific until the child grows older. Given the brevity of many early social interactions (Holmbeg, 1980), attention getting may be a more important skill for infants and preschoolers, with adults taking the responsibility for maintaining the interaction, while attention holding may become increasingly important for older children (Keane & Conger, 1981) in more reciprocal relationships. Similarly, for young autistic children expectations for social behavior may be based on their ability to get attention from anticipating adults. In this case, social motivation may be one of the most critical distinguishing factors in how socially impaired a child is judged to be. For older children and adolescents with autism, for whom *some* social motivation is established, issues of social competence (e.g., attention holding) may become more important.

In contrast to quantitative measurement of peer interactions for autistic children, qualitative observations have been even more limited both in the amount of research performed and in the number of variables studied. In relation to the distinction between attention getting and attention holding, Martini (1980) observed two 8-year-old autistic children in a classroom grouping with four other severely socially impaired classmates and two teachers during free play. She found that the boys engaged in fairly frequent "contacts" (1.13 per minute), but that these contacts were very brief and seldom sustained for longer than 20 seconds. It should be noted that these contacts included behaviors such as looking or changes in body orientation, as well as overt behavioral approaches, so that it is not clear if the children were "making contact" and then withdrawing because the other child responded too little or too much (which is Martini's interpretation) or whether the children simply never went beyond the first step of "onlooker" behavior to a more overt form of interaction.

In a series of papers, McHale and others (McHale, Olley, & Marcus, 1981a; McHale, Olley, Marcus, & Simeonsson, 1981b; McHale, 1983) also attempted to look at qualitative aspects of autistic children's play and interaction with nonhandicapped peers. In one study (McHale et al., 1981a), five nonverbal severely to moderately retarded autistic children between 5 and 8 years of age were observed playing with each other, with a group of five nonhandicapped peers and with their teacher. The autistic children most frequently displayed asocial and stereotypic play with their autistic classmates and cooperative play with the nonhandicapped children.

In another study (McHale, 1983), 10 small groups of nonhandicapped second and third graders participated in daily play sessions with six autistic children for a period of a week. The interactive and communicative behavior of the nonhandicapped children increased over the week in which their group visited the autism classroom. The autistic children showed increases in the amount of social interaction and decreases in the amount of solitary activity, but these could be measured only over the course of the 10-week period, since variability was so great. There were no significant changes in the frequency of communication or appropriate play of the children with autism. However, the study did yield some interesting observations. The children played mostly in pairs. They spent over half their time using gross motor toys (i.e., tricycles) as opposed to constructive toys (i.e., blocks) or sensorimotor materials (i.e., tops). Because of high variability, the limited number of variables, and the lack of a control group, the conclusions that can be drawn from the study were limited. Yet, overall the results were promising. By the end of the 10-week period, the autistic children spent about 75% of their time interacting with other children.

For the present research, a number of qualitative measures of social behavior (and behaviors suggested to serve as precursors to active social interactions) were identified as potentially relevant to very early peer interactions. These variables, listed in Table II, include a measure of proximity, visual attention to others, time spent in self-stimulatory activities, and time spent in appropriate solitary play.

C. Interactive Measures

A third kind of unit of analysis is necessary to measure the relationship between the *type* of behaviors of interacting children. Obviously, this kind of analysis is often highly dependent on both quantitative and qualitative measures described above, but it goes beyond asking what individual aspects of the target-child's behavior or of the situation allow one to predict whether he or she will interact, to asking which relationships among aspects of both children's behavior allow prediction of successful interactions. For example, marked differences have been noted in the responsiveness of very young children to different kinds of initiations and in different contexts. Tremblay *et al.* (1981) found a much higher rate of response to overtures for rough and tumble play than to vocalized calls for attention in preschool children. The presence of toys has been found to trigger more frequent initiations in some situations, especially in groups, but to decrease the amount of social interaction in dyads of normally developing children (see Rogers, 1982) compared to situations in which there were no toys. Certain types of activities during day-care such as house corners and teacher-directed reading have been shown to promote social interaction more than others (Rubin, 1977). Holmberg (1980) found that increases in the number of elaborate interchanges among peers from 12 to 42 months old could be accounted for by more joint use of objects maintained over several initiation–response sequences as well as by a greater number of conversations involving purely verbal exchanges. Verbal initiations were the most obvious social act that increased with age of peer in Holmberg's study. Interestingly, verbal overtures did not increase at the expense of object-oriented behaviors, but in addition to them. Further, the relative frequency of negative or "assertive" acts as compared to positive social behaviors

Table II

*Qualitative Measures of Behaviors Serving
as Precursors to Interaction*

Maintenance and toleration of proximity to others
Time attending to others
Time spent in self-stimulatory activities
Time in solitary play

---

peaked at about 30 months in Holmberg's group of normally developing subjects, but the absolute number of negative initiations did not change from 12 to 42 months. Overall, Holmberg (1980) characterized the age change in peer interactions from 1- to 3½-year-old children as a gradually expanding number of different types of behaviors (from giving and taking, to imitating simple uses of objects, to joint use of objects and conversations) that allowed for longer, more complex interchanges and gave the children more options from which to select successful ways of initiating or responding to a particular playmate.

Studies that measure interactive aspects of behavior in autistic children with peers are very few. While no specific measurements were taken, McHale and her coauthors (McHale et al., 1982a,b) commented that, in their group study, the nonhandicapped children who were the most directive and persistent in their style of play were the most successful in eliciting social responses from the children with autism. Similarly, an experimental study by Clark and Rutter (1981), although not with peers, showed that when the experimenter made more interpersonal demands in terms of questions and explanations, autistic children responded with more relevant speech and more frequent adult-related behavior. These findings parallel the classroom studies of Bartak and Rutter (Bartak & Rutter, 1973; Rutter & Bartak, 1973) in which greater social responsiveness was observed in classrooms where there were high and consistent demands for appropriate social behavior.

Yet, as Wing pointed out, when placed in the context of peer interactions, autistic children are triply handicapped in playgroup contexts by their specific social deficits (e.g., their very lack of the initiating skills described by Vandell in normally developing 6 month olds), their language deficits, and their limited abilities to play or use objects creatively. Their options are hence even more limited not only when the tasks are unstructured, but also when they require some spontaneous use of objects and some reciprocal interaction, as in play between nonhandicapped children. A major problem in designing treatment programs for these deficits is that it is difficult even to identify reasonable units of observations and analysis in the face of so many entangled problems. However, for the present research, based on the normal developmental literature, a number of interactive measures of social behavior were identified as potentially relevant to changes usually occurring during early childhood. These variables, summarized in Table III, include measures of the types of behaviors that serve as social responses, the children's manner of initiating interaction, and their flexibility in responding to a variety of initiations. Distinctions were made on the basis of five factors: mode of behavior (e.g., verbal), imitation, positive/negative, appropriateness, and position in behavioral sequence (e.g., beginning versus continuing).

Table III

Interactive Measures

Behaviors which were categorized	Factors used to categorize behavior types
Types of responses made by autistic child	Verbal vs motor-gestural vs object oriented
Types of initiations made by autistic child	Imitative vs nonimitative
Types of initiations receiving a response	Positive vs negative
from autistic child	Appropriate vs inappropriate
	Beginning vs continuing

In summary, quantitative, qualitative, and interactive measures of social behaviors have been drawn from research on the development of peer interactions in normally developing children from infancy through the preschool years, in order to describe the social interactions of preschool and school-age autistic children. The research reported below utilized these variables to provide systematic description of the social behavior of a number of children with autism. The next step was to design treatment programs using knowledge from developmental studies of the contexts in which positive social behaviors between young peers are likely to occur.

IV. Techniques for Intervention: Overall Approach

One of the first steps in designing a treatment program for the peer-related behavior of autistic children was to evaluate existing programs to teach social skills. A number of carefully designed programs exist for the treatment of children described as socially isolated or aggressive (Wanlass & Prinz, 1982), but it rapidly was apparent that these programs were not appropriate for the population we wished to serve. First, especially for the socially isolated children, the assumption was generally made that the withdrawn children possessed the skills they needed in order to participate in more interaction, but did not use these skills. In fact, results from several studies have indicated that, when they do initiate interaction, many withdrawn children are as successful as others, but that the critical difference between other children and them was the extent to which they responded to others (Greenwood, Todd, Walker, & Hops, 1978). For autistic children, it did not seem fair to assume that performance factors, such as general responsiveness, were the major issue. Second, and probably more important, available social skills programs, even for preschoolers, have tended to be *very* verbal (Gottman, Gonso, & Schuler, 1976; Greenwood *et al.*, 1978; LaGreca & Santogrossi, 1980; Spivack & Shure, 1974). Analyzing hypothetical situations and role playing are major techniques. Although these techniques might be of value for a certain number of high-functioning older children and adolescents with autism, they did not seem applicable to most preschool or school-age autistic children.

V. Study 1: The Social Behavior of Autistic Children in Same-Age and Mixed-Age Dyads

A recurring statement about the social deficits experienced by autistic children with peers is that they have no friends. While friendship has many meanings, two characteristics of children's relationships seem amenable to deliberate manipulation and might be used to help children with autism to develop a friendship. First, as the friendship develops, children seek each other out and have more extended and varied experiences with each other (Hartup, 1977). Thus, research with normally developing children has shown that much of peer interaction in preschool children occurs during self-defined dyads even in the midst of groups (Holmberg, 1980; Vandell, 1977). Though it sounds obvious that friends would spend at least some time interacting in pairs, for children with autism for whom opportunities for *any* interaction with nonhandicapped children are limited, opportunities for the undivided attention of a normally developing child in a dyad are almost nonexistent. Furthermore, by being without many of the basic attention-getting skills discussed earlier, autistic children often cannot create a dyad where interactions can develop beyond attracting attention in order to participate in more reciprocal and elaborate interchanges (Holmberg, 1980). Among a similar vein, Sinson and Wetherick (1981) suggested that the reason why children with Down's syndrome, who were quite sociable when in a special nursery, had almost no social interaction with peers in an integrated setting was that the children with Down's syndrome inadvertently discouraged any initial interactive attempts by refusing to look at other children as they approached. Most of the previous research on play and peer interaction of children with autism used groups of children ranging from 2 autistic children and a nonhandicapped playmate (Strain et al., 1979) to groups of as many as 10 children (McHale, 1983). Thus, one simple technique selected for the treatment programs reported here was to create dyads with the autistic children as members, by providing them with the opportunity to play with a series of nonhandicapped playmates one at a time. Only the two children were in the room at one time, so neither had any alternative social companions. The autistic children did not have to compete for attention with other more responsive or interesting partners.

A second aspect of friendships in normally developing children is familiarity. Friendships do not develop instantaneously (Lewis & Rosenblum, 1975). Once they have developed, even by age 4 or 5 years, they tend to remain stable over at least several weeks (Marshall & McCandless, 1957) and several different situations (Hartup, 1975). A number of authors have stressed the importance of familiarity as children learn similar response repertoires which promote the maintenance of further social interaction (Doyle *et al.* 1980) and establish mutual rules for relating (Holmberg, 1980). Children playing with familiar partners have been shown to imitate each other more often and so to expand the ways that they play more than children interacting with unfamiliar playmates (Doyle *et al.*, 1980). Some authors have identified reciprocal imitation as the basis for friendships, particularly between handicapped and nonhandicapped children (Snyder, Apolloni, & Cooke, 1977). For autistic children who have little contact with nonhandicapped children, there are typically few opportunities for enough contact with the same child that sufficient familiarity can develop. Some children have a great deal of interaction with siblings which may compensate for this, but many do not have normally developing siblings readily available or willing to participate.

In previous research with autistic children, several studies rotated nonhandicapped peers frequently (McHale, 1983), while others set up interactions with clearly defined adult-determined styles of interaction (Strain *et al.*, 1979). These manipulations left little room for development of mutual rules within the social group, and not surprisingly, few long-lasting changes were observed from peer exposure.

For the studies conducted here, it was decided to allow the dyads some time together every day over a period of several weeks. An interval of 15 minutes per day was selected as a reasonable amount of time for the nonhandicapped children to be out of class that also fit within the attention span of the children with autism. Since previous research indicated that the immediate effect of adult interruptions was often to stop ongoing peer interactions (Strain, 1981), it was decided that adults would interfere with the children's play only if absolutely necessary. No specific instructions were given to the children except to play with each other. It was felt that this approach could provide information about the effect of growing familiarity on the relatively natural interactions of a number of autistic children and nonhandicapped peers.

A. Subjects

Six children (5 boys, 1 girl) with autism were selected for the initial study (Hopkins & Lord, 1981), out of 17 children attending a categorical program for children with autism and related disorders in a public elementary school. The children all met Rutter's (1978c) and *DSM III* (American Psychiatric Association, 1979) diagnostic criteria for autism. They all had receptive language sufficient to understand simple oral directions in familiar contexts. They were seldom self-injurious or aggressive. They formed a relatively homogeneous group in chronological age (10–12 years), intellectual level (Leiter IQs of 35–45; Arthur, 1952), and scores on the Childhood Autism Rating Scale (moderate to severe ranges of autism) completed independently by two psychologists (Schopler, Reichler, DeVellis, & Daly, 1980). The children were representative of children who attended categorical programs for children with autism in the geographical area.

A major methodological issue concerned the selection of playmates for the children with autism. Same-sex partners were selected, because even during the preschool years most peer interactions occur between members of the same sex (Hartup, 1980; Parten, 1932). However, choosing the age of the playmate, both absolute and relative to the age of the child with autism, was more difficult. Recently, in a number of studies with nonautistic children as well as with animals, it has been suggested that younger playmates promote interaction with socially deficient individuals more effectively than do older peers. The logic behind this suggestion included the belief that the younger playmates would be better models of simple, early-developing play skills than older children would be and that, being less assertive, younger peers would provide socially handicapped individuals with greater opportunities to be "leaders" (Furman, Rahe, & Hartup, 1979; Suomi & Harlow, 1972). Since in our experience, autistic youngsters between 5 and 12 years of age attending elementary school in this geographical area were often placed into integrated kindergartens, and since cognitively, kindergartners (out of all the nonhandicapped children attending school) most closely matched the available autistic subjects in terms of nonverbal mental age, 5- to 6-year-old normally developing children were selected to serve as one group of playmates.

On the other hand, the advantages of same-age playmates were also considered. Nonhandicapped children matched in chronological age to the children with autism would be between the ages of 10 and 12 years and thus cognitively functioning at much higher levels than the autistic children. The 10- to 12-year-old nonhandicapped children (referred to as same-age partners) would be expected to be more assertive than younger playmates and to perhaps involve the autistic children in more play (Greenwood et al., 1981). Same-age playmates might provide more structure and explicit guidance (Clark & Rutter, 1981) than younger children and be more flexible in their social repertoire and more able to suit the needs of their playmates. Discrepancies between the levels of the handicapped and nonhandicapped children could have a positive influence, since several studies have found that when a discrepancy existed between cognitive levels of interacting children, the play of the less competent children began to resemble that of the more competent children more often than the reverse (Guralnick, 1981; Lougee, Grueneich, & Hartup, 1977).

Hence, in Study 1, the autistic children were each paired with two non-handicapped children of the same sex, one child from grade 4–6 matched to within 6 months of the autistic child's chronological age and one child from kindergarten. Nonhandicapped children were volunteers from classes in the school housing the program for autistic children. Thus, there were six 10- to 12-year-old children with autism, each of whom was assigned to two nonhandicapped playmates of the same sex, one a kindergartner and one from grade 4–6. Two autistic children were randomly assigned to a control group and received no special treatment except for control observation sessions with the nonhandicapped peers and daily visits to the treatment room with the teacher. These visits were matched in frequency and spacing to the actual treatment sessions of another subject.

B. Procedures

A number of other procedural decisions about treatment, in addition to subject-related decisions, were also influenced by the normal developmental literature. As it was known that space restrictions can increase the likelihood of interaction in normal children (Mueller, 1972; Smith, 1978), one end of an extra classroom in the school was marked off into 1-ft squares to create a 15 × 15-ft play area. Familiar toys were available such as blocks, bowling pins, hats, vehicles, and very large puzzles. Large gross motor toys (e.g., tricycles, climbing apparatus) were avoided because of suggestions that social behavior decreases in the presence of these toys (McHale, 1983; Smith, 1978). For the first 5 minutes, the children were encouraged to select their own toys; for the second 5 minutes, they were asked to play together with the vehicles and blocks (although this was not enforced once they set up the blocks); and for the third 5 minutes, they were told they could play with whatever they wanted. Previous research with nonhandicapped children had suggested that more social interaction occurred using vehicles, in a house corner, or in teacher-led groups than in other contexts (Rubin, 1977). Requiring the children to spend some time with the blocks and vehicles was an attempt to see if these findings held true in this setting.

Treatment consisted of 10 daily 15-minute sessions during which the autistic child and peer were asked to play together in the special classroom. Nonhandicapped children were asked to "help the autistic child learn to play." Autistic children were told to "go play." An adult familiar to the children was present at all times, but sat reading at a desk behind a screen.

Baseline data on the social-behavioral variables described below were collected by videotaping the autistic children in groups of three playing in the treatment room for 15 minutes on the day before treatment was initiated and by taping each autistic child playing with one nonhandicapped peer for 15 minutes on the first day of treatment (day 1). The order in which the different-age peers played with the autistic children was counterbalanced. On the sixth and tenth day of treatment, videotapes were again made of the treatment dyads and the control dyads. After 10 days of treatment there was a week-long break without treatment, during which another 15-minute tape was made of the threesomes of autistic children. After the break, each autistic child in the experimental condition played with the other peer assigned to him, again for 10 consecutive days for 15 minutes each day. Videotapes were made of treatment and control dyads on the first day (day 11), middle day (day 16), and last day of treatment (day 20). A final 15-minute observation was made of all autistic children in classroom groups of three the following week.

Videotapes were scored in 15-second time samples ("intervals") by two observers not familiar with the purposes of the research project. Reliability was established on practice videotapes of children not included in the study and then checked by having the observers unknowingly code four of the same tapes at various times during the data analysis. Reliability coefficients for individual codes were always above .80 and were generally between .88 and .92.

Potential measures of quantitative, qualitative, and interactive aspects of social behavior, drawn from studies of normal social development, were discussed earlier. As shown in Table I, quantitative measures included the number of intervals in which the autistic child was observed interacting with the playmate, the number of initiations made by the autistic child (these included only overt visible or audible approaches), and the average number of intervals per continuous interaction in which the children were engaged in a single activity. Initiations included any active approach to the other child, such as throwing a ball, calling his or her name, or handing him or her an object. Responses included imitating an action within 15 seconds of its original occurrence, accepting an offered object, or following an instruction. Because any *active* approach was scored as an initiation even if the child had also made a separate response, the number of initiations included not only attempts to start interactions but also active attempts to maintain them. Thus, initiations were coded as "beginning" or "continuing." The ratio of responses made by the autistic child (within 15 seconds of his partner's overture) to his playmate's initiations was also computed.

As shown in Table II, qualitative measures included the absolute distance between the children, whether or not the autistic child's face was oriented towards his playmate at the time of the 15-second time sample, and the number of intervals including self-stimulatory behavior and/or solitary play.

Interactive measures, as shown in Table III, included the types of responses (e.g., gestural, verbal, positive, negative) and initiations made by each child and the relationship (e.g., imitative, beginning) between the kind of behaviors shown by one child and the kind of behavior shown by the other. Different types of initiations and responses were coded separately, but a child only received credit for one initiation and one response in a 15-second interval. A child who caught a ball tossed by his partner, said "thank you," and tossed it back to him was scored as responding to his playmate's nonverbal offer of an object (a beginning initiation) by accepting the object and making a positive verbal statement (a verbal plus nonverbal object-related response), and then offering the object to him (an imitative object-offer as a continuing initiation).

C. Use of Baseline Data for Treatment Goals

The process of using developmental trends to identify specific changes in these measures which would serve as goals for treatment in Study 1 involved two steps. First, by observing the children with autism prior to treatment, their social behavior could be placed on a series of continua, derived from Wing and Gould's categories of social deficit, which had some correspondence with developmental sequences. Second, predictions could then be made of behaviors most likely to change.

Before treatment began, the autistic children were observed in two groups (corresponding to the two classrooms from which they were drawn) of three children interacting with each other in the treatment room. There was very little variability in behavior among the children. No child made more than four initiations or more than four responses in 15 minutes. The average distance between a child and the child closest to him was over 4 ft. The children only spent from 2 to 6 out of 60 intervals engaged in appropriate solitary play with objects. However, they did spend from 25 to 30% of the time oriented toward each other. This could have been chance, because there were four walls and if they had simply rotated every minute to turn to look at a different wall, the same result could have occurred. Overall, the behaviors of all the children would seem to be considered *aloof* on the basis of quantitative measures. However, few opportunities even to be *passive* occurred, since the children rarely approached each other.

When they were observed during Session 1, interactions between the autistic and nonhandicapped children also occurred at very low rates, in accordance with the observations of other severely handicapped children by other authors (Guralnick, 1981). In fact, for all but one autistic child, the initial interaction with the unfamiliar nonhandicapped playmate was even less successful (i.e., greater distance, less interaction) than with familiar autistic classmates during the pretreatment observation. For five of the six autistic children, reciprocal interactions with the nonhandicapped peers occurred in fewer than 4 out of 60 15-second intervals. Only one autistic child made any initiations. The children with autism responded to less than 25% of their partner's attempts to get them to play. A typical interaction consisted of a single initiation made by the nonhandicapped child and, in one out of four cases, a response by the autistic child. However, there was only one negative interaction between an autistic child and a nonhandicapped playmate. Active avoidance on the part of the autistic children consisted of maintaining distance and self-stimulating. The autistic children generally remained at least 6 ft (out of 15 possible) away from their playmate.

Over half of each of the autistic children's time was spent unoccupied (i.e., not interacting with the playmate or using any of the toys). On the average, some kind of self-stimulatory activity occurred during 11 out of 60 intervals. Five out of six autistic children showed no cooperative play; however, the same children were observed in simple but appropriate solitary play during 10–21 intervals (out of 60). They were also each observed to be oriented toward the other child at least 25% of the time.

Although Wing and Gould (1979) would probably have labeled five out of the six children as *aloof*, there were three findings that suggested that the autistic children were showing some passive interest in social activity. (1) The autistic children did engage in more appropriate solitary play in the presence of nonhandicapped partners than they had when with autistic classmates. (2) They responded positively and very rarely negatively to *some* of the nonhandicapped playmates' overtures. (3) They spent some time oriented to their partners, without any prompting or specific instruction to do so. Thus, treatment goals included further modification of preinteractive behaviors (i.e., proximity, attention, self-stimulatory behavior) that might lead to increased responsiveness (and thus, initiation and time in interaction) for these children. In addition, it was hoped that solitary play might show further increases as the autistic children observed new ways of using the materials by watching their playmates (Doyle *et al.*, 1980).

One autistic child, David (Subject 4), was quite different from the other children from the start of the sessions. From the start, David responded to almost 75% of his playmate's overtures. In fact, his rate of response was almost identical to that of his nonhandicapped partner and the other nonhandicapped playmates. On the other hand, David was quite self-stimulatory and made many fewer initiations (i.e., 4 out of 60 possible) than did his partner, who approached him during 36 intervals. Interactions between David and his partner were quite brief and the average distance between them was similar to that of other dyads. Overall, David's behavior seemed more accurately described as *passive* than *aloof*. Yet in most ways, David's nonhandicapped partner's behavior appeared to be no different from the other same-age playmates, though he produced more initiations during this first session than any of the other partners.

Expectations for David in response to treatment included increased frequency of initiating activities and engaging in solitary play, and longer interactions. The difference between David's behavior (which was definitely *aloof*) with his familiar autistic classmate and his behavior with his first nonhandicapped playmate suggested that generalization or failure to find generalization would be heavily dependent upon the social behaviors of both children in the dyad. Measures in which the potential for generalization seemed less confounded with the peer's behavior than in a total interaction score were solitary play, toleration of proximity, and time spent oriented toward the other child.

D. Results and Discussion

For the autistic children in the treatment condition (Subjects 1–4), a number of changes were observable after only 10 sessions. As shown in Fig. 1, the number of interactions increased markedly for three out of four children from day 1 to 10 and for a different three out of four dyads from day 11 to 20.

In addition, as depicted in Fig. 2, the average distance between the children decreased to less than 3 ft by day 20 for all children in treatment. Self-stimulatory behavior decreased for all four autistic children in the treatment condition. Time attending to the other child increased until all of the autistic children in the treatment group were oriented toward the other child during more than 75% of the intervals during the last session. Time spent in noninteractive play and appropriate object use increased for three out of four children during each set of dyads; ceiling effects occurred for the other two dyads because of their high frequency of interaction. These results are portrayed in Fig. 3.

The percentage of their playmates' initiations to which they responded increased for all four autistic children in treatment from a mean of 36% at day 1 to a mean of 94% at day 20. The number of interactions that were longer than a single initiation–response episode increased from a mean per session of just over zero, to four. Nevertheless, initiations made by the autistic children were still relatively rare (the mean was less than six per session, modes = 1–2) and were quite variable across time and subject (range = 0–23). Except for David, almost all of the autistic children's initiations were beginning approaches. For David, the proportion of initiations that began interactions rather than continued them gradually decreased from 90 to about 50%. Charles (Subject 3) also began to produce a few continuing initiations but only in the last set of sessions.

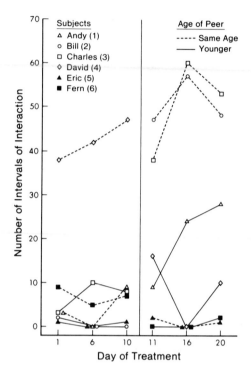

Fig. 1. Number of intervals of interaction across days of treatment (Study 1).

For the control dyads (Subjects 5 and 6), no consistent pattern of change emerged. No changes in the amount of interaction or in any of the qualitative measures were observed. Appropriate solitary play increased for one child in one dyad, decreased for one other, and remained steady for the children in the other two dyads. Responsiveness increased in two of the four dyads from a mean response:initiation ratio of about .25:1 to ratios of .40:1 and .52:1, but decreased for one dyad down to .20:1 and remained virtually unchanged for the other.

Generalization from one nonhandicapped playmate to another was measured by comparing data collected during initial sessions with the first nonhandicapped child (day 1) with data from the initial sessions with the second partner (day 11). Scores on day 11 as compared to day 1 indicated more time spent oriented toward the other child and more consistent responsiveness for all four autistic children in treatment, and more interaction for three out of four treatment dyads. These differences were not observed for the two children who served as controls.

Generalization was also assessed by observing the autistic children's behavior with their autistic classmates. All autistic children in the treatment

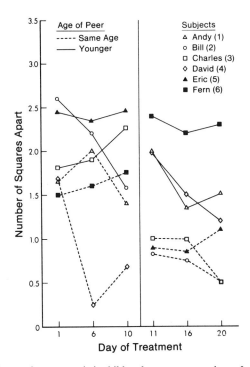

Fig. 2. Mean distance between autistic child and partner across days of treatment. (Distance was measured across 1-ft squares marked on the floor.)

group showed decreases in distance from other children (from a mean of over 4 ft to less than 3), increased time attending to another child (mean of 23 intervals to 34; see Fig. 4), and more frequent solitary play (mean of 4 to 25 intervals out of 60). Amount of interaction increased very slightly for each treatment subject (from a mean of 4 intervals to 9). No changes occurred for the control group, except for slight decreases in distance between the children.

Comparisons between same-age and mixed-age dyads were generally quite consistent across subjects. While relative age differences held true for playmates in treatment and control conditions, the absolute scores became increasingly different with treatment. Only treatment dyads are described below in order to minimize confusion. Same-age playmates initiated interaction five times more often than younger playmates (means = 30 vs 6 out of 60 intervals, respectively) and were almost twice as likely to respond to the autistic child (99 vs 58% response rate, respectively). Given these findings, it is not surprising that, for three out of four treatment pairs, the rate of interaction was consistently higher for same-age dyads than the mixed-age peers (see Fig. 1). As shown in Fig. 2, distance between play-

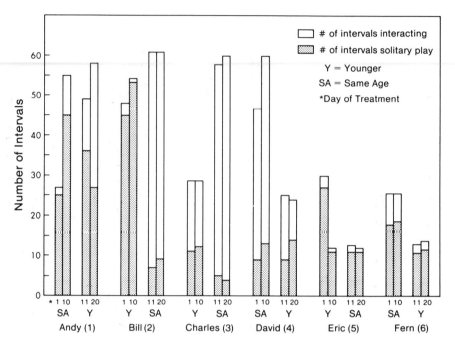

Fig. 3. Number of intervals spent in interactive and noninteractive but appropriate play for individual autistic children on first and last day in each dyad.

mates was almost always greater for mixed-age pairs than same-age pairs. The autistic children made more initiations (means = 10 vs 3) and spent more time oriented (means = 47 vs 30 out of 60 intervals) toward same-age children and younger children. The number of initiations made by each autistic child also increased over time within the same-age dyad, although there was a great deal of intersubject variability. Interactions of autistic children with same-age playmates were typically sustained without interruption in one activity longer than were interactions with kindergartners. Further, children with autism responded to same-age playmates at a rate of over 80% and to kindergartners at a rate of 55%, though there were no differences in the rate of self-stimulatory behavior in the presence of either peer.

Qualitative measures helped to clarify the nature of the interaction with different-age playmates. Of the initiations made by nonhandicapped peers in the treatment condition, 17% were vocalizations alone, 51% were purely nonverbal, and 32% were combinations of vocal and nonverbal behaviors. Of the nonverbal behaviors, two-thirds involved the offer of an object or demonstration of its use with a gesture of approach, about one-third were

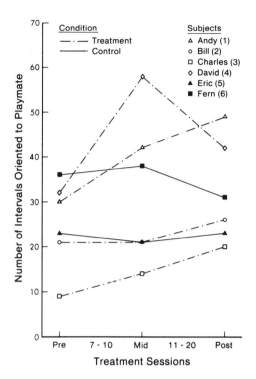

Fig. 4. Number of intervals during which autistic children attended to one or more autistic classmates, as measured pre-, mid-, and posttreatment.

purely gestural without an object, and only a few involved physical contact. Younger playmates used more vocalization alone and in combination with nonverbal behaviors than did their older counterparts. Same-age playmates appeared to reduce the number of vocalizations made without accompanying gestures over the 10 sessions, but younger playmates did not.

All of the responses made by the autistic children in the treatment condition to their playmates' overtures were nonverbal. Over 98% of the responses involved accepting materials (58%) or imitating an action with an object (40%). The frequency of these behaviors was variable over the course of the study primarily because the children selected different materials on different days. There was no effect of the 5-minute "block and vehicle" period, except that the children did play with the blocks and vehicles during this time more often than with other toys. There were no identifiable relationships between specific toys and specific behaviors. However, there were significant differences in the rates at which the autistic children responded to different types of initiations. Whereas 92% of nonverbal initiations and 84% of initiations that involved both a vocalization and a nonverbal gesture received a response, only 24% of the initiations that were vocalizations alone did so.

Of the initiations made over the course of the study by the autistic children, all but five involved offers or use of materials without speech. The nonhandicapped playmates responded to 92% of these initiations. The five other overtures by autistic children all involved a vocalization alone. None of these initiations received a response, perhaps because most of them occurred out of context or were virtually incomprehensible (e.g., mumbled, poorly articulated) except to someone who knew the child well. The playmates typically responded to initiations by using the objects (85% of responses overall, 20% in imitation of the autistic children), gesturing only (11%), or touching the autistic child (4%). There were no purely vocal responses. Only 3% of the autistic children's nonverbal responses were accompanied by vocalization.

Observation suggested that, apart from age, the playmates who were the most effective at including their autistic partners in play were the children who were the most active and intrusive. A stepwise multiple regression including various measures summed over sessions of each nonhandicapped peer's behavior showed that the number of initiations made by the nonhandicapped peer accounted for over 50% of the variance in predicting the number of initiations the autistic child made. To control for the possibility of the reverse effect, namely that the nonhandicapped children were modeling the more active behavior of the autistic children, the same analysis was run using the change score for the number of autistic initiations from the first to last session within the dyads. This time the playmate's initiations accounted for over 60% of the variance in the autistic children's initiations. A similar analysis using change scores from the nonhandicapped peers yielded a regression coefficient of .15.

Individual differences among the children with autism were maintained throughout the first set of dyads (days 1–10) in level of interaction. David (Subject 4), who had been much more responsive than his classmates during Session 1, continued to show a much higher rate of interaction than did the other children with autism. This difference could be attributed both to his greater responsiveness and also to his partner's intrusiveness, since his nonhandicapped playmate produced more initiations than any of the other partners during Session 1. (He initiated 23 out of 60 intervals; the next highest initiation rate was 16, with a mean of 9 and a range of 1–23.) However, by the end of Session 10, the other autistic child in treatment who was playing with a same-age peer (Andy, Subject 1) was attending to his partner and responding to his partner's initiations at a rate equal to David. By Session 10, for those autistic children playing with younger partners, frequency of attention to the other child had also increased to just below that showed by David during Session 1. Rates of responsiveness increased over the 10 sessions for the autistic children with younger partners, but did not ever equal those with same-age partners.

Overall however, frequency of interaction remained higher for David than for the other children, because his partner continued to initiate interactions at a higher rate (31 out of 60 intervals) and because, interestingly, David began to make more initiations himself. Thus, as hoped, David did move up Wing and Gould's (1979) quasi-developmental progression to become more active, producing 18 initiations during Session 20. As predicted, length of interaction also increased to a mean of more than two initiation–response sequences per uninterrupted interaction for David and his partner. There was a ceiling effect for solitary play. On the other hand, after the first 10 sessions, the other autistic children would no longer have been called *aloof*, as they had become quite responsive to their partners. Their behaviors corresponded to the *passive* behavior of David at the beginning of the study.

In the second set of dyads (days 11–20), the two autistic children who played with same-age playmates showed even greater increases in responsiveness than they had with the kindergartners. They also began to have longer sustained interactions. Both Bill (Subject 2) and Charles (Subject 3) showed some increase in initiations, with Charles making 23 overtures to his playmate during Session 20. By the end of treatment, like David, Charles could no longer be called *passive*. He was actively engaged in playing with his partner.

During Sessions 11–20, Andy (Subject 1) was paired with a kindergartner who behaved much more like five of the six same-age partners than had Andy's first same-age playmate. This kindergartner made almost as many initiations as did the other children. He frequently offered materials. Andy became quite responsive and attended to this playmate, but never did make many initiations.

David's experience with his second and younger playmate represented one of the disadvantages of encouraging a *passive* autistic child to become more *active*. In the first session, David made nine initiations, most of which the kindergartner did not even acknowledge. These initiations included speaking to the kindergartner in very poorly articulated sentences, throwing a ball at him, and waving a puzzle piece at him without clearly indicating his purpose. In some instances, the kindergartner appeared frightened by the approaches of this much older and larger handicapped child. In the next sessions, both children made fewer and fewer overtures. However, as the nonhandicapped child became more comfortable, he (the kindergartner) became more assertive and some interaction was reestablished (see Fig. 1).

In summary, Study 1 investigated the interactions of six 10- to 12-year-old children with autism playing with autistic classmates and in dyads with nonhandicapped partners of the same chronological age or from kindergarten. Initial sessions contained very little interaction, except for one autistic child. With opportunities for daily interaction, the four children in treatment showed consistent gains in responsiveness, attentiveness, and appropriate precursor behaviors such as solitary play. The control group showed no equivalent changes.

While substantial gains were made over the course of treatment, the quality of the interactions remained different from interactions typically described in dyads of nonhandicapped children. There was little use of language, and interaction occurred at a relatively low rate in these dyads. The categories of *aloof, passive*, and *active but odd* proved to be quite useful in describing the quantitative aspects of the constellation of social behaviors in the autistic children. Variables related to these categories could be reliably measured, providing some empirical validation for these concepts. However, one caveat about the categories emerged. All of the children with autism changed categories at least once across observations and several changed many times. The categories in which the children's behavior fell were not stable across playmates or even across time with the same playmate.

The particular behaviors that an autistic child showed at any given time related both to qualities intrinsic to himself and also to the behavior of his playmate. For example, David (Subject 4) was very responsive from the start of treatment. This responsiveness may have contributed to his partner's high rate of initiation, which could have then fed into David's increasingly high rate of initiation. However, with an unfamiliar kindergartner, David's active behavior was more frightening than stimulating. Thus, interactions between them dwindled to almost none, until the kindergartner began to take the lead and David responded more passively.

All four autistic children were very responsive to at least one partner who showed a high rate of initiations (three of the same-age playmates and one younger partner), but only two of the four autistic children themselves began to initiate. Though concurrent changes occurred for some variables, a uniform increase in all social behaviors did not occur. At a minimum, both the opportunity to interact and some level of interest or skills in initiating on the part of the autistic children (as shown by Charles and David, but not by Andy and Bill) seemed to be necessary but not sufficient to produce social interaction. Opportunities for interaction were provided by the treatment program in general, and by persistent initiations by peers specifically. These results would support the use of Wing and Gould's broader conceptualization of the triad of social impairment, since differentiating purely on the basis of social behavior between autistic and nonautistic children with severe social deficits would seem to be very difficult (although Wing and

Gould also used elaborate routines to make this differentiation for their population and the present data do not address this issue).

VI. Study 2: A Replication, with Higher Functioning Autistic Children

A. Subjects, Procedures, and Goals

Because the first study involved only six subjects who were drawn from a single program serving autistic children, the next step was to see if the results reported above could be replicated with another group of children (Hopkins & Lord, 1981). Thus, the second study was a replication of Study 1 using higher functioning children with autism in a different school setting. Two autistic boys were selected (Subject 7, Greg, and Subject 8, Hank) aged 8 years and 10 years old, respectively, who were in a categorical class for children with autism and related disorders. Both scored in the Borderline/ Low Average range of intelligence (76 and 83, respectively) on the Leiter International Performance Scale (Arthur, 1952) and in the mild range of autism on the Childhood Autism Rating Scale (Schopler et al., 1980). Both boys met DSM III (American Psychiatric Association, 1979) and Rutter (1978c) criteria for autism. Both boys were able to produce sentences five to seven words long and to understand fairly complex directions, but they differed in the amount of language they produced spontaneously. One boy, Greg, spoke fluently and frequently. He also exhibited quite complex though repetitive patterns of play. The second child, Hank, spoke very rarely. He spent much of his unstructured time rocking, humming, and looking at visual patterns while turning his head.

Procedures for Study 2 were similar for Study 1 except that children from grades 3 and 5 (instead of grades 4–6) were used as same-age playmates in addition to the younger kindergartners. Because of the limited availability of subjects and the complete lack of change occurring in the controls in Study 1, no control group was run. The autistic children were observed on three occasions (pre-, mid-, and posttreatment) in groups of three, with two other autistic-like children drawn from their classroom. They were also videotaped on days 1, 6, 10, 11, 16, and 20 with nonhandicapped partners.

From the outset of Study 2, the behaviors of the two children with autism were quite different from each other. As shown in Fig. 5, Greg began Session 1 with a much higher rate of interaction (25 out of 60 intervals) and a higher rate of response (.77 responses for every initiation) than Hank, or any of the subjects in Study 1 except David. Also, like David, Greg made some initiations on day 1 (i.e., 9), but many fewer than his partner, who

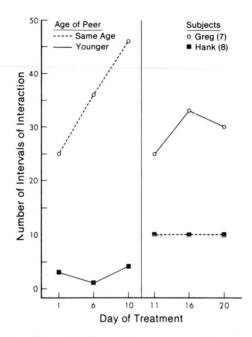

Fig. 5. Number of intervals of interaction across days of treatment (Study 2).

made 27. Several of the other aspects of his behavior, such as the time Greg spent oriented toward his playmate and his tolerance of the other child's proximity, were similar to the subjects in Study 1. However, he differed from all of them in that he engaged in frequent solitary play from the beginning and did not show any self-stimulatory behavior. He was also sometimes quite negative (which usually consisted of yelling "no"), unlike the children in the other study. Using Wing and Gould's categories, Greg could be considered *passive*. The same expectations held for him as for David in that it was predicted that his role as an active initiator would increase in response to treatment. More specific qualitative and interactive aspects of Greg's behavior are discussed below.

In contrast, Hank was much more like the children in Study 1. He made no initiations on day 1. His response rate was actually the lowest of any child observed (.12 responses per initiation). He showed very little solitary play and his rate of self-stimulation was very high (33 out of 60 intervals). On the average, he stayed almost 5 ft away from the other child, although the amount of time Hank spent attending to his playmate was similar to subjects in Study 1 (27 out of 60 intervals). Altogether during Session 1, Hank was the clearest example of an *aloof* child observed in either study.

B. Results and Discussion

Not surprisingly, the response to treatment of the two boys with autism was somewhat different. For Greg, who began day 1 with a high rate of interaction, response rate remained high but variable (between .67 and .93 responses per initiation). However, Greg's rate of initiation increased steadily with the same-age partner (from 9 to 27 out of 60) and with somewhat more variability with his younger playmate (from 19 to 24 intervals). Negative behaviors decreased with the same-age playmate only. As shown in Fig. 6, length of interaction increased with both partners, as did the number of continuing initiations Greg made.

While his attention to the same-age playmate increased gradually (from 24 to 46 out of 60 intervals), Greg's attention to the younger child remained lower than one might expect from Study 1 (around 30 intervals). This occurrence may have been due to Greg's interest in the toys. Greg was almost never unoccupied; his frequency of solitary play remained high throughout the study. His play not only varied in accordance with how much he wanted to interact with the other child, but his likelihood of interacting with his playmate was also affected by how intent he was in his play.

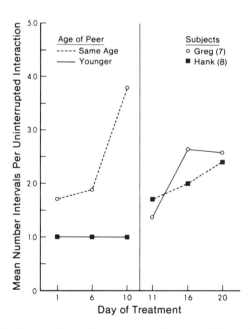

Fig. 6. Mean number of intervals per uninterrupted interaction.

In contrast, Hank (Subject 8) showed consistent improvements in how frequently he attended to the other child, increasing from 27 to 43 out of 60 intervals when with the younger playmate, to a ceiling of 52 to 54 out of 60 intervals with the same-age partner. Hank made initiations during only two sessions over the course of the study. His response rate per initiation increased from .12 at day 1 to .36 by day 10, remained at .28 for Session 11, and exceeded .75 by Sessions 16 and 20. His rate of self-stimulation remained relatively high through Session 11, but did gradually decrease to 18 out of 60 intervals on day 20. In addition, the amount of time Hank spent in appropriate solitary play steadily increased from 4 to 42 intervals by day 20. Distance from the playmate also decreased for each partner to less than 2 ft.

In their classroom groups observed pre-, mid-, and posttreatment, the two boys also showed different responses. Greg showed increasing orientation (from 13 to 32 out of 60 intervals) and responsiveness (from .55 to .70 responses per initiation) to his autistic classmates. Hank showed a decrease in self-stimulatory behavior and in the distance from his classmates. There were no changes in frequency of interaction in their classroom groups for either child. Negative incidents, which occurred regularly for both boys, decreased gradually from 8 and 2 on day 1 for Greg and Hank, respectively, to 4 and 0 on day 20.

As shown in Fig. 5, results contrasting the nonhandicapped playmates by age were very similar to Study 1. Both boys with autism interacted more with the same-age playmate than the younger one. They were more often oriented toward the same-age partner, closer to him, and more responsive to him. As shown in Fig. 6, sustained interactions lasting longer than two initiation–response sequences occurred more often with the same-age partner than with the younger child. Hank, who was quite self-stimulatory, showed fewer self-directed behaviors with the same-age playmate than the younger child. The same-age playmates were more consistently responsive than the younger ones and were more likely to approach the children with autism.

Specific characteristics of successful initiations and responses in interactions with the nonhandicapped kindergartners were similar to those of the autistic children with the kindergartners in Study 1. In both dyads in Study 2, over half of the younger nonhandicapped children's initiations were nonverbal offers of materials, imitations, or gestures without any accompanying vocalization. Similar to subjects in Study 1, all of Hank's responses to these overtures involved accepting offered objects or imitating the other child's action with the same or similar object. All of Hank's responses to the younger peer occurred after object offers; Hank did not respond to other types of interactions by his younger playmate at all. With the same-age partner, he responded twice as often to silent offers of materials than to verbal or verbal and gestural overtures. However, he did at least respond at a rate of about 40% to initiations involving language. As with his younger playmate, the pattern of nonverbal responses also held true for Hank's interactions with the same-age playmate. He made only one initiation himself over the course of treatment with each partner; these initiations consisted of throwing a ball to the other child and handing the other boy a puzzle piece (both coded as object offers).

From the perspective of the nonhandicapped playmates, Hank's same-age partner used more vocalizations with material offers (22%) and alone (47%) than did his younger playmate, who used vocalization alone or along with material offers only 28% of the time overall. The average length of interaction in terms of number of initiation–response sequences was 1.0 for Hank and the kindergarten child, but increased steadily with the same-age partner from 1.6 to 2.0 to 2.4 initiation–response sequences by day 20.

Greg's behavior with both nonhandicapped playmates differed in three significant ways from the behavior of Hank and the children in the previous study. Differences occurred in (1) the extent to which both partners spoke, (2) the extent to which they responded to each other's verbal attempts at communication, and (3) the length of time over which a particular interaction was sustained. Unlike Hank and the subjects in Study 1, with playmates of both ages Greg responded with approximately equal frequency to all types of verbal and nonverbal initiations except for touching, to which he responded negatively or not at all. With the younger partner, Greg's responses consisted primarily of accepting objects or imitating their use. However, with the same-age playmate, only one-quarter of his responses were purely nonverbal, with the remainder about equally split between purely verbal and simultaneous verbal and object-use behaviors. In turn, Greg's same-age partner produced more initiations that consisted of vocalizations alone (37%) and vocalizations plus nonverbal behaviors (48%) than did any of the other nonhandicapped playmates in either Study 1 or 2. Nearly half of Greg's responses were also verbal (46%) or verbal and object oriented (17%).

Greg himself made proportionately even more purely verbal overtures to both of his partners (compared to nonverbal or both verbal and nonverbal initiations) than the nonhandicapped playmates made to him. The type of initiation Greg used made no difference to the same-age partner's likelihood of response. However, the kindergartner responded to Greg's purely nonverbal offers of objects and gestures at a significantly higher rate (92–100%) than to his verbal only and nonverbal plus verbal overtures (56–68%). Almost all of the kindergartner's responses (94%) consisted of accepting objects or acting upon them in imitation without any vocalization.

The average length of uninterrupted interaction increased steadily for each dyad except Hank and the kindergartner, as shown in Fig. 6. By the tenth day together, almost one-half of Greg's interactions with his playmates went beyond an initiation and response sequence. By day 20 this was also the case for Hank and his same-age partner.

C. Overview of Study 1 and 2

One clear subjective impression that may not be immediately evident amid all the data presented here is how social the autistic children looked in the last few sessions of both studies, especially with the same-age peers. Negative interactions and some inappropriate behavior did occur, but they were very rare. Social responses and approaches scored on appropriateness were not reported, because obvious socially directed inappropriateness (e.g., unusual topics, monologues, inappropriate touching) never occurred more than two or three times in a session and only in a few sessions. This is not to say that these children were never socially inappropriate. In other settings, such as during an integrated gym or lunch period, particularly the most active children often behaved in quite bizarre ways, but they did not typically do so in this study.

What was it about this situation that contributed to these effects? It cannot be overemphasized how generally calm these sessions were. They occurred for short periods of time, on a daily basis, in a familiar environment. There were no adult demands except for staying within a restricted space, and no requirements that the children with autism sit still for long periods of time or attend to language or other difficult content areas. There was little verbal interaction except in the dyads in which *both* playmates were quite competent in their use of language. Cognitive demands were generally low and were very much determined by the children.

Activities were often quite repetitive. By being able to turn away or walk across the room in order to terminate an interaction, the child with autism had a significant amount of control over the interactions that occurred. As indicated by the data, for many of the dyads the pace of interaction increased very gradually. The general trend was to shift from little interaction or none at all to more frequent positive interaction, still often at a lower rate than one might expect with adults. Growing familiarity between the partners had effects in the treatment studies similar to those in research reported in the developmental literature (Doyle *et al.*, 1980). The autistic children gradually attended and responded to each other more. They began to imitate their partners' behavior more often over the course of treatment. They became more ready for social interaction (Mueller, 1972) by tolerating physical proximity and decreasing self-stimulatory behaviors. When they were not interacting, they engaged in more solitary play as well. Sometimes they even began to take an active role in initiating interactions; however, this was the least consistent change across subjects and situations.

This is not to claim that either the nonhandicapped playmates or the autistic children were behaving "normally." In normal circumstances, the nonhandicapped playmates may have paid little attention to the autistic children and certainly would not have put out the huge effort many of the playmates exerted in order to get the handicapped children to play. However, the nonhandicapped playmates were usually quite successful in creating situations that, as compared to those of adults, characterize peer relations in young children: egalitarian, repetitious, object-oriented interactions. The interactions that occurred in this study were in some ways not that different from a preschool child who plays with a toddler from next door for a few minutes at a time in his own home.

By the end of treatment, the autistic children did not look "normal." They still had difficulty in coordinating aspects of social behaviors (such as looking at someone before handing him something), they seldom used language, they were still primarily passive, and they still used objects in very limited ways. They responded more positively to the structure and intrusiveness of the same-age playmates than they did to the "opportunities for leadership" provided by the younger children. However, most of the social behaviors the autistic children did produce were surprisingly appropriate. These observations suggest that in those situations in which most bizarre social behaviors toward peers are typically observed (e.g., in public places, during lunch in a noisy cafeteria, in an integrated art class, meeting unfamiliar friends or siblings), the autistic children may be responding to the behavioral and cognitive demands of the entire situation as well as to the specific requirements for peer interaction. Integrating autistic children into relatively large, confusing, cognitively demanding regular school classrooms may be necessary and important for a number of reasons, but on its own it may not be the most effective way of allowing positive social behaviors toward peers to develop (Gresham, 1982; Guralnick, 1981).

Social competence and appropriateness, though obviously related, may also develop separately to some extent. In these sessions, while the children avoided obvious inappropriateness in most cases, they still had difficulty producing effective social approaches. Thus, although clear improvements occurred in responsiveness and in precursors to social behaviors for all the autistic children in treatment, increases in the number of initiations made by the children with autism were much less consistent.

One question that arose out of the first two studies was whether there was a way to reduce some of the variability in the peers' behavior in order to encourage more initiative on the part of the autistic children. Two findings from the earlier studies provided working hypotheses. First, it was observed in the first two studies that two of the three autistic children who consistently made some initiations (one of whom, Charles, was the only child to show a steady increase in initiations over the course of treatment) began the study as more responsive and spending more time in solitary play than the other autistic children.[2]

On the one hand, it may have been that children with some social skills benefit more from treatment than children with almost none. On the other hand, one could ask whether, by structuring the intervention, one can devise situations that produce the same kind of changes in all of the children as those that occurred in the one child, including children with more significant social deficits. If more solitary play and greater responsiveness could be produced in *aloof* autistic children, would they then be in a better position to participate more actively in peer interactions?

Second, high correlations were observed, not only between the number of initiations that were made by each autistic child within a dyad, but also between the number of initiations made by the nonhandicapped playmate and the increase in initiations (from day 1 to 10 or day 11 to 20) by the child with autism. On the basis of these findings, Study 3 was designed to structure the treatment so that the nonhandicapped peers reliably initiated frequent interactions from the start (increased quantity) and also made these initiations in such a way as to maximize the chances that the autistic children would respond (improved quality of interactive characteristics). Given the experience of Strain (Strain *et al.*, 1979), in which little generalization was observed even after marked improvements with a "trained" peer, an additional question for Study 3 concerned the extent to which improvements in these structured dyads would generalize to other playmates.

VII. Study 3: Explicitly Trained Peers and the Social Behavior of Autistic Children

A. Study Design

1. SUBJECTS

Four middle-class white males, all of them between 9 years and 11 years of age in a public school program for youngsters with autistic-like behavior, and who met the criteria described below, were selected from two class-

[2]One could argue that these children were simply less autistic than the other subjects and just showed fewer social deficits in general. In fact, as discussed earlier, Lorna Wing would probably have classified two of the children as *passive* (and so *not* autistic by her criteria for autism), becoming more *active but odd* over the course of treatment. It is important to note

rooms. According to the independent judgments of two psychologists, the autistic subjects all were categorized as severely autistic on the Childhood Autism Rating Scale (Schopler *et al.*, 1980) and met Rutter's (1978c) diagnostic criteria for autism. In addition, each child frequently showed sensory peculiarities and some self-stimulatory behavior (*DSM III*). The autistic children ranged in age of 9 years:1 month to 11 years:10 months, scored in the moderate to severe range of retardation on the Leiter International Performance Scale (Arthur, 1952), and scored between 2½ and 3½ years (age equivalents) on the Peabody Picture Vocabulary Test (Dunn, 1965). All the autistic children understood a limited amount of language such that they could follow simple directions in a familiar context. Two of the autistic children spoke in simple phrases; two other children each used a small number of manual signs.

The teachers of the fourth-grade classes in the same public elementary school were asked to recommend 12 nonhandicapped boys who were normally developing socially and cognitively, and who could afford to miss 15 minutes of class each day for 6 weeks. All nonhandicapped children were white, middle-class males ranging in age from 9:6 to 10:11. The children were randomly assigned to groups of three nonhandicapped playmates and one autistic child. Within a group, the nonhandicapped peers were randomly assigned to a training condition, an untrained baseline, or an untrained generalization condition. There were no age differences by condition of playmate.

As in the studies previously discussed, the design of Study 3 consisted primarily of within-subject modifications with each autistic child as his own control. Each autistic child played with a different untrained peer before treatment (designated as baseline) and a day or two after treatment ended (designated as untrained generalization). During the same period he also played with one of the trained peers who had played with another autistic child during treatment (trained generalization). The order of untrained generalization and trained generalization was counterbalanced across children. During treatment sessions, each autistic child played with one trained nonhandicapped playmate for two series of 10 15-minute daily sessions, separated by a 2-week vacation. Videotapes were made every 5 days before and after the treatment holiday from day 1 until day 20 (1, 6, 10, 11, 16, 20). Videotapes were also made of the baseline session (1 day before treatment) and of untrained and trained generalization sessions (1 or 2 days after treat-

---

that each of these boys had at some point been considered extremely unresponsive and aloof from peers; however, between age 5 and 7 years some of them had shown noticeable improvements. However, it certainly may be true that it is easier to help a mildly autistic or socially impaired child than it is to help a severely autistic child.

ment ended). One month after treatment ended, a follow-up session with the initial trained playmate was also recorded.

Before the first treatment session, each nonhandicapped playmate was trained to initiate social interaction by prompting appropriate behaviors and reinforcing the autistic child's appropriate actions. After 10 sessions, there was a 2-week-long break, during which time each autistic child was given a one-session refresher training course. Pre-, mid-, and posttreatment data were also collected for interactions among three of the autistic children who were from the same classroom.

Before each session, nonhandicapped playmates were told to show the autistic child how to play and to get him to play as best they could. The same instruction was given before baseline, both types of generalization, and follow-up sessions. All treatment took place in an extra classroom 12 × 20 ft in size, marked off into a 12 × 15-ft play area, similar to that used in Studies 1 and 2.

2. TRAINING SESSIONS

Initial peer training, patterned after Strain *et al.* (1979), occurred during three separate 10- to 20-minute sessions between an adult research assistant and each nonhandicapped playmate individually. During the first training session, the nonhandicapped playmate was shown around the playroom and informed of the purpose of the study and the procedures to be used. The second training session consisted of the demonstration of simple requests and gestures as means of prompting social interaction and initiating play, and the demonstration of simple language and smiles, claps, hand shaking, and touching as means of reinforcing appropriate play or social interaction. Prompts were defined as clear verbal statements of the behavior desired from the autistic child accompanied by a gesture or use of an object. Reinforcements were defined as positive statements made within 3 seconds of the autistic child's action that stated explicitly what was being reinforced. These statements were always accompanied by a gesture or use of an object.

Role playing, with the experimenter acting as the autistic child, was used to give the peer 10 opportunities to initiate and prompt play using a simple request and a gesture or object offer. On five of these occasions, the experimenter complied with the request. On five other occasions, the experimenter ignored the peer for 20 seconds, and then reminded him that he must keep trying to get the child to play even if the child would not play at first (Strain *et al.*, 1979). Subsequently, during five role-playing situations, the experimenter displayed appropriate behavior (e.g., throwing a ball back, building a block tower, working on a puzzle) and the nonhandicapped partner was expected to reinforce the behavior. If after 3 seconds the nonhandicapped playmate did not reinforce the behavior, the experimenter reminded him of the importance of telling or showing the autistic child what he was doing well. On five of the occasions, the experimenter displayed an inappropriate action such as rocking, hand flapping, or talking to herself about an inappropriate topic. If the peer attempted to reinforce these actions, the experimenter reminded him not to reward inappropriate behavior.

The third training session began with the experimenter first modeling the use of prompting and reinforcement with a confederate autistic child. The confederate autistic child was a higher functioning, verbal 10-year-old boy with a visual impairment from the same class as most of the autistic subjects. At first, each nonhandicapped partner watched the experimenter play with the confederate autistic child. The nonhandicapped playmate then practiced playing with him. Peers were reminded to use prompts and reinforcement. The experimenter allowed the nonhandicapped playmate and the autistic confederate to play together until she had observed the nonhandicapped child make 10 attempts at initiating play through prompts and give 10 reinforcements.

Measures, coding procedures using 15-second time samples, and procedures for establishing reliability were identical to those in previous studies, except for the addition of the variables of prompts and reinforcements, as defined earlier.

3. BASELINE SESSIONS

During the first baseline session with untrained playmates, the autistic children looked very similar to the children in Study 1. Only one of the four children made any overt initiations to the nonhandicapped playmate. Three of the four children with autism spent almost two-thirds of their time totally unoccupied. The average distance between playmates was again over 6 ft. The autistic children responded to less than 30% of their partners' attempts to get them to play. Similarly, they spent about 30% of their time oriented toward the other child. The only marked difference between this group of autistic children and the children in Study 1 was that only one of the children in Study 3 engaged in overt self-stimulatory behavior during more than five intervals.

Similar to the previous studies, all the children would have been categorized as *aloof* during the baseline sessions on the basis of the quantitative measures. The one child who violated Wing and Gould's descriptions did not do so because of his social behavior, but because of his behaviors with toys. This child, Ian (Subject 9), was very interested in the materials and set to play almost immediately. While his play was quite simple and repetitious for an 11-year-old child, he was notably different from the other autistic children in the rate and fervor with which he built block towers, rolled the bowling ball, and pushed the barrel.

Nonhandicapped children who played with the autistic children during the untrained baseline session also behaved in much the same way as the same-age nonhandicapped peers did in the first session in Study 1. They were quite responsive to any approaches of the autistic child; the nonhandicapped children responded to every one of the autistic children's overtures. In addition, the untrained playmates made some initiations (range was 12–36 out of 60 intervals; mode = 12). These initiations were primarily nonverbal and usually involved objects or gestures. No reinforcements occurred during these dyads.

Interactions among the three autistic children were almost identical to those in Study 1. No more than three interactions occurred during baseline for any child. There was little solitary play, although there was also less overt self-stimulatory behavior than observed previously. Most of the time the autistic children wandered around the room or did nothing.

As discussed earlier, goals for treatment included not only increasing rate of interaction, solitary play, and qualitative precursors to interaction, but also increasing the rate at which all of the autistic children produced initiations. One important question also concerned whether, if these changes occurred, they would be maintained in the presence of an untrained playmate who did not provide the structure and example (Clark & Rutter, 1981) of the trained partners.

B. Results and Discussion

From their first contact with the autistic partners, the nonhandicapped playmates who had been trained used what they had been taught; they were far more active and intrusive than the untrained children, averaging 30 initiations as opposed to 18 in their first session and 42 initiations in their last, as contrasted to 12 during untrained generalization. General responsiveness for the autistic children did not differ since it hovered around 99–100% for all playmates, but playmates who had been taught to reinforce the autistic children's approaches with specific active social behaviors (e.g., making positive statements, touching the other child, or clapping) were much more likely to respond in this way (average 17 intervals per session) than the naive playmates (this never occurred spontaneously).

Differences in the behavior of the autistic children were immediately observable in their first session with the new playmate who had been trained to "get them to play," as compared to their behavior in baseline sessions. The average distance between playmates dropped to less than 3 ft for autistic children as soon as they began to play with the trained partner. All of the autistic children spent over 40 out of 60 intervals oriented toward the trained playmate, even in the first session. The percentage of peer initiations to which the autistic children responded rose to over 60% for all the children. As shown in Fig. 7, reciprocal interactions occurred in a minimum of 24 out of 60 intervals in Session 1.

The least change in the autistic children's behavior was observed in initiations, but even there, three out of the four children with autism made at least one overture to their new "trained" playmate in their first session with him. These results are shown in Fig. 8. Generally, the behavior of the autistic subjects in Study 3 playing with trained partners for the first time looked very much like the behaviors of the autistic subjects in Study 1 after 10 sessions.

The quantity of social interaction continued to increase over the course of treatment for three of the dyads; for the fourth, with Ian (Subject 9), a ceiling of 56 out of 60 intervals in cooperative play was reached during day 1 of treatment and maintained throughout the sessions. For the other autistic children, the session during which a stable rate was achieved varied

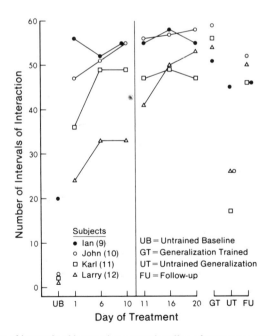

Fig. 7. Number of intervals of interaction across baseline of treatment, generalization, and follow-up (Study 3).

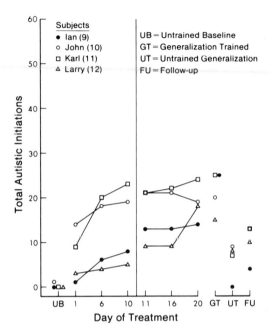

Fig. 8. Number of positive initiations made by each autistic child across baseline, treatment, generalization, and follow-up.

from day 10 for Karl (Subject 11) to day 11 for John (Subject 10); for Larry (Subject 12) increases were still shown on the last day of treatment. These increases did not seem to be dependent with any one-to-one correspondence on the behavior of the nonhandicapped playmates, who had all established quite stable rates of initiation by day 6 (range 39–51, out of 60 intervals containing initiations) and rates of response (range 94–100%) on day 1. For one autistic child, John (Subject 10), the increases in interaction closely paralleled his increases in responsiveness to his partner. However, in general rates of responsiveness were high from the start (range 63–94%). In contrast to the previous study, all four autistic children gradually increased the number of spontaneous initiations they made over the course of treatment (see Fig. 8).

After the final day of treatment, generalization sessions with an unfamiliar *trained* peer (i.e., the trained partner of another autistic child) and an unfamiliar *untrained* peer were held. As shown in Figs. 7 and 8, generalization to the unfamiliar trained peer was excellent, not only in general measures of presocial behavior and responsiveness, but also in the number of initiations made by the autistic children.

In contrast, sessions with *untrained* peers suggested some improvements in responsiveness compared to baseline sessions with a naive playmate (the minimal level of responsiveness of any child was up to .83 responses per initiation). However, as shown in Fig. 7, there was markedly less interaction with untrained playmates than with the trained peers. When the behaviors of individual autistic children were compared across baseline and generalization sessions (both with naive playmates), improvements occurred for only the distance between the children, the time the autistic children spent oriented toward their partner, and responsiveness.

Follow-up sessions between each autistic child and his original trained playmate (from Session 1) showed maintenance of high levels of interaction and at least some initiating by the autistic child 1 month later (see Figs. 7 and 8).

Generalization for three of the autistic children from the same classroom when playing together showed consistent improvements in orientation, proximity, and solitary play. Although the amount of interaction and scores on presocial measures were radically lower among this group than in the dyads, during posttreatment sessions the autistic children stayed within an average of 2 ft of their classmates, looked at each other during over half the intervals, and each engaged in some solitary play (with the appropriate use of toys) for at least one-third of the time. There were no consistent changes in rate of interaction, however.

Qualitative and interactive measures served mostly to confirm that the nonhandicapped playmates were using their training. The most effective initiation for eliciting a response from the autistic children was a verbal statement either specifying a desired action or commenting on a previous action accompanied by the use or offer of a toy (88% were responded to). Offers of materials without any verbal statements also received a high rate of response (70%). Purely verbal initiations received many fewer responses proportionately (39%). Major changes in the behavior of the trained playmates over the course of the study involved decreases in the number of purely verbal interactions (which were consistently less successful), increases in the number of joint verbal and nonverbal initiations, and increases in the number of times the playmates specifically reinforced an initiation made by the autistic child as compared to reinforcing his general use of objects. All of the autistic children's responses and all but one of their initiations were nonverbal.

Because of the high rate of initiation by the trained peer, solitary play was almost nonexistent. Length of sustained interactions was most often higher (greater than three initiation–response sequences) in dyads including trained peers than in any of the other dyads in this study or in Study 1 or 2. However, these scores were quite variable from session to session. Because the nonhandicapped peers were such avid "prompters," they sometimes changed activities when they did not get as immediately positive a response as they expected. This behavior often produced a series of brief interactions until the children settled on an activity in which they were both interested (Keane & Conger, 1981). This sometimes resulted in lower average lengths of interaction than in previous sessions. Comparisons between beginning and continuing initiations were also variable for the same reason, though the proportion of continuing initiations, not surprisingly, was much higher for all subjects (range 50–80% of initiations) than in other studies. Even when continuing initiations were excluded, subjects in Study 3 still made more beginning initiations than were typically made in Study 1 and 2.

C. Overview of Study 3

In summary, when interacting with same-age playmates who had been taught to prompt and reinforce social behaviour, all four autistic children showed high rates of response and made some attempts at initiating. As with the autistic children in Clark and Rutter's (1981) experiment, the more socially demanding the situation, the more the children with autism interacted. It is important to note, however, that this situation was socially demanding in terms of the other child's repeated initiations and positive responses, *not* in terms of cognitive requirements or demands for complex behavior with many people.

The structure provided by the trained playmates' behavior had an immediate effect very similar to the effect of familiarity in Studies 1 and 2 on the behavior of the autistic children. The similarity between the effects of structure and familiarity could be due to the autistic children's ability, in both cases, to identify the salient cues exhibited by the other children that required responses and to know what to do in response. In Study 1 and 2, this knowledge was acquired over a series of interactions during which the same-age nonhandicapped peers gradually modified their behaviors to make these cues more obvious, and the autistic children began to attend to them more carefully. In addition, in Study 1 and 2 the autistic children, through watching their partner, acquired some object-oriented play behaviors that they could use in response to his approaches. In Study 3, through training, the nonhandicapped playmates had been taught beforehand many of the same behaviors spontaneously acquired by the nonhandicapped peers in Studies 1 and 2. The autistic subjects were able to begin treatment with the cues and possibilities laid out for them.

One interesting finding was that for the children in Study 3, vocalizations enhanced the likelihood of a response to a gesture or object offer, whereas in Study 1 vocalizations lessened the chance of a response. One possible explanation for this discrepancy was that in Study 3 almost all vocalizations accompanying gestures or object use were either clear requests for specific behaviors or positive statements of reinforcement about specific behaviors of the autistic children. These had been the techniques taught in training. These verbalizations were quite different from the more conversational and less specific comments made by the untrained partners in Study 1. It should be noted, however, that in both Study 1 and 3 vocalizations without any accompanying use of objects received the lowest rate of response by far.

The strong generalization that occurred from interactions from one trained nonhandicapped peer to another trained peer suggested that general, structuring behaviors consistent across playmates allowed transfer of levels of interaction. However, these cues did not easily transfer to (or were not available from) the *untrained* unfamiliar peer in the last generalization session. As in Studies 1 and 2, generalization across all the different settings occurred for responsiveness and for measures of behaviors considered to be precursors to social interaction.

The failure of the increases in initiation observed with the trained peers to generalize to less structured interactions with untrained peers provides some insight regarding why autistic children may not spontaneously generalize social skills acquired with adults to peer interactions. In fact, the interactions here between trained and untrained peers were far more similar (e.g., same room, same toys, same rules) to each other than typically are other interactions between peers to those with adults. While, in Study 3 especially, the behavior of the playmates could not be considered very natural, there were important commonalities among the various dyads, such as the lack of external rewards and the object-oriented, repetitious quality of the interactions. Even so, only passive social behaviors, such as responsiveness, attention, and other precursors to interaction, generalized. Though the autistic children seemed to have learned (or to be more motivated) to attend to social cues from their peers, they appeared to need more specific direction as to what to do than other children typically provided. Since at some point the goal of an intervention is to help autistic children deal with the natural environment more effectively, these findings represent a major problem. It is not known whether increases in initiation might have occurred if the autistic children had been given the opportunity to become familiar with their last new untrained partner in more than one session. Similarly, a greater number of initiations might have been maintained if the prompt and reinforcement procedure had been faded in a deliberate way (Romancyzk et al., 1975). Direct teaching to the autistic children of some of the initiating behaviors gradually acquired by the subjects in Study 3, followed by the opportunity to use these behaviors with peers, would be another approach to test.

VIII. General Discussion

A. The Applicability of Normal Developmental Research

In Section II the question had been raised of the usefulness of information about normal social developmental in observing and modifying the social behavior of children with autism. Three areas had been identified for which normal developmental research might be helpful: defining the units of observation and analysis, designing intervention techniques, and identifying goals for treatment.

Units of analysis and measurements drawn from the literature on normal development proved to be quite useful in the preceding studies. Quantitative and qualitative measures served to differentiate dyads on the basis of familiarity and characteristics of the playmate (e.g., age, training). Interactive measures helped clarify the role of specific behaviors in increasing the amount of interaction between children.

Yet selecting the most appropriate level of analysis of observational data is always a difficult decision. From a theoretical point of view, more specific hypotheses concerning the contribution of specific behaviors of the peer or the autistic child should be studied in terms of the part they play in series of initiations and responses and in the maintenance of interactions. To do so, additional levels of analysis are needed, including both finer descriptive measures of behavior (e.g., facial expressions, specific uses of objects) and more sequentially oriented measures (e.g., time-sequential series). From a more clinical perspective, another approach would specify the behavioral outcome for children with autism by the end of treatment and work backward to select measures that would allow documentation of how these behaviors were acquired.

Several decisions about methods of intervention drawn from studies of normal development appeared successful. The use of dyads who played together long enough to achieve some familiarity produced stronger effects than had been reported in earlier studies using larger, more frequently rotating groups (McHale, 1983). The restriction on space appears to have been important, although this variable was not specifically manipulated in the studies reported here. A somewhat surprising finding was that among the toys provided in these three studies, there were no systematic differences in the behavior of the children while using them. However, there were so many other factors to be taken into account, it may be that the effects of these relatively similar toys were not sufficiently strong to appear independently in such short time periods.

In all probability, both relative and absolute age of the playmate made a difference. One kindergartner was very interactive and one grade 6 child was not. Whether the absolute or relative age of the nonhandicapped peers

(5–6 vs 9–12 years) was the source of the difference could not be directly answered from Studies 1 and 2. However, on the whole, the kindergarten peers often seemed a bit overwhelmed with their job. This observation held true even for those kindergarten children who played with two of the 9–10 year olds who were small for their age and not much bigger physically than the kindergartners. Other researchers have used grade 2 students and have not reported the same problems (McHale, 1983). One might wonder if there might be certain *absolute* requirements for certain social skills, which are often but not always associated with age, necessary to promote interactions with these highly socially deficient children (McHale *et al.*, 1981a). On the other hand, for some of the kindergarten pairs, the size difference between the nonhandicapped 6-year-old and the autistic 12-year-old child was quite pronounced. In these cases particularly, the factor of relative size did seem to reduce the initiative taken by the smaller, nonhandicapped child.

The studies reported here contained a number of limitations, and hence care must be taken in interpreting the results. Sample sizes were small and the number of observations per child was limited; appropriate statistics could not always be carried out. The children with autism represented only some of the many groupings of autistic children defined by factors such as age, intelligence, severity of autism, and language deficit. For example, it is not clear how higher functioning children with autism would have responded to the behavior of the trained playmates in Study 3. Finally, the time periods were quite short. It is also not known whether behaviors with the untrained playmate during the generalization period in Study 3 would have improved if observed over a longer time. Nevertheless, a start has been made which now requires replication, expansion, and refinement.

Though Wing and Gould's categories of social deficit were quite useful in organizing quantitative aspects of the children's behavior, the social skills and deficits of the autistic children did not fall into a simple pattern. From general observation, the data seemed well characterized by Wing and Gould's (1979) three categories, when one considered a child's behavior during a single treatment session. However, the children did not remain in the same category over time or across playmates. Most commonly a child moved "up" one category (i.e., from *aloof* to *passive*) over the course of treatment. There did not appear to be any particularly significant stability to the category of *aloofness*, or unusualness in the shift from *aloofness* to *passivity*, at least with this age children, to warrant using this distinction to separate Kanner-type autism from the more generally defined triad of social impairment. Thus, as Wing and Gould have suggested, standard settings (including variables such as the age, familiarity, and behavior of the interactive partner targeted for observation) must be identified in order to allow reliable use of these categories for diagnostic purposes. Descriptions of the dyadic interactions in these studies required reference not only to each individual partner, but also to characteristics of the children's relationship both on a molar level (i.e., relative age) and on a molecular level (e.g., first child A did this, then child B responded in this way).

Although one goal of the present research was to study directly social behaviors in peer interactions, the complex interrelationships among the language, cognitive, and social deficits of children with autism proved impossible to ignore. For example, under some circumstances use of language made the peer interactions proceed more smoothly; when the playmates could talk to one another (as in Study 2) or when the nonhandicapped peer used clear verbal instructions or praise for specific behaviors (as in Study 3), interactions lasted longer and initiations were more successful in eliciting responses. The use of language, when modified to suit the social and communicative needs of the autistic children, facilitated the autistic children's knowing what their partners wanted them to do and allowed the children with some expressive language skills to respond quickly to their partners and build rapidly on their partners' responses to them. This finding revealed a similar facilitative role of language to that described by Holmberg (1980) in the peer interactions of normally developing 3 year olds. In contrast, for the autistic children with more limited receptive skills, language was primarily a negative factor, except in Study 3 in which the playmates were very careful in how and why they spoke. Even for one high-functioning child (Greg in Study 2) and for several of the nonhandicapped kindergartners, language was not a useful way of eliciting a response from them or allowing them to initiate. The language demands of different kinds of social interactions should clearly be included in planning treatment or descriptive studies. This consideration is particularly important in studies of integrated classrooms, where language demands may be quite different from those of other experiences of an autistic child coming out of a highly structured one-to-one program.

Similarly, the use of objects in play was also an important dimension in the peer interactions observed. Autistic children with better developed play skills were generally more immediately interactive and sometimes took more initiative (Strain & Fox, 1981) than other children with autism. Solitary play, as opposed to unoccupied time, increased with treatment for almost all children, except when high levels of interaction produced ceiling effects. Toys were definitely the tools for interaction. There was almost never an interaction that did not involve some joint use of an object. Thus, as for normally developing preschool children, play with toys did serve to facilitate social interaction; play was not one more self-directed activity. Again, the skills of the individual children need to be kept in mind when selecting toys and activities. Preconceptions of what other children of the same age would typically do with the toys may not be helpful, unless one considers the developmental level of the individual child with autism. Given the generalization of gains in solitary play that occurred from the treatment dyads to the classroom groupings in many cases, good potential exists for the direct teaching of play skills in order to maximize initial social contacts. It also seems fair to assume that socially acquired play skills will transfer to leisure activities in less structured settings, at least to some extent.

In a recent paper (1983), Rutter emphasized the cognitive problems in processing social meanings experienced by children with autism. He identified two major facets of this cognitive impairment, specifically deficits in reciprocity and in attachment or bonding. Both deficits were apparent in the children studied here. The notion of reciprocity requires that the child with autism attend to social cues, know what they mean, know what he or she should do in response, and then do so, using social behaviors that are comprehensible to his or her partner. The children in these studies were placed in contrived situations in which activities were familiar and cognitive demands for play were low. With familiarity or structure through training, the autistic subjects came to attend to social cues, presumably to know what they meant (although this was not tested directly since the situation was designed to limit alternatives), knew what to do in response, and did so. One interpretation of these findings is that the changes in the behavior of the autistic children were predictable and systematic responses to reductions in cognitive demands of the peer interactions. In addition, when the non-handicapped peers were particularly intrusive and responsive, *in some cases* the autistic children were able to move beyond passive processing and responding to produce meaningful initiations of their own.

Normal developmental research could be used to establish a sequence of expected difficulty based on the cognitive demands of social situations. Such a cognitive sequence could be used to identify ways of facilitating the autistic child's processing of social meaning. Again, a related implication is that an autistic child's social behavior with peers cannot be considered without taking into account the cognitive demands of the situation. For example, when a child is placed in a group of children, not only do the social rules change, but so do the requirements for rapid processing of input from many different sources. Often the specific tasks are quite different as well. These cognitive demands may have an equally great, if not greater, effect on an autistic child's behavior as do the social needs.

B. Other Friendship Dimensions

Yet, apart from the differences in the dyadic interactions that can be accounted for by differences in social cues or cognitive aspects of structure provided by nonhandicapped playmates, other characteristics of the children with autism emerged as contributing factors. The autistic children studied here varied among each other, especially in their initiating behavior, even when the behaviors of their peers were highly similar. While not formally observed, the degree to which the autistic child was motivated to interact with or "cared about" his or her partner may have been an important factor. Knowing how to interact and wanting to do so were two different components of social behavior. Though often what first appeared as a lack of interest could be shown to be lack of knowledge, there still remained differences among the children with autism and among the particular dyads that could not be accounted for solely by cognitive factors. Perhaps these were precursors to more abstract concepts of bonding, friendship, and empathy. In less contrived situations in which it is not the "job" of the nonhandicapped peer to play with his or her autistic partner, it may be factors such as these that determine the reciprocity from the nonhandicapped child's point of view.

It seems possible to link differences in reciprocal interaction at this level to colloquial distinctions between acquaintances and friends. The behavior of the autistic children could be placed in a developmental sequence for much of the acquisition of the more cognitive–behavioral aspects of friendship or acquaintanceship (i.e., attention, imitation, joint use of objects), but in many cases, the children with autism still differed from normally developing children in taking less direct initiative in the relationships. The autistic children failed to use, or did not use effectively, very basic social and affective behaviors that are typically observed in normally developing 7- to 9-month-old infants (Rutter, 1980). Although attention to the other child and responsiveness to him almost always improved concurrently, the development of initiations seemed to be a separate phenomenon, at least as influenced by familiarity and the interactive behavior of the partner, the two major factors studied here. Apart from the importance of considering the contribution of language, as well as cognitive development and specific aspects of the ability to play, there still remained important *social* dimensions necessary to describe accurately the interactive behavior of the autistic children. Through environmental manipulations and direct teaching, one can create situations in which autistic children will interact and enjoy doing so. It is not known whether this can be done without requiring so much peer effort, often in the absence of much positive feedback from the autistic playmate, so that the nonhandicapped child will continue to want to interact with the autistic child.

We have some incidental data relevant to this last question (Hopkins & Lord, 1981). In a study of two 8- to 10-year-old moderately retarded autistic boys, we monitored every day 5 minutes of daily 15-minute play sessions, organized much the same as the previous studies. The nonhandicapped peers had been taught to reinforce the social behaviors of their partners. Our goal was to identify when interaction and initiation rates were stable and then to introduce a new, untrained peer and follow the course of their interactions. However, for neither of the dyads were interaction rates ever stable for more than 3 days. The number of intervals of interaction per 5 minutes increased steadily for the first 9–13 days. Initially, the nonhandicapped children took more and more initiative in beginning interactions. Gradually the autistic children also began to make some initiations. However, after the amount of time they spent in interaction had reached between 70 and 80% of the intervals, the initiations made by the *nonhandicapped* children began to decrease. The autistic children continued to make approaches until the response rates of their partners fell as well, at which point we ended the study.

Our interpretation of the results was that the nonhandicapped playmates were exhausted. In the previous studies, breaks and an endpoint had always been built into the schedule. We had underestimated their importance for the nonhandicapped children. We had also overestimated the endurance of the nonhandicapped children in the face of a very difficult job. Clearly, other factors could have been involved as well and further study is needed, but this result unfortunately mirrors several findings by investigators working with other populations (Gresham, 1982). We are not suggesting that it is impossible to motivate nonhandicapped children to play with children who are both autistic and retarded, but that a great deal of care may be required in providing some incentives (e.g., changing the toys, providing refresher training, being more deliberate about social rewards) for the playmates.

Lewis and Rosenblum (1977), in attempting to define the concept of friendship, suggested that the overt function of peer relations is to provide opportunities for positive interaction between individuals who operate at comparable levels of complexity. If this is the case, the autistic child with a very uneven pattern of development is at a particular disadvantage in finding a partner with similar skills. On the other hand, friends do not have to be identical in every respect. It may be true that, if the autistic child's specific "processing" difficulties can be minimized by environmental manipulations and direct teaching, and if social learning experiences can be provided for him, the child with autism may be in a position similar to any other person with unusual patterns of abilities or deficits. Like anyone who is obviously handicapped or different from other people in a significant way, the autistic person may find fewer people willing to accept his differences but still may himself be capable of friendship.

However, friendships are typically defined by children according to the reciprocity of the partners liking for each other and the reinforcing behavior of each child to the other (Hartup, 1977). Even the most careful match-making and developmentally modulated opportunity for interaction may still not be sufficient for friendship to develop, if the autistic child cannot give the other child the sense that he or she is cared for. Yet many of the autistic subjects in these studies gave clear indications that they did care about their partners (as did *some* of the nonhandicapped children), for example, by asking for them, looking for them, or crying when there was no play session. Furthermore, as Radke-Yarrow (1975, p. 302) described in her observations of infants' emotional responses to other people, often for young children "events themselves propel the child into an activity. Once the child is *in* the activity, the structure of the activity makes it interactive with tones of affect. Although the child may not have initiated the feeling of help or sympathy [or friendship], he ends up feeling that way. The event . . . transforms the impersonal into the personal."

An autistic child who has never been given the opportunity to have an intense series of active, meaningful (on his language and cognitive level) experiences with another child is doubly isolated, both by his original deficits and his lack of experience. Perhaps one role of the study of normal development is to identify essential aspects of this experience that need to be deliberately made to happen even for handicapped children. Placing a handicapped child with a nonhandicapped child does not equal "normal interaction" (Gresham, 1982; Guralnick, 1981). Identifying the significant characteristics of interactions and friendships between children and attempting to facilitate their occurrence in the social contacts of autistic children may be more valuable in the long run.

C. The Importance of Context

Obviously, research on social behavior in nonhandicapped children can be valuable in identifying patterns of development to be facilitated. Yet often the use of the developmental literature is manifested primarily in the listing of the *social* behaviors the handicapped child needs to learn. It is not clear, given the complex nature of the deficits associated with autism, that this approach will be very fruitful. In part, the difficulties of borrowing specific goals from normal developmental literature have to do with the nature of social behavior itself. The appropriateness of different social behaviors is highly dependent on the larger context and the behavior of other people involved in the interaction. Even for an autistic child with very limited social skills, teaching all-purpose behaviors such as eye contact, greeting, or smiling will not foster social interaction unless these behaviors are used with the appropriate partner and appropriate timing. Because many autistic children are clearly different from other children in many ways, it is not fair to assume that the general environments in which they interact or the specific actions of others to them are, or ever will be, the same as for a nonautistic person of the same age and sex. Expectations and social needs may be quite different for children or adolescents with autism than for other children. Wing (1978) commented that the *passive* autistic child is often considered more socially acceptable than the *active but odd* child. Thus, behaviors that primarily involve simple responses to other people's actions may be the most useful skills for autistic children in situations with high cognitive demands or that have clear behavioral requirements such as at school or in public places. Goals for social behaviors in more informal, individualized environments such as at home may also differ depending on whether the goal is to decrease the autistic child's dependence on adults or other authorities (such as by providing activities for leisure time that could be carried out with a partner or alone without much supervision) or to increase the ability of the child to control his own social environment (such as by actively approaching others and sustaining interactions with them). Direct social skills training may be useful in helping the child *learn* new skills, but if in the long run these skills are to be truly effective socially, the relationship of these skills to other behaviors and to the interpersonal contexts in which they are to occur has to be considered.

Descriptions of social behavior in nonhandicapped children highlight the complexity of setting up treatment goals and the importance of always remembering that the ultimate goal is *social* interaction, not producing an isolated behavior out of context. Concepts taken from normal developmental literature such as reciprocity, friendship, and the specific value of peer relations may be more useful in planning goals for social situations than any list of sequentially acquired social behaviors. Expected levels of difficulty for cognitive, language, and play-related aspects of the interaction drawn from studies of nonhandicapped children may be more helpful than similar sequences for purely social behaviors. Thus, developmental research may be more helpful in the long run in specifying the factors, social and otherwise, that one needs to consider in identifying treatment goals and methods than in delineating those goals specifically.

For example, the importance of the behavior of the other person in an interaction is illustrated by the discrepancy, discussed in Section I, in how autistic children interact with adults versus other children. On the basis of the studies reported here, one wonders if at least part of what is described as improved social behavior with adults is not just increased responsiveness to *anyone* who approaches. Adults, particularly parents and teachers, are presumably more likely to initiate interaction with an autistic child than are other children. However, when another child attempts to interact with an autistic child, at least in these studies, children of 9–12 years of age typically responded at least 25% of the time even to an unfamiliar peer. In addition, adults are probably more likely than children to make approaches in a form so as to maximize the autistic child's ability to process the social meaning or to "make her feel comfortable", [as the mother of the girl with autism said in DeMyer's (1979) book]. As shown in the research here, when children made these adjustments either spontaneously or with training, the autistic children responded very well. Clearly other factors discussed earlier, such as familiarity, are also at work, but the discrepancy in autistic children's reactions to adults and to children seems better described as a discrepancy in their response to particular behaviors in specific contexts than as a general social deficit related to the age of the other person included in the interaction (Rheingold & Eckerman, 1975). Helping autistic children come to interact more successfully with other children may be better accomplished by identifying the contexts in which peer interactions are likely to occur and promoting the use of different behaviors in these contexts by *both* partners, or by modifying the contexts to facilitate the use of skills the children already possess, rather than by trying to transfer a list of social behaviors rotely learned in artificial contexts with adults.

Research in the area of social development in children with autism has far to go. Longitudinal studies, larger samples of children with autism of various age and abilities (especially in language and play), and closer observation of autistic children in a variety of contexts are all much needed. The relationship of experiences with family members and teachers to peer-related behavior is an interesting issue. Interventions using a combination of direct teaching and less structured opportunities for practice would seem to have potential. In addition, interventions involving manipulation of contexts for interaction occurring during everyday routines such as in the classroom, at recess, or during activities with siblings would also be valuable. The effects of interventions such as those described here on social behaviors outside the classroom also need to be evaluated.

In the past, much attention has been focused on the numerous social behaviors that autistic children did not have and on the more bizarre behaviors that they showed. Yet, comparisons to research on normal development show much that is positive about the social behavior of children with autism. Although having *some* social skills is not the same as being "normal," the autistic children observed in these studies not only showed surprisingly little negative behavior, but also showed systematic, gradual improvements after a very short time in relatively unobtrusive interventions. In order to occur, these changes required the careful manipulation of the social contexts and the cognitive and language demands of the situation. However, the social behavior of the autistic children did "get better" and in some ways it stayed "better" across a number of variations in context. As we are able to relate the positive skills that autistic children possess to the social goals that we want for them, the design of appropriate treatment methods and educational modifications should come more easily. Identifying significant experiences in normal social development and analyzing the components of these experiences that are potentially most important for the child with autism may allow us to prevent some of the secondary deficits that occur as the result of lack of experience or opportunity to learn. Autistic children *can* develop peer relations, if goals for social behavior with other children are considered in relation to other areas of development, and if appropriate social contexts are made available to them.

Acknowledgments

Much of this work was done in collaboration with other people. Foremost in importance were Mike Hopkins, who submitted portions of Study 1 to the University of Minnesota as his master's thesis in educational psychology, and Linda Bream, who submitted portions of Study 3 to the University of Minnesota as an honor's thesis in psychology. Others directly involved in the research were Phil Sievers and Betsy Butler. Portions of this manuscript were presented at the International Meetings of the National Society for Autistic Children and the biannual meeting of the Society for Research in Child Development, both in Boston in 1981.

Thanks are extended to the parents and children who participated in the studies and to the teachers and administrators in the public school systems of St. Paul, Minneapolis, and Glen Lake. Gratitude is also due to Joanne Tymkow and Deborah Hay for help in putting this article together.

References

American Psychiatric Association. *Diagnostic and statistical manual of mental disorders* (3rd ed.). Washington, D.C.: American Psychiatric Association, 1980.

Arthur, G. *The Arthur adaptation of the Leiter international performance scale.* Chicago, Illinois: The Psychological Service Center Press, 1952.

Barker, R. G., & Wright, H. F. *Midwest and its children.* New York: Harper, 1955.

Bartak, L., & Rutter, M. Special educational treatment of autistic children: A comparative study. I. Design of study and characteristics of units. *Journal of Child Psychology and Psychiatry*, 1973, **14**, 161–179.

Becker, J. M. T. A learning analysis of the development of peer-oriented behaviour in 9 month old infants. *Developmental Psychology*, 1977, **13**, 481–491.

Belsky, J. The effects of context on mother-infant interaction: A complex issue. *Quarterly Newsletter of the Laboratory of Comparative Human Cognition*, 1979, **1**, 29–31.

Bronson, W. C. Developments in behaviour with age-mates during the second year of life. In M. Lewis & L. A. Rosenblum (Eds.), *Friendship and peer relations.* New York: Wiley, 1975. Pp. 131–152.

Cantwell, D., Baker, L., & Rutter, M. A comparative study of infantile autism and specific developmental receptive language disorder. IV. Analysis of syntax and language function. *Journal of Child Psychology and Psychiatry*, 1978, **19**, 351–362.

Castell, R. Physical distance and visual attention as measures of social interaction between child and adults. In S. J. Hutt & C. Hutt (Eds.), *Behaviour studies in psychiatry*. Oxford: Pergamon, 1970.

Clark, P., & Rutter, M. Autistic children's responses to structure and to interpersonal demands. *Journal of Autism and Developmental Disorders*, 1981, **11**, 201–217.

Clark-Stewart, A. Recasting the lone stranger. In J. Jilck & A. Clarke-Stewart (Eds.), *The development of social understanding*. New York: Gardiner, 1978.

Davison, G. A social learning therapy programmed with an autistic child. *Behaviour Research and Therapy*, 1964, **2**, 149–159.

DeMyer, M. K. *Parents and children in autism*. New York: Holt, 1979.

Donnellan, A. M. An educational perspective of autism: Implications for curriculum development and personal development. In B. Wilcox & A. Thompson (Eds.), *Critical issues in educating autistic children and youth*. Silver Springs, Maryland: U.S. Dept. of Education, 1980.

Doyle, A. B., Connolly, J., & Rivest, L. P. The effect of playmate familiarity on the social interactions of young children. *Child Development*, 1980, **51**, 217–223.

Dunn, L. M. *Expanded manual for the Peabody picture vocabulary test*. Minneapolis, Minnesota: American Guidance Service, 1965.

Eckerman, C. O. The human infant in social interaction. In R. B. Cairns (Ed.), *Social interaction: Methods, analysis and illustrations*. Hillsdale, New Jersey: Erlbaum, 1979.

Eckerman, C. O., & Whatley, J. L. Toys and social interaction between infant peers. *Child Development*, 1977, **48**, 1645–1656.

Eckerman, C. O., Whatley, J. L., & Kutz, S. L. Growth of social play with peers during the second year of life. *Developmental Psychology*, 1975, **11**, 42–49.

Ferster, C. B. Positive reinforcement and behavioral deficits of autistic children. *Child Development*, 1961, **32**, 437.

Flavell, J. H. Structures, stages, and sequences in cognitive development. In W. A. Collins (Ed.), *The concept of development. Vol. 15: The Minnesota symposium on child psychology*. Hillsdale, New Jersey: Erlbaum, 1982.

Furman, W., Rahe, D. F., & Hartup, W. W. Rehabilitation of socially withdrawn preschool children through mixed-age and same-age socialization. *Child Development*, 1979, **50**, 915–922.

Goldfarb, W. *Childhood schizophrenia*. Cambridge, Massachusetts: Harvard Univ. Press, 1961.

Gottman, J., Gonso, J., & Schuler, P. Teaching social skills to isolated children. *Journal of Abnormal Child Psychology*, 1976, **4**, 179–197.

Greenwood, C. R., Todd, N. M., Walker, H. M., & Hops, H. *Social assessment manual for preschool level (SAMPLE)*. Eugene, Oregon: Center at Oregon for Research in the Behavioral Education of the Handicapped, 1978.

Greenwood, C. R., Walker, Todd N. M., & Hops, H. Normative and descriptive analysis of preschool free play social interaction rates. *Journal of Pediatric Psychology*, 1981, **6**, 343–367.

Gresham, F. M. Validity of social skills measures for assessing social competence in low-status children: A multivariate investigation. *Developmental Psychology*, 1981, **17** (4), 390–398.

Gresham, F. M. Misguided mainstreaming: The case for social skills training with handicapped children. *Exceptional Children*. 1982, **48** (5), 422–433.

Guralnick, M. J. The social behaviour of preschool children at different developmental levels: Effects of group composition. *Journal of Experimental Child Psychology*, 1981, **31**, 115–130.

Hartup, W. W. Peer interaction and social organization. In P. H. Mussen (Ed.), *Carmichael's manual of child psychology*. New York: Wiley, 1970. Pp. 361–456.

Hartup, W. W. The origins of friendship. In M. Lewis & L. A. Rosenblum (Eds.), *Friendship and peer relations*. New York: Wiley, 1975. Pp. 11–26.

Hartup, W. W. Peer interaction and the behavioral development of the individual child. In E. Schopler & R. Reichler (Eds.), *Psychopathology and child development*. New York: Plenum, 1976.

Hartup, W. W. Peer relations and family relations: Two social worlds. In M. Rutter (Ed.), *Scientific foundations of developmental psychiatry*. London: Heinemann, 1980. Pp. 280–291.

Hermelin, B., & O'Connor, N. *Psychological experiments with autistic children*. Oxford: Pergamon, 1970.

Holmberg, M. C. The development of social interchange patterns from 12 to 42 months. *Child Development*, 1980, **51**, 448–456.

Hopkins, J. M., & Lord, C. The social behavior of autistic children with younger and same-age nonhandicapped peers. In D. Parke (Ed.), *Papers and reports from international meetings of the National Society for Autistic Children*. Boston, Massachusetts: NSAC, 1981.

Howlin, P. The assessment of social behaviour. In M. Rutter & E. Schopler (Eds.), *Autism: A reappraisal of concepts and treatments*. New York: Plenum, 1978.

Hutt, S. J., & Hutt, C. (Eds.). *Behaviour studies in psychiatry*. Oxford: Pergamon, 1970.

Hutt, C., & Ounsted, C. The biological significance of gaze aversion with particular reference to the syndrome of infantile autism. *Behavioural Science*, 1966, **11**, 346–356.

Kanner, L. Autistic disturbances of affective contact. *Nervous Child*, 1943, **2**, 217–250.

Keane, S., & Conger, J. The implications of communication development for social skills training. *Journal of Pediatric Psychology*, 1981, **4**, 369–381.

Koegel, R. L., Firestone, P. B., Cramme, K., & Dunlap, G. Increasing spontaneous play by supressing self-stimulation in autistic children. *Journal of Applied Behaviour Analysis*, 1974, **7**, 521–528.

Kubicek, L. F. Organization in two mother-infant interactions involving a normal infant and his fraternal twin who was later diagnosed as autistic. In T. M. Field, S. Goldberg, D. Stern, & A. M. Sostek (Eds.), *High risk infants and children: Adult and peer interactions*. New York: Academic Press, 1980. Pp. 99–112.

LaGreca, A. M., & Santogrossi, D. A. Social skills training with elementary school students: A behavioural group approach. *Journal of Consulting and Clinical Psychology*, 1980, **48**, 220–227.

Langdell, T. Recognition of faces: An approach to the study of autism. *Journal of Child Psychology and Psychiatry*, 1978, **19**, 255–268.

Lewis, M., & Rosenblum, L. A. Introduction. In M. Lewis & L. A. Rosenblum (Eds.), *Friendship and peer relations*. New York: Wiley, 1975. Pp. 1–9.

Lord, C., Bream, L., & Hopkins, J. M. *Autistic children's interactions with nonhandicapped peers*. Paper presented at the Society for Research in Child Development, Boston, 1981.

Lougee, M. D., Grueneich, R., & Hartup, W. W. Social interactions of same-age and mixed-age dyads of preschool children. *Child Development*, 1977, **48**, 1353–1361.

Lovaas, O. I., Koegel, R., Simmons, J. Q., & Long, J. S. Some generalization and follow-up measures on autistic children in behaviour therapy. *Journal of Applied Behaviour Analysis*, 1973, **6**, 131–166.

Lovass, O. I., Schaeffer, B., & Simmons, J. O. Experimental studies in childhood schizophrenia. *Journal of Experimental Research and Personality*, 1965, **1**, 99–109.

Mahler, M. On early infantile psychosis. The symbiotic and autistic syndromes. *Journal of the American Academy of Child Psychiatry*, 1965, **4**, 554–568.

Marshall, H. R., & McCandless, B. R. A study in predictors of social behavior of preschool children. *Child Development*, 1967, **28**, 149–159.

Martini, M. Structures of interaction between autistic children. In T. M. Field, S. Goldberg, D. Stern, & A. M. Sostek (Eds.), *High risk infants and children: Adult and peer interaction*. New York: Academic Press, 1980. Pp. 257–292.

Masur, E. F. Preschool boys' speech modifications: The effects of listeners' linguistic levels and conversational responsiveness. *Child Development*, 1978, **49**, 924–927.

McHale, S. M. Social interactions of autistic and nonhandicapped children during free play. *American Journal of Orthopsychiatry*, 1983, **53**, 81–91.

McHale, S. M., & Olley, J. G. Using play to facilitate handicapped children's social development. *Topics in Early Childhood Special Education*, 1982.

McHale, S. M., Olley, J. G., & Marcus, L. M. *Variations across settings in autistic children's play*. Paper presented at biannual meetings of the Society for Research in Child Development, Boston, 1981. (a)

McHale, S. M., Olley, J. G., Marcus, L. M., & Simeonsson, R. J. Nonhandicapped peers as tutors for autistic children. *Exceptional Children*, 1981, **48**, 263–265. (b)

Moore, N. V., Ever.tson, C. M., & Brophy, J. E. Solitary play: Some functional reconsiderations. *Developmental Psychology*, 1974, **10**, 830–834.

Mueller, E. The maintenance of verbal exchanges between young children. *Child Development*, 1972, **43**, 930–938.

Mueller, E., & Brenner, J. The growth of social interaction in toddler play-groups: The role of peer experience. *Child Development*, 1977, **48**, 854–861.

O'Neill, P. J., & Lord, C. Functional and semantic characteristics of the child-directed speech of autistic children. In D. Parke (Ed.), *Papers and reports from international meetings of the National Society for Autistic Children*, Boston, Massachusetts: NSAC, 1981.

Parten, N. B. Social participation among preschool children. *Journal of Abnormal and Social Psychology*, 1932, **27**, 243–269.

Radke-Yarrow, M. Some perspectives in research on peer relations. In M. Lewis & L. A. Rosenblum (Eds.), *Friendship and peer relations*. New York: Wiley, 1975. Pp. 298–306.

Ragland, E. U., Kerr, M. M., & Strain, P. S. Effects of social initiations on the behaviour of withdrawn autistic children. *Behaviour Modification*, 1978, **2**, 565–578.

Rheingold, H. L., & Eckerman, C. O. General issues in the study of peer relations: Some proposals for unifying the study of social development. In M. Lewis & L. A. Rosenblum (Eds.), *Friendship and peer relations*. New York: Wiley, 1975. Pp. 293–298.

Richer, J. The partial non-communication of culture to autistic children—An application of human ethology. In M. Rutter & E. Schopler (Eds.), *Autism: A reappraisal of concepts and treatment*. New York: Plenum, 1978. Pp. 47–61.

Ricks, D. M., & Wing, L. Language communication and use of symbols. In L. Wing (Ed.), *Early childhood autism*. Oxford: Pergamon. Pp. 93–134.

Rogers, S. J., Developmental characteristics of young children's play. In G. Ulrey & S. J. Rogers (Eds.), *Psychological assessment of handicapped infants and young children*. New York: Thieme-Stratton, 1982. Pp. 65–83.

Romanczyk, R. G. Diamant, C., Goren, E. R., Trunell, G., & Harris, S. L. Increasing isolate and social play in severely disturbed children: Intervention and post-intervention effectiveness. *Journal of Autism and Childhood Schizophrenia*, 1975, **5**, 57–70.

Roper, R., & Hinde, R. A. Social behavior in a play group: Consistency and complexity. *Child Development*, 1978, **49**, 570–579.

Rubin, K. H. Play behaviours of young children. *Young Children*, 1977, Pp. 16–24.

Rutter, M. Diagnosis and definition. In M. Rutter & E. Schopler (Eds.), *Autism: A reappraisal of concepts and treatment*. New York: Plenum, 1978. (a)

Rutter, M. Developmental issues and prognosis. In M. Rutter & E. Schopler (Eds.), *Autism: A reappraisal of concepts and treatment*. New York: Plenum, 1978. (b)

Rutter, M. Diagnosis and definition of childhood autism. *Journal of Autism and Developmental Disorders*, 1978, **8**, 139-161. (c)

Rutter, M. Attachment and the development of social relationships. In M. Rutter (Ed.), *Scientific foundations of developmental psychiatry*. London: Heinemann, 1980. Pp. 267-279.

Rutter, M. Cognitive Deficits in the pathogenesis of autism. *Journal of Child Psychology and Psychiatry*. 1983 (in press).

Rutter, M., & Bartak, L. Special educational treatment of autistic children: A comparative study. II: Follow-up, findings and implications for services. *Journal of Child Psychology and Psychiatry*. 1973, **14**, 241-270.

Schopler, E., Reichler, R., DeVellis, R. F., & Daly, K. Toward objective classification of childhood autism: Childhood autism rating scale. *Journal of Autism and Developmental Disorders*, 1980, **10**, 91-104.

Sigman, M., & Ungerer, J. Attachment and social behaviors in autistic children. Paper presented at the biannual meeting of the Society for Research in Child Development, Boston, 1981.

Sinson, J. C., & Wetherick, M. E. The behaviour of children with Down's syndrome in normal play groups. *Journal of Mental Deficiency Research*, 1981, **25**, 113-120.

Smith, P. K. A longitudinal study of social participation in preschool children: Solitary and parallel play re-examined. *Developmental Psychology*, 1978, **14**, 517-523.

Snyder, L., Apolloni, T., & Cooke, T. P. Integrated setting at the early childhood level, the role of non-retarded peers. *Exceptional Children*, 1977, **43**, 262-266.

Spivack, G., & Shure, M. B. *Social adjustment in young children*. San Francisco, California: Jossey-Bass, 1974.

Strain, P. S. Peer-mediated treatment of exceptional children's social withdrawal. *Journal Exceptional Education Quarterly*, 1981, **1**, 93-105.

Strain, P. S., & Cooke, T. P. An observational investigation of two elementary age autistic children during free play. *Psychology in the Schools*, 1976, **13**, 82-91.

Strain, P. S., & Fox, J. J. Peers as behavior change agents for withdrawn classmates. In B. B. Lahey & A. E. Kazdin (Eds.), *Advances in clinical child psychology* (Vol. 4). New York: Plenum, 1981. Pp. 167-198.

Strain, P. S., Kerr, M. M., & Ragland, E. U. Effects of peer-mediated social initiations of prompting/reinforcement procedures on the social behaviour of autistic children. *Journal of Autism and Developmental Disorders*, 1979, **9**, 41-54.

Suomi, S. J., & Harlow, H. F. Social rehabilitation of isolate-reared monkeys. *Developmental Psychology*, 1972, **6**, 487-494.

Tremblay, A., Strain P. S., Hendrickson, J. M., & Shores, R. E. Social interactions of normal preschool children: Using normative data for subject and target behaviour selection. *Behaviour Modification*, 1981, **5**, 237-253.

Vandell, D. L. Boy toddlers' social interaction with mothers, fathers, and peers (Doctoral dissertation, Boston University, 1977). *Dissertation Abstracts International*, 1977, **37**, 6309B-6310B.

Vandell, D. L., Wilson, K. S. & Buchanan, N. R. Peer interaction in the first year of life: An examination of its structure, content and sensitivity to toys. *Child Development*, 1980, **51**, 481-488.

Wanlass, R. L., & Prinz, R. J. Methodological issues in conceptualizing and treating childhood social isolation. *Psychological Bulletin*, 1982, **92** (1), 39-55.

Wing, L. Social, behavioral and cognitive characteristics: An epidemiological approach. In

M. Rutter & Schopler (Eds.), *Autism: A reappraisal of concepts and treatment*. New York: Plenum, 1978.

Wing, L., & Gould, J. Severe impairments of social interaction and associated abnormalities in children: Epidemiology and classification. *Journal of Autism and Developmental Disorders*, 1979, **9**, 11–29.

Wing, L. K. *Early childhood autism*. Oxford: Pergamon, 1976.

STUDIES OF STRESS-RESISTANT CHILDREN:

METHODS, VARIABLES, AND

PRELIMINARY FINDINGS

Norman Garmezy and Auke Tellegen

DEPARTMENT OF PSYCHOLOGY
UNIVERSITY OF MINNESOTA
MINNEAPOLIS, MINNESOTA

*Applied Developmental
Psychology, Volume 1*

ISBN 0-12-041201-2

I. Introduction

Two decades ago Lois Murphy (1962) in *The Widening World of Child-hood* posed a paradox that is now slowly being resolved. How, she asked, was it possible that our literature of childhood was so replete with children's problems, failures, and adjustment difficulties, and so neglectful of the manner in which threats can be overcome, corrected, or counterchallenged? The source of the research bias was evident—the language was the contribution of clinicians concerned with maladaptation. An alternative emphasis on adaptation and competence which might have served a compensatory function was not a central concern of most developmental psychologists during the 1950s and 1960s. If a termination of the neglect now appears underway it is in part because of the growing interest of many developmentalists in the study of social competence (Kent & Rolf, 1979), prosocial behaviors (Staub, 1978; Radke-Yarrow & Zahn-Waxler, 1983), social-emotional development (Cairns, 1979; Maccoby, 1980), cognitive styles (Kogan, 1976), problem solving (Shure & Spivack, 1978; Spivack, Platt, & Shure, 1976), ego resilience (Block & Block, 1980; Werner & Smith, 1982), parenting (Schaffer, 1977; Lamb, 1982), temperament and individual differences in children (Thomas & Chess, 1977; Westman, 1973), and related areas.

But research in these areas is not the exclusive province of developmental psychologists. The research interests of psychopathologists have also been turned to the study of adaptation and to the creation of programs of prevention aimed at training persons to cope more effectively with adversity.

Studies of children at risk for psychopathology (Watt, Anthony, Wynne, & Rolf, 1984) have led to an increased emphasis on competence as a result of repeated observations that the dire anticipations of a disordered future, based on adverse circumstances during childhood, have often been refuted by indications of adaptiveness in adulthood (Bleuler, 1978).

Our experience at Minnesota has followed a similar course. Over the past decade Minnesota's *Project Competence* was one of several programs conducted in this country and abroad that focused on children presumed to be vulnerable to psychopathology. Multiple subject groups were studied over the past decade including children born to mothers who had once received a diagnosis of schizophrenia, a nonpsychotic affective disorder, or a personality disorder. In addition, groups of children were studied whose antisocial behavior, isolative or asocial behavior, or hyperactivity in most instances had brought them to the attention of school authorities often with subsequent referral to a community clinic. Matched and random controls drawn from the same classrooms that housed these presumably vulnerable children were also selected. Attention was given to the social competence of these various child cohorts as indexed by the sociometric judgments of their classmates (Garmezy & Devine, 1984).

Tests of the basic hypothesis of the index children's vulnerability to behavior disorder, following more than a decade of research, suggested that many of the children (particularly those of previously or currently mentally disordered parents) gave little, if any, indication of current signs of pathology or incompetence, and, by extension, were not the most likely candidates for future failure. Indeed, many showed clearly adaptive social behavior and work patterns. The longitudinal clinical studies of other investigators that carried the offspring of schizophrenic parents into adulthood clearly demonstrated their competence in work and marriage (Bleuler, 1978). Turning over the coin of vulnerability seemed to reveal facets of "invulnerability" or resilience that had hitherto been neglected.

The term *stress resistant* was used by our research group when we initiated our program of research with children who met two criteria: (1) exposure to sustained and intense life stressors, and (2) the maintenance of mastery or competence despite the presence of such disturbing events. We discontinued use of the term *invulnerable* for it promised more than it provided. Strictly speaking the word *invulnerable* indicates an impregnable quality which has given rise to an even less appropriate term, *superkids* (Kauffman, Grunebaum, Cohler, & Gamer, 1979).

It would be best now to relinquish these concepts for the more prosaic but more accurate descriptions of children as "resilient" as used by the Blocks (1980) or "stress resistant" as adopted by the Minnesota group (Garmezy, 1981).

The concept of invulnerability has undeniably captured the imagination of many. For the mass media it evokes images of heroism and unusual achievements under grim circumstances. Among ordinary citizens it elicits an immediate response of recognition ("Yes, I know someone just like that"). To the researcher it promises the comfort and reward of witnessing the positive side of persons under stress. Most of all, to school personnel it brings a welcome message of hope that they can successfully nurture the competencies of receptive children whose families are buffeted by poverty, unemployment, illness, spousal loss or separation, parental death, or disaster—competencies that will free them from their "at risk" status.

Given these evocative virtues it is curious how sparse the clinical, let alone the experimental, literature is on the subject. Case reports are available and these provide descriptions of the behavior of individuals exposed to various types of stress such as poverty (Coles, 1972), the holocaust (Epstein, 1979), uprooting and migration (Zwingman & Pfister-Ammende, 1973), child abuse (Kempe & Helfer, 1980), disaster (Erikson, 1976), divorce (Wallerstein & Kelly, 1980), severe mental disorder (Schatzman, 1973), and chronic disease and disability (Gliedman & Roth, 1980).

A number of volumes provide examples of creative attainment under adversity such as *Cradles of Eminence* (Goertzel & Goertzel, 1962), *Three Hundred Eminent Personalities* (Goertzel, Goertzel, & Goertzel, 1978), and *Lessons from Childhood* (Illingworth & Illingworth, 1966). But their framework is a limited one for studying stress resistance. The attainments of eminent figures of the past distance us from the reality of ordinary people who cope with distress. One cannot build a literature of stress resistance on the achievements of giants when the same phenomenon has a high incidence in the lives of millions of adults and children.

These case reports present the stimulus side of stress. They reflect the *stressors* of poverty, unemployment, unnatural wars and natural disasters, uprooting, social isolation, stigmatization, parental abuse, bereavement, separation, and loss. It is a litany of today's ills for which the case study provides an unsystematized if fascinating study of lives. In its emphasis on competent behavior amid disadvantage it is a welcome antidote to an earlier emphasis on deficit, disability, and disadvantage.

The orientation is not a new one. Past voices of major figures have gone unheeded. More than 30 years ago Henry Murray (OSS, 1948) issued a challenge in which he urged that we supplement our knowledge of the pathogenic and strive to gain

a much clearer understanding of the positive, creative and health building forces which so often succeed in checking, counteracting, or transforming the complexes of early life in such a way as to produce characters which in certain respects are stronger than they otherwise would have been. The question is, what determinants must be taken into account in predicting whether this or that hurtful occurrence will impede or encourage the development of an effective personality. (p. 168)

Many questions remain unanswered when the case study is the only method of studying stress-resistant behavior. First, antecedents are cited, outcomes are noted, but the processes or mechanisms that link the two remain unidentified. Second, conclusions about processes are invariably highly inferential. Typically, the role of protective factors that might account for adaptation in situations where incompetence is anticipated is usually not discussed. Third, cases are rarely aggregated in a search for commonalities. To do so requires a more systematic study of individuals exposed to the same types of stressful experiences. When this is done the role of protective factors may become evident. For example, in their volume *Psychological Deprivation in Childhood,* Langmeier and Matêcjêk (1975) have provided evidence of some possible protective factors that may enhance adaptation in children exposed to a severe and almost universal stress experience. In writing of the Blitz on London during World War II they noted,

Although evacuation, with all its demands and consequences produced a considerable amount of stress and certain behavior problems in the majority of children, the incidence of disorder and maladaptation, relatively speaking, was considerably lower than we might expect.

Their review of research led them to conclude that an important protective factor may have operated.

Generally, children who had healthy positive relationships with their parents tolerated evacuation with relative ease. It is clear that this relationship with their parents provided the basis for security which helped them to adapt to the new situation. (pp. 152–153)

In this same volume, reports of children who were imprisoned in Nazi concentration camps suggested that psychological damage was less severe in those children who retained contact with their families. Thus retention of the parent–child bond apparently served to contain anxiety and breakdown. But the authors also suggested the presence of other protective factors as indexed by a recurrent emphasis drawn from their literature search citing "stable families," "happy early lives," a prior history of having been "mentally very healthy," the possession of "character traits developed in early childhood," and more fundamental constitutional dispositions that may have made some children more resistant to adverse life conditions.

Epidemiological considerations are of special importance in the study of risk and resistance. Epidemiology, writes one of its world leaders, Johns Hopkins' Ernest Gruenberg (1981), is the "basic science of public health practice and preventive medicine" whose traditional focus of inquiry is framed by these questions: Who gets sick? Who doesn't? Why? (i.e., What are the risk factors?) What can be done to reduce the incidence of disorder? (This implies a knowledge of protective factors and intervention methods.) "Who gets sick?" emphasizes the need to identify *predisposing* factors. "Who doesn't?" directs attention to those *protective* and ameliorating factors that allow some individuals to make surprisingly healthy adaptations despite seemingly debilitating circumstances. The question "Why?" implies the need to understand the *processes* that determine the presence or the absence of disorder under similar background and exposure conditions. And finally, "What can be done about it?" focuses upon *prevention,* the "inoculation" that follows the identification of a population at risk and the mechanisms underlying the disorder.

The data generated by epidemiological research are of great significance in studying stress-resistant qualities in children who are presumed to be at risk for psychiatric disorder. An illustrative example may help. Rutter and his colleagues (Rutter, 1979; Rutter, Cox, Tupling, Berger, & Yule, 1975a; Rutter, Yule, Quinton, Rowlands, Yule, & Berger, 1975b) collected a considerable body of epidemiological data on the incidence of psychiatric disorder in 10-year-old children residing in two strikingly different demographic and geographic areas, the Isle of Wight and an inner borough of London. In the course of their investigations they identified six "risk" factors associated with childhood psychiatric disorders: (1) severe marital discord, (2) low social status, (3) overcrowding or large family size, (4) paternal criminality, (5) maternal psychiatric disorders, and (6) admission into the care of local authority.

Families were categorized on the basis of the number of risk factors exhibited. Rates of psychiatric disorder in the offspring were then examined as a function of the frequency count of these risk factors. The findings were quite striking: when one risk factor was present the likelihood of the child having a psychiatric disorder was not appreciably greater than for those children whose families were free of risk. Two risk factors, however, provided a fourfold increase in the likelihood of a child having a psychiatric disorder, whereas four factors and above increased this risk 10-fold.

Rutter (1979) reports that this relationship between incidence of psychiatric disorder and the severity of risk exposure may hold for acute stressors as well as for chronic familial ones. Thus, multiple hospital admissions of a child increased greatly the risk for psychiatric disorder in comparison with children who had had only a single hospital admission. An interaction of chronic and acute stress could also produce a greater likelihood of psychiatric disorder as well as more long-term adverse effects.

What role do protective factors play in the context of the high degree of risk reflected in negative familial attributes in the two samples? Rutter (1979) took his clue from studies of children in institutions. These indicated that if a child had established a stable relationship with an adult (not necessarily the parent), then the child was more likely to achieve a better social adjustment. Since marital discord and parental psychopathology constituted strong risk factors in the earlier studies, Rutter and his associates chose a sample of children who were living with their biological parents and who met these twin criteria. Since all children were living in severely discordant households the investigators then evaluated a subset of children whose relationship with one parent was marked by warmth and the absence of severe criticism. When comparing children who had the benefit of some degree of parental affection with a group marked by the absence of a good relationship with either parent, the investigators noted that the incidence of a conduct disorder in the children was 25% in the first group of children compared with approximately 75% in the second. These results received further support in another study (Rutter, 1971) in which children from homes marked by discord and severe family problems were moved from their homes in early childhood and placed elsewhere. Rutter then examined the prevalence of conduct disorder in children whose foster homes were marked by discord versus those who had been housed with harmonious families. The latter group had approximately two and a half times fewer cases of conduct disorder when compared with the former group (approximately 20 vs 50%).

Rutter's data on the reversibility of the trauma of separation gain support from Kadushin's (1967) study of the follow-up of 91 highly stressed children who had been placed for adoption when they were 5 years of age or older. Prior to their permanent adoption these children, who had been removed from their biological parents because of neglect and/or abuse, had been further subjected to considerable trauma including multiple foster home placements. Their early childhood had been marked by poverty, poor housing, family discord, and parental pathology including promiscuity, alcoholism, imprisonment of a parent, psychosis of a parent, etc. Only one-third of these children had been in homes characterized by normal parental warmth and acceptance. Neglect was evident in 70% of the sample.

Interviews with the adoptive father and mother by trained social workers indicated that in 87% of the cases the adoptive parents expressed satisfaction with the adoption. Presumably then these children who had been traumatized so consistently and so early in their lives were able to adapt satisfactorily in adoptive homes in which the parents were supportive and affectionate.

Studies such as these reflect initial excursions into the exploration of protective factors in the response of children to stress and disadvantage. In summarizing a brief review of his and other investigators' relevant studies,

Rutter (1979) noted that the investigation of protective factors was not at a stage where definitive conclusions could be drawn.

> What is clear, though, is that there is an important issue to investigate. Many children do *not* succumb to deprivation, and it is important that we determine why this is so and what it is that protects them from the hazards they face. The scanty evidence so far available suggests that when the findings are all in, the explanation will probably include the patterning of stresses, individual differences caused by both consitutional and experiential factors, compensating experiences outside the home, the development of self-esteem, the scope and range of available opportunities, an appropriate degree of environmental structure and control, the availability of personal bonds and intimate relationships, and the acquisition of coping skills. (p. 70)

These suggestions, eminently reasonable and backed by data, provide an agenda for future research. It is not possible that any one investigative team will be able to complete the broad canvas set in place by Rutter. But a start is necessary. With that in mind the remainder of this article is devoted to a description of an ongoing research program, Project Competence, begun in 1979 on the campus of the University of Minnesota with the generous support of the William T. Grant Foundation and the National Institute of Mental Health. What follows is a sequential story of the development of that project, the concepts it employed, the different cohorts of children who were studied, the types of dependent variables that were used, and some preliminary findings based upon our ongoing data analyses. The article concludes with a critical appraisal of the successes and failures we encountered in trying to comprehend the elusive nature of stress resistance in children.

II. Project Competence: Studies of Stress-Resistant Children

Origins

A variety of studies completed over a span of many years reveals the long-term interest of our research group in stress-resistant children. First came the experimental demonstration that the competence qualities of children and the quality of familial integration transcended the low socioeconomic status of families (DePree, 1966; Weintraub, 1973). These studies were followed by a literature review (Nuechterlein, 1970; Garmezy & Nuechterlein, 1972) that focused on the personal and familial attributes of competent black children living in America's urban ghettos. A summary of the behaviors associated with such children and their families has recently been reported (Garmezy, 1981). In turn, a long-range program of research on children vulnerable to psychopathology was mounted in which the major dependent variables were social competence and attentional functioning of such children. The various cohorts studied included the biological offspring of (1) schizophrenic mothers and (2) affectively disordered and personality-disordered mothers, and children who were (3) conduct disordered, (4) internalizing, and (5) hyperactive, together with (6) matched and (7) randomly selected adaptive peers who were classmates of the children who comprised the various risk groups. Results of this decade-long program of research will shortly be published in a series of chapters that are part of a definitive volume devoted to research with children vulnerable to schizophrenia (Watt *et al.,* 1984). Evidence that many of the targeted children (with the prominent exception of the antisocial group) behaved in ways indistinguishable from control children added impetus to our decision to study stress resistance in childhood. While it is true that some children of schizophrenic mothers did show attentional dysfunctions (Marcus, 1972; Nuechterlein, 1983) and low peer acceptance (Rolf, 1972), other children of similar risk status were indistinguishable from controls.

The most recent precursors to our large scale study were two pilot studies involving selected children who met the twin criteria for stress resistance status, namely manifest stressful events in their own lives or their parents, with evidence of maintained competence in the face of such adversity.

Using a representative case approach we first attempted to learn whether school personnel could help us to identify such children. Our entry into the schools was facilitated by 15 previous years of collaborative research in the city school system. This period of tenure was strengthened by an earlier offering by the senior author of two tuition-free, credit-granting graduate seminars designed for school principals and centered on the study of vulnerable and invulnerable children, the role of competence skills acquired in school, and preventive intervention efforts that schools could undertake. The culminating requirement of the course was the preparation of a case report by each principal describing a stress-resistant child in their school. These case presentations were discussed in the seminar, with particular reference to the school as a possible protective factor that might attenuate the stress the child was experiencing.

Our initial case approach to stress resistance in children was straightforward. We traveled to different schools, interviewed principals, social workers, and counselors, briefed them on the purpose of our visit, sought permission to tape their comments about unnamed children in their schools, and promised an anonymity that was never violated. We communicated the twin criteria for stress resistance to school personnel in a nontechnical manner ("Can you tell us of any children in your school about whom you were very concerned when you first learned about some of the outside pressures they were experiencing, but now having seen how they get along in school you are delighted whenever you see them in the halls?") In this somewhat homey manner we communicated our interest in hearing about adaptive children who (1) were encountering difficult circumstances beyond the halls of the school building, but (2) were manifestly competent in the school as a workplace.

These interviews, so cooperatively given, were taped, transcribed, and then discussed fully in our research group in an effort to learn how best to categorize the stressors, to record the achievements of the children, and how to categorize their efforts to cope with their difficult circumstances.

Here in a somewhat disguised fashion is a composited account of children described to us in the course of our school visits.

> A fifth grade 11 year old boy is one of many offspring in a family beset by numerous problems. The father is a marginal worker who has been alcoholic for years. He is usually unemployed and when he does work the jobs he holds are transient and very unskilled. The mother has a low level, part-time job distributing advertising leaflets and also does outside housework to add to the meager family income. She is obese and dyslexic and maintains the run-down house, which is little more than a shack, in which the large family lives. The house is messy, disorganized and smells of urine. The family does not receive welfare assistance.
>
> The offspring are a large and troubled group. One brother has been involved in crime and currently is serving a prison sentence. Another brother living at home is hyperactive, still another is mentally retarded, and still another has been severely assaulted under mysterious circumstances. A number of sibs have been dismissed from high school because of malicious behavior, destructive aggressiveness, and chronic truancy.
>
> The mood of the parents is one of despondency and defeat. Life is perceived as a sequence of disastrous events which leave the mother with a sense of ever present hopelessness.
>
> But the child who has met the interviewer's dual criteria is described by his principal in this manner.
>
> "He is a resilient boy who gets along well with others. He is a good athlete and has won several trophies in difference sports. Everyone in school likes him because he is well-mannered and a bright student. He never misbehaves and so he has never come to the attention of the police or the juvenile court. He comes to school in worn but presentable clothing. He tells us that he prepares his own breakfast in the morning. He is a good kid."

One is caught up in the drama of such a recital and therein lies a danger. Cases such as the above are peripheral examples of a phenomenon that probably has broader representation among school children who may not meet the criterion of *very severe* stress exposure that our instructions probably conveyed to school personnel. Were we to select only children from families as severely stressed as the ones described above, even a lengthy search of an entire city school system might well produce such a small number of cases available for study as to make a research program untenable. We had to conclude that the logistical problems posed by such stringent criteria would probably defeat our effort before it began.

Therefore, we initiated a second pilot study[1] in which we concentrated on a single central city school and sought to take advantage of a more representative sample of school children. Our choice was a school whose principal and teachers were particularly action oriented in trying to ensure the well-being of their children. With complete cooperation of staff we launched our study by providing teachers who were to rate their children with criteria described in brief essays defining our twin concepts of *stress/pressure*, and *adaptation*. Teachers were interviewed about the children in their classrooms and their descriptive vignettes were recorded by hand with code numbers substituted for the children's names.

We collated the material obtained on each child from sessions with teachers, social workers, counselors, and principal, and placed these verbatim contents on a single sheet with the child's code number. Three members of the research team independently read and rated the severity of stress exposure to which the child had been subjected either directly through personal experience or indirectly via the experiences of the family. Raters were allowed the option of withholding a rating if they thought that their available information was insufficient.

The teachers were also asked to rate the adaptation of the children in three areas of functioning: *academic performance, work habits* (without regard to academic ability), and *personal–social behavior.* They also provided a global rating of adaptation for each child. Combining scores obtained from the stress and adapatation ratings resulted in assignment of children to one of four groups, formed by dividing the sample into high vs low stress and high vs low adaptation subgroups.

Three months later teachers again rated the children in their classrooms as well as a second group of children with whom they had contact because of the modular structure of the school curriculum. This enabled us to determine interteacher reliability at a single temporal point and intrateacher reliability at two points spaced 3 months apart.

Class members also provided sociometric ratings of their peers using the "Class Play" procedure devised by Bower (1969) and subsequently modified by Rolf (1972) in a doctoral study of children at risk for psychopathology.

In addition, parental permission was obtained to secure information from a small number of students who occupied each of the four cells. Among the additional measures were a standardized achievement test, an abbreviated *WISC-R* comprised of the Block Design and Vocabulary subtests, the *Porteus Maze,* and a test of role-taking ability that Chandler, Green-

[1]The investigative team consisted of V. Devine, N. Garmezy, M. O'Dougherty, D. Fox, D. Pellegrini, and K. Dwyer.

span, and Barenboim (1974) had used to measure social competence in disturbed institutionalized children.

In summarizing the results of this suggestive (but nondefinitive) pilot study Garmezy (1981)[2] noted

> The low stress/high adaptation group obtained the highest scores on most measures; the high stress/high adaptation . . . group was practically identical to its low stress counterpart on peer sociometric ratings and only slightly lower on achievement test scores. The peer ratings of the two high adaptive groups were markedly different from the ratings of the two low adaptive groups, the mean positive peer choice scores being almost three times greater for these groups. By contrast, the two low adaptation groups performed significantly more poorly across all competence measures, with the low adaptation/low stress group evidencing the poorest performance of all. This should not be surprising since the adaptation ratings tapped into several of the areas rated by the competence indicators. But it was encouraging to learn that peers viewed the high stress/high adaptation and the low stress/high adaptation groups in a comparably favorable manner, particularly so since the categorizations of the children were chosen, not on the basis of peer selection, but on the basis of teacher's judgment. (p. 255)

An interesting sidelight of the study resulted when we informed all parents that we would willingly share the results with them at an evening meeting to be held at the school at their convenience. A positive response came from many of the parents of the high-adaptive children irrespective of their high or low stress status, while there was a notable lack of responsiveness by parents of the two groups of low-adaptive children.

III. The Ongoing Research Program

In 1979 a large scale program of research was begun which, in part, took advantage of what we had learned in the course of the pilot investigations. We began our research by formulating three questions.

1. Could we successfully identify several different cohorts of stress-resistant children whose lives were marked by exposure to different types of stressors?

2. Were there identifiable and characteristic patterns of competence-related behaviors in such children that differed from those found in their less adaptive counterparts despite the similarity of the stress experiences to which both groups had been exposed?

A related question concerned a more distant and integrative goal: If such

---

[2]This summary was adapted from a report prepared by the investigative team that created and completed the pilot study.

patterns could be identified, were they similar to those exhibited by other stress-resistant children who had been exposed to different types of stress experiences?

3. Were there developmental factors that differentiated these stress-resistant children from their less adaptive peers?

These difficult questions presented the research group with problems of definition. First, to identify the child cohorts we had to specify the stressful events to which different groups of children had been exposed. Second, by defining stress resistance as adaptation in the face of adversity, it was necessary to develop measures of competence that we believed reflected such adaptive behavior.

A. The Cohorts[3]

From the inception of the study we sought to include different cohorts of children in which the type of stress events that defined each cohort was identifiably different. Three such cohorts were included in the present program: (1) Cohort I, a community-based group of approximately 200 families drawn from two schools located in the central city, (2) Cohort II, a small group of 32 children whose infancy and early childhood were marked by the stress of a profound, life-threatening congenital heart defect, and (3) Cohort III, a group of 29 severely physically handicapped children who faced the stress of leaving the special school for the handicapped they had attended to meet the challenge of being "mainstreamed" in a regular classroom of a larger public school. This article is an account of our research with Cohort I.

B. The Community Cohort

The central city, community-based cohort (Cohort I) consisting of 200 families has received the heaviest concentration of our research activity. The word *central,* as opposed to *inner,* is used to describe the locus of our activity in order to denote the greater heterogeneity in socioeconomic and racial composition that mark the neighborhoods of our city in comparison with the large ghetto districts of many large American cities.

The families who have participated in our studies constitute a volunteer group who have joined in all aspects of the project. This includes 6 hours

[3]This article presents a preliminary report solely of Cohort I. A forthcoming publication authored by O'Dougherty, Wright, Garmezy, Loewenson, and Torres (1983) will describe results obtained with Cohort II. Results obtained with Cohort III have been reported in recently completed doctoral dissertations of Silverstein (1982) and Raison (1982).

of interviewing of mothers and 2 hours of additional interviewing of the index children, accompanied by cognitive and personality studies of these children that were designed to measure their adaptational qualities: the *Peabody Individual Achievement Test* (PIAT), an abbreviated intelligence test (Cummings & Mulrooney, 1981a,b) consisting of the Block Design and Vocabulary subtests of the WISC-R, which correlates strongly with the Full Scale IQ measure ($r = .88$); in half the group, laboratory procedures were employed to measure social cognition, problem solving, divergent thinking, humor (including the ability to generate it), and measures of delay of gratification and impulsivity–reflectiveness.

The selection of children for this larger cohort was determined by the willingness of their families to participate in the study. The children were enrolled in grades 3–6 of two schools (A and B) housed in the same architectural complex in the central city. These schools are located in a neighborhood of working class families, with a heavy blue-collar representation, and a substantial number of single parents in which the mother as head of household typically was receiving some form of governmental assistance. In School A, for example, intact families made up 46% of the 76 participating families, "reconstituted" families made up 21% of the sample (this includes mother and stepfather, or mother and a "significant other" living together in the household), while single-parent households accounted for 33% of the sample. Minority representation of the school children was estimated at 44% at the time the study was initiated, but the number of families represented by these children was 26%. The estimate was based on a sight count used by the school system to establish the children's racial identity. The largest proportion of children (31%) were black, approximately 7% were American Indian, with Hispanic and Asian children accounting for 4% and 2%, respectively.

The two schools, A and B, are very similar in the demographic composition of the families of the children who attend them. The educational philosophy of School A is a traditional one emphasizing the assignment of children to a specific homeroom in which a single teacher provides the bulk of daily instruction. School B emphasizes modular programming and team teaching.

IV. The Measurement of Stress

A. The Overall Approach to Analyzing the Data

Our intent was to explore relations among a number of major but tentative environmental and individual variables, each anchored to multiple candidate indicators. Our overriding interest was in the underlying variables rather than single indicators as such. This focus (strengthened by our concern not to multiply measures and relations such that their number would be unduly large relative to our sample size) naturally led us to devote the first stage of our analysis to *data reduction within each of several specified domains,* typically through extensive correlational and factor-analytic explorations of the internal structure of a domain. The end result was the replacement of many single indicators by a smaller number of composite measures representing major dimensions of such domains as competence, reflectiveness–impulsiveness, socioeconomic status, and stress. In the following pages some examples of this reduction process are presented.

We then proceeded with the next step in our analysis, the exploration of relations *between* domains, for example, social class and cognitive variables in relation to measures of competence, or social class and stress combined with measures of social cognition in relation to competence. For this second phase we have relied primarily on multiple regression procedures, specifically, the planned, so-called hierarchical, methods described in detail by Cohen and Cohen (1975). This approach allows one to treat measures from one or more domains as independent variables and, upon entering these in a specified order preferably suggested by theoretical considerations, determine their distinctive contribution to prediction of a dependent variable from a different domain. Used judiciously this type of analysis can be a basis for evaluating both predictive main effects and interactions among predictors, and can be used both to test prespecified hypotheses and, in a more exploratory vein, to generate new hypotheses for future work. Again several examples are discussed.

If there is one point of agreement among stress researchers it is that there is no agreement as to how best to define the concept. Mason (1975), a distinguished researcher, in describing the history of the stress area, presented the problem in the opening paragraph of his essay.

> Perhaps the single most historical fact concerning the term "stress" is its persistent, widespread usage in biology and medicine in spite of almost chaotic disagreement over its definition. This fact alone would seem to suggest both that the term has a curiously strong popular or intuitive appeal and that it fills widely recognized needs for describing biological phenomena not adequately covered by other generic terms at present. It is sometimes said that durability provides a good index of the validity or usefulness of scientific concepts. If this is true, then the durability of stress concepts in the face of so much confusion over terminology suggests that a continuing search for what is solid and valid in these concepts may eventually prove rewarding. (p. 6)

In the meantime *stress* continues to have multiple meanings. It has been used to represent stimulus, response, and mediating variables. It has been linked to, and sometimes equated with, anxiety, conflict, frustration, emotional distress, tension, arousal, harsh environmental and interpersonal deprivations, ego and physical threat, physical trauma, illness, and injury. Yet, as Mason has noted, the concept, despite all its definitional confusion, has demonstrated remarkable staying power.

However, to use the concept in research on stress resistance requires some empirical anchoring. With Cohorts II and III we defined stress in terms of the presence of shared physical disabilities in the children. For Cohort II this was a specific life-threatening congenital heart defect in infancy and childhood successfully modified by open-heart surgery. For Cohort III the children's severe physical handicaps with the physical restrictiveness it imposed, plus the added experience of placement in a regular classroom after a lengthy period in a special school, served as the common stressors.

B. Measuring Life Events

Cohort I, unlike the other two cohorts, was designed to be a larger and more heterogeneous sample selected from within a typical central city community. For this sample we had to have some method that would enable us to survey the community rapidly to measure the severity of stress our volunteer families had encountered during the previous year. We turned to a self-report procedure which, during the past 15–20 years, has become increasingly popular as a measure of stress exposure—*the life events method* (Dohrenwend & Dohrenwend, 1974).

There is a lengthy history to the effort to create a scale of stressful life events from which one could infer the severity of stress that a respondent had encountered. Included in that history would be Cannon's (1929, 1932) investment in recording the somatic consequences of significant events and situations in a person's life, Meyer's (1919) construction of a life chart derived from mental patients' histories in an attempt to search out temporal contiguities between critical events and specific psychosocial experiences of patients with the appearance of symptoms of their psychiatric disorders, and Selye's (1946) General Adaptation Syndrome (GAS) based on his laboratory demonstrations of the role of induced trauma and anatomical changes following the organism's exposure to prolonged stress.

During the past two decades a central contribution has been made by Holmes and Rahe (1967) and their associates, who constructed a *Schedule of Recent Events* (SRE) and a *Social Readjustment Rating Questionnaire* (SRRQ) designed initially to assess the frequency of occurrence of 43 significant life events. Later, a magnitude estimation scaling procedure derived from methods of psychophysical measurement was used to develop scale values ranging from 0 to 100 for each of the 43 events. The scaling procedure required a large number of raters (394) to compare each event with marriage, which was assigned a value of 100. The judges were asked to assign event values based on two questions: Is this event indicative of more or less readjustment than marriage? Would the readjustment take longer or shorter to accomplish? High scores were assigned if the readjustment required of a person (as judged by raters) was more intense and protracted than marriage; proportionately smaller values were assigned if the event was perceived as less intense and of briefer duration. On the basis of this rating procedure the most stressful events reliably implicated were (1) *strains in family relationships* such as marriage, death, divorce, separation, pregnancy, and new family members; (2) *work problems* such as loss of a job by discharge or retirement, or business readjustments; and (3) *personal misfortunes* such as sustaining an injury or going to jail. Events that require minor readjustments and therefore have earned lower scale values include vacations, Christmas, and minor legal violations.

Although there is a surprising degree of concordance in the scale values assigned by Japanese, Scandinavian, Spanish, and Western European raters, there is evidence that cultural differences can influence rating. Reliability of judgments based on short-term test–retest ratings appear adequate (Herzog, Linder, & Samaha, 1981). Validity of the instrument is attested to by a plethora of studies relating high scale scores to a variety of ills and physical disorders (Rabkin & Struening, 1976). Reviews of these research studies are numerous (Dohrenwend, 1981), as are criticisms of the method itself (Dohrenwend & Dohrenwend, 1977, 1978; Rutter, 1981).

The utilization of the life events method with children was fostered by the appearance in 1972 of Coddington's *Social Readjustment Rating Scale for Children* (1972a,b). This scale borrowed heavily from the original work of Holmes, Rahe, and others but was modified by inclusion of a list of experiences that were more applicable to groups of preschoolers, elementary, junior high school, and senior high school students. More recently, Coddington (unpublished) has revised the scale that had been administered to a large number of adolescents in many different settings ranging from community centers to jails. The adolescents' life-change-unit scores, corrected for extreme deviance, are reported to be consonant with those provided by professional judges including teachers, pediatricians, and mental health workers. Coddington reports that scale scores provided by 3620 children show no social class or racial differences in the assignment of values to the 51 events that constitute the scale.

Research reports (Heisel, 1972; Heisel, Ream, Raitz, Rappaport, & Coddington, 1973) indicate that children with different forms of childhood illness (juvenile rheumatoid arthritis, hemophilia, and general pediatric, surgical, and psychiatric cases) show elevated life events scores relative to a normative group. Similar results have been obtained by investigators studying chronically ill (Bedell, Giordani, Amour, Tavormina, & Boll, 1977) and accident-prone (Padilla, Rohsenow, & Bergman, 1976) children.

Criticisms of the life events method are numerous and implicate objections based on empirical, methodological, and conceptual limitations of the scaling procedure and the data derived from research with them (Brown, Harris, & Peto, 1973; Brown, Sklair, Harris, & Birley, 1973; Dohrenwend & Dohrenwend, 1977, 1978; Uhlenhuth, Balter, Lipman, & Haberman, 1977; Herzog unpublished). Here is a sampling of critics' objections.

1. Correlations reported between scale scores and illness status, while positive, are typically quite modest.

2. The causal role of an event is ambiguous. Although presumed causes, they may also be consequences of the behaviors of less adaptive individuals. Two-way causal connections may make it impossible to differentiate clearly antecedents from consequents.

3. Some events are objective statements of occurrences, but others demand subjective assessment by judges. The global stress score is therefore not without ambiguity.

4. The sampling of life events is inadequate. When respondents are invited to suggest events, the seriousness of content omissions becomes evident (Yeaworth, York, Hussey, Ingle, & Goodwin, 1980; Herzog, unpublished).

5. Many studies of life events and their relationships to physical and emotional states are cross-sectional rather than longitudinal, retrospective rather than prospective, with all the disadvantages inherent in such methods (cf. Garmezy & Devine, 1977).

6. The normative data for these scales are quite inadequate for various ethnic, cultural, and racial groups.

7. A summated score of positive and negative events adds to the ambiguity of the global rating. There is strong evidence that the significance of negative and positive events for adaptive behavior is quite different (Herzog *et al.,* 1981).

8. Overgeneralizations based on life events research pose a danger. All major life events do not necessarily lead to physical or mental disorders; in turn, disorders are not necessarily preceded by stressful life events. All studies indicate that a wide range of individual differences characterize responses to such experiences. Furthermore, as Rutter (1981) has noted "there is a great paucity of evidence on the possible importance of stressful life events in the genesis of psychiatric disorders of childhood." The same statement can be made for the physical disorders of childhood.

These are some of the criticisms that have been put forward, and others can be added. Why then did our research group decide to use a modification of the Coddington scale to secure a first rough measure of stress exposure in those families that were to constitute the community sample? The reason was a pragmatic one.

We needed a rapid survey that would offer the research group a first approximation to the distribution of stress scores characterizing those families that would agree to collaborate in the projected research program. A Life Events Questionnaire (LEQ) seemed the most apt method for achieving this end. But mindful of the limitations of these instruments we had also decided in planning the study to engage the participating mothers in a series of three 2-hour interviews to be described later. We planned to use one of the sessions for a lengthy discussion with each mother of the context surrounding the occurrence of each stressful life event.[4]

The procedure we followed was to modify the Coddington scale excluding several of the original events and adding 16 others that reflected some items more appropriate to a working class sample. We also added a number of positive items to negate any set developed by respondents on reading the LEQ that the project's focus was on psychopathology rather than competence. To derive weights for these newly added events the following procedures were employed. Forty clinical judges were provided with 35 life events from Coddington's original list, rank ordered according to their presumed impact on a typical elementary school child. New events were presented to the judges in random order with instructions to insert each event into the original rank-ordered sequence in terms of its judged comparative impact upon a child. These judgments were averaged and each item was assigned a weight according to its placement in that original sequence. The 50 descriptive event items of the scale, 30 of which are negative, 11 positive, and 9 ambiguous with regard to their desirability or undesirability (which could only be determined from the mother's interview), were then reworded into declarative sentences that emphasized the child's perspective of these events (e.g., "The child's mother began to work sometime during the past year"). Parent informants were asked to check those events which occurred *within the past year* (Herzog et al., 1981). A copy of the modified Coddington Life Events Questionnaire (LEQ) appears in Table I.

---

[4]A report of the results obtained in this session with School A families is now being prepared by Mr. Harvey Linder as a portion of his doctoral dissertation. In addition, the other 4 hours of interviews with the mother included a lengthy inquiry into family and parental backgrounds, family relationships, caretaking patterns and child-rearing practices of the mother, and her perceptions of the participating child including his or her early developmental history and current adaptation. These extensive data are currently being analyzed.

The LEQ was then mailed together with an explanatory letter about the project to all parents or guardians of children enrolled in grades 3–6 of School A. Subsequently the same procedure was followed for School B. A set of complete instructions accompanied the LEQ mailing, together with a supporting letter from the school principal and a request for permission to collect cumulative school record data and teacher's ratings of the child. Permission slips and a stamped self-addressed envelope for return to the Project office accompanied the mailing. Parents were paid $5.00 immediately upon receipt of the questionnaire, or $7.50 if separate LEQs had to be completed in the event that more than one offspring in the family was enrolled in grades 3–6.

The LEQ was mailed to 256 families of all 302 children enrolled in grades 3–6 of School A. There followed in turn another mail solicitation, followed by a final effort at contact. These three consecutive solicitations brought a return of 122, 26, and 36 LEQs, respectively. These 184 LEQs represented the participation of 158 families, for an approximate rate of return of 61% of the total sample.

Table I

Life Events Questionnaire: Scoring for 50 Items[a]

Item number	Description	Source[b]	Status[c]	LCU[d]
1	Move to new school district	C	A	46
2	Outstanding personal achievement	C	P	39
3	Failed grade or held back	C	N	57
4	Suspended from school	C	N	46
5	Did not make extracurricular activity	PC	N	38
6	Became church member	C	P	25
7	Father away from home more due to job	C	N	45
8	Mother began work	C	A	44
9	Change in financial status	C	A	29
10	Parent hospitalized	C	N	55
11	Child hospitalized	C	N	62
12	Sibling hospitalized	C	N	41
13	Child in serious accident	PC	N	61
14	Acquired physical handicap	C	N	69
15	Congenital physical handicap	C	N	60
16	Parent died	C	N	90
17	Grandparent died	C	N	38
18	Sibling died	C	N	68
19	Close friend died	C	N	53
20	Sibling born	C	A	50
21	Adult joined family	C	A	41
22	Child began to date	PC	A	44
23	Change in peer acceptance	C	A	51
24	Vacation	PC	P	27

Table I (*Continued*)

Item number	Description	Source[b]	Status[c]	LCU[d]
25	Close friend moved away	PC	N	46
26	Child's pet died	PC	N	44
27	Child learned of own adoption	C	N	52
28	Sibling left home	C	A	36
29	Child broke up with boyfriend/girlfriend	PC	N	46
30	Parents divorce	C	N	84
31	Marital separation	C	N	78
32	New stepparent	C	A	65
33	Increase in parent–child arguments	C	N	51
34	Decrease in parent–child arguments	C	P	27
35	Increase in arguments between parents	C	N	51
36	Decrease in arguments between parents	C	P	25
37	Child involved with drugs/alcohol	C	N	61
38	Unmarried sister pregnant	C	N	36
39	Recognition for athletics	PC	P	38
40	School play or performance	PC	P	36
41	Parent lost job	C	N	38
42	Parent's minor jail sentence	C	N	44
43	Parent's major jail sentence	C	N	67
44	Child placed in "gifted" program	PC	P	44
45	Award at school	PC	P	37
46	Family evicted	PC	N	48
47	Sibling involved with drugs/alcohol	PC	N	40
48	Funds cut off by government agency	PC	N	44
49	Award outside of school	PC	P	37
50	Leadership position	PC	P	40

[a] Modified from Coddington (1972a).

[b] Source of life events, either Coddington (1972a) (C) or Project Competence (PC).

[c] Status of life events, either Positive (P), Negative (N), or Ambiguous (A), according to clinical judges' ratings.

[d] Life change units: weighted values.

Of the original number of families contacted, 84 (33%) of these accounting for 100 children (33%) failed to respond to our initial mailing and all subsequent efforts to engage them. The final effort at contact was a series of structured telephone calls to as many of the nonresponders as we could reach. Because of our concern whether we had evoked a negative response in the community due to our interest in specific life stressors, we inquired in this telephone interview about the reasons for nonparticipation. Only 11 families indicated a negative response to the survey and of these only 6 could be classified as actively hostile to the research effort. Four of these 6 families gave "invasion of privacy" as the basis for their refusal to participate. While numerous reasons were given for rejection, only a very small number indicated that their rejection was an active, negative one.

One year later a second LEQ was mailed to participating families to cover events of the immediate past year. A follow-up reminder and telephone calls produced a total of 135 LEQs from 113 families.

For School B two sets of LEQs were collected in a somewhat comparable manner, but there was one significant modification in our procedures that resulted in a significant increase in the number of participating families.

The reason for our change in solicitation of families is an important one, for it deals with the critical problems of subject attrition and sampling bias. But before reporting these observations a brief mention should be made of an additional rating of stress that was used by the Project staff.

C. An Additional Stress Score

In addition to a Stress score derived from the LEQ, a second score was obtained by having the interviewers, who had spent 6 hours with the mother, rate the stress experiences of the family. This measure, *Interviewer's Rating of Stress* (Larsen, unpublished), was designed as an adjunct to the estimate of life stress derived from the LEQ and was scaled ranging from 1 (low stress) to 5 (high stress). The time period covering these ratings was the same for both the LEQ and the interviewer's rating. Each stress rating was accompanied by a confidence rating to reflect the clinical judge's certainty or uncertainty about her rating. Few nonconfident ratings were obtained. Where two raters were involved, independent ratings were obtained. Training sessions on initial cases were held to provide interviewers with the opportunity to set up criteria for rating the interview protocols.

The correlations between the Interviewer's Rating of Stress scores and the LEQ Negative/Ambiguous Events scores for School A ranged from +.45 to +.49.

D. Subject Attrition and Sampling Bias

The fear of significant attrition of our participating families was a constant source of concern to the research team. The possibility for an increase in the number of dropouts was possible at two points in our efforts to solicit families. The first time (T_1) was in response to our letter of solicitation inviting parents to complete the LEQ and requesting permission for the research group to review the children's academic records. The second time (T_2) was the invitation of families to participate in the extensive research program that followed the collection of the second LEQ a year later. Of the two invitations, the second was the more challenging, and a strong collective effort was made to construct a letter that focused attention on the importance of learning how children come to cope with their stressful world. Details of the various studies to be conducted were provided as a supplement to the letter of invitation, and families were urged to call the principal investigators if they had any questions to ask. It was at this critical point that our subject attrition increased. Eighty-three families of the original 158 LEQ responders (53%), representing 100 children of the prior group of 184 (54%), agreed to join the project. By comparing the participants and nonparticipants (from the original responder group) it became possible to see whether our losses were random or nonrandom. The data clearly demonstrated that the final study sample was not entirely representative of the initial sample that was originally solicited for the project. Two pieces of evidence warranted this conclusion.

1. It was possible to compare the average competence scores of children of the original LEQ responders and nonresponders. Children of families who completed the LEQ showed a trend toward greater competency in terms of the ratings of peers and teachers, although the results were not statistically significant.

2. When families that had completed the initial LEQ but subsequently declined to participate in the project were compared in terms of their LEQ scores, those who elected to continue their participation reported significantly fewer stressful life events than those who had terminated their participation ($\bar{x} = -.189$ vs 2.44, $t = -.290$, $p = .044$). Similarly the children of those who chose to participate showed significantly higher ratings of academic, social, and behavioral competence as indexed by their cumulative records, and peer and teacher ratings.

Thus, in comparison to the original sample, the participating group shared some reduction in the range of manifest competence in these children as well as in the reported stress experience scores of their parents.

E. Overcoming the Problem of Attrition with the School B Sample

It had always been the plan of our research group to hold School B in reserve until the study of School A had been completed, with the intention of remedying any mistakes in procedures that had occurred in the course of our initial contacts in the community.

Aware of the sample bias that had crept into our School A sample (Sample A), we did not allow that situation to reoccur with the School B sample (Sample B). We were able to predict the likelihood of a repetition because our proportions of responders and nonresponders in School B closely paralleled those observed in School A.

The key to the solution of attrition lay in a report prepared by the leader of our interviewing team[5] urging rapid and direct contact with nonresponding families of School B. Our interview team paid visits to the nonresponding families, presumably with the aim of ascertaining their reasons for deciding not to participate in the project. Ms. Larsen's report indicated that the implementation of this strategy required an extraordinary degree of pursuit. Repeated visits had to be made to the homes before contact was finally established. Often the nonresponding families had moved several times since the inception of the study, a sign, Ms. Larsen noted, that in itself was probably an indication of a family caught up in a more stressful set of experiences.

The results of this intensive effort at direct contact proved striking. An attempt was made to reach a total of 48 nonresponding families from School B. Nine of this group responded to an additional mail solicitation. This required that visits be made to 39 families representing 45 school children. Of this group, on the basis of home visits, 33 families with 39 children (71%) were enlisted into the project in 1 month's time. Since only 4 families of the 48 families could not be contacted, we could account for 90% of the families and 91% of the children. The sample size for School B was increased by 46% due to the extended efforts of our interview team to contact directly the recalcitrant families. Recognizing the possibility of a fragile commitment to the study, we gave first priority to interviewing this group of families.

F. Refining the Measurement of Stress

The problem of measuring the stress experiences of the participating families was of primary concern to our research group ever since the original decision was made to employ a Life Events Questionnaire as a preliminary survey instrument.

As mentioned previously, two members of the research group[6] designed a sequence of three 2-hour interviews with the mothers, the final portion of which involved a follow-up contextual inquiry into the specific stressful life events, particularly the most significant negative ones. These interviews clearly indicated that the stresses experienced by the families of the School A sample were not truly attenuated in the manner suggested by the distri-

[5]Credit goes to Ms. Andrea Larsen whose (unpublished) report, *The home visit as a method to elicit continued participation in a family stress study,* provided the research group with a method for partially solving the dropout problem.

[6]Using other available instruments H. Linder and N. Garmezy arranged the contents of the 6 hours of interviewing of mothers that were conducted by Linder and research members.

bution of the original LEQ scores. Interviewing brought out additional stressful experiences that had occurred to the participating families of School A during the previous year—revelations made easier as parents developed a close relationship with the interviewers.

The initial analyses of our numerous dependent variables were structured in terms of the original LEQ scores. Eventually we will reanalyze our results on two bases: (1) the revised clinical ratings of stress as derived from the contextual interview plus other data obtained in the course of 4 hours of interviewing that was focused on family background, mother–child relationships, and other contents which brought in their wake a recital of other stress experiences not recorded on the LEQ, and (2) the Interviewer's Rating of Stress for the family as deduced from 6 hours of prolonged contact with the parent(s).

The families of School A are not strangers to stress. The clinical data obtained during the lengthy interviews with the mother now stand us in good stead in deriving two revised stress scores that will probably provide more valid indices of the distress our families have known over the past several years than will the Life Events Questionnaire which formed the basis of our initial stress evaluations.

In addition, our results will allow other investigators to compare the stress scores obtained for our samples from the structured LEQ with the interview-based scores of these same respondents derived through the more open-ended clinical method of inquiry which characterized a portion of the interviewer's exchange with the mother.

G. Reliability and Stability

The correlations between the first and second administrations of the LEQ (spaced 1 year apart) in Schools A and B were moderately high and statistically significant. For Negative/Ambiguous Events scores and Total Events scores the School A correlations were .60 and .62, respectively; for school B these values were .53 and .64, respectively. All correlations are statistically significant below the .001 level.

H. Cohort Attributes: The Measurement of Socioeconomic Status[7]

Social status has received considerable research attention as a moderator of the effects of stress (Sandler, 1980). Studies by Dohrenwend (1970) and Dohrenwend and Dohrenwend (1969) indicate that stressful events have a greater impact on lower class individuals than on those of higher socioeco-

---

[7]The variable of socioeconomic status, its contents, and measurement are described extensively in a Project Competence Technical Report (Linder et al., 1981).

nomic status (SES) (Kessler, 1979). In a study in which educational level was used as an indicator of social status, Dohrenwend (1973) found a significant correlation between the number of recent life stresses and psychological disorder for lower social class groups but not for higher ones.

Generally, this differential impact of stress in lower SES groups has been explained by the paucity of resources available to poor people (Dohrenwend & Dohrenwend, 1970; Cobb, 1976). However, lack of resources is unlikely to explain fully the variability that characterizes groups of lower SES individuals who differ in their adaptability in the face of stress. Kessler (1979) concluded that the impact of stress has other moderators such as efficacy of coping strategies, gender, and marital status. For example, women, particularly if unmarried, are more affected by stress than others of comparable SES, possibly because they lack buffers that could serve to attenuate a distressing event. The study of "protective" factors is of recent origin. Its expansion over the next decade should hasten the development of more effective prevention strategies in the behavior disorders (see Rutter, 1979; Garmezy, 1982).

The empirical findings that the lower one's social class status, the more deleterious (in general) the effects of stress, necessitated inclusion of this variable in evaluating the effects of our stress measures. But this required the use of a reliable index of social class which, in turn, would provide an opportunity to study variations in coping strategies within given social class levels, and thus control for competence variations that could be explained as a function of socioeconomic status.

To collect data on SES level, the mother's occupational classification was ascertained together with her work history, level of job satisfaction, arrangement for child care while working, etc. The large proportion of single mothers in our sample dictated the decision to forego extensive data gathering on the biological fathers' employment history in those families—a decision not easily arrived at but one which was logistically necessary in the light of the many hours of interviewing that had already been scheduled.

The determination of which SES classificatory system to use was made difficult by the following realities:

1. Most, if not all, classificatory schemas now in use are based primarily on the classification of *male* heads of households. Not only is this in itself becoming an outdated criterion, but in 42% of our sample the sole head of the family was a female.

2. The two systems considered were the Duncan *Socioeconomic Index* (SEI) developed in cooperation with the National Opinion Research Center (see Duncan, 1961; Hauser & Featherman, 1977), and the Hollingshead *Index of Social Position* (ISP) (Hollingshead, 1957; Watt, 1976). Neither

made provision for families receiving government assistance—a status shared by a substantial portion of our community sample.

3. These systems also failed to provide a classification for "housewife," which comprised 15% of the sample.

4. In an effort to avoid overintrusiveness in regard to family economics, we decided to use broad categories of income ($5000 intervals), which did not allow for a more well-defined classification.

The problem of assigning social class status was discussed with consultant sociologists,[8] and the following consensus was obtained.

1. The current trend is often to examine relationships among occupation, education, income, and related dependent variables in separate analyses rather than to treat them as a single global aggregate of SES.

2. The currently most widely used aggregate method is the Duncan Socioeconomic Index (SEI).

3. There appears to be no adequate provision for classifying families on welfare, or women who identify themselves as "housewives."

4. Both occupation and education are viewed as the best predictors of a wide range of variables.

5. If both parents in an intact family work, the higher status occupation of the two is frequently used. In those instances in which the mother lives with a man to whom she is not married, his occupation may be used if (1) he plays a significant role in supporting the family and (2) is perceived as a family member.

With these consideration in mind, the decision was made to use Duncan's SEI as the index of socioeconomic status. A further important consideration was that the Duncan Index discriminates better within middle- and low-SES groups—categories which by virtue of the educational and occupational status of our sample had the largest membership. Furthermore, the Duncan index allowed for more precise occupational classification than did the Hollingshead scale.

Information used in providing an SES assignment was based on the first of the lengthy parent interviews (see p. 264) in which inquiry was made of the occupational title, job description and duties of jobs held by mother and father, education of mother and father (which was solicited by phone), family income including that of the separated parent, family size, and a home rating index. Information on father's occupation was collected for

[8]We acknowledge with appreciation the assistance provided by Dr. Helena Lopata (Loyola University) and Drs. Jaylean Mortimer and David Mangan (University of Minnesota).

stepfathers and/or foster fathers as well. These were used if the biological father was no longer in the home.

There is an elaborate set of statistics based on SES classification (Linder, Silverstein, & Samaha, 1981) which cannot be detailed in this brief article. Some general statements, however, can be made based upon those analyses.

1. Interrater agreement is 94% and above for coding mother's and father's occupation and 100% for coding parental education.

2. Correlations between Duncan codes and Hollingshead codes for different methods of determining social class status, based on occupation in Schools A and B, are consistently high for mothers (>.70), fathers (.79), and head of household (>.75).

3. The distributions of educational and occupational level achieved show marked variability. For education the modal level in both Schools A and B is high school graduation, but substantial proportions of mothers and fathers have not completed high school or are only junior high school graduates.

In general, the educational/occupational distributions indicated a broad range of social status with three major categories. (1) The largest proportion of participating families were of lower to middle class status including blue-collar and to a lesser extent skilled-worker assignments. (2) There was a sizable proportion of indigent mothers who were receiving governmental assistance. (3) A small proportion (10%) of parents occupied a more solid middle-class niche by virtue of their education and professional, semi-professional, or managerial occupational roles. The justification for not using "inner city" but rather "central city" as the description of the geographical locale of the study (see p. 243) was supported by this distribution of socioeconomic levels.

4. SES correlations with achievement measures, PIAT scores, and IQ fell in the neighborhood of +.30. Its correlation with stress scores (combined Negative and Ambiguous Events) is negative and statistically significant, but moderately low (−.18 to −.24) with different administrations of the LEQ in the two samples. The correlations with stress ratings of families derived from interview data is in the same direction and somewhat higher.

V. The Measurement of Children's Competence

A. Measures of Competence Used

To evaluate children's competence it was decided to collect a number of distinctive measures of the child's functioning in school.

Permission was secured from participating parents that allowed the research team to derive three such measures of functional competence for the children who participated in the study. These included the following:

1. *Work (academic) competence.* This component of competence was based initially on independent clinical ratings provided by four judges who applied a set of decision rules to their analyses of each child's cumulative school record. A 5-point rating scale (superior to poor) used by the judges produced high interrater agreement. In 37 of 159 cases judges reached perfect agreement, half-point differences were present in 80 cases, and 37 other cases were separated by a full point. Alpha coefficients of reliability were computed (treating judges as items) and produced a coefficient for School A cumulative record achievement ratings of $+.98$.

Nevertheless, cumulative records vary considerably in completeness, types of test scores administered and present in the record, and grades. These differences were particularly apparent among the many students who transferred into central city classrooms. In addition, the group-administered achievement tests that appear on the cumulative record are particularly onerous for children from deprived families or those who have reading deficits. Therefore, it was decided to administer to each child the Peabody Individual Achievement Test (Dunn & Markwardt, 1970). Its virtues are many: the use of pictorial and spatial comprehension items are helpful to children who have difficulty in verbal expression; coverage is wide ranging; the test emphasizes power rather than speed in providing a rapid and rough estimate of general educational level; and it is a useful instrument for providing parents with information regarding their child's school achievement. (We had indicated a willingness to share information with the parents about their children's test performance, but not the contents of the child's interview with project staff or the teacher's ratings).

Our analysis of PIAT and school achievement ratings provided further confirmation of the effects of subject attrition in the School A sample. Children of parents who had declined participation in the study had significantly lower mean achievement score ratings than those whose parents had consented to participate ($p < .001$).

The intercorrelation between PIAT ratings and cumulative record achievement score ratings was $+.83$. On the basis of this intercorrelation the PIAT was selected to serve as a measure of work achievement (Cummings & Mulrooney, 1981a).

2. *Behavioral competence,* the second measure of children's competence, was indexed by teacher ratings of the children using a well-standardized instrument, the *Devereux Elementary School Behavior Rating Scale* (Spivack & Swift, 1967). Studies and reviews (Littell, 1972) indicated that this instrument not only provided the broadest behavioral coverage of various

teacher ratings scales but offered the most extensive documentation of reliability and validity of the scale, and the adequacy of the standardization
data (Finkelman & Ferrarese, 1981). The scale is composed of 47 items, 26
of which are rated on a 5-point scale, the other 21 on a 7-point scale. These
individual items are assigned to 11 different factor scales containing three,
four, or five items each. The 11 factor scores are standardized and combined into a profile.

Our appraisal of the Devereux data, based on two administrations of the
scale in School A and one in School B, indicated large differences between
classroom means on all 11 factors, despite the fact that the children in these
classes had not been assigned by ability level. It appeared that much of the
variation we found was probably due to differences in rating styles among
teachers. Therefore scores within classes were standardized separately to
control for classroom differences. All statistical analyses were performed
using within-class standardized scores.

A principal components analysis performed on Devereux Scale scores obtained from the combined School A and B samples suggested four major
dimensions. A varimax rotation of the first four principal factors to simple
structure resulted in dimensions that we termed *Disruptive-Oppositional*
(18 items), *Poor Comprehension-Disattention* (14 items), *Cooperative-
Initiating (8 items),* and *Performance Anxiety* (4 items). The internal consistency of these factors as reflected in coefficient alphas was high (ex-
ceeding .80).

Test–retest reliabilities, spanning 17 months, of the first three factors
ranged from .52 to .69. The fourth factor scale, Performance Anxiety, had
a lower test–retest reliability correlation of .27.

Correlations of these Devereaux factor scores with academic achievement, IQ, LEQ scores, and socioeconomic status of the participating samples were variable and generally low but often were statistically significant
because of the substantial number of subjects tested.

3. *Interpersonal (social) competence* was derived from a sociometric technique employed with classroom peers, a modification of the Class Play designed by Bower (1969). This procedure is based upon peer judgments and
requires that each child in a classroom view himself or herself as the director
of a class play and cast his or her classmates in various positive and negative
play roles. The method has been employed by Project Competence (Masten
& Morison, 1981) personnel for more than a decade in the schools without
the occurrence of a single untoward experience, despite the participation of
thousands of school children in the project during that span of time.

Because previous experience had indicated marked sex differences in the
overall number of roles assigned (girls tend to receive fewer votes) and in

the sex distribution for particular roles, we decided to administer the Class Play twice in each classroom, with members first assigning roles for either boys or girls, followed by role assignments for the opposite sex. All references to sex were eliminated from the individual play-role descriptions.

The Minnesota Revision of the Class Play consists of 30 roles, 15 positive and 15 negative. The rational categories represented by these roles include Leadership, Aggression, (Prosocial/Antisocial), and Sociability (Gregariousness/Social Isolation).

Factor analyses of item z scores for the 30 roles indicated that a three-factor solution was most meaningful: Factor 1 is identified as *Sociability-Leadership,* Factor 2 as *Aggressive-Disruptive,* and Factor 3 as *Sensitive-Isolated.* These factors are the same for both boys and girls. Three basic scores are derived for our purposes: a *Positive* score based on the 15 positive roles of Factor I, a *Disruptive* score based on 7 roles of Factor II, and an *Isolated* score based on 7 other roles in Factor III. All scores were standardized within classroom and sex to adjust for unequal sex and classroom size distributions. The roles that form the basis for each of these scores are indicated in Table II.

The intercorrelations and alpha reliability coefficients reveal the scales to have high internal reliability and low to moderate intercorrelations.

Test–retest correlations over a 6-month interval are $+.87$ for Positive, $+.77$ for Disruptive, and $+.80$ for the Isolated score. After 12 and 18 months the scores continue to remain moderately stable despite changes in the school year and new assignments of the children to different classrooms. The 12-month correlations are .71, .69, and .69 for the three scores; at 18 months they drop slightly to .63, .64, and .66, respectively.

Moderately high correlations were found among peer perceptions, teacher perceptions (Devereux ratings), academic achievement, and IQ.

B. Compositing and Intercorrelating the Competence Variables

One of our aims was to reduce the number of dependent variables by constructing a smaller number of composite variables. Three sociometry factors, four Devereux factors, and two academic achievement scores were considered too many for inclusion in regression analyses.

Factor analyses of the peer and teacher ratings resulted in two major factors. Loading highly on the first factor were the following measures: from the sociometry scores, Sociability-Leadership (positive loading) and Sensitive-Isolated (negative loading), and from the Devereux, Cooperative-Initiating (positive loading) and Poor Comprehension-Disattention (negative loading). (If included, the academic achievement scores also load on

Table II

Roles Included in the Sociometry Scores
Derived from the "Class Play"

Positive score

Is a good leader
Has good ideas for things to do
Is someone you can trust
Has many friends
Will wait their turn
Everyone listens to
Plays fair
Has a good sense or humor
Is polite
Makes new friends easily
Helps other people
Everyone likes to be with
Can get things going
Is usually happy
Likes to play with others

Disruptive score

Gets into a lot of fights
Loses temper easily
Shows off a lot
Interrupts when others are speaking
Is too bossy
Teases other children too much
Picks on other kids

Isolated score

Would rather play alone than with others
Has feelings that get hurt easily
Has trouble making friends
Can't get others to listen
Is very shy
Is often left out
Is usually sad

---

this first factor.) This bipolar factor reflects the extent to which the child is actively engaged in the work of the classroom. We have titled this factor *Engaged–Disengaged*.

Loading highly on the second factor are the sociometry score Aggressive–Disruptive and the Devereux score Disruptive–Oppositional. This factor appears to reflect disruptive or negative social behavior and has been labeled *Classroom Disruptiveness*.

On the basis of these and additional analyses two new composites were created, titled *Engage* and *Disrupt*. Their scoring operations are as follows:

ENGAGE = Sociometry Factor 1 (Sociability-Leadership)
plus (+)
Devereux Factor 3 (Cooperative-Initiating)
minus (−)
Sociometry Factor 3 (Sensitive-Isolated)
minus (−)
Devereux Factor 2 (Poor Comprehension-Disattention)

DISRUPT = Sociometry Factor 2 (Aggressive-Disruptive)
plus (+)
Devereux Factor 1 (Disruptive-Oppositional)

(The Devereux score Performance Anxiety was not included in the composite scores for several reasons, including a reduced N and weaker psychometric properties.)

The retest coefficients of these two factor scores over an 18-month span in School A indicate a reasonable degree of stability with values of .75 and .71, respectively for Engage and Disrupt. These social/behavioral competence composites were correlated with our measures of work competence. In School A the correlation between Engage with PIAT and IQ is .62 and .54, respectively, and for Disrupt, $r = -.20$ and $-.07$ (ns), respectively. Eighteen months later these r values are Engage/PIAT, $+.69$, Engage/IQ, $+.62$, Disrupt/PIAT, $-.30$, and Disrupt/IQ, $-.23$. Although all correlations are significant it is Engage that bears the more meaningful relationships with tested achievement and intellectual test performance.

VI. Interviews with Families

From the time of the initial formulation of the research program, we viewed two areas as central to our investigation: the lengthy set of interviews with our volunteer mothers and the briefer ones with the target offspring.[9]

A. *The Parent Interviews*

For the mothers, arrangements were made to schedule three 2-hour interviews to be conducted in the home at times that were convenient. For Sample A, a male and a female interviewer were present for most of the

[9]Portions of the mothers' interviews were borrowed with permission from prior interviews constructed by Drs. Michael Rutter, Fred Jones, George Brown, and Erlenmeyer-Kimling and her associates. The children's interviews included contents derived from interviews constructed by Drs. Diana Baumrind, Eliot Rodnick and Michael Goldstein, C. J. Kestenbaum, and H. R. Bird. The Project team gratefully acknowledges the contributions of these investigators and their associates.

interviews, allowing for alternation in interviewing and note taking. With the respondent's permission all interviews were tape recorded. For Sample A this involved 486 hours of interview time spent with 81 mothers of 96 children in the School A sample. At the time of this report the voluminous data collected have been coded and computer output obtained as have a substantial number of the interviews with 108 mothers of 120 children of Sample B.

Each of the three interview sessions was given over to specific areas designed to move from informational items to more intimate contents related to family problems and stressful events. Interview I focused on *demographic data and family background* with inquiries related to the following areas: family composition, housing, parent employment and work patterns, neighborhood and community activities, social contacts of the family, nuclear family contacts, social responsibilities of the parents, mother's early childhood and family background, parents' schooling, parents' work history, marital history, marriage and family life, history of family illnesses and accidents, and a home rating scale which was completed by the interviewer based upon observations made during the home visits.

Interview II focused on the *target child's developmental history and current behavior*. These contents included a developmental history which was completed by mother, based upon her recall of the period of pregnancy and birth, the child's early physical development, temperament indicators, feeding practices, and health history. No assumptions were made that recall would be veridical. Other items included were caretaking, early and current schooling, social and peer behavior, behavior at home, patterns of family communication, parent–child and surrogate relationships, current behavior problems, and sex-related behaviors.

Two general goals were set for Interview II: (1) to investigate the mother's perceptions of her child's competence and (2) to obtain a general view of the family's socialization practices and philosophy of child rearing with a specific emphasis on the target child. The interview, which required a minimum of verbatim recording, was structured to be readily coded by the interviewers. Several minor revisions were made in the interview format to improve clarity and coding after several initial interviewing experiences.

Interview III was essentially a *life-events-in-context* interview. Each negative and ambiguous life event initially reported in the Life Events Questionnaire (LEQ) became a focus of special inquiry aimed at providing a contextual background against which to evaluate, and if necessary to modify, the stress valuation placed upon a specific event. The following format was used, although the description of potential moderators (anticipation, preparation, etc.) was worded differently for different stress experiences.

1. General description of the event.
2. Anticipation and preparation for the event (if any).
3. Control or noncontrol over the events.
4. Immediate reactions of family members as reflected in their attitudinal and behavior changes.
5. Implications and/or consequences of the event for the family and the child.
6. Resources/help available at the time of, and subsequent to, the event.
7. Index child's behavior during and following the event, in comparison with other family members including siblings.

Here is one example of the structured inquiry for a specific life event drawn from the LEQ. If mother had checked the item *Serious illness requiring hospitalization of a parent* as having taken place during the previous year, the typical procedure was to ask the following set of questions in Interview III:

1. Has anyone in the family been ill during the past year or so?
2. Have you or your husband had any illnesses?
3. Was anyone admitted to or left in a hospital during the last year for any type of physical disability or mental handicap? (Probe: How long? How serious? How acute? Loss of work? Emergency or routine? Anyone beyond the immediate family?)
4. Were there any early signs of the illness, so that you anticipated that it might happen?
5. Were the children prepared for it? How?
6. (If hospitalization of a parent or child occurred.) How did the family members react? (Check out the index child.)
7. What were the consequences of the illness? (Probe: financial indebtedness, loss of job, threat of recurrence, separation of family.)
8. Were there any long lasting effects of the illness, such as a visible physical handicap?
9. Did you require and receive assistance of any kind, financial or personal, during the period of the illness?

Basically, then, the ratings of context are dependent upon answers to questions related to *foreknowledge, preparation, alteration of normal routine, control, past experience, emotional impact,* and *availability of resources or social support.*

The contextual interviews (Interview III) for Sample A and their analyses are now nearing completion and will be reported in a later publication.

Analyses of the first two interviews with the mothers are also proceeding. The breadth and diversity of the contents of these two sessions have posed a problem of data reduction, and this has been achieved by collating questions distributed throughout the first two interviews into various content categories, and then determining the scoring of the range of responses given by the respondents to these various inquiries. An example of a prominent content category drawn from Interview I is one of *maternal history and background*. Within this category are various types of historical information including family living arrangement, the mother's (and father's) history of schooling and related activities, mother's perceived abilities and deficits, her plans beyond school and success or failure in realizing them, employment history, marriage, births, and pregnancies. Another category titled *change* records the parent's history of jobs held, level of work activity, places and length of residences, and number of family moves. *Marriage, mother–child* and *father–child relationships, family milieu, rearing rules and discipline patterns in the home, parental participation in community organizations and activities, social supports and friendships, recreation,* and *entertainment activities* are other examples of categories for which data analyses have been completed. These and other contents provide evidence of patterns of parental competence, early and later levels of socioeconomic status, family and outside social networks, family cohesion and warmth, family discord and dissolution, and parent–child relationships. These and related contents will be correlated with such variables as family stress levels, the index child's competence qualities, the child's view of family, and her or his performance on laboratory tasks.

B. The Child Interviews

Unlike the more highly structured interviews provided for mothers, the child interview was deliberately made more open ended. We sought a broad overview of the child's world as seen from the child's point of view. In particular, one aim of the two sessions was to seek information about the nature of this child's competence qualities, reactions to stress, and modes of coping. During the course of the interview inquiries were made about stressful events such as family moves, school changes, parental divorce or separation, and illnesses and deaths in the family.

Interviews were conducted with 93 children from the School A sample and 111 children from School B. For School A two interviewers, a male and a female, each interviewed approximately equal numbers of boys and girls. All interviews were tape recorded. Each child was asked a core set of questions with probes aimed at securing better in-depth responses to important or overly brief answers that the child provided.

The first 52 cases were completely transcribed generating some 4000 pages of text. Subsequently, the staff moved to dictating extensive summaries of the content areas and from there to formal narratives of the interview contents for Sample B.

Twelve areas of inquiry made up the contents of the children's interview.

1. School.
2. Outside activities.
3. Chores and responsibilities.
4. Money and work.
5. Friends and peers.
6. Family and home.
7. Boys and girls.
8. Fantasies and dreams.
9. Future perspectives.
10. Self-concept.
11. Emotions and problems.
12. Other life events.

We illustrate the content area, *Money and work,* with a partial list of some of the questions asked the child: Do you get an allowance? How much do you get? How often do you get it? Do you have to do anything to earn it? Do your parents ever give you money? (If so) When? What for? How much? What do you do with your money? What else? Do you save any of your money?

Finkelman (1983) then constructed a series of 173 rating scales on which to rate various contents of the transcripts. Some of the scales are quite specific, others more global, and several tap behaviors evidenced by the child during the interview (e.g., "expresses self in a clear and coherent manner"). Two clinical judges rated the contents of each interview using the various scales.

On the basis of a series of factor analyses Finkelman reduced his multiple scales down to three factor scores. Factor I bears a resemblence to the composited children's competence score we had termed Engaged–Disengaged. These are children who are open with close friends and family members and are judged to have a high degree of closeness with their families. The correlation between Factor I and the global competence factor Engaged is .58. Factor II appears to measure a dimension similar to the second composited competence dimension, Disruptive. Its correlation with the Disruptive factor is +.51. Factor III consists of scales that tap motivation, striving, and level of aspiration. It too is highly related to Engaged-

Disengaged ($r = .59$); however, Factor III is less related than Factor I to the IQ score.

Interrater reliability coefficients were quite high for all three factor scores (Factor I = .89; Factors II and III = .84), as were the internal consistency reliability measures (coefficient alpha for Factor I = .95, Factor II = .94, and Factor III = .81).

Using hierarchical multiple regression with Engaged–Disengaged as the dependent variable, Finkelman has reported that Factor I of the children's interview scales makes a small and nonsignificant contribution to the prediction of competence in the child after the independent variables of age, sex, IQ, and socioeconomic status have been entered. Factor III (motivation/striving) does, however, contribute significantly to the prediction of Engaged–Disengaged when the same independent variables are considered. The greater contribution of Factor III after IQ effects are considered is partly due to the fact that Factor I shares more variance with IQ than does Factor III. In a similar hierarchical regression analysis, Factor II makes a significant contribution to the prediction of global Disruptiveness, accounting for 22% of the variance. Additional analyses of these interviews are available in a recently completed doctoral dissertation (Finkelman, 1983).

VII. Experimental Laboratory Measures

As another part of the research program we sought to develop a set of measures of basic processes as well as to assess the child's functioning in different settings. As explained above, for the home we used interview techniques and for the school we employed differing measures of competence in the work, social, and behavioral domains using formal test scores, peers, and teachers as our sources of information. Our third approach was to observe the children in the laboratory under more controlled conditions. Three major studies were run to evaluate factors that were hypothesized to temper stressful experiences for the child.[10]

Pellegrini (1980) examined the role of social cognition. Ferrarese (1981) explored the dimensions of reflectivity–impulsivity and delay of gratification. Masten's (1982) research centered on an exploration of two related areas of ability not measured by traditional tests of intelligence, creative (divergent) thinking and humor.

We offer below only an abbreviated review of these laboratory studies;

[10]In this section we have summarized only several components of the complex and informative doctoral dissertations conducted by Pellegrini (1980), Ferrarese (1981), and Masten (1982). We are grateful to these colleagues for allowing us to present a limited number of findings in advance of the complete reports of their studies which are now being prepared for journal publication.

the principal investigators involved will be providing more detailed reports in subsequent journal publications.

A. Social Cognition and Stress Resistance (Pellegrini, 1980)

If one had to point to the essential talents needed for coping with stressful events, one would undoubtedly be the individual's effectiveness in social and cognitive problem solving. The former is at least partially dependent upon a sensitivity to others—an interpersonal awareness by the child of the thoughts, feelings, intentions, and needs of others. This awareness has been termed "perspective taking" and, as with cognitive development, it too shows a developmental progression through a sequence of stages, initially marked by the young child's characteristic egocentrism or failure to differentiate their own point of view from that of another person. By early adolescence this has changed to a more objective perspective of a differentiation between self and others accompanied by a growing social sensitivity. Selman (1976) has projected an even higher stage of social development which is marked by an abstract, broader societal perspective on human relations.

Attributes of this order are a significant component of social competence and maturity, which in turn bear a relationship to effective personality integration and adaptation. The linkages of such factors to freedom from incapacity, maladaptation, and behavior pathology and, conversely, its evident tie to effective coping under stress (Jahoda, 1958) led to Pellegrini's (1980) doctoral study of the social-cognitive qualities of stress-resistant children.

The instruments he chose to study these relationships were the *Selman–Jaquette Interpersonal Awareness* measure (see Selman, 1976, 1982) and the *Means–End Problem-Solving Test* (MEPS) devised by Shure and Spivack (1978). The former utilizes interpersonal-moral dilemmas for assessing developmental stages in a child's awareness of the nature of (1) persons, (2) friendships, and (3) group organization. The presentations of dilemmas and their resolution are followed by a semistructured clinical interview, in which interviewer probes allow for the assignment of scores and the derivation of an estimate of a child's social-cognitive maturity within each of the three domains as well as a global awareness score. The MEPS test is presumed to tap skills that are learned through experience with others, and most particularly, with the child's rearing figures. Such factors as a sensitivity to social problems, an awareness of causal relations, the search for alternative solutions, the ability to perceive immediate and long-range consequences of one's actions, and the planning of steps necessary to research a goal or resolve a situation marked by obstacles and conflict are all believed to be implicated in satisfactory performance on this simple test, which utilizes hypothetical social dilemmas. This child is presented with six brief stories (Pellegrini modified these since two were somewhat antisocial in content) with only the beginning and the outcome provided by the investigator. The child's task is to fill in how the outcome was achieved and the dilemma resolved. For his study Pellegrini devised special rules for rating which gave greater emphasis to alternative solutions presented by the child.

Interpersonal Awareness scores showed a moderate positive relationship with positive peer perceptions and academic achievement and a somewhat lower relationship with positive teacher ratings of classroom behavior. Social problem-solving ability showed a stronger relationship to positive sociometric status and teacher assessments of competence. Interpersonal Awareness scores and social problem-solving ability showed a moderate relationship to each other.

Hierarchical multiple regression analysis (Cohen & Cohen, 1975) was employed to test the hypotheses relating social cognition to competence and to competence under stress. Pellegrini found that both the Interpersonal Awareness and the MEPS scores made significant, independent contributions in accounting for variance in manifest competence even after the contributions of sex, age, and intellectual ability are accounted for. Of the two social cognition tasks, the explanatory power of the MEPS test was greater. Pellegrini's analysis of significant interaction effects from the regression analyses provided some interesting and potentially important findings.

> An interaction between interpersonal awareness and social problem-solving suggests that combined inadequacy in both social-cognitive domains are related to negative sociometric status, while adequacy in either one of the domains may compensate for inadequacy in the other with regard to this aspect of competence. An interaction between interpersonal awareness and stress suggests that increasing stress is associated with decreasing behavioral competence, but only where interpersonal awareness is deficient. In the context of mature interpersonal awareness, behavioral competence appears to increase slightly with increasing stress. Finally, an interaction between intellectual ability and stress suggests that increasing stress is associated with decreasing academic competence, but only where intellectual ability is deficient. In the context of above-average intellectual ability, academic competence actually appears to increase with increasing stress. The latter two interactions provide initial clues to some of the important characteristics of stress-resistant children. (Pellegrini, 1980, p. iv)

B. The Significance of Reflection and Impulse Control for the Manifestation of Competence (Ferrarese, 1981)

Exponents of widely differing viewpoints, ranging from classical psychoanalysis to contemporary social learning theory, appear to agree on the critical significance of a developmental process through which children acquire in varying degrees the ability and disposition to monitor and modulate the expression of their impulses. Theorists are likely to disagree on the nature of the particular tendencies that are of central concern, or on the particular learning or maturational processes through which the initial behavior repertoire may be transformed. Such consensus as emerges from different theories centers primarily on the general idea that a constellation of characteristics, variously referred to as "ego control," "reflectiveness," "frustration tolerance," and "capacity for delay of gratification," represents the desirable pole of a continuum of individual differences, the undesirable extreme of which has been given such labels as "undercontrol," "impulsiveness," or "immaturity."

This area of individual differences which, following Kagan, Rosman, Day, Albert, and Phillips (1964), we will refer to as Reflectiveness–Impulsiveness (R–I), was the object of study of a doctoral thesis by Ferrarese (1981) conducted within the framework of our project. The central issue addressed by Ferrarese was whether the qualities reflecting R–I were relevant to the manifestation of competence under varying levels of stress.

The 96 participants (45 boys, 51 girls) in the special procedures conducted in this study were all recruited from School A. Because these children took part in the larger project, measures of stress, competence, intelligence, and achievement were already available.

These data, however, had originally been collected about a year earlier. An attempt was made, therefore, to obtain this information a second time, approximately concurrently with the conduct of the present study. Unfortunately, data could be collected on only about 65 of Ferrarese's original sample of 96 (the precise number varies with the measure). A comparison of this final group with the sample that originally had been approached for participation in our project indicated (as pointed out earlier) that the former is not a random sample. Participating children tended to receive higher competence ratings and their families lower stress scores, which suggests a restriction of range and possible attenuation of the relationship of concern in this study, a limitation to be borne in mind when appraising the results presented below.

The procedures Ferrarese (1981) selected for assessing R–I is described only briefly since they are elaborated in his doctoral dissertation. Following that, we present results bearing on the dimensional structure of R–I as it emerged from the correlations among its various indicators. Finally, we present and discuss findings concerning the relevance of R–I to competence and achievement and its relationship to measures of stress and socioeconomic status.

1. ASSESSMENT OF REFLECTIVENESS–IMPULSIVENESS

In this study R–I was treated as a still relatively open concept of as yet unknown dimensionality. A number of different and alternative assessment methods were employed, allowing the data to play a critical role in further shaping our conception of R–I with respect to both its internal structure and its relevance to competence.

The specific measures of R–I were derived from three separate procedures: (1) a modification of Kagan's *Matching Familiar Figures Test* (MFFT), (2) two administrations of the *Porteus Maze Test,* one using the standard method and one an adaptive method devised for this study, (3) a *Delay of Gratification* procedure (see Weintraub, 1973). These three procedures were individually administered in two sessions typically 3–4 days apart, with each session lasting approximately 50 minutes. The first session began with an introduction stressing the length of time Project Competence had been active and would continue to be in the future. This was done to reinforce the child's expectation that any delayed gift earned would indeed be received as promised. Next, the Matching Familiar Figures Test was administered followed by the standard administration of the Porteus Mazes. The second session consisted of an adaptive administration of the Porteus Mazes followed by the Delay of Gratification procedure. As indicated earlier, measures of stress, intelligence, achievement, and competence were obtained from the subjects as participants in the larger project at about the same time as the R–I measures. Measures of socioeconomic status were also available.

a. Matching Familiar Figures Test (MFFT). The MFFT is a perceptual performance task requiring subjects to scan a series of sets of very similar but subtly differing pictures of familiar objects and to select the one that is identical to a simultaneously presented standard stimulus.

The MFFT has been widely used in a variety of studies. Findings have been interpreted as showing that children scored as impulsive are less bright, more distractible, more physically active, externalizing in their behavioral patterns rather than internalizers, more likely to be learning disabled, delinquent and aggressive, and more emotionally responsive (Ferrarese, 1981).

As designed by its originators (Kagan *et al.,* 1964) each form of the MFFT consisted of 12 items, and the accuracy and latency of each item response was recorded. The total accuracy and latency scores were classified as either above or below the median to yield a 2 × 2 typology, such that children in one quadrant were classified as fast–accurate and those in the opposite quadrant as slow–inaccurate. The inclusion as subjects of children in the remaining two quadrants was not recommended.

Subsequently this method of scoring has been criticized. Block, Block, and Harrington (1974) have argued that only accuracy was related to differences between "impulsive" and "reflective" children. The fourfold typology can certainly also be criticized on purely psychometric grounds. Not only does it preclude an analysis of the distinctive predictive contributions of the separate accuracy and latency measures, the dichotomization of scores amounts to relinquishing a great deal of the information contained in the original quasi-continuous scores. In the present study, as in other more recent ones, latency and accuracy were therefore retained as separate measures, without dichotomization.

The test procedure itself also contained several modifications of the original MFFT method that were introduced by Weintraub (1968). Briefly stated, the number of alternatives per item was increased from 6 to 8, and the number of items from 12 to 23. The use of booklets was replaced by projection of the standard stimulus and test stimuli on a screen. Latencies were monitored electronically rather than with a stopwatch. Finally, rather than informing the child of the correctness of the first response to each item and requiring a second response when the first one was incorrect, which could conceivably introduce an uncontrolled factor of failure–frustration, one response only was requested to each item, and no feedback was provided.

Two scores, then, were derived from the MFFT: (1) MFFT Accuracy, or number of correct responses, and (2) MFFT Latency, or average response latency per trial.

b. *Porteus Maze Test*. As indicated earlier, two test administrations were employed. The first one followed the standard procedure (Porteus, 1933, 1942, 1955). For the second administration the so-called Extension Series of Mazes was administered in an adapative rather than in the standard consecutive manner. Under this procedure, whenever a child failed a scored maze, an easier maze was inserted until one was successfully traversed. In this manner a successful trial was ensured immediately prior to each scored trial.

In addition to using the standard scoring procedure, the latency of the child's first marking of each maze following its presentation was recorded in both administrations. Consequently, three scores were available from both administrations: (1) Porteus Test Age, or age equivalent score, (2) Porteus Q score, or Qualitative (i.e., carelessness) score, and (3) Porteus Latency, or average latency per maze.

c. *Delay of Gratification*. This procedure was modeled after DePree (1966) and Weintraub (1968, 1973), and consisted of two tasks, the toy preference task and the delay of gratification procedure proper. First, the toy preference test is briefly described. Its purpose was to have the children closely examine and evaluate, and thus become thoroughly familiar with, a set of 12 toys, in preparation for the delay task. Different but overlapping sets of toys were used for boys and girls. Both sets of 12 demarcated approximately equal-appearing intervals of attractiveness across the age range represented in the study and had been selected previously from a larger set of 20 toys on the basis of ratings and ranking by a group of children similar in age and socioeconomic background as the experimental subjects.

The children in the present study were asked to rate and then rank the

12 toys in a manner designed to capture the child's attention. A rating scale in the form of an engaging display board was used, and in the process of rating, the child actively handled each toy.

Next the actual delay of gratification task was introduced. The children were told that they would now play a game in which they would actually win as a prize one of the toys just rated. It was explained to them that they would be shown 18 pairs of toys and that they were to decide each time whether they wanted the toy designated "Today" or the one designated "Two Weeks." They were told to decide very carefully because one of their 18 choices would be their prize. If the prize happened to be a "Today" toy they would receive it on that same day after school; if it was a "Two-Weeks" toy it would be given to them after a 2-week delay.

Following these instructions and three practice trials each child completed the 18 test trials in the manner just described. The members of each of the 18 pairs of prizes differed in ranked attractiveness, and the "Today" toy was always the less attractive of the two. Next the children selected their prize by picking blindly 1 out of 18 tags that presumably identified each of their choices. In reality this "lottery" was so designed as to ensure that the children would win either their second-ranked "Two-Weeks" or their third-ranked "Today" choice. If the children won a "Today" choice they received it at the end of the school day. If they won a "Two-Weeks" choice the experimenter delivered it after school 2 weeks later. The gifts were wrapped and a hand-written note was given to the child to take home to the parents to explain that the toy was indeed a gift.

Three scores were derived from the Delay procedure: (1) Delay Choice, or number of delay choices out of 18 trials, (2) Delay Choice Latency, or mean response latency per trial, and (3) Toy Rank Time, or total time taken to rank the 12 toys.

2. Internal Structure of R–I Measures

In order to derive a more parsimonious set of R–I indicators, the 11 original variables were intercorrelated and subjected to factor analysis. The slope of the magnitudes of the principal components indicated the presence of two main dimensions. Accordingly, the two first principal factors were rotated to a varimax simple structure.

The results clearly indicated that Factor I is a Performance Adequacy (or *Performance*) dimension. It is primarily associated with MFFT Accuracy, with the adaptive as well as standard Porteus TA and Q scores, and with MFFT Latency. Of these markers only the last one is a speed measure (and of all the latency variables it is the only one measuring total response time on a task structured to have one correct response). Factor II was readily interpreted as a *Latency* dimension, reflecting individual differences in time taken to initiate a response or reach a decision. With the exception of MFFT Latency, all latency measures, namely, the two Porteus latencies, the Delay Choice Latency, and Toy Ranking Time, are clear Factor II markers.

On the basis of these results the original 11 variables were replaced in Ferrarese's main analyses by a smaller set of three variables: scores representing the two rotated factors and derived by summing the z scores of their respective markers, labeled R–I Performance and R–I Latency, respectively; and the Delay Choice measure. The latter was retained as a separate measure because of its theoretical importance and because it was not adequately represented by either factor. As expected, the correlations among the three measures are relatively low, the highest absolute value being .28.

3. RELATIONSHIP OF R–I TO COMPETENCE, STRESS, AND SOCIOECONOMIC STATUS

The correlations between the three major R–I variables and measures of competence, intelligence, rated stress, and socioeconomic status exhibited two salient features. First, of the three R–I measures, R–I performance is the one most clearly related to competence and the other measures just mentioned. Specifically, it has meaningful correlations with four out of five competence measures (namely, $+.45$ with Engage, $-.42$ with Performance Anxiety, $-.50$ with Poor Comprehension–Disattention, and $+.37$ with the PIAT), whereas the corresponding correlations for Delay Choice are comparatively weak, and those for R–I Latency are negligible. R–I Performance is also moderately correlated with the stress and socioeconomic indicators, with Delay Choice showing comparable but lower correlations. With IQ partialed out, only the correlations involving R–I Performance remain significant and of meaningful magnitude; those with Delay Choice were now comparable to the near-zero R–I Latency correlations (a result that we may attribute in part to the relatively high correlations of Delay Choice with IQ).

Second, of the five competence measures only Disruptive is not significantly related to R–I. This may be something of a surprise since Disruptive emerged as one of two major dimensions of competence based on peer nomination and peer ratings. This finding, however, indicates that disruptiveness in the sense of fighting, teasing, and being bossy and a show-off, although suggesting a quality of insufficiently controlled *interpersonal* behavior, is largely independent of the kind of *cognitive* control tapped by measures of R–I, and should not be confused with it in the assessment of competence.

The relationship of R–I to competence was further examined in a series of hierarchical regression analyses. Sex, age, and IQ were entered first in these analyses, allowing a determination of how much of a contribution any subsequently entered variables, including R–I measures, could make that was not attributable to these three basic variables. (R–I Latency was excluded from the multiple regressions because of its uniformly low correlations with the dependent variables of concern.)

It was evident from the results that IQ makes a significant and substantial contribution to all competence measures other than Disruptive. The results also showed that apart from IQ, only R–I Performance contributed significantly, confirming our earlier impression based on the zero-order correlations.

Furthermore, the one significant interaction revealed by the regression analysis is between R–I Performance and IQ in relation to Performance Anxiety. Although a sporadic interaction such as this one is more in need of replication than interpretation, we view it tentatively as indicating that children who are either reflective and intelligent or impulsive and relatively less intelligent are, all other things equal, more likely than others to experience Performance Anxiety. In sum, of three major R–I measures, one, R–I Performance, reflecting individual differences in performance quality rather than mere performance speed, appears most relevant to manifestations of competence even when IQ is controlled for.

The role of IQ itself warrants further comment. It is obvious that its contribution to competence is pervasive. In fact, in the regression analyses IQ preempts a substantial portion of the potential contribution of measures such as R–I Performance and Delay Choice, reflecting, of course, the partial overlap of these measures. Should one, to the extent that this is the case, regard the R–I variables as less informative and less interesting to the researcher? We do not think so. One salient characteristic of R–I Performance markers, such as MFFT Accuracy and the Porteus TA and Q scores, is that they reflect success with problems that are not inherently difficult and that are in principle soluble given enough patience, since no time limits are imposed. We suggest that any partial overlap between these R–I variables and IQ indicates that one important ingredient of measured intelligent behavior may be just this willingness to allocate the time needed for an adequate response.

A similar point can be made about the Delay Choice measure. Its fairly substantial correlation with IQ suggests the possibility that intelligence can *in part* be construed as readiness to forego the convenience of an immediate gratification in favor of a more substantial later reward. In other words, the results lead us to entertain the view that certain R–I variables may affect competence *through* their contribution to intelligent behavior. The advantage of this perspective on intelligence is, of course, that it suggests some specific and promising approaches to fostering intelligent behavior by strengthening specific and teachable problem-solving behaviors (e.g., Kendall & Wilcox, 1980).

Turning now to the role of environmental variables, we had found that R-I Performance was moderately correlated with both Rated Stress ($r = -.42, p < .01$) and the Socioeconomic Index ($r = +.33, p < .01$). Consistent with this, the regression analyses indicated that neither Stress nor Socioeconomic Index made a significant predictive contribution when placed *after* R-I Performance and Delay Choice in the regression sequence. The converse is true as well; when in parallel analyses Rated Stress and socioeconomic status were inserted *prior* to the R-I measures, the former and not the latter added significantly to the multiple correlations. Also, no significant Stress × R-I interactions were found.

It appears, then, that the contributions to competence made by R-I, particularly R-I Performance, may be inseparable from environmental factors such as stress and socioeconomic background. The data are entirely consonant with what would seem to be a reasonable view that these variables *mutually influence* one another. One implication would be that methods of promoting habits of adaptive reflectiveness will not suceed unless designed in full awareness of the broader environmental context in which the child is expected to make an adaptation. Even if reflectiveness could be strengthened through special instruction, the resulting improvement might not be retained in the long run unless encouraged and sustained by the child's broader environment.

C. The Significance of Children's Creative Thinking and Sense of Humor for Manifestations of Competence under Stress (Masten, 1982)

This laboratory study was the last of the experimental investigations conducted with the children who composed the School A sample. The following summarizes a portion of Masten's findings.

Her subjects included 93 of the original sample of School A children who at the time of this investigation were in grades 5–8.[11] Thus, many of the children had to be interviewed in the junior high schools they were then attending. The children were seen individually for two testing sessions in their schools.

Masten selected two trait characteristics that she identified from the literature as potentially relevant to the use of more mature coping and problem-

---

[11]The change in the number of grades of the participating children is a function of the time delay in generating and concluding this third major laboratory study.

solving strategies by competent children under stress. The first was creative (or divergent) thinking which she sought to assess by use of the Wallach–Kogan battery of tests reported by these investigators in their 1965 volume, *Modes of Thinking in Young Children*. The second was an understudied but intriguing aspect of personality—a sense of humor (see as examples of serious approaches to humor, volumes by Chapman & Foot, 1976, 1977; Goldstein & McGhee, 1972; McGhee, 1979; McGhee & Chapman, 1980).

Masten's major hypotheses were these. First, on the assumption that divergent thinking (DT) reflects cognitive flexibility and a potential richness of problem-solving strategies, she postulated that such thinking, if linked with intellectual ability, would be strongly associated with competence under stress. Second, she hypothesized that creative and humorous thinking reflect a common mode which would be represented by a relationship that exceeded their shared variance with a g factor of general intellectual ability. Third, humor as an attribute with three components of comprehension, appreciation, and generation combined both the cognitive and the affective—an interaction that should provide for effective coping and mastery in the school setting and under conditions of stress. Humor was assessed by Masten through assembling a set of humorous "Ziggy" cartoons as well as control cartoons in which the humor had been removed.[12] Ratings of funniness, comprehension (with a subset of stimuli graded for difficulty level), and the ability to generate funniness in altered cartoons were all part of a series of tasks devised by Masten.

There are many findings of interest in Masten's work which she will be reporting in depth in forthcoming publications. Here in very reduced form are several of them:

1. Ideational fluency and the ability to generate humor are significantly related to teacher ratings of "cooperative-initiating" behavior. Ideational fluency has a stronger relationship than intellectual ability with this teacher rating.

2. Children high in both IQ and DT scores are particularly advantaged. A low–high pattern of these two scores is associated with peer ratings of disruptive–aggressive behavior, and the high–high pattern with sociability and leadership.

3. Of the three humor variables, humor generation shows the strongest relationship to competence. After sex, age, and IQ effects are accounted

---

[12]Appreciation is expressed to Tom Wilson, the creative parent of Ziggy, and the Universal Press Syndicate for granting permission to create a humor test with Ziggy serving as its hero and central participant.

for, the measure of creative humor still shows a modest, positive relationship to global competence. Children who generate humor are less likely to be judged sensitive–isolated by peers. Creative humor ability appears to be more strongly related to good quality thinking in general than to divergent thinking per se. Children who can generate humor may be high-quality thinkers. But there may be other important processes involved, since humor generation does not tap cognition alone but also the integration of affect and cognition in producing a response that may well be of inestimable value in coping with stress.

4. An exploratory analysis of subgroups of children whose families were viewed as markedly stressed by our interviewers, and who varied in competence as indexed by global scores on the Engage variable, suggested that high-stress competent children had higher humor generation scores than did their high-stress, lower competence counterparts.

VIII. Some Concluding Remarks

Much has been left unstated in this article. We have not commented on the research of our colleagues Frank Wright and Margaret O'Dougherty in their follow-up studies of the psychological, neurological, and neurophysiological qualities of children who, born with the life-threatening heart defect of Transposition of the Great Arteries, had had successful open-heart surgery. These children of Cohort II returned to the University hospital years later at Dr. Wright's invitation to participate as a component cohort of our project, during which time an effort was made to ascertain their neurological status and the quality of their adaptation, psychologically and academically.

A major achievement of that research project has been the creation of a cumulative risk model composed of medical variables (e.g., duration and severity of hypoxia, weight and height growth failure, duration of hospitalization) drawn from the presurgery medical record. This model has proved to be strongly predictive of more subtle measures of children's cognitive performance and attentional adequacy years after successful open-heart surgery (O'Dougherty, 1981).

We have left for publication elsewhere findings of the adaptation of children with severe physical handicaps who underwent the stress of being mainstreamed into regular classrooms after prolonged stays in a special school for the disabled (Cohort III). Two doctoral dissertations have formed the framework for our investigations of this group. Silverstein (1982) engaged in 6 hours of interviewing parents exploring the family life of these children, the adaptations demanded, and the stressors undergone by family and child. In the course of her research she collected a wealth of clinical commentary in addition to demographic and quantitative data that reflected the impact of severe physical disability of a child on the lives of their families. Concurrent with that interview study was one performed in the classroom by Raison (1982). This consisted of a rigorous, ethological-observational study of these children and their classmates in both the mainstreamed and the special schools. The method used was a complex observational system devised by our University colleague, William Charlesworth, a developmental psychologist–ethologist. This method (Charlesworth, 1978, 1979) can be used to evaluate problem-behavior analysis of children in response to situational blocks or problems arising in the classroom or in other settings. Using this technique during a span of 90 hours of observation, Raison demonstrated the adaptiveness of handicapped children in their mainstream setting, whose behavior proved to be quite similar to that of their nonhandicapped classmates.

Underway is an effort by Silverstein and Raison to integrate their two studies, using the data collected on the families at home and on the children in the school to provide us with a greater understanding of how children and families cope with severe physical handicap in two markedly different ecological settings.

Still to be carried out are more comprehensive analyses integrating findings from the three experimental laboratory studies of Cohort I bearing on the cognitive and motivational characteristics of the children. These analyses may help us improve our discriminations among competent children through a series of data-related questions such as these: Is there a relationship between cognitive problem solving and divergent thinking? Is interpersonal awareness related to humor and to social intelligence? What relationship do these factors bear to conceptual tempo, delay of gratification, and reflectiveness? Which competence qualities of the parent are best reflected in competence qualities of their offspring as revealed within the classroom, the family, and the neighborhood?

We have only begun to so analyze the parent and child interview data which in turn will also be related to our laboratory studies and to a more integrated view of the mother–child relationship.

We have available behavior ratings of the children that were completed by all members of our research group who had contact with them whether in the course of experimental studies, personality, intellectual and achievement assessments, interviews, etc. These will be collated and related to more informal observations of the children's attributes as judged by those members of our team who observed and worked with the children. For example, the rating profile included two behavioral humor items provided by Masten so that direct observations of mirth and spontaneous humor in the other experimental and interview settings can be compared with the expression and appreciation of humor by the child in a laboratory context.

There is much more as yet undone in this program of research that has sought to stimulate interest in and to contribute to efforts to undertand the processes that underlie resilience in children exposed to a stressful world. When we first grew interested in this fascinating phenomenon a decade ago, one of us wrote an article (Garmezy, 1971) based on our work with children of disturbed parents and our candid discussions with school personnel. That context was a departure from psychopathology in that it focused on the unanticipated adaptations of children who were perceived to be at risk for disordered behavior. Perhaps it bears repeating in the context of this initial effort to present an overarching view of our project.

> In the study of high-risk and vulnerable children, we have come across another group of children whose prognosis could be viewed as unfavorable on the basis of familial or ecological factors but who upset our prediction tables and in childhood bear the visible indices that are hallmarks of competence: good peer relations, academic achievement, commitment to education and to purposive life goals, early and successful work histories. We have seen such children in our inner-city schools. . . . School principals not only believe they can identify such children but they resonate to the hopefulness suggested by the concept. . . . They can produce instances from within their own school settings of children whose intellectual and social skills are not destroyed by the misfortunes they encounter at home and on the street.
>
> Were we to study the forces that move such children to survival and adaptation, the long range benefits to our society might be far more significant than our many efforts to construct models of primary prevention designed to curtail the incidence of vulnerability. (p. 114)

Acknowledgments

Preparation of this article was facilitated by a Research Career Award to the senior author from the National Institute of Mental Health (MH 14914), by research grants to the authors and coinvestigator V. Devine from the NIMH (MH 33222), and by the William T. Grant Foundation. A start-up grant from the Graduate School and additional funding from the University of Minnesota Computer Center are gratefully acknowledged.

The research reported in this article would not have been possible without the dedicated efforts of the Project Competence research team members. Included within our group are graduate students completing their doctoral dissertations, some of whom have been mentioned in this article, honors undergraduates, and staff personnel. The invaluable contributions of all of these participants are recorded in the Technical Reports of the project (Project Competence, 1981).

Only some of these individuals have been cited in this article, but others, too, have contributed to the research effort. Unfortunately with some 25 additional names to be noted we must forego specifying all of the individuals who have been involved in the program. But we would be remiss if we failed to mention the following persons. In alphabetical order they are T. Cross, R. Davis, K. Larkin, L. Pettersen, and J. Samaha. We acknowledge with appreciation the important work performed by D. Pellegrini, A. Masten, and P. Morison who served successively as Project Coordinators. J. Abraham performed with distinction in her role as Administrative Secretary.

References

Bedell, J. R., Giordani, B., Amour, J. L., Tavormina, J., & Boll, T. Life stress and the psychological and medical adjustment of chronically ill children. *Journal of Psychosomatic Research,* 1977, **21**, 237–242.

Bleuler, M. *The schizophrenic disorders: Long-term patient and family studies.* New Haven, Connecticut: Yale Univ. Press, 1978.

Block, J. H., & Block, J. The role of ego-control and ego-resiliency in the organization of behavior. In W. A. Collins (Ed.), *Development of cognition, affect, and social relations. The Minnesota symposia on child psychology* (Vol. 13). Hillsdale, New Jersey: Erlbaum, 1980.

Block, J., Block, J., & Harrington, D. M. Some misgivings about the Matching Familiar Figures Test as a measure of reflection-impulsivity. *Developmental Psychology,* 1974, **10**, 611–632.

Bower, E. M. *Early identification of emotionally handicapped children in school* (2nd ed.). Springfield, Illinois: Thomas, 1969.

Brown, G. W., Harris, T. O., & Peto, J. Life events and psychiatric disorders: II. Nature of causal link. *Psychological Medicine,* 1973, **3**, 159–176.

Brown, G. W., Sklair, F., Harris, O. T., & Birley, J. L. T. Life events and psychiatric disorders. *Psychological Medicine,* 1973, **3**, 74–87.

Cairns, R. B. *Social development: The origins and plasticity of interchanges.* San Francisco, California: Freeman, 1979.

Cannon, W. B. *Bodily changes in pain, hunger, fear and rage* (2nd ed.). New York: Appleton, 1929.

Cannon, W. B. *The wisdom of the body.* New York: Norton, 1932.

Chandler, M. J., Greenspan, S., & Barenboim, C. Assessment and training of role-taking and referential communication skills in institutionalized emotionally disturbed children. *Developmental Psychology,* 1974, **10**, 546–553.

Chapman, A. J., & Foot, H. C. *Humour and laughter: Theory, research and applications.* New York: Wiley, 1976.

Chapman, A. J., & Foot, H. C. (Eds.), *It's a funny thing, humour.* Oxford: Pergamon, 1977.

Charlesworth, W. R. Ethology: Its relevance for observational studies of human adaptation. In G. P. Sackett (Ed.), *Observing behavior: Proceedings of a conference* (Vol. 1). Baltimore, Maryland: Univ. Park Press, 1978.

Charlesworth, W. R. An ethological approach to studying intelligence. *Human Development,* 1979, **22**, 212–216.

Cobb, S. Social support as a moderator of life stress. *Psychosomatic Medicine,* 1976, **38**, 300–314.

Coddington, R. D. The significance of life events as etiologic factors in the diseases of children: I. A survey of professional workers. *Journal of Psychosomatic Research,* 1972, **16**, 7–18. (a)

Coddington, R. D. The significance of life events as etiologic factors in the diseases of children: II. A study of a normal population. *Journal of Psychosomatic Research,* 1972, **16**, 205–213. (b)

Cohen, J., & Cohen, P. *Applied multiple regression/correlation analysis for the behavioral sciences.* Hillsdale, New Jersey: Erlbaum, 1975.

Coles, R. *Migrants, sharecroppers, mountaineers. Children of crisis* (Vol. 2). Boston, Massachusetts: Little, Brown, 1972.

Cummings, L., & Mulrooney, S. The measurement of achievement: The achievement ratings and the Peabody Individual Achievement Test. *Project Competence: Studies of stress-resistant children: Technical reports* (N. Garmezy, PI). University of Minnesota, September 1981. (a)

Cummings, L., & Mulrooney, S. The measurement of general intellectual ability. *Project Competence: Studies of stress-resistant children: Technical reports* (N. Garmezy, PI). University of Minnesota, September 1981. (b)

DePree, S. *Time perspective, frustration-failure, and delay of gratification in middle-class and lower-class children from organized and disorganized families.* Unpublished Ph.D. dissertation, University of Minnesota, 1966.

Dohrenwend, B. P., & Dohrenwend, B. S. *Social status and psychological disorder.* New York: Wiley, 1969.

Dohrenwend, B. P., & Dohrenwend, B. S. Class and race as related sources of stress. In S. Levine & N. A. Scotch (Eds.), *Social stress.* Chicago, Illinois: Aldine, 1970.

Dohrenwend, B. P., & Dohrenwend, B. S. The conceptualization and measurement of stressful life events: An overview of the issues. In J. S. Strauss, H. M. Babigian, & M. Roff (Eds.), *The origins and course of psychopathology: Methods of longitudinal research.* New York: Plenum, 1977.

Dohrenwend, B. S. Social class and stressful events. In E. H. Hare & J. K. Wing (Eds.), *Psychiatric epidemiology.* London and New York: Oxford Univ. Press, 1970.

Dohrenwend, B. S. Social status and stressful life events. *Journal of Personality and Social Psychology,* 1973, **28,** 225–235.

Dohrenwend, B. S. (Ed.), *Stressful life events and their contexts.* New York: Neale Watson, 1981.

Dohrenwend, B. S., & Dohrenwend, B. P. (Eds.), *Stressful life events.* New York: Wiley, 1974.

Dohrenwend, B. S., & Dohrenwend, B. P. Some issues in research on stressful life events. *Journal of Nervous and Mental Disease,* 1978, **166,** 7–15.

Duncan, O. D. A socioeconomic index for all occupations. In A. J. Reiss, O. D. Duncan, P. K. Hatt, & C. C. North (Eds.), *Occupations and social status.* Glencoe, Illinois: Free Press, 1961.

Dunn, L. M., & Markwardt, F. C. *Peabody Individual Achievement Test.* Circle Pines, Montana: American Guidance Service, 1970.

Epstein, H. *Children of the holocaust.* New York: Putnam, 1979.

Erikson, K. T. *Everything in its path.* New York: Simon & Schuster, 1976.

Ferrarese, M. J. *Reflectiveness-impulsivity and competence in children under stress.* Unpublished Ph.D. dissertation, University of Minnesota, 1981.

Finkelman, D. *The relationship of children's attributes to levels of competence in familial stress.* Unpublished Ph.D. dissertation, University of Minnesota, 1983.

Finkelman, D., & Ferrarese, M. The measurement of classroom behavioral competence: The Devereux Teacher Ratings. *Project Competence: Studies of stress-resistant children: Technical reports* (N. Garmezy, PI). University of Minnesota, September 1981.

Garmezy, N. Vulnerability research and the issue of primary prevention. *American Journal of Orthopsychiatry,* 1971, **41,** 101–116.

Garmezy, N. Children under stress: Perspectives on antecedents and correlates of vulnerability and resistance to psychopathology. In A. I. Rabin, J. Aronoff, A. M. Barclay, & R. A. Zucker (Eds.), *Further explorations in personality.* New York: Wiley, 1981.

Garmezy, N. *Stress-resistant children: The search for protective factors.* Presented at the 10th International Congress of the International Association of Child Psychiatry and Related Professions, Dublin, July 1982.

Garmezy, N., & Devine, V. T. Longitudinal vs. cross-sectional research in the study of children at risk for psychopathology. In J. S. Strauss, H. M. Babigian, & M. Roff (Eds.), *The origins and course of psychopathology: Methods of longitudinal research.* New York: Plenum, 1977.

Garmezy, N., & Devine, V. Project Competence: The Minnesota studies of children vulnerable to psychopathology. In N. F. Watt, E. J. Anthony, L. C. Wynne, & J. Rolf (Eds.), *Children at risk for schizophrenia: A longitudinal perspective.* London and New York: Cambridge Univ. Press, 1984, in press.

Garmezy, N., & Nuechterlein, K. Invulnerable children: The fact and fiction of competence and disadvantage. *American Journal of Orthopsychiatry,* 1972, **42,** 328–329. (Abstract)

Gliedman, J., & Roth, W. *The unexpected minority: Handicapped children in America.* New York: Harcourt, 1980.

Goertzel, M. G., Goertzel, V., & Goertzel, T. G. *Three hundred eminent personalities.* San Francisco, California: Jossey-Bass, 1978.

Goertzel, V., & Goertzel, M. G. *Cradles of eminence.* Boston, Massachusetts: Little, Brown, 1962.

Goldstein, J. H., & McGhee, P. E. (Eds.), *The psychology of humor: Theoretical perspectives and empirical issues.* New York: Academic Press, 1972.

Gruenberg, E. M. Risk factor research methods. In D. A. Regier & G. Allen (Eds.), *Risk factor research in the major mental disorders.* Washington, D.C.: U. S. Government Printing Office. DHHS Publication No. (ADM)81–1068, 1981.

Hauser, R. M., & Featherman, D. L. *The process of stratification: Trends and analysis.* New York: Academic Press, 1977.

Heisel, J. S. Life changes as etiologic factors in juvenile rheumatoid arthritis. *Journal of Psychosomatic Research,* 1972, **16,** 411–420.

Heisel, J. S., Ream, S., Raitz, R., Rappaport, M., & Coddington, R. D. The significance of life events as contributing factors in the diseases of children: III. A study of pediatric patients. *Journal of Pediatrics,* 1973, **83,** 119–123.

Herzog, J., Linder, H., & Samaha, J. The measurement of stress: Life events and the interviewer's ratings. *Project Competence: Studies of stress-resistant children: Technical Reports* (N. Garmezy, PI). University of Minnesota, September 1981.

Hollingshead, A. B. *Two-factor index of social position.* Copyright privately printed and circulated. Yale University, 1957.

Holmes, T. H., & Rahe, R. H. The social readjustment rating scale. *Journal of Psychosomatic Research,* 1967, **11,** 213–218.

Illingworth, R. S., & Illingworth, C. M. *Lessons from childhood.* Edinburgh: Livingstone, 1966.

Jahoda, M. *Current concepts of positive mental health.* New York: Basic Books, 1958.

Kadushin, A. Reversibility of trauma: A follow-up study of children adopted when older. *Social Work,* 1967, **12,** 22–33.

Kagan, J., Rosman, B. L., Day, D., Albert, J., & Phillips, W. Information processing in the child: Significance of analytic and reflective attitudes. *Psychological Monographs,* 1964, **78** (1, Whole No. 578).

Kauffman, C., Grunebaum, H., Cohler, B., & Gamer, E. Superkids: Competent children of psychotic mothers. *American Journal of Psychiatry,* 1979, **136,** 1398–1402.

Kempe, C. H., & Helfer, R. E. (Eds.). *The battered child* (3rd ed.). Chicago, Illinois: Univ. of Chicago Press, 1980.

Kendall, P. C., & Wilcox, L. E. Cognitive-behavioral treatment for impulsivity: Concrete versus conceptual training in non-self-controlled problem children. *Journal of Consulting and Clinical Psychology,* 1980, **48,** 80–91.

Kent, M. W., & Rolf, J. E. (Eds.). *Primary prevention of psychopathology: Social competence in children* (Vol. 3). Hanover, New Hampshire: Univ. Press of New England, 1979.

Kessler, R. C. Stress, social status, and psychological distress. *Journal of Health and Social Behavior,* 1979, **20,** 259–272.

Kogan, N. *Cognitive styles in infancy and early childhood.* Hillsdale, New Jersey: Erlbaum, 1976.

Lamb, M. (Ed.). *The role of the father in child development* (2nd ed.). New York: Wiley, 1982.

Langmeier, J., & Matějcek, Z. *Psychological deprivation in childhood.* New York: Halstead, 1975.

Linder, H., Silverstein, P., & Samaha, J. The measurement of socioeconomic status. *Project Competence: Studies of stress-resistant children: Technical reports* (N. Garmezy, PI). University of Minnesota, September 1981.

Littell, W. M. Review of the Devereux Elementary School Behavior Rating Scale. In O. K. Buros (Ed.), *Seventh mental measurements yearbook* (Vol. 1). Highland Park, New Jersey: Gryphon, 1972.

Maccoby, E. E. *Social development: Psychological growth and the parent-child relationship.* New York: Harcourt, 1980.

Marcus, L. M. *Studies of attention in children vulnerable to psychopathology.* Unpublished Ph.D. dissertation, University of Minnesota, 1972.

Mason, J. W. A historical survey of the stress field. Part I. *Journal of Human Stress,* 1975, **1,** 6–12.

Masten, A. *Humor and creative thinking in stress-resistant children.* Unpublished Ph.D. dissertation, University of Minnesota, 1982.

Masten, A., & Morison, P. The measurement of interpersonal competence: The class play. *Project Competence: Studies of stress-resistant children: Technical reports* (N. Garmezy, PI). University of Minnesota, September 1981.

McGhee, P. E. *Humor: Its origin and development.* San Francisco, California: Freeman, 1979.

McGhee, P. E., & Chapman, A. J. (Eds.). *Children's humour.* London: Wiley, 1980.

Meyer, A. The life-chart. In *Contributions to medical and biological research* (dedicated to Sir William Osler, in honor of his seventieth birthday). New York: Hoeber, 1919.

Murphy, L. B. *The widening world of childhood.* New York: Basic Books, 1962.

Nuechterlein, K. H. *Competent disadvantaged children: A review of research.* Unpublished summa cum laude thesis, University of Minnesota, 1970.

Nuechterlein, K. H. Signal detection in vigilance tasks and behavioral attributes among offspring of schizophrenic mothers and among hyperactive children. *Journal of Abnormal Psychology,* 1983, **92,** 4–28.

O'Dougherty, M. M. *The relationship between early risk status and later competence and adaptation in children who survive severe heart defects.* Unpublished Ph.D. dissertation, University of Minnesota, 1981.

O'Dougherty, M. M., Wright, F. S., Garmezy, N., Loewenson, R. B., & Torres, F. A risk model for predicting neuropsychologic outcome in children with congenital heart disease. *Child Development,* 1983, in press.

OSS (Office of Strategic Services) Assessment staff. *Assessment of men: Selection of personnel for the Office of Strategic Services.* New York: Holt, 1948.

Padilla, E. R., Rohsenow, D. J., & Bergman, A. B. *Pediatrics,* 1976, **58,** 223–226.

Pellegrini, D. *The social-cognitive qualities of stress-resistant children.* Unpublished Ph.D. dissertation, University of Minnesota, 1980.

Porteus, S. D. *The maze test and mental differences.* Vineland, New Jersey: Smith, 1933.

Porteus, S. D. *Qualitative performance in the maze test.* Vineland, New Jersey: Smith, 1942.

Porteus, S. D. *The maze test: Recent advances.* Palo Alto, California: Pacific Books, 1955.

Project Competence: Studies of stress-resistant children: Technical reports (N. Garmezy, PI). University of Minnesota, September 1981.

Rabkin, J. G., & Struening, E. L. Life events, stress, and illness. *Science,* 1976, **194** (4269, Dec. 3), 1013–1020.

Radke-Yarrow, M., & Zahn-Waxler, C. Roots, motives and patterns in children's prosocial behavior. In J. Reykowski, J. Karylowski, D. Bar-Tal, & E. Staub (Eds.), *The development and maintenance of prosocial behaviors: International perspectives.* New York: Plenum, 1983, in press.

Raison, S. B. *Coping behavior of mainstreamed physically handicapped students.* Unpublished Ph.D. dissertation, University of Minnesota, 1982.

Rolf, J. E. The academic and social competence of children vulnerable to schizophrenia and other behavior pathologies. *Journal of Abnormal Psychology,* 1972, 80, 225–243.

Rutter, M. Parent-child separation: Psychological effects on children. *Journal of Child Psychology and Psychiatry,* 1971, **12,** 233–260.

Rutter, M. Protective factors in children's response to stress and disadvantage. In M. W. Kent & J. E. Rolf (Eds.), *Primary prevention of psychopathology: Social competence in children* (Vol. 3). Hanover, New Hampshire: Univ. Press of New England, 1979.

Rutter, M. Stress, coping, and development: Some issues and some questions. *Journal of Child Psychology and Psychiatry,* 1981, **22,** 323–356.

Rutter, M., Cox, A., Tupling, C., Berger, M., & Yule, W. Attainment and adjustment in two geographical areas: I. The prevalence of psychiatric disorder. *British Journal of Psychiatry,* 1975, **126,** 493–509. (a)

Rutter, M., Yule, B., Quinton, D., Rowlands, O., Yule, W., & Berger, M. Attainment and adjustment in two geographical areas: III. Some factors accounting for area differences. *British Journal of Psychiatry,* 1975, **126,** 520–533. (b)

Sandler, I. N. Social support, resources, stress, and maladjustment of poor children. *American Journal of Community Psychology,* 1980, **8,** 41–52.

Schaffer, R. *Mothering.* Cambridge, Massachusetts: Harvard Univ. Press, 1977.

Schatzman, M. *Soul murder: Persecution in the family.* New York: Random House, 1973 (Signet Edition, 1974).

Selman, R. L. A structural approach to the study of developing interpersonal relationship concepts. In A. Pick (Ed.), *10th Annual Minnesota Symposia on Child Psychology.* Minneapolis, Minnesota: Univ. of Minnesota Press, 1976.

Selman, R. L. *The growth of interpersonal understanding: Developmental and clinical analyses.* New York: Academic Press, 1982.

Selye, H. The General Adaptation Syndrome and the diseases of adaptation. *Journal of Clinical Endocrinology,* 1946, **6,** 117–230.

Shure, M. B., & Spivack, G. *Problem-solving techniques in childrearing.* San Francisco, California: Jossey-Bates, 1978.

Silverstein, P. R. *Coping and adaptation in families of physically handicapped school children.* Unpublished Ph.D. dissertation, University of Minnesota, 1982.

Spivack, G., Platt, J. J., & Shure, M. B. *The problem-solving approach to adjustment.* San Francisco, California: Jossey-Bass, 1976.

Spivack, G., & Swift, M. *Devereux Elementary School Behavior Rating Scale Manual.* Devon: The Devereux Foundation, 1967.

Staub, E. *Positive social behavior and morality: Social and personal influences* (Vol. 1). New York: Academic Press, 1978.

Thomas, A., & Chess, S., *Temperament and development.* New York: Brunner/Mazel, 1977.

Uhlenhuth, E., Balter, M. D., Lipman, R. S., & Haberman, S. J. Remembering life events. In J. S. Strauss, H. M. Babigian, & M. Roff (Eds.), *The origins and course of psychopathology: Methods of longitudinal research.* New York: Plenum, 1977.

Wallach, M. A., & Kogan, N. *Modes of thinking in young children: A study of the creativity-intelligence distinction.* New York: Holt, 1965.

Wallerstein, J. S., & Kelly, J. B. *Surviving the breakup: How children and parents cope with divorce.* New York: Basic Books, 1980.

Watt, N. F. *Two factor index of social position: Amherst modification.* Denver, Colorado: Univ. of Denver Press, 1976.

Watt, N. F., Anthony, E. J., Wynne, L. C., & Rolf, J. (Eds.), *Children at risk for schizophrenia: A longitudinal perspective.* London and New York: Cambridge Univ. Press, 1984.

Weintraub, S. A. *Cognitive and behavioral impulsivity in internalizing, externalizing and normal children.* Unpublished Ph.D. dissertation, University of Minnesota, 1968.

Weintraub, S. A. Self-control as a correlate of an internalizing-externalizing symptom dimension. *Journal of Abnormal Child Psychology,* 1973, **1**, 292–307.

Werner, E. E., & Smith, R. S. *Vulnerable, but invincible: A study of resilient children.* New York: McGraw-Hill, 1982.

Westman, J. C. (Ed.). *Individual differences in children.* New York: Wiley, 1973.

Yeaworth, R. C., York, J., Hussey, M. A., Ingle, M. E., & Goodwin, T. The development of an adolescent life change event scale. *Adolescence,* 1980, **15**, 91–97.

Zwingmann, C., & Pfister-Ammende, M. *Uprooting and after . . .* Berlin and New York: Springer-Verlag, 1973.

AUTHOR INDEX

SUBJECT INDEX

A

Achievement, composite study activities and, 84–87
Achievement Anxiety Test, 89
Age, study activities and, 87–88
Allport-Vernon value scale, 91
Anxiety, study activities and, 89–90
Attention, visual
  active, 130–131
  comprehension and, 133–135
  continuous, 128
  reactive, 129–130
  to television, 128–137
Attentional inertia, in television viewing, 152–154
Attitude, study activities and, 91
Autism, social deficits and, 166–170
Autistic children
  social behavior in same-age and mixed-age dyads, 184–206
  social behavior with trained peers, 206–215
  social development in, 170–173

B

Background context characteristics, 92–95
Basic school tasks, *see* Tasks, basic school

Behavioral competence, 259–260

C

California Psychology Inventory, 91
Child development, *see also* Social development
  comparisons across contexts, 14
  history of study of, 4–11
  laboratory studies of, 11–14
Child development research, applicability to autistic children, 216–219
Child interviews, 266–268
Cognition
  development of, TV viewing and, 117–119
  laboratory studies of, 11–14
Cognitive continuity, 154–158
  television viewing and, 121–127
Cognitive development, television viewing and, 124–127
Cognitive processing of television, development of, 154–157
Common branches, *see* Tasks, basic school
Competence
  measurement of, 258–263
  reflection and impulse control and, 270–277
Comprehensibility, cues to, 135–137